Sir Matthew Hale (1609–76) was the greatest common lawyer of his age, and the most universally admired. Although he held office under Oliver Cromwell, this barely affected his standing in Restoration times.

A study of Hale's life and thought necessarily illuminates the central role of the common law in Stuart politics. This book explains Hale's political ideas, and his subtle understanding of the peculiar character of an 'unwritten' law. It also covers his extensive writings on scientific and religious questions, writings which document a shift from puritan to liberal Protestantism. His acute but equivocal response to the science of Descartes and Boyle reveals a fascinating interplay between his 'latitudinarianism' and the new natural philosophy. The result is a unique case study, and a comprehensive portrait of a seventeenth-century mind.

Cambridge Studies in Early Modern British History

SIR MATTHEW HALE (1609–1676)

Cambridge Studies in Early Modern British History

Series editors

ANTHONY FLETCHER

Professor of Modern History, University of Durham

JOHN GUY

Professor of Modern History, University of St Andrews

and JOHN MORRILL

Reader in Early Modern History, University of Cambridge, and Fellow and Tutor of Selwyn College

This is a series of monographs and studies covering many aspects of the history of the British Isles between the late fifteenth century and the early eighteenth century. It includes the work of established scholars and pioneering work by a new generation of scholars. It includes both reviews and revisions of major topics and books which open up new historical terrain or which reveal startling new perspectives on familiar subjects. All the volumes set detailed research into our broader perspectives and the books are intended for the use of students as well as of their teachers.

For a list of titles in the series, see end of book.

SIR MATTHEW HALE
1609–1676

Law, religion and natural philosophy

ALAN CROMARTIE

Trinity College, Cambridge

CAMBRIDGE
UNIVERSITY PRESS

Published by the Press Syndicate of the University of Cambridge
The Pitt Building, Trumpington Street, Cambridge CB2 1RP
40 West 20th Street, New York, NY 10011–4211, USA
10 Stamford Road, Oakleigh, Melbourne 3166, Australia

First published 1995

Printed in Great Britain by Antony Rowe Ltd

A catalogue record for this book is available from the British Library

Library of Congress cataloguing in publication data
Cromartie, Alan.
Sir Matthew Hale (1609–1676): law, religion, and natural philosophy / Alan Cromartie.
p.   cm. – (Cambridge studies in early modern British history)
Includes bibliographical references and index.
ISBN 0 521 45043 8 (hc)
1. Hale, Matthew, Sir, 1609–1676. 2. Lawyers – England – Biography.
3. Law – England – History. 4. Hale, Matthew, Sir, 1609–1676 – Views on religion.
5. Hale, Matthew, Sir, 1609–1676 – Views on science.
I. Title. II. Series.
KD621.H34C76 1995
340'.092 – dc20   94–9611   CIP

ISBN 0 521 45043 8 hardback

In memory of my father

CONTENTS

ACKNOWLEDGEMENTS

This book has its origins in (and wholly supersedes) a somewhat uneven doctoral dissertation ('Sir Matthew Hale', Cambridge 1991). I am extremely grateful to Richard Tuck, my supervisor; to my examiners, Professor Gerald Aylmer and Mr David Yale; and to the British Academy, which paid for three years of research. Part of the last revision took place in time stolen from other projects during happy short-term fellowships at the John Carter Brown and Folger Shakespeare Libraries. Trinity College, Cambridge has housed, fed, and protected me for the best part of a decade, latterly as a Fellow, elected under Title 'A'. Like many Cambridge graduate students over recent years, I doubt I would have persevered without the consistent kindness of John Morrill. As an unusually disorganised reader, I have benefited greatly from the goodness of the staff in the Bodleian Library, Oxford, the University Library, Cambridge (especially the Rare Books Room), the Public Record Office, Chancery Lane, Lambeth Palace Library, Lincoln's Inn Library, Gloucester Record Office, and the London Library. The then librarian of Lambeth Palace, Dr Geoffrey Bill, made my researches feasible by letting me read the Hale papers in an unbound, uncatalogued state. I owe a special debt to Colin Armstrong for reading the *Church Times* and telling me this archive had become available. Exasperated readers should exonerate all the above of the responsibility for anything to be found in the following pages which strikes them as dull, or erroneous, or stupid. Things would have been much worse without the criticisms of an anonymous reader, my copy-editor, Mary Richards, and the editors of this series. Inadequacies which remain are nobody's fault but my own.

Introduction: a summary life

'That incomparably learned, upright man and just'[1] Sir Matthew Hale, Chief Justice of King's Bench, was born on 1 November 1609, at the village of Alderley in Gloucestershire. By the time of his death, on Christmas Day of 1676, he had come to embody an ideal of piety and probity and learning. He was 'good Sir Matthew Hales', 'the just and pious ... Hales', 'that excellent good man', a figure whose reputation, in itself, would justify a study of his career.[2] This introduction will set out, as economically as possible, the facts of the life that occasioned this chorus of praise.

The little that is known about Hale's background suggests it was respectable, but socially entirely unpretentious. The nearest town to Alderley was Wotton-under-Edge, a centre of the clothing trade just under the scarp of the Cotswolds. The effective founder of his family was a clothier of Wotton, a certain Robert Hale, who left £10,000 between five sons.[3] This character's only mark on local history had a certain symbolic appropriateness, given the nature of his grandson's fame; he was thrown off a jury, in 1573, for refusing to have any part in a false declaration.[4] His second son, also a Robert (?1563–1612), was educated at Broadgates Hall in Oxford, matriculating in April 1580, and was called to the bar, at Lincoln's Inn, in February 1594.[5] He married Joan Poyntz of Alderley in

---

[1] *Memoirs of the Verney Family during the seventeenth century*, ed. F. P. Verney, 1907, vol. IV, p. 321. All books published in London unless otherwise stated. The annotation of this introduction is largely restricted to matters of fact.

[2] A. B. Grosart (ed.), *Prose works of Andrew Marvell*, 1875, vol. IV, p. 315; John Gadbury, *The just and pious scorpionist or the nativity of that thrice excellent man Sir Matthew Hales*, 1677; *The diary of John Evelyn*, ed. W. Bray, 1907, vol. II, p. 63. For a printed tribute in verse, see *A poem of the history of Queen Hesther, an elegy on the death of the Lord Chief Justice Hales and other occasional poems*, For William Leech, n.d., pp. 4–5. For a rare discordant view, alleging that he was republican, see 'Quaeries on Chief Justice Hales' (Bodleian library, MS Dom. b. 8, pp. 557–8).

[3] Gilbert Burnet, *The life and death of Sir Matthew Hale*, 1682, p. 1

[4] E. S. Lindley, *Wotton-under-Edge: men and affairs of a Cotswold wool town*, 1977, pp. 38–9, 214.

[5] *Alumni Oxonienses: the members of the University of Oxford 1500–1714*, ed. Joseph Foster 1891; Burnet, *Life*, 2.

1

1599, and built the house at Alderley where his only child Matthew was born.[6] As a barrister, he never appeared in court (he had a 'chamber practice'), because he was rather hesitant in speech, and also much too scrupulous to add 'colour' to a case.[7] He was addicted, Matthew later wrote, to studying theology and the scriptures, and chose a guardian for his son who ensured that these tastes were passed on.[8]

Matthew Hale was brought up, from the age of two, by Antony Kingscot of Kingscot (d. 1654) a man of strongly puritan opinions.[9] Kingscot was much admired by the local antiquarian Smyth of Nibley (1567–1640), because 'he and his lineal ancestors have continued in this little manor now above 500 years, never attainted nor dwelling out of it elsewhere; nor hath the tide of his estate higher or lower flowed or ebbed in better or worse condition ...'[10] The manor in question was extremely modest, suggesting little more than yeoman status, for Kingscot's father Christopher had lands worth £80 p.a. when he died in 1607.[11] In economic terms, Hale was roughly his guardian's equal, inheriting lands worth £100 p.a., less £20 p.a. that his father had tied to local charities.[12]

These facts exhaust our knowledge of the younger Hale's social position, perhaps without serious loss to our knowledge of Hale. If Kingscot had a long-term influence, it derived from his religion not his income. His views can reasonably be gauged from the will he left in 1654, which denounced and disinherited his son for joining 'the Popish army, the enemies of God, his Church and this nation'.[13] The sources are agreed that Hale's early education was under puritans, and not, as would have been more natural, in Wotton's grammar school.[14] His tutor at Oxford's Magdalen Hall was Obadiah Sedgwick (?1600–58), who was later a noted puritan divine, but who left no discernible intellectual trace. The only certainties upon this topic are his matriculation, on 20 October 1626,[15] and his entry into Lincoln's Inn on 18 May 1629.[16]

At Lincoln's Inn, Hale soon made friends with a number of distinguished older men, including William Noy (d. 1634), the authoritarian Attorney-General, William Prynne (1600–69), the puritan antiquary, and

---

[6] Edmund Heward, *Matthew Hale*, 1972, p. 14.   [7] Burnet, *Life*, 2; Lambeth 3516, 2.
[8] Lambeth 3516, 2.   [9] Burnet, *Life*, 3.   [10] *Berkeley MSS*, 409.
[11] H. P. R. Finberg (ed.), *Gloucestershire studies*, Leicester 1957 p. 164.
[12] Burnet, *Life*, 3. This figure is taken from Burnet, Hale's first biographer, who was writing in the early 1680s. The only other evidence is a letter Hale wrote in 1633, expressing willingness to exchange his land for an annual income of £100 (Lambeth MSS 3516, fo. 205).
[13] *Finberg, Gloucestershire studies*, 164.
[14] Burnet, *Life*, 5; Wood, *Athenae Oxonienses*, 3rd edn, 1813, vol. III, p. 1091.
[15] Joseph Foster, *Alumni Oxonienses: 1500–1714*, 4 vols., Oxford 1891–92. Hale chose to describe himself as 'armiger'; his father was content with just 'plebeian'.
[16] *Records of the Honourable Society of Lincoln's Inn: the Black Books*, 1898, vol. II, p. 285.

also, most importantly, John Selden (1584–1654), a man of almost universal learning, whose theories were to dominate much of his later thought.[17] Hale was called to the bar in 1636, after the usual seven years of training, but our knowledge of his professional career begins in the middle of 1641. His earliest known client was a judge, one of those who pronounced for the king in the notorious 'Ship Money' decision (1638), which legalised emergency taxation.[18] If the case had come to trial, such judges would have been accused of treason, a crime on which Hale soon developed a special expertise. In the course of the next ten years, he argued for a series of defendants, including the king's chief minister Archbishop Laud (1643–44),[19] his Scottish ally the Duke of Hamilton (1649),[20] and the presbyterian royalist Christopher Love (1651).[21] In the course of the same period, he was working on a learned manuscript (discussed in Chapter 3) which makes it clear that he himself was intellectually a royalist.

For all his theoretical adherence to the king, Hale prospered in the later 1640s; he was rich enough by 1648 to be able to find £4,200 to spend on a purchase of land.[22] He already had about him a kind of moral charm that enormously impressed his generation. No evidence historians are likely to unearth could convey this quality better than a story John Aubrey (1626–97) records:

I remember about 1646 (or 1647) that Mr John Maynard (now Sir John and serjeant) came into Middle Temple Hall, from Westminster-Hall, weary with business and hungry, when we had newly dined. He sat down by Mr Bennet Hoskyns (the only son of Serjeant Hoskyns, the poet) since baronet, and some others; who having made an end of their commons, fell unto various discourse, and what was the meaning of the text (Rom. v 7) 'for a just man one would dare to die; but for a good man one would willingly die.' They asked Mr Maynard what was the difference between a just man and a good man. He was beginning to eat and cried: 'Hoh! you have eaten your dinners and now have leisure to discourse; I have not. He had eat but a bit or two when he replied: 'I'll tell you the difference presently: Serjeant Rolle is a just man, and Matthew Hale is a good man', and so fell to make an end of his dinner. And there could not be a better interpretation of this text. For Serjeant Rolle was just, but by nature penurious; and his wife made him worse: Matthew Hale was not only just, but wonderfully charitable and open handed, and did not sound a trumpet neither, as the hypocrites do.[23]

[17] Burnet, *Life*, 14; John Aubrey, *Aubrey's brief lives*, ed. Andrew Clark, 2 vols., Oxford 1898, vol. II, pp. 21, 225; Lambeth 3516, 203.
[18] *The autobiography of Sir John Bramston*, Camden Society 1845, p. 78.
[19] T. B. Howell (ed.), *A complete collection of state trials*, 1810 (hereafter cited as Cobbett, *State trials*), vol IV, p. 653.
[20] Cobbett, *State trials*, IV, 1162–65; Hale's own notes for his argument survive in Lambeth 3479, 164–75.
[21] Cobbett, *State trials*, V, 206–46.   [22] Lindley, *Wotton-under-Edge*, 212.
[23] *Aubrey's brief lives*, II, 203–4.

It was this enviable reputation, allied to his extraordinary learning, that gave his attitude to the Republic its great political significance.

The execution of King Charles seems not to have interrupted Hale's career. He consented to take the Engagement to be 'true and faithful to the Commonwealth without a King and a House of Lords',[24] and was a leading figure in the so-called Hale commission (1652) to examine the state of the laws. In January 1654, at the start of the Cromwellian regime, he accepted a place as a judge, and he sat in Cromwell's parliament that autumn. He made it clear he favoured a 'single person's' rule, but seemed perfectly content that the single person should be Oliver. A major-general commented, in 1656, that 'I never knew a man at his own cost more willing to serve the present government than he'.[25] At Cromwell's death, however, he at once resigned his post, and maintained himself instead by 'chamber practice'.[26]

Hale sat in the parliament called by Richard Cromwell (1659), but he appears to have played no significant part; in the Convention parliament (1660), however, he was a highly influential figure. Though he welcomed the king's return, he 'feared the detestation of the latter extreme under which we last smarted ... will carry us over to the former extreme'.[27] He is said to have made a speech suggesting a conditional restoration, and certainly hoped to modify the church to meet long-standing puritan demands. He later became a close personal friend of the presbyterian[28] leader Richard Baxter (1615–91), and he was the author, in 1668, of an abortive 'comprehension'[29] bill.

Suspicion of the new regime proved no bar to resuming a successful judicial career, first as Chief Baron of the Exchequer (November 1660), and then as the Chief Justice of King's Bench (May 1671). In December 1672, for reasons that have never been explained, the council decided in principle to sack him.[30] The plan was dropped, however, presumably because the king opposed it, and Hale was unmolested till he resigned, pleading ill health, in February of 1676. Among the politically minded, attitudes to his time upon the bench depended very largely on attitudes to nonconformity, for in cases that related to the interests of dissent Hale was almost invari-

---

[24] Cobbett, *State trials*, V, 211.   [25] *Thurloe state papers*, IV, 686.

[26] *Calendar of the Clarendon state papers preserved in the Bodleian library*, 5 vols., Oxford 1932, vol. IV, p. 160.

[27] J. B. Williams, *Memoirs of the life character and writings of Sir Matthew Hale*, 1835, p. 63.

[28] 'Presbyterian' is used, throughout this book, in the loosest of its seventeenth-century senses, to refer to nonconformists who wanted an intolerant national church.

[29] 'Comprehension' set out to enlarge the church by making concessions to scrupulous puritan minds.

[30] Public Record Office, S.P. 104/177, fo. 101.

ably found on the liberal side. The Tory Roger North (1653–1734) regarded him as 'demagogical', though he admitted that 'when Hales was Chief Baron of the Exchequer, by means of his great learning, even against his inclination, he did the Crown more justice, in that court, than any others, in his place, had done with all their good will and less knowledge.'[31] To most of his contemporaries, however, he remained an emblematic paragon, the type of the upright judge and pious layman, combining enormous legal erudition with a puritan-tinged but rational religion. This was the view cemented by his earliest biographer Gilbert Burnet, whose Low Church hagiography *The life and death of Sir Matthew Hale* (1682) has set the tone for subsequent discussions.

There are competent biographies of Hale, and the facts of his public career are undisputed.[32] His private life seems to have been unhappy, though the evidence is little more than gossip; the first of his wives, Anne Moore, made a 'great cuckold' of him, if Aubrey's 'brief life' is to be believed.[33] He is said to have had ten children by this marriage, of whom six survived to early adult life.[34] His second marriage, in 1667, was to a second Anne, who appears to have been a servant of some kind.[35] North gleefully alleged that

this great man was most unfortunate in his family; for he married his own servant maid, and then, for an excuse, said there was no wisdom below the girdle. All his sons died in the sink of lewdness and debauchery; and if he was to blame in their education, it was by too much of rigour, rather than of liberty . . .[36]

With a handful of his other characteristics, we are on surer ground. We know he had to force himself to condemn convicted felons, and that his tenderheartedness extended even to his animals;[37] that he dressed with ostentatious shabbiness;[38] that he spoke extremely softly and chose his words with care;[39] and that he needed spectacles for reading.[40] This handful of details apart, the sources are uninformative about the personality that so impressed all his contemporaries. Hale is presented in this book as the mass of historical evidence presents him, as the bearer of opinions in

---

[31] North, *The life of the Rt. Hon. Francis North Baron of Guilford*, 1742, p. 61.
[32] Edmund Heward, *Matthew Hale*, 1972; J. B. Williams, *Memoirs of the life, character and writings of Sir Matthew Hale*, 1835.
[33] *Aubrey's brief lives*, I, 278.
[34] Burnet, *Life*, 109. Heward, *Hale*, 33, 112–14 has traced the details of his family.
[35] Hale, *Works*, I, 89. The scurrilous 'Quaeries on Chief Justice Hales' describes him as 'marrying his scullion-wench to make himself a cuckold' (Bodleian library MS Dom. b. 8, 558).
[36] North, *Life of Guilford*, 63.   [37] Burnet, *Life*, 99; Hale, *Works*, II, 273–4.
[38] Burnet, *Life*, 12–13; Hale, *Works*, I, 89..
[39] North, *Life of Guilford*, 62; Style 204 (Law reports are cited, where possible, from the standard reprint, *The English reports*, 1900–11.); Hale, *Works*, I, 97.
[40] Lambeth 3493, 88v.

politics, philosophy, theology, and law. He is treated as a Protestant, a constitutional royalist, and a dabbler in natural science, but never, for example, as a landowner in south-east Gloucestershire.

To lawyers, of course, his importance has always been clear: not only was he a great judge, but his *Historia placitorum coronae* (first published 1726) became an unchallenged authority on English criminal law, while his *History of the common law of England* (1713) gave a sketch of the legal past that was unrivalled for two centuries. His other legal writings (just one of which was published in his lifetime) included treatises about the customs and the House of Lords considered as a court, and an *Analysis* of the whole system, as well as no fewer than three attempts to write a work on the prerogative. No one was better equipped to articulate the views of his profession, and no one gives more insight into the intellectual implications of the constitutional role of common law.

Hale's non-professional manuscripts are not of the same stature, but they have an extraordinary interest for the more general history of ideas. He wrote one famous printed book, the *Primitive origination of mankind* (1677), which was praised by Dr Johnson, but has been rather more revered than read. There were also three short scientific pamphlets, as well as a number of brief devotional tracts, published without consent, but not without his subsequent approval. His claim to attention, however, is not his printed output, but the extraordinary range of surviving manuscript material, from edifying private meditations, through writings on the physics of the magnet, to works about the nature of the soul. His longest single treatise, the ten part, five volume 'De Deo', tries to show the existence of God by reference, amongst other things, to metaphysics, physics, ethics, providence, prophecy and the voice of conscience.

None of these manuscripts was meant for print, and most convey the impression of being an aid to private meditations. His great friend Richard Baxter, who actually saw him at work, said that he wrote with amazing fluency, needing only 'to tap his thoughts and let them run', preparing himself at most with a jotted plan.[41] He wrote, by his own account, to 'fix' his thoughts,[42] and the resultant faults of all these writings are a great boon to the historian. He repeated himself so often that his meaning was rarely in doubt, and he tried to be exhaustive in stating rival views. His papers thus give an unusually intimate access to an unusually methodical mind.

Perhaps their greatest merit is the sense that they give of a culture's situation. Hale was born into a stable monarchy, where philosophy was Aristotelian, and theology was firmly Calvinist. The collapse of all these

---

[41] Hale, *A discourse of the knowledge of God and of ourselves*, 1688, ed. Richard Baxter, sig. A4v; Hale, *Contemplations moral and divine*, 1676, sig. A2.

[42] Lambeth 3509, 70; Lambeth 3493, ii.

certainties was reflected in the pages of his works, and so was the inter-relation of beliefs in all three of these spheres. He could touch, in a single brief work 'On the nature of laws', on the origins of property, the nature of the will, and the hope that virtuous pagans might be saved.[43] His purpose (in the non-professional writings) was invariably religious; he chose to consider some aspect of the world for the sake, as he usually put it, of 'carrying up' his mind to his creator. Although his subject matter was so varied, his topic of the moment was always intended to strengthen Christian faith.

Hale's output aspired to unity, but this book has been divided in three parts, treating 'law', and then 'religion', and lastly 'natural philosophy'. Though the section on 'law' is designed as an essay on Hale, it traces the development of an entire approach to politics. It explains why all the parties, in the turmoil of the English revolution, appealed to an unwritten legal system, and how the operations of that system made a republic unsustainable. It is only incidentally concerned with Hale's technical legal achievements, though it of course contains much information of interest to historians of law. The sections on 'natural philosophy' and 'religion' can be read quite independently of the first half of the book, but they should, if at all possible, be taken in conjunction with each other. Not the least of Hale's great virtues was ignorance of the boundaries segmenting our own, more timid, mental lives.

[43]British Library, Hargrave 485.

Part I

LAW

Coke: the appeal to reason

Hale was a noted judge, in a period respectful of judges, a 'man of great authority'[1] for his expertise in law. His career and his writings exemplified an obvious but very puzzling feature of seventeenth-century English political life. The culture to which he belonged was deeply constitutionalist in feeling: participants assumed, that is to say, that the purpose of debate was always to establish what the law of England was, not what it ought to be. In itself, this was hardly a matter for surprise; there was a sense, in late Renaissance Europe, in which every political argument was legal. The law, as Justinian's *Institutes* had put it, was 'the knowledge of things human and divine';[2] it included every principle that was relevant to administering a state. Particular local arrangements (*ius civile*) were open to supplementation and correction with reference to rules (described as the 'laws' of nature and of nations) that were binding on all humanity in every place and time. By the outbreak of the English civil wars, most of Hale's countrymen had come to a very much odder belief: that the repository of all this wisdom was their esoteric and unwritten system, the unapologetically provincial common law.

Hale would in any age have been a great professional technician; there were few other periods, however, in which his mastery of legal practice would have given him such political importance. The lawyers were grammarians, to extend a now conventional metaphor, of the dominant 'language of political thought', and therefore of the legitimacy of an extraordinary range of polemical claims. Thinkers as far apart as Thomas Hobbes and the Leveller John Lilburne attempted, on occasion, to cast their very radical suggestions as an interpretation of the existing law.[3] Not

---

1 'Vir magnae apud nos authoritatis'. The natural philosopher Henry Oldenburg, on the subject of Hale's late scientific writings (*The correspondence of Henry Oldenburg*, ed. and tr. A. R. and M. B. Hall, 1977, vol. XI, p. 313).
2 R. W. Lee, *The elements of Roman law: with a translation of the Institutes of Justinian*, 4th edn, 1956, p. 43 (*Institutes*, I, i, 2).
3 For Hobbes, see below, pp. 98–100.

even the republicans (as Chapters 4 and 5 will try to show) were exempt from the urge to present their cause in broadly legal terms. The English treated common law, in fact, as a kind of political science, describing not just how things were, but how they ought to be. They did not turn away from rational political debate:[4] they turned towards a body of ideas they supposed to be supremely rational. If Hale is to be understood, then so must the brilliant publicist who lodged this expectation in the national consciousness. The foundation of his legal and political ideas was the achievement of Sir Edward Coke (1552–1634).

For forty years, as lawyer or Crown servant, Coke had a central role in public life. He was Elizabeth's Attorney-General (1594–1606), James' Chief Justice of Common Pleas (1606–13) and then of the King's Bench (1613–16) and a prominent figure, after James had sacked him, in the troubled parliaments of the 1620s.[5] He was no more consistent, over this lengthy period, than would be expected of a politician, but his writings showed unwavering commitment to a powerful general conception of the law. The jurisprudence that he popularised (and probably to some extent invented) was continually implied, and occasionally eloquently stated, in the course of eleven volumes of *Reports* (1600–15), followed, more systematically, by the four parts of his *Institutes of the common law* (1628–44).[6] They constitute an extended justification of a kind of 'judge-made law'. The great judge was an arbiter of every political question because he had internalised, through his professional training, what amounted to an infinity of wisdom, becoming the mouthpiece of natural law and even, perhaps, of God. This position was undoubtedly extreme, by the standards of his or any other time, but it was very deftly integrated into much less contentious legal matter. The link, and his claim to attention, was a theory about legal thinking: an account, with remarkable power, of what lawyers actually did.

The common law proper (that is, excluding statute) was an unwritten system, which drew, as most practitioners agreed, on two separate authoritative sources: on the principles of natural law but also on 'general custom' (which was technically defined to include all rules observed, throughout

[4] For some admirably succinct reflections on this topic, see Johann P. Sommerville, 'History and theory: the Norman Conquest in Stuart political thought', *Political Studies*, 34 (1986), 249–61.

[5] There is still no scholarly biography, but S. D. White, *Sir Edward Coke and the grievances of the commonwealth*, Manchester 1979, covers the 1620s parliaments.

[6] The twelfth and thirteenth parts of the *Reports* (first printed 1656 and 1659) contain much interesting material, but only those writings Coke certainly opted to publish are relevant to this chapter's argument. On the sources of the *Reports*, see J. H. Baker, 'Coke's notebooks and the sources of his reports' in J. H. Baker, *The legal profession and the common law*, 1986, pp. 153–69.

the land, since 3 September 1189).[7] The first was essentially rational, and therefore intrinsically binding; the second was enacted by popular consent. The first resembled the truths of mathematics; the second was a kind of tacit statute. It was possible, however, to combine the two ideas. The inherent adaptability of custom (unlike a rigid, because written, law) could be seen as a guarantee that the system it created was a rational response to local needs. This was certainly the view of Sir John Davies (1569–1626), who wrote that the English had 'made their own laws out of their wisdom and experience (like a silkworm that formeth all her web out of her self only)'.[8] It was the possibility that J. G. A. Pocock describes: that 'custom might be idealised and described as perfect equity; the English common lawyers virtually reached this point.'[9] The idea was extremely attractive (not least to Matthew Hale), but Coke had a different approach.

The problem Coke addressed was best articulated by St German (*c.* 1460–1541). For the great Henrician jurist, the common law proper was 'divers general customs of old time used through all the realm, which have been accepted and approved by our sovereign lord the King and his progenitors and all their subjects'.[10] A chapter later in the same discussion he mentioned the main problem that this definition raised. The general customs were 'the strength and warrant' (the Latin version has 'auctoritas') of a number of rules he called 'maxims', which were unknown outside the Inns of court.[11] 'Authority', he had earlier explained, was crucial to the making of every human law, because 'the sentence of a wise man doth not bind the commonalty if he have no rule over them'.[12] These maxims were

---

[7] Sir John Fortescue, *De laudibus legum Angliae*, ed. S. B. Chrimes, Cambridge 1949, pp. 37–41; Sir John Dodderidge, *The English lawyer*, 1631, pp. 153, 194; 1 Plowden 9 (Law reports are cited, where possible, from the standard reprint, *The English reports*, 1900–32.).

[8] Davies, *Irish reports*, Dublin 1762, p. 6. J. G. A. Pocock, *The ancient constitution and the feudal law: a study in English historical thought: a reissue with a retrospect*, Cambridge 1987, pp. 32–5.

[9] Pocock, *Ancient constitution*, 24.

[10] St German, *St German's Doctor and Student*, ed. T. F. T. Plucknett and J. L. Barton, Selden Society, 1974, p. 45.

[11] St German, *Doctor*, p. 59. For a careful definition of the maxim see John Guy, *St German on chancery and statute*, Selden Society supplementary series, no. 6, 1985, p. 87. More generally, see Peter Stein, *Regulae juris: from juristic rules to legal maxims*, Edinburgh 1966.

[12] St German, *Doctor*, 26–7. For a very interesting contrasted view, see Glenn Burgess, *The politics of the ancient constitution: an introduction to English political thought 1603–1642*, 1992, esp. pp. 27–57. Burgess believes that all of common law was seen as both reason and custom, though many of the customs were only known among the common lawyers (pp. 34–5). He implicitly denies that the making of a custom in the first place demanded a general popular consent. This theory is probably true of most earlier lawyers; we are told that 'nowhere in the theory of Pecock and Fortescue or in the Year Books can be found statements which regard the consent of the community as the basis for national custom, the common law' (Norman Doe, *Fundamental authority in late medieval law*,

not part of natural law, but nor were they created by consent. It might be said (and was) that they were ultimately customary: that they did no more than organise a mass of principles agreed by custom.[13] But the presentation was authoritative, and the problem then recurred at one remove. If they were interpreting custom (often in highly counter-intuitive ways) they must have some authority to do so.

The dilemma was painfully clear. Common law was supposed to rest upon consent but its details were extremely technical, and plenty of its rules were surprising or even abhorrent to the layman. The training of professionals was based in part on oral exercises, and the common law literature, such as it was, was written either in Latin or Norman French.[14] The knowledge of the law, to a very large extent, was the knowledge of various technical procedures, of the availability, in particular situations, of certain royal 'writs'. It was custom, of course, in a weak sense (the people acquiesced), but it was devised and developed in the courts of Westminster Hall.[15]

The esoteric nature of the law was related to its utter formlessness.[16] There was no convenient synthesis of all this scattered learning, so the great common lawyers spent much of their lives in reading and excerpting from the Year Books, medieval accounts of what earlier lawyers had done. The most important works of reference, the *Abridgements* of Brooke and Fitzherbert, were really no more than lists of legal points, somewhat haphazardly set out under loose thematic headings. No one was born a

Cambridge 1990, p. 22). In the time of Hale's youth it was equally true of the great Attorney-General William Noy (Noy, *A treatise of the principal grounds and maxims of the laws of this kingdom*, 1641, pp. 20–1). In the case of St German, however, it is mistaken. Burgess believes (p. 31) that St German's concept of a 'law of reason secondary particular' contains 'all laws which the English thought rational [i.e. all peculiarly English laws]'. In fact St German holds that this 'law of reason secondary' consists in laws that are 'grounded' and 'derived upon' the statutes, customs, and maxims (*Doctor*, 33–5). It cannot be identical with custom, because it is composed of rules deduced from the principles of positive law. There is a sense, of course, in which custom can be seen as rational: it does not actually conflict with reason, or else it would not be a law at all. But many rules which satisfy this test lack the authority to bind as laws.

13 This was the theory of Thomas Hedley, in E. R. Foster (ed.), *Proceedings in parliament 1610*, vol. II, House of Commons, Yale 1966, p. 176.

14 The best account of legal training and the social history of law is Wilfrid R. Prest, *The rise of the barristers: a social history of the English bar 1590–1640*, Oxford 1986, and the same author's *The Inns of court*, 1972. On its probable consequences for the law see J. H. Baker, 'The Inns of court and legal doctrine', in T. M. Charles-Edwards *et al.* (ed.), *Lawyers and laymen: studies in the history of law presented to Professor Dafydd Jenkins*, pp. 274–83.

15 The discussion that follows owes a large but unspecifiable debt to A. W. B. Simpson's immensely helpful essay, 'The common law and legal theory' in Simpson (ed.), *Oxford essays in jurisprudence*, 2nd series, Oxford 1973.

16 For a frank admission of this, see William Lambarde, *Eirenarcha, or of the office of justices of the peace*, 1619, p. 511.

lawyer, as Coke on occasion remarked,[17] and no one could become one through reading a few books. He was led to the very interesting conclusion that law acquired authority in the place that it acquired a rational form: in the mind of a common law judge.[18]

His own most elaborate treatise deliberately exemplified the system's most obvious faults. Justinian's *Institutes* were meant to be a legal primer, but the first part of Coke's *Institutes*, his learned commentary on Littleton, made no concessions to the mere beginner. Littleton (1402–81) was a fifteenth-century judge who wrote a little treatise about tenures, a masterpiece of clarity that was obviously and usably a textbook;[19] Coke obfuscated Littleton's achievement by surrounding it with a jumble of ingenuity and erudition that ranges unpredictably over the common law. The product was a kind of anti-textbook, a work whose very form denied that legal knowledge could be organised. The original edition could not be used for reference purposes, as Coke had published it without an index, on the grounds that 'tables and abridgements are most profitable to them that make them'.[20] It is a book to be 'read in' and lived with, rather than consulted, a monument to the uselessness of merely written knowledge unless it is internalised in a trained professional mind.

This raised the question in what sense, if any, the law the professionals practised could be traced to the popular will. The substance of the law, as known to the judges, was not just unknown but unknowable outside the Inns of court. In the late medieval period, it seems that no one saw this as a problem. E. W. Ives has pronounced, with reference to the early sixteenth century, that 'authority lay in the collective mind of the profession, past and present',[21] while Norman Doe has written that 'judicial usage and consent, rather than popular consent, made the common law (though occasionally a fiction was employed, notably by St German, that the community of the realm had consented to the common law)'.[22] The probable explanation of this fact is that almost all the sources we possess were produced by professionals talking among themselves. For a courtroom lawyer's purposes, the authority of judges was simply presupposed.

In the time of Coke, however, the common lawyers had acquired a wider

[17] Coke, *The first part of the Institutes of the laws of England*, ed. C. Butler and F. Hargrave, 138.
[18] He once remarked that a certain rule was 'good law, if it be well understood; for non in legendo sed intelligendo leges consistunt' (*Eighth reports*, 167a).
[19] For many interesting reflections on the relationship between legal literature and jurisprudence, see A. W. B. Simpson, 'The rise and fall of the legal treatise: legal principles and the forms of legal literature', *University of Chicago Law Review*, 48 (1982), 632–79.
[20] Coke, *First institutes, fo. 395a*.
[21] E. W. Ives, *The common lawyers of pre-Reformation England: Thomas Kebell: a case study*, Cambridge 1983, p. 161.
[22] Doe, *Fundamental authority*, 26.

audience; they needed to offer some kind of explanation why the customs observed by the bench should bind upon the nation as a whole. They therefore acknowledged, in theory, that the positive rules enforced by the court system enjoyed their legal status by popular consent.[23] Coke was the one significant exception to this rule. He never denied, though he certainly did not stress, that the 'general customs' of England were part of common law.[24] But he was most reluctant to allow the nation as a whole a legislative power, even (as we shall see) when it assembled in a parliament. The role that 'custom' played within his thought was as 'the best interpreter of laws', rather than as a legislative force.[25] The essence of his theory was the belief that common law was 'reason', containing nothing arbitrary at all.[26]

The association between law and reason was hardly a novel idea. 'Law', Cicero had said, 'is the highest reason (*ratio summa*) implanted in nature, which commands what ought to be done and forbids the opposite. This reason, when firmly fixed and developed (*confirmata et confecta*) in the human mind, is law'.[27] It was, however, broader than any local system of merely 'civil' law. It was the principle that distinguished good and evil, that 'came into existence simultaneously with the divine mind' (*orta est simul cum mente divina*),[28] that 'when it is full grown and perfected (*cum adolevit et perfecta est*) is rightly called wisdom'.[29] Coke was familiar with these platitudes, and mobilised them to promote a much more curious personal belief: that every claim the Roman made for 'law' could be applied to English common law, and that the wisdom Cicero described existed in its 'perfect' form in the common lawyer's mind. The system's great internal harmony was a mark of its exalted origin, for 'without question *lex orta est cum mente divina*, and this admirable unity and consent in such diversity of things proceeded from God the fountain and

---

[23] Henry Finch, *A description of the common laws of England*, 1759, pp. 52–3; Sir John Dodderidge, *The English lawyer*, 1631, p. 103.

[24] For a casual admission of this fact, see *Ninth reports*, 75b.

[25] Coke, *Second reports*, 81a; *Sixth reports*, 5b. There were also, of course, local customs, but even these had to be 'reasonable', that is, to be accepted by the judges of Westminster Hall.

[26] On the common law concept of reason, see J. U. Lewis, 'Sir Edward Coke (1552–1633): his theory of artificial reason as a context for modern basic legal theory', *Law Quarterly Review*, 84 (1968), 330–42; C. M. Gray, 'Authority and the imagination: the jurisprudence of Sir Edward Coke', in Perez Zagorin (ed.), *Culture and politics from puritanism to the enlightenment*, Berkeley 1980, pp. 25–66; and Gray, 'Parliament, liberty and the law', in J. H. Hexter (ed.), *Parliament and liberty from the reign of Elizabeth to the English civil war*, Stanford 1992, pp. 85–121. For the idea's earlier history, see Doe, *Fundamental authority*, 108–31.

[27] 'lex est ratio summa insita in natura, quae iubet ea, quae facienda sunt, prohibetque contraria. eadem ratio cum est in hominis mente confirmata et confecta, lex est.' Loeb Classical Library, *The works of Cicero*, vol. XVI (*De republica, De legibus*) tr. C. W. Keyes, 1928, pp. 316–17.

[28] Cicero, *De legibus*, 382–3.   [29] *Ibid.*, 320–1.

founder of all good laws and constitutions.'[30] It followed that the common law of England had an answer to every question which it faced, and that the master of this legal system, a learned judge like Coke or Matthew Hale, was the natural arbiter of politics.

Coke's assertions depended, in part, upon a mere coincidence of words: that 'reason' was not just rationality, in absolute and eternally binding form, but the name usual among common lawyers for the intellectual method they employed.[31] Reason distinguished what was law from what, as it happened, was not. Local customs upheld by the courts were 'customs reasonable' and rules that they struck down were often said to be 'unreasonable', but the 'reason' concerned was not to be confused, the professionals hastened to stress, with the layman's 'natural reason'. It was the faculty acquired by training that extracted some workable rules from a formless body of immemorial knowledge, knowledge transmitted largely through accounts, excerpted from three centuries of 'Year Books' and Reports, of what earlier lawyers had done. The law, Coke maintained, was an art, the province of a craftsman (Latin: *artifex*). The practitioner's skill, his 'artificial' reason, was the way to make sense of this chaos.

Understanding of Coke's position demands a close analysis of the full range of his equivocations. Consider, for example, his dazzling exposition of the old tag 'ratio est anima legis':

the reason of the law is the life of the law, for though a man can tell the law, yet if he knows not the reason thereof, he shall soon forget his superficial knowledge. But when he findeth the right reason of the law, and so bringeth it to his natural reason, that he comprehendeth it as his own, this will not only serve him for the understanding of that particular case, but also many others, for cognitio legis est copulata et complicata,[32] and this knowledge will long remain with him.[33]

This passage uses 'reason' in at least five distinguishable senses:
(1) Absolute rationality, the law of nature.
(2) The rationality or ordering principle intrinsic to a given subject matter.
(3) The justification of a particular rule.
(4) The lawyer's 'natural reason' (his intellectual faculty).
(5) The idea in the mind of the lawyer.
The phrase 'right reason of the law', for instance, refers both to the 'reason' of any particular rule (3) and to the rationality internal to the

---

[30] *Third reports*, iv, from Coke, *The reports of Sir Edward Coke, Knt.*, ed. J. H. Thomas and J. F. Fraser, 1826 (the *English reports* reprint omits his prefaces).

[31] Finch, *Description*, 52; Dodderidge, *English lawyer*, 242; William Noy, *A treatise of the principal grounds and maxims of the laws of this Kingdom*, 1641, p. 1, cited in Burgess, *Politics*, 40. See the excellent short discussion of 'the common law as reason' in J. P. Sommerville, *Politics and ideology in England 1603–40*, 1986, pp. 92–5.

[32] 'Knowledge of the law is interconnected and folded together.'

[33] Coke, *First institutes*, 183b.

system as a whole (2), but it also suggests 'recta ratio', the absolute rationality (1) of writers such as Cicero or Aquinas. If the lawyer had argued correctly, this reason was not just a feature of the system, but also the thought (5) in his mind (4). As Coke explained in a closely parallel statement:

> ratio est anima legis, for then we are said to know the law when we apprehend the reason of the law, that is when we bring the reason of the law so to our own reason, that we perfectly understand it for our own; and then, and never before, we have such a perfect and inseparable property and ownership therein, as we can neither lose it, nor any man take it from us, and [as] will direct us (the learning of the law is so chained together) in many other cases.[34]

The great judge drew authority from the intellectual labours of the whole of the profession that he led: 'ratio est radius divini luminis,[35] and by reasoning and debating of grave learned men the darkness of ignorance is expelled, and by the light of legal reason the right is discerned, and thereupon judgement is given according to the law, which is the perfection of reason.'[36] The phrase 'the perfection of reason' thus referred to both process and product: the activity of lawyers, as well as the wisdom achieved.

This picture of the common law, the starting point of Hale's, was not so much the outcome as the presupposition of all truly legal thought. One of the purposes of Coke's reports was to sort out contradictions within the common law 'for that it cannot be, but in so many books written in so many several ages there must be ... some diversity of opinions and many doubts left unresolved.'[37] The sources were to be interpreted to reveal their underlying harmony:

> the office of an interpreter is to make such construction not only that one and the same author be not against himself, but also that the resolutions of judgements reported in any one book be not by any literal interpretation expounded against any resolution or judgement reported in any other, but that all si fieri possit should stand together.[38]

Only a trained professional could hope to accomplish this feat, because only a mind that was soaked in legal detail could hope to preserve the coherence of the system as a whole. A significant implication of this view (with consequences that we shall return to) was that a knowledge of the whole was somehow prior to a grasp of its various constituent principles.

The presumption of rationality in the existing law became a useful intellectual tool. The law could be presumed, as a supremely rational

---

[34] *Ibid.*, 394b.   [35] 'Reason is a ray of divine light.'
[36] Coke, *First institutes*, 232b.
[37] Coke, *Third reports*, xxx.   [38] *Ibid.*, 84b.

creation, to have certain desirable features. Coke thus imputed reason to the law, and saw the professional's task as that of revealing its wisdom. This occasionally involved him in an arrogant rejection of good but isolated precedents, which he would treat as 'sudden' (hasty and unconsidered) acts or judgements.[39] But even in discerning virtues allegedly inherent in his system, the great judge was inevitably led to develop and enhance his heritage. He needed to discover consistent principles that explained away the discord of his sources, and that could be extended to answer his contemporary needs. As S. E. Thorne remarked,

> sentences beginning 'for it is an ancient maxim of the common law', followed by one of Coke's spurious Latin maxims, which he could manufacture to fit any occasion and provide with an air of authentic antiquity, are apt to introduce a new departure. Sentences such as 'And by these differences and reasons you will better understand your books', or 'And so the doubts and diversities in the books well resolved' likewise indicate new law.[40]

The great advantage of Coke's legal theory was that 'certainty' and intellectual beauty (the elegant rationalisation of a chaotic field) were invariably the marks of legal truth.

Coke saw the history of common law as that of a move from arbitrary judgement to a system with enough sophistication to be predictable, providing the anxious litigant, in a much favoured phrase, with 'certainty the mother of repose'.[41] The people of Israel were governed by natural law alone, 'before the law was written by Moses, who was the first reporter or writer of law in the world'.[42] This was the general rule, and not a peculiar privilege of the Jews, because kings were originally judges: 'before judicial or municipal laws were made, Kings did decide cases according to natural equity, and were not tied to any rule or formality of law, but did dare jura.'[43] The system's evolution did not break the link with reason; it became more reasonable not less, matured indeed into 'the perfection of reason', in the course of its formalisation by the lawyers.

In England's case, notoriously, Coke thought this process had been very long: that the common law had reached an asymptote of rationality by the time of King Edward I, but that the fundamentals of the system had been observed in Saxon, if not druidic times.[44] Because of its long continuous

---

[39] *Second reports*, 67a; *Third reports*, 13b; *Ninth reports*, 89b.

[40] S. E. Thorne, *Essays in English legal history*, 1985, p. 227.

[41] *Second reports*, 75a; *Third reports*, 91b; *Eighth reports*, 53a.

[42] Coke, *Seventh reports*, Calvin's case, 12b.

[43] *Ibid.*, 13a.

[44] Glenn Burgess elegantly argues (*Politics*, 6–7, 26–7, 76–7) that Coke conflated two ideas about unwritten law. He agreed, on the one hand, with Davies, that it adapts itself to circumstance, and that a long development will produce a wise result. On the other, he quoted an argument of Sir John Fortescue's (discussed below, p. 34) which visualised

history, the lawyer could be confident in imputing a near-infinity of reason to the tradition he inherited. The method of the judge, with its confidence in common law's resources, thus presupposed a certain vision of the English past (this point will be further discussed in the context of Hale's own historical outlook). For practical judicial purposes, the great antiquity of common law meant that any of its rules, however foolish, could be defended against criticism: 'if all the reason that were dispersed into so many heads were united into one, yet would he not make such a law as the law of England is, because by many successions of ages it hath been fined and refined by so many learned men.'[45] In another kind of writer, the defender of some limited positive system, this would have been a mere conservative bromide; in Coke, who regarded common law as omnicompetent, it amounted to a claim to political power.

Coke thought, in fact, that there was no such thing as a question undecidable within the common law.[46] A layman might have expected, for example, that the judges would be baffled by the problem of the status of 'post-nati', the Scottish subjects of King James born after he ascended the throne of the neighbouring realm. The issue had prompted Sir Edwin Sandys (1561–1629), a member of the Commons, to make a quite conventional appeal to natural law:

[he] showed that this case was proper to be consulted with the law of nations, which is called 'ius gentium'; for there being no precedent for it in the law 'lex deficit' and 'deficiente lege recurritur ad consuetudinem'[47] and 'deficiente consuetudine recurritur ad rationem naturalem',[48] which 'ratio naturalis' is the law of nations called 'ius gentium'.[49]

The test case, known as Calvin's case (1607) was given an elaborate report, translated from Coke's usual French into a sonorous English. He delivered a magisterial riposte to those who thought like Sandys:

if the said imaginative rule be rightly and legally understood, it may stand for truth, for if you intend ratio for the legal and profound reason of such as by diligent study and long experience and observation are so learned in the laws of

---

the common law as static. It is clear that law's adaptability is quite essential to his argument; the notion that its principles had remained the same for many hundred years is at most an unnecessary flourish. As Burgess rightly notes (p. 76–7), 'when he came to discuss more detailed matters ... he often tacitly abandoned his more extreme claims'.

[45] Coke, *First institutes*, 97b.

[46] One of a number of interesting parallels with the thought of Ronald Dworkin, particularly as expounded in *Law's Empire*, Harvard 1986.

[47] 'The law is wanting, [and] when the law is wanting one resorts to custom.'

[48] 'When custom is wanting one resorts to natural reason (*ratio naturalis*).'

[49] Cobbett, *State trials*, II, 563. For another use of the same argument, see British Library, Harleian MSS 5220, fo. 4v. The author, Sir John Dodderidge, was writing in the last years of Queen Elizabeth's reign. He proposed to use this method to discover the rights of the Crown.

this realm as out of the reason of the same they can rule the case in question, in that sense the said rule is true; but if it be intended of the reason of the wisest man that professeth not the laws of England, then (I say), the rule is absurd and dangerous.[50]

It followed that the law had a response to all of the dilemmas thrown up by social life, and that there could be no appeal, however unusual the case, to the authority of lay opinions.

Coke did not hold, of course, that lawyers had nothing to learn from other people. The judge, however learned, was not omniscient, and there was no shame, in specialised concerns, in taking advice from the appropriate experts:

seeing that [common] laws do limit, bound and determine of all other humane laws, arts and sciences I cannot exclude the knowledge of any of them from the professor of those laws; the knowledge of any of them is necessary and profitable. But forasmuch as if a man should spend his whole life in the study of those laws, yet he might add somewhat to his understanding of them: therefore the judges of the law in matters of difficulty do use to confer with the learned in that art or science, whose resolution is requisite to the true deciding of the case in question.[51]

The judge had the privilege, however, of integrating all these forms of knowledge, and stamping their conclusions with his own authority. To recognise a principle as legal was to have grasped its rationality: the way it could be harmonised with the 'reason' of the system as a whole. In Calvin's case, for instance, Coke made a reference to 'the law of nature', describing it as a 'part of the law of England'.[52] He was entitled to this move, though the layman Sandys was not, because his view of nature was moulded by his prior understanding of the law.

Coke's enemy was always 'natural' reason, reason unguided by professionals, personified, he may have thought, by the presumptuous layman who was his lawful king.[53] It was impossible, in principle, to arrive at a legal conclusion without the use of legal argument. It necessarily followed that there was no such thing as equity, if equity was an independent science, a form of natural justice which might correct and supplement the law. An equitable court (such as the court of Chancery led by his greatest enemy Lord Ellesmere) presumed to be more reasonable than reason, and was therefore looked upon with great distrust. The chancellor's strictly equitable powers dated only from the time of Henry VI, and they lacked

---

[50] Coke, *Seventh reports*, Calvin's case, 19a. Lord Ellesmere's judgement also mentions Sandys, or at least another member who made the same remark (Knafla, *Law and politics*, 220).

[51] Coke, *Third reports*, xxxviii.   [52] Coke, *Seventh reports*, Calvin's case, 12b.

[53] For their most famous clash, see Coke, *Twelfth reports*, 65. Coke's own account of this dramatic scene, as R. G. Usher proved, was an account of what Coke wished he said. Usher, 'James I and Sir Edward Coke', *English Historical Review*, 18 (1903), 664–73.

the slightest statutory foundation.[54] Coke's theoretical hostility was not unprecedented, but it differed from the attitude of his most authoritative predecessor. For Christopher St German, existing law was fully equitable (it drew on equitable principle), and therefore immune from correction.[55] But St German had also quite clearly believed that there were areas outside the law, fields where the chancellor's conscience was the only appropriate judge. His famous legal book took the form of a respectful dialogue 'betwixt a doctor of divinity and a student in the laws of England', an interchange between experts in overlapping but autonomous fields. There was a place, where common law was silent, for the lawyer to attend to lay ideas.

Coke is probably best contrasted, in general philosophical as well as legal terms, with a prominent absolutist who was later (as Lord Chancellor) a judge in equity. Coke's view of legal knowledge was bound to be opposed by Francis Bacon (1561–1626), if only because Bacon saw knowledge in every form as constructed out of isolated facts. Bacon presented law in different terms: as a dependant of the sciences, rather than as their queen. His argument on Calvin's case

showed that it was a singular commendation to the laws of England, that it was not insociable, but contented to hear and be advised by other sciences in matters of dependency upon them; as in cases of exposition of words by grammarians; in matters of matrimony, deprivation, bastardy, by civilians; in minerals by natural philosophers; in uses by moral philosophers.[56]

The matters on which the common law was intended to be 'content to be advised' included the rights of the king. There was a separate sphere of political knowledge, whose conclusions were arrived at independently of law, but which were binding upon common lawyers. In Bacon's case, at least, the maxims that resulted were likely to be authoritarian.[57] It was

---

[54] Coke, *The second part of the Institutes of the laws of England . . . the second part . . . the third part . . . the fourth part*, ed. Brooke, 1797, *Fourth Institutes*, 82. Coke admitted, however, that there was a place for equity in 'matters of trust and confidence' (*Second reports*, 78b). On the practice of King's Bench, which was more accommodating than Coke's theory would suggest, see Charles M. Gray, 'Boundaries of the equitable function', *American Journal of Legal History*, 20 (1976), 192–226. W. J. Jones, 'Conflict or Collaboration? Chancery attitudes in the reign of Elizabeth', *American Journal of Legal History*, 5 (1961), 12–54, and Jones, *The Elizabethan Court of Chancery*, 1967, paint a peaceful picture of the common law's normal relations with equity. Coke's conduct in 1616 is convincingly defended, at least from a jurisprudential standpoint, in J. H. Baker, *The legal profession and the common law*, 1986, pp. 205–29.

[55] The details of his thought are very much harder to pin down. See J. A. Guy, *St German on chancery and statute*, Selden Society, Supplementary series, no. 6, 1985, esp. pp. 83–93.

[56] Cobbett, *State trials*, II, 563.

[57] For an exploration of Bacon's thought, relating his absolutist stance to his legal and philosophical ideas, see Julian Martin, *Francis Bacon, the state and the reform of natural philosophy*, Cambridge 1992.

ideas like his (as Chapter 2 will show) that provided ammunition for the lawyers of the Crown.

The essence of Coke's theory, and its besetting weakness, was that the law's authority was based upon 'reason' alone. The intellectual method of the lawyer was the only judge of what was rational, and therefore what was binding on the English. His reluctance to speak of common law as custom was a mark of a reluctance to see it as in any sense an arbitrary creation, a series of positive rules which were arrived at by consent. Hale's writings on the law, culminating in his *History of the common law of England*, drew heavily upon Coke's legal thought. The difference between them was in Hale's theory of obligation, which based the law's authority on contracts that were made between the people and their king. The heart of the whole matter was Coke's unusual attitude to English written law and therefore to the parliaments in which that law was made.

Though for judicial purposes Coke saw the law as unimprovable, he was not a blind opponent of the idea of parliamentary legislation. The powers and procedures of parliament were after all a part of common law.[58] He tacitly admitted that there was a place for a legislative body, whose purpose was to remedy the 'mischiefs' the existing system caused. His objection was to clumsy legislation, in ignorance of the existing law, which tended to cause more problems than it solved. Some statutes gave no trouble, because they were nothing but 'declaratory' (they affirmed or else restored the common law), but others were 'introductory', and a very fertile source of social danger.[59] The history of the law, at least as Coke surveyed it, was a history of oscillation round a mean. Time and again, for superficial reasons, the English would depart from common law; time and again, the law would be restored 'with great applause'.[60] The ignorance of laymen was the cause of the uncertainty in law, and the remedy was statutes drawn up by qualified professionals:

if Acts of parliament were after the old fashion penned, and by such only as perfectly knew what the common law was before the making of any Act of parliament concerning that matter, as also how far forth former statutes had provided remedy for mischiefs and defects discovered by experience, then should very few questions in law arise.[61]

Statute could be as salutary as the unwritten law, so long as it was guided by someone with a grasp of legal reason. In practice this seldom occurred, but parliamentary wisdom was still an essential presumption of his theory. If law and reason were identical, and parliament was a legislative body,

---

[58] Coke, *First institutes*, 11b.
[59] Coke, *Eighth reports*, xxiii; Coke, *Third reports*, xxxiii; *Fourth reports*, v–vi.
[60] Coke, *Third reports*, xxxiii.   [61] Coke, *Second reports*, ix–x.

then the institution had to be regarded as the supreme authority on reason: in other words as something like a court.

Coke's attitude to parliament has been much misunderstood, even by writers broadly sympathetic, because of an assumption that Englishmen were rising towards a 'modern' view of sovereignty. It has occasionally been claimed (most notably by C. H. McIlwain),[62] that Coke's ideas on statute should be seen as a kind of survival: an unchanged relic of a period when parliament was a judicial body, entrusted with 'finding' the law. In fact, if anything, Coke was a very daring innovator. There seems to have been a consensus, in the later years of Elizabethan England, on a rather familiar view of parliament. Unlike unwritten law, which was intimately linked with natural reason, the statute law was wholly 'positive'.[63] The parliament was a court, at least in name, but it functioned as a modern legislature, acting by representative consent.[64] As William Lambarde (1536–1601) put it: 'forasmuch as every man, from the highest to the lowest, is there either in person or by procuration, every man is said to be bound by that which doth pass from such an assembly.'[65] A conventional way to make this conventional point was to depict the parliament as uniting all the forces of the body politic. Sir Thomas Smith (1513–77) said that it 'representeth and hath the power of the whole realm both the head and the body. For every Englishman is intended to be there present'.[66]

Coke's theory was rather different. In the fourth part of his *Institutes*, composed at the end of his life, he carefully described the role that parliament should play. Like Smith, he used the simile of a 'body politic', but he gave it a different twist:

as in the natural body when all the sinews being joined in the head do join their forces together for the strengthening of the body there is ultimum potentiae, so in the politique body when the king and Lords spiritual and temporal, knights, citizens and burgesses are all by the king's command assembled and joined together under the head in consultation for the common good of the realm, there is ultimum sapientiae.[67]

---

[62] In *The high court of parliament*, 1910.
[63] For the word 'positive', see *A discourse upon the exposition and understanding of statutes*, ed. S. E.Thorne, San Marino 1942, p. 103 and Thorne's learned note.
[64] For an authoritative verdict, see G. R. Elton, *The parliament of England 1559–81*, Cambridge 1986, p. 39. It should be noted, however, that Elton is committed to a strictly functional analysis. He analyses, with great thoroughness, the parliament's administrative role. 'The rest was pretence, even if that pretence could at times deceive the pretenders' (p. 379). It might be protested, of course, that erroneous beliefs very frequently determine political acts.
[65] Lambarde, *Archeion, or the High Courts of Justice in England*, 1635, p. 245. See also D. M. Dean and N. L. Jones, *The parliaments of Elizabethan England*, pp. 2–3.
[66] Sir Thomas Smith, *De republica anglorum*, ed. L. Alston, Cambridge 1906, p. 49.
[67] Coke, *Fourth institutes*, 3.

The function of representation was to ensure that parliament was wise.[68] Nowhere in the *Fourth institutes* did he treat the legislature as a means for securing popular assent. His treatment of its power to bind the absent was an excellent example of this point. He confined himself to saying that a statute was generally binding, because 'the law intends that every person hath knowledge thereof, for the parliament represents the body of the whole realm'.[69] He stressed presumed knowledge of statute, where Smith and Lambarde stressed presumed consent.

Coke would not have been unusual if he had tried to denigrate the statutes. Most people held that common law was in a vague sense 'higher' than the laws that a parliament made, if only because it was mingled with principles derived from natural justice.[70] Coke's strategy was to exalt the statutes by tracing their authority to the 'reason' of unwritten law. By presuming they were rational, in a sense to be determined by the judges, he brought them under professional control. It was the lawyer's duty, as he frequently confessed, to implement the parliament's intention, but the way he reconstructed that intention very often in practice subverted the parliament's will.[71] His most detailed account of the process ran as follows:

Four things are to be discerned and considered:
1st. What was the common law before the making of the Act.
2nd. What was the mischief and defect for which the common law did not provide.
3rd. What remedy the parliament hath resolved and appointed to cure the disease of the commonwealth.

---

68 A counter-argument might be attempted, based on the maxim used in the *Reports* that 'an Act of parliament to which the Queen and all her subjects are parties and give consent, cannot do a wrong' (*Ninth reports*, 107a; weaker versions at *Sixth reports*, 27b and *Eighth reports*, 137a). But on the one occasion that he elaborates upon this point (*Eleventh reports*, 14a) he concentrates on the assembly's wisdom: 'it was also urged that if the said act ... [should have a particular effect, then] it would do a wrong; and as it is said in Plowden [1 Plowden 398] the parliament is a court of the greatest honour and justice, of which none ought to imagine a dishonourable thing, and the *Doctor and student* [p. 300] it cannot be thought that a statute that is made by authority of the whole realm, as well of the King and of the Lords temporal and spiritual, as of all the Commons, will do a thing against the truth'. A quotation from Fortescue follows, to much the same effect. He very noticeably does not argue that no one can be wronged by their own consent.

69 Coke, *Fourth institutes*, 26. This was not a new idea (see for example Richard Crompton, *L'authoritie et jurisdiction des courts de la majestie de la roygne*, 1594, fo. 16). What is significant is that it was Coke's only use of the notion of representation.

70 Cobbett, *State trials*, II, 581; S. E. Thorne (ed.), *A discourse upon the exposition and understanding of statutes: with Sir Thomas Egerton's additions*, San Marino 1942, p. 1.

71 The source of Coke's approach was probably Edmund Plowden, whose *Commentaries* (1571) were a model for the *Reports*. Appeals to 'the intent of the Act' are a recurring feature of this work (see, for example, 1 Plowden 10, 18, 57, 205). Plowden also had a tendency, to judge from a superficial scrutiny, to assimilate the reason of a statute to the reason of the system as a whole. His definitive discussion is a short essay on statutory interpretation appended to his treatment of Eyston v. Studd (2 Plowden 465–8). On the rise of a stress on intentions, see the introduction to Thorne, *Discourse upon the statutes*.

And 4th. The true reason of the remedy; and then the office of all the judges is always to make such construction as shall suppress the mischief, and advance the remedy, and to suppress subtle inventions and evasions for continuance of the mischief, and pro privato commodo, and to add force and life to the cure and remedy, according to the true intent of the makers of the Act, pro bono publico.[72]

There was an ambivalence in Coke's position. On a sympathetic reading, he claimed that professional learning equipped the lawyer to identify the intended purpose of a given measure, and so to determine whether or not it covered a particular situation. Unsympathetic readers might plausibly accuse him of using sensitivity to the presumed intentions of the law as a mask for prejudices of his own. The presumption that law promoted 'public good' gave the ruthless judge a very powerful weapon. Lord Chancellor Ellesmere (1540–1617) complained that he and his judicial colleagues '[made] construction of [statutes] according to equity, varying from the rules and grounds of law, and enlarging them *pro bono publico*, against the letter and intent of the makers.'[73] Authority drained, in other words, from the fallible makers of statute towards a wiser parliament, existing in the minds of common lawyers. If Ellesmere is to be believed, a similar group of presumptions effectively de-personalised the king, who was continually supposed to will the nation's good, as opposed to the short-term interests of the Crown. As the chancellor tartly put it, 'he hath stood so much in phrase upon the King's honour, as in his resolutions he hath had no respect to the King's profit'.[74] Coke's actual sovereign was replaced, for legal purposes, by a constructed monarch who was far-sighted and benevolent.[75]

His theory's consequences for the king were worked through (much to Hale's dismay) in the revolution years. From the point of view of parliament, there was also a very worrying implication. Coke grudgingly allowed, in the *Fourth institutes*, that parliament was omnipotent *de facto*, but his position's logic pointed another way.[76] Parliamentary authority derived (to recapitulate) from precisely the same source ('reason') as the authority of other courts. The institution was presumed to deliberate in reasonable ways, and operated most effectively when the experts on reason, the judges, were consulted. It was at least conceivable that a parliamentary statute might simply contradict what reason said. In such a

---

[72] Coke, *Third reports*, 7b.
[73] McIlwain, *High court*, 294–5. Ellesmere was referring to the Magdalen College case, in which Coke had cited the principle quoted above (*Eleventh reports*, 74a).
[74] Knafla, *Law and politics*, 302.
[75] See also, on this theme, the remarks by Clayton Roberts on the maxim that the 'King can do no wrong', in his brilliant, unread *The growth of responsible government in Stuart England*, Cambridge 1966.
[76] Coke, *Fourth institute*, 36–8.

case the opinion of King's Bench was surely preferable to that of laymen. There was thus a possibility that the court might choose to overrule a statute. This was the claim Coke made in Bonham's case.

Dr Bonham had been gaoled, by order of the College of Physicians, for practising their trade without a licence. Its powers in the matter, granted by royal charter, had been confirmed by parliamentary statute. It was objected, amongst other things, that these powers made the college a judge in its own cause. The evidence for Coke's beliefs is contained in a single sentence of his judgement (delivered 1610):

> it appears in our books, that in many cases the common law will control Acts of parliament, and sometimes adjudge them to be utterly void; for when an Act of parliament is against common right and reason, or repugnant, or impossible to be performed, the common law will control it, and adjudge such Act to be void.[77]

It is possible he never spoke these words, a possibility which adds to their obvious intrinsic interest.[78] If the dictum was interpolated later, grossly distorting the original, then Coke must have felt very strongly about the idea.

Coke's claim was so sensational that it has been exhaustively discussed. A number of great lawyers have examined the Year Book precedents he used, and come to broadly similar conclusions.[79] If Coke's decision argued in good faith (the tacit assumption that these writers share), then he seems to have seen the statute as 'repugnant' (self-contradictory). An Act that made the college a judge in its own cause was not a mistake; it was nonsense. Coke was not overturning what parliament said, because parliament had failed to say anything at all. At most he was interpreting the law so it amounted to a contradiction. The case was not a precedent, it followed, for judicial review of the substance of legislation.

On any reading of the crucial sentence, this highly ingenious view is rather strained. 'Against common right and reason, or repugnant, or impossible to be performed' is a strikingly elaborate formulation. 'Against common right and reason', used anywhere else in Coke's works, would carry the meaning 'against common law', as indeed would the more ambiguous 'against reason'.[80] It makes no natural sense to take the words 'repugnant or impossible to be performed' as just an explanation of the

---

[77] Coke, *Eighth reports*, 118a.

[78] Charles Gray, 'Bonham's case reviewed', *Proceedings of the American Philosophical Society*, 116 (1972), 36.

[79] 12 Modern 687–8 (the great Chief Justice Holt); C. H. S. Fifoot (ed.), *The letters of Frederic William Maitland*, Selden Society, Supplementary series, vol. I, 1965, p. 6; S. E. Thorne, 'Dr Bonham's Case', *Law Quarterly Review*, 54 (1938), 543–52.

[80] Coke, *Eighth reports*, 125b–26a, for example, contrasts the expression 'common right' with merely local custom.

earlier part of the phrase.[81] Reluctance to believe that Coke meant what he said has rested in part on ingrained positivism, and partly on a related prejudice: that the apparent claim (if it was made) was a survival from medieval times.[82] The natural progression, it has always been assumed, is from a court's 'law-finding' to the conscious legislation of a sovereign. If the interpretation sketched here is correct, Coke's dictum was not a last stand but a premeditated innovation, designed to bring the written law under stricter judicial control. If the purpose of his judgement was to establish a new principle, quite alien to the spirit of contemporary law, then study of the precedents is unlikely to reveal his true intentions.

The dictum was largely ignored (a sign that Coke's opinions were embarrassingly extreme) but the scanty evidence suggests that the rest of the legal profession took his words in their literal sense.[83] At least one contemporary writer gives strong support to the same interpretation. Henry Finch (d. 1625) described the common law by quoting Cicero's *De legibus*; he characterised the system, in much the same spirit as Coke, as 'refined reason, which when it is grown up, and is perfect, is rightly named wisdom'.[84] He clearly distinguished natural from artificial reason.[85] He then made the conventional point that 'laws positive, which are directly contrary to the laws native, lose their force, and are not to be reputed as laws at all'.[86] Not even the most barbarous of races has any right to legalise a crime against natural law.

And this is sufficiently plain and manifest to all, being of such things as are against the law of nature. But inasmuch as the law of reason is known but by such as can judge well, and by these also but imperfectly known (as we have shown before) for this reason a case is the more difficult to be known, what laws shall be said to agree, or disagree to the same; only in general (as suffices in this case and to our present purpose) it is truly said, and ought to be assented to by all, that the laws which do in reality contradict the law of reason, are null and void, as well as those which contradict the law of nature.[87]

---

[81] Plowden uses a similar triplet, giving equal weight to each of its components: 'if [a] remainder had been appointed to commence upon an impossibility precedent, or upon a thing against law, or upon a repugnancy ... there the remainder should be void, for such a condition shall always be void' (1 Plowden 32).

[82] Thorne, *Discourse upon the statutes*, 85–92; McIlwain, *High court*, 286–92.

[83] Gray, 'Bonham's case reviewed', 51–6. For summaries of the case ignoring its most famous dictum see Sir Thomas Ireland, *An exact abridgement in English of the eleven books of reports of Sir Edward Coke*, 1651, pp. 314–6; Sir John Davies, *A perfect abridgement of the eleven books of reports*, 1651, pp. 202–3.

[84] Finch, *Description*, 53. The words are quoted from Cicero, *De legibus*, 320: 'quid est autem non dicam in homine, sed in omni caelo atque terra ratione divinius? quae cum adolevit atque perfecta est, nominatur rite sapientia'.

[85] Finch, *Description*, 52.   [86] *Ibid.*, 53.

[87] *Ibid.*, 53. The *Description* is a translation of the Law French *Nomotechnia* (1613). On the history of this work see Wilfrid Prest, 'The dialectical origins of Finch's *Law*', *Cambridge Law Journal*, 36 (1977), 326–48.

The judgement in Bonham's case showed that a theory of common law as 'reason' had anti-parliamentary implications. Coke had the politics of a Chief Justice, who privileged the opinions of judges like himself. Although he was a constitutionalist in thinking that even the king was subject to the rule of common law, he was suspicious of the institution that offered the best prospect of controlling royal power. For later constitutionalists like Selden (the other major influence on Hale), his exaltation of the bench's role was at best embarrassing. It was no doubt annoying for James to be told that his pronouncements were valueless in law, but the judges, his employees, were unlikely to pose a long-term threat to the interests of the Crown.[88] In at least one well-known respect, Coke's own career exemplified this truth. In 1628, when he was a disaffected parliament man, he opposed the Crown's prerogative of imprisoning opponents without cause; when he was on the bench, he had taken quite the opposite opinion.[89] It was not surprising, then, that thinkers of Hale's generation appealed from the law's spirit to its letter, and from judicial reason to the will of parliament.

[88] As Sommerville remarks, *Politics and ideology*, pp. 96–7.
[89] White, *Grievances*, 231–4.

2

Selden: the appeal to contract

To be a lawyer, Coke believed, was to understand the law as rational: to grasp the function of particular rules in the light of their place in the system as a whole. This understanding had the disadvantage that it was legal not historical; Coke claimed, no doubt quite seriously, to reconstruct intentions behind particular rules, but his view of the past was dictated by his professional presuppositions. A theory of the common law as reason greatly discouraged any sense that its origins were messily contingent. In depicting law as rational (that is, in understanding it as law) he denied its actual roots in arbitrary arrangements entered into by consent. Hale's great achievement, as a legal thinker, was to combine Coke's insights into the character of common law with a genuinely historical perspective. His starting point, in this and other areas, was his friend Selden's (1588–1654) thought.

John Selden was a barrister, and earned some money by conveyancing, but he was really, by the time Hale knew him, a professional antiquarian with a passion for the law.[1] His trenchant *Table talk*, from the period of their friendship, gives a sense of his vigorous mind.[2] His interests were bafflingly various, embracing jurisprudence, history, and all the oriental languages which were at that time studied in the West, but there was nonetheless a common concern. The law of particular places, created by local consent, was defended against rival codes with universal claims. The common law of England, the English 'municipal' law, was immune from supplementation and correction, whatever its divergence from sophisti-

---

[1] His consistency, over more than a forty-year period, is obviously open to dispute. It will remain so, in view of the range of his interests, until a detailed study is produced. David S. Berkowitz, *John Selden's formative years*, Washington 1988 is a mine of information but not a useful guide. On Selden's earlier thought see Paul Christianson, 'Young John Selden and the Ancient Constitution *c.* 1610–18', *Proceedings of the American Philosophical Society*, 128 (1984), and 'Royal and parliamentary voices on the ancient constitution *c.* 1604–21', in Linda Levy Peck (ed.), *The mental world of the Jacobean court*, Cambridge 1991.

[2] Recorded by one Richard Milward, who 'had the opportunity to hear his discourse twenty years together' (presumably the period 1634–54). *Table talk of John Selden*, ed. Frederick Pollock, 1927, pp.1–2.

cated thought. He was equally unmoved, in this respect, by Catholic and Protestant voices, by the *Digest* of Justinian, the canonists' *Decretum*, and even the Bible itself.

An advantage of this way of thinking, from the standpoint of a constitutionalist, was in coping with the tactics of the Crown. The political experience of the lawyers, over the generation before the civil war, was dominated by three major cases. In each of them the king laid claim, by an appeal outside the common law, to an inalienable prerogative. In Bate's case (1606), this prerogative was the right to levy customs without parliament's consent; in the case of the Five Knights (1627), it was imprisonment of his opponents without revealing cause; in R. v. Hampden, the Ship Money case (1638), it was the power of emergency taxation. The prerogative in question was to be known from general principles, often referred to as 'ius gentium'.[3]

As Chief Baron Fleming (1544–1613) pronounced, in his judgement on the first of these great cases, there were 'reasons ... not extracted out of the books of law ... reasons of policy; for "rex est legalis et politicus"; and reasons politic are sufficient guides to judges in their arguments ...'[4] Fleming believed, in other words, that there was a knowledge of 'policy', in fact a political science, quite independent of the common law. This was roughly (it will be remembered) what Bacon also held. It was nonetheless quite difficult for constitutionalists who thought like Coke to challenge a judgement like Fleming's. Appeal to other sciences was regarded by Coke as quite legitimate, so long as it was guided by a learned professional's knowledge of the 'reason' of the law. Fleming's views were undoubtedly crude, but his opinions about politics had an authority denied to 'the wisest man that ever professed not the law of England'.

For Selden, no such problem could arise, though his argument, in some respects, was rather close to Coke's. He agreed with Coke, at all events, that there was no appeal from common law to supposedly more general principles; there was no extra-legal sphere within which 'higher' rules could be consulted. For English purposes, at least, the common law interpreted the dictates of nature itself. The *Notes on Fortescue* (1616), his principal meditation on the subject, referred to it as 'limited law of nature':

although the law of nature be truly said immutable yet it is as true, that it is limitable, and limited law of nature is the law now used in every state. ... But the divers opinions of interpreters proceeding from the weakness of man's reason, and the several conveniences of divers states, have made those limitations, which the law hath suffered, very different.[5]

---

[3] For interesting reflections on this habit, see Burgess, *Politics*, esp. 144–7, 160, 203–7.
[4] Cobbett, *State trials*, II, 388.   [5] Selden, *Opera*, III, 1891.

The difference between them was that Coke had created a space for judicial discretion. The judge could draw on every science, and make extensive use of their conclusions, in the light of his presuppositions about the system's rationality. Coke had strongly held opinions about the nature of the public good, and presumed that the law, being perfect, would agree.

Seldenian jurisprudence cast doubt on the premise that English law could be considered perfect. Coke thought the wisdom of the common law was owed to its lengthy development by the professionals, its 'fining and refining by so many learned men'. Selden denied, by contrast, that it made sense to boast about the system's comparative age: 'all laws in general are originally equally ancient. All were grounded upon nature, and no nation was, that out of it took not their grounds, and nature being the same in all, the beginning of all laws must be the same.'[6] All laws were both natural and ancient, so none could claim more reason than the others; they were interpretations of natural principles, imposed by the authority of a legislating 'state'. Selden dismissed

the trivial demand, 'When and how began your common laws?' Questionless it is fittest answered by affirming, when and in like kind as the laws of all other states, that is, 'When there was first a state in that land, which the common law now governs'. Then were natural laws limited for the conveniency of civil society here, and those limitations have been from thence increased, altered, interpreted, and brought to what they now are; although perhaps, saving the meerly immutable part of nature, now, in regard of their first being, they are not otherwise than the ship, that by often mending had no piece of the first materials . . .[7]

For Selden, as much as for Coke, the common law was the natural law for England, and was thus the proper language of political debate. The difference between their approaches was in the authority by which this English natural law was to be known. For Coke, the Lord Chief Justice, authority stemmed from the logic of the system, which was something that only professionals could hope to apprehend. It was therefore common lawyers who were the appropriate experts on the way in which the country should be ruled. For the antiquarian Selden, the proper method was historical. The English 'limitations', the local expression of nature, were less evolutions of reason than authoritative actions of the 'state'.

It might have been expected, in the light of this distinction, that they would use the past in different ways. Both men were constitutionalists, who held that royal powers were defined by common law, and both of them had theories that were vulnerable to historical research. Coke needed to show that the law was the product of a long development; Selden had to rebut the view that the English legislator was the unaided king. The focus of their anxieties was the year 1066.

[6] *Ibid.*, 1891   [7] *Ibid.*, 1891–2.

This is, of course, a topic much discussed, ever since the publication of J. G. A. Pocock's classic work, *The ancient constitution and the feudal law* (1957; 're-issued with a retrospect' 1987). Pocock believed that English historical thought had been conditioned by a 'common law mind', and that a symptom of this 'mind' was the denial of the Norman Conquest. The intellectual habits created by the English legal system, which was deemed to be immemorially ancient, made it hard to grasp that English institutions had been imported wholesale from feudal Normandy. Hale's masterpiece of the Restoration years, *The history of the common law of England*, offers one of the best examples of the apparent blindness this involved. Hale's attitudes will be discussed in their chronological place, but a mildly digressive discussion is clearly called for here.

As Pocock demonstrated, a host of writers vigorously denied that William had been a conqueror, but their reasons for so doing were far from obvious. He mentioned, it is true, a train of thought which would account for their anxiety:

if Duke William, even for a single instance, had been an absolute ruler – if he had been king by ius conquestus – then . . . all that had been done – even to increase the sphere of reason and law, had been done by virtue of his unfettered will, on which his grants depended, and on which (transmitted to his descendants) the laws and liberties of England for ever afterwards must depend likewise. To admit a conquest was to admit an indelible stain of sovereignty upon the English constitution.[8]

But this argument is seldom or never found in the royalist propaganda of the period, 'certainly with insufficient frequency to justify the incessant refutations which appeared'.[9] As a writer in general reluctant 'to transform a *mentalité* into a series of "moves"',[10] Pocock refused to reduce his 'common law mind' to a political convenience.

An early article by Quentin Skinner (who had a theoretical commitment to recovering the 'intentions' behind a given text) disputed Pocock's main empirical finding. He showed there was a contemporary tradition, that of the unpretentious 'chronicles', which was happy to speak of a conquest in 1066; and that it depicted King William as altering the law in virtue of his rights as conqueror.[11] It was only in the context of political debate, and of

---

[8] Pocock, *Ancient constitution*, 53.

[9] *Ibid.*, 54. Johann Sommerville lists exceptions to this rule, but they are clerics or civilians (Sommerville, 'History and theory', 255–7). The claim that William was a conqueror did not impinge on the mainstream of political debate. See the comment by Glenn Burgess, *Politics*, 84–5.

[10] Pocock, *Ancient constitution*, 262.

[11] Quentin Skinner, 'History and ideology in the English revolution', *Historical Journal*, 8 (1965), 150–78. Pocock has not unreasonably objected that '[Skinner] did not produce many writers before 1640 who had argued from the fact of a Norman Conquest to the present absolute prerogative of a King of England, which was what I had contended was nearly unknown' (*Ancient constitution*, 283).

histories informed by politics, that conquest was routinely and perhaps somewhat hysterically denied. This suggested that it was appropriate to seek a political motive for such views, presumably a terror of the 'stain of sovereignty'. Skinner's article rather intemperately implied that the Whig orthodoxy was a conscious 'fabrication' of a convenient but 'bogus' past.[12] The two varieties of explanation are not, however, mutually exclusive; it is entirely possible that fear of an inherited sovereignty accompanied rather than caused the eccentric historical outlook produced by Pocock's 'mind'. Coke's writings at all events show that the latter could exist without the former.

In the works of Edward Coke, King William was a conqueror *de jure*. In Pocock's terminology, he was 'King by ius conquestus', and therefore had a right to an absolute power. Coke quoted a famous argument which actually depended on this point. According to Sir John Fortescue (*c.*1394–1476),

the kingdom of England was first inhabited by Britons; then ruled by Romans, then possessed by Saxons, who changed its name from Britain to England. Then for a short time the kingdom was conquered by Danes and again by Saxons, but finally by Normans, whose posterity hold the realm at the present time. And throughout the period of these nations and their kings, the realm has been continuously ruled by the same customs as it is now, customs which, if they had not been the best, some of these kings would have changed for the sake of justice or by the impulse of caprice and totally abolished them, especially the Romans, who judged almost all the rest of the world by their laws. Similarly, others of these aforesaid kings, who possessed the kingdom of England only by the sword, could, by that power, have destroyed its laws.[13]

Coke quite agreed with Fortescue that William had the right to change the law. The triumphant duke had the prerogative of legislating for his conquered realm, but English arrangements were obviously ideal, and he would have been ill-advised to do so. He therefore set out to discover the Saxon laws 'the sum of which, composed by him into a Magna Carta ... he blessed with the seal of security and wish of eternity'.[14]

This statement can be clarified with the aid of his report on Calvin's case. When a Christian prince has conquered a nation of heathens, its laws are abrogated quite automatically 'for that they be not only against Christianity, but against the law of God and of nature'; Christian laws could be changed 'at his pleasure', but they remained in force until he did so.[15] Coke thought that laws were binding in virtue of their rationality. A Christian polity was presumed to be based upon reason, and so its institutions were

[12] Skinner, 'History and ideology', 154, 160.
[13] Fortescue, *De laudibus*, 39, quoted in Coke, *Third report*, xxi.
[14] Coke, *Eighth reports*, v.   [15] Coke, *Seventh reports*, Calvin's case, 17b.

presumed to be well-suited to its needs. In the immediate aftermath of conquest, there was admittedly a *ius conquestus*, but conquerors often decided to respect the constitutions that they found. In kingdoms acquired by descent (like those of James I) law-making was by parliament alone.[16] Coke does not clearly state (and probably did not in fact believe), that nothing changed at about King William's time. The point about the 'sum of law' the Conqueror had made was not so much its details as the fact it was informed by legal reason. The threat that was represented by the Normans, so far as the Chief Justice was concerned, was the breach in the continuity of the law's 'reasonable' development.

Selden was probably just as sure as Coke that William had the right to change the law. He certainly believed that 'by law of war, regularly all rights and laws of the place conquered, be wholly subject to the conqueror's will'.[17] One of his very earliest books, the *Analecton Anglo-Britannicon* (completed 1607 but unpublished till 1615), treats William as the founder of a completely new political order ('respublica nova'), who diminished England, in effect, to nothing but a 'Norman colony'.[18] For practical administrative reasons, he chose to retain quite a number of Saxon laws, 'more, however, because they were very well suited to civil administration than as a concession to the wretches' pleas'.[19] Two years later, however, in *Jani Anglorum facies altera* (1610), he had toned down this view.[20] Both works make use, for instance, of the same brief Latin tag:

> The law's old age stands firm by royal care
> Statutes resume their ancient grey hair
> Old ones are mended with a fresh repair
> And for supply some new ones added are.[21]

The *Analecton* added that these verses were not in all respects appropriate, in view of the king's inordinate exactions;[22] *Janus Anglorum* cited it without perceptible ironic feeling. The later treatise showed no interest in Norman expropriation of the English, or in the legislation designed to hold the vanquished Saxons down.[23] This suggests he had become more sensitive to the perils of the 'stain of sovereignty'.

[16] *Ibid.*   [17] Selden, *Opera*, III, 1333. He cites from Calvin's case to this effect.
[18] Selden, *Opera*, II, 949. He saw 1066, in fact, as a 'Machiavellian moment', and refers to the Florentine's advice (*Discourses*, Book I, Chapter 25–6) to a new prince in William's position.
[19] 'Magis tamen quod ad civilem erant administrationem aptissimae quam miserorum precibus annuendo'. (Selden, *Opera*, II, 948).
[20] See especially the contrast between *Opera*, II, 999 and *ibid*, 950–1.
[21] 'Firmatur senium juris, priscamque resumunt/ Canitiem leges, emendantur vetustae/ Acceduntque novae' (Translation from *Tracts written by John Selden*, 1683, tr. Redman Westcot, p.50).
[22] 'Haud tamen undiquaque placet illud acrostichon' (Selden, *Opera*, III, 951).
[23] By contrast with Selden, *Opera*, III, 948, 951.

Janus Anglorum also clearly stated (unlike the *Analecton*) that William's title to reign was as King Edward's rightful heir.[24] It nonetheless implied that he was free to legislate, and indeed made a number of changes in the law.[25] What was really important to Selden was that this phase was clearly terminated when the invader promised to respect the Saxon laws.[26] By the time of the *History of Tithes* (1618), his views were quite clearcut: William was not a conqueror, but the inheritor of Edward's power, and 'such of [the Saxon laws] as are now abrogated were not at all abrogated by his conquest, but either by the parliaments and ordinances of his successors, or else by non-usage and contrary custom'.[27]

At this point, an objection may be raised. Selden was quite untroubled by almost total change in common law, comparing the law to 'the ship that by often mending, had no piece of the first materials'. The English legal history that *Janus Anglorum* sketched out involved frequent and extensive alterations. The powers enjoyed by William might seem quite as irrelevant as the earlier materials of the ship. Hale's *History of the common law*, which learnt a lot from Selden, was to approach an indifference of this kind.[28] The least unconvincing reply to this objection is that the English law's development was the fruit of the English legislator's nature. The community considered as a whole, the shipwright of the ship analogy, had often modified the existing system without more than tacit assent from the king. The problem with a conquest was that it threatened the authority by which these silent changes could be made.

Selden's beliefs about the Norman conquest were typical of his approach to principles of alien origin. He was always quite indifferent to the history of particular legal rules, so long as their authority was reception by consent. One implication of this view, which had a powerful influence on Hale, was in the attitude taken towards English jurisdictions that practised foreign law. A difficulty, for the common lawyer, was the presence, in the bishops' courts, of an imported code. The answer Coke and others found was shared by many writers; it might be termed the 'Anglican' solution, and it was still accepted in the time of Bishop Stubbs (1825–1901).[29] Faced with this alien system, which was the fruit of papal legislation, Coke laid stress on reception by the English. As a Jesuit complained, 'he runneth everywhere to this shift, that the pope's ecclesiastical and canon laws, being admitted to England, may be called the king's ecclesiastical laws for

---

[24] Selden, *Opera*, II, 997.   [25] *Ibid.*, II, 998.   [26] *Ibid.*, II, 998–9.
[27] *Ibid.*, III, 1336.
[28] Pocock, *Ancient constitution*, 175–80.
[29] F. W. Maitland, *Roman canon law in the Church of England: Six Essays*, 1898, pp. 52–3.

that they are admitted and allowed by him and his realm.'[30] The common law was essentially rational, the product of an immemorial wisdom, but the canon law was 'admitted', at particular moments in known history, and was therefore the creation of particular acts of consent.[31]

Coke used the notion of consent to denigrate a competing professional group, but Selden's was a subtler and a more balanced view. A characteristic example of the latter's arguments was his treatment of the English law of probate. The rules about probate of wills (as opposed to the rules concerned with enforcement of the legacies themselves) were drawn from the secular part of civil law. In England and only in England (as Selden was delighted to point out), this function was entrusted to the courts run by the church.[32] This control over probate developed at the time of King Henry II. The authority behind it was the same as the authority behind the common law:

It hath like antiquity and original as other parts of the common law, that is, immemorial custom [its arrival pre-dated, of course, the 'time of memory', 3 September 1189]. For although it be exercised according to the civil and canon laws in the spiritual courts with some reference had to the customs of England, yet it is clear that the power which the spiritual courts have to exercise it is merely by the common law, although we find not when it came first to them, no more than we find [the original of] divers of our settled customs and maxims in the common law, touching which yet we can without much difficulty prove that at such or such times they were not in practice; as perhaps in the more ancient ages this was not in these courts.[33]

The law of England shifted, but the power that made the law was always its reception by the English and their king. A particular rule of the church was binding only when it was accepted, and the role of common law was as the record of consent.

The time of Selden's greatest influence, in purely political terms, was probably the parliament of 1628. There was a perfect fit, at the time of this assembly, between his view of alien law and the needs of the more discontented members. The greatest political issue was probably the government's abuse of martial law. Selden denied that martial law could claim to be a law of any kind: 'there are no laws in England but are made laws either by custom or Act of parliament. Can any man show me that martial law is confirmed by either of these ways?'[34] Selden's insistence on this principle left him unmoved by precedents supporting the government's case. Royal delinquencies were always common, but their example had no

---

[30] 'A Catholic divine' [Robert Parsons], *An answer to the fifth part of reports lately set forth by Sir Edward Coke, Knight ...*, 1606, p. 3.

[31] Coke, *Fifth reports*, 16a-b. [32] Though even Parsons knew this: *Answer*, 302.

[33] Selden, *Opera*, III, 1671.

[34] R. C. Johnson *et al.*, *Commons debates 1628*, vol. II, p. 575.

legal force. As his *Table talk* maintained: 'In all times the princes in
England have done something illegally to get money, but then came a
parliament and all was well, the people and prince kissed and were friends,
& so things were quiet for a while.'[35] It was in parliament, if anywhere,
that prince and people had to come to terms, and so it was the parliament
that embodied what he meant by the English 'state'.

There was much more to Selden than pedantic antiquarian scholarship.
His work was animated, as his behaviour showed, by a moral, if not a
religious, commitment to the rule of common law. He was one of those, in
1629, who had delayed the adjournment of the Commons, keeping the
House in session by forcibly preventing the Speaker from leaving his chair.
He suffered for this gesture, as he spent two years in gaol, and he seemed
to have been chastened by his treatment. But his next major treatises, on
apparently innocent topics, gave English constitutionalist theories the
backing of coherent philosophical ideas. The focus of these writings, and
his most important legacy to Hale, was his conception of *ius gentium*.

Ius gentium was the obvious location of those political principles alleged
by the Crown to stand outside the rules of municipal law. It consisted in
those practices observed by every people (with a few exceptions known
from travellers' tales) that were not exactly rules of natural law.[36] The
original civilian distinction between 'ius gentium' and 'ius naturale' was
that natural law applied to everything, but *ius gentium* only to humans.[37]
The common lawyers were more influenced, so far as a generalisation can
be ventured, by the Thomist understanding, which treated this puzzling
category as a deduction from *ius naturale*, given the human wish to live at
peace.[38] They spoke, at all events, of a kind of 'secondary natural law',
deduced from the natural law proper, and distinct from mere positive
rules.[39]

One feature of the concept should be noted, a feature of obvious
importance to thinkers about common law. It was known from the 'consensus' of mankind, a consensus that might be understood either as registering a natural truth, or as creating universal custom. This ambiguity
between reason and custom mirrored the ambiguity within the common

---

[35] Selden, *Table talk*, 83.
[36] For some very shrewd remarks on the distinction, see Sir Robert Filmer's 'Observations
upon H. Grotius *De jure belli et pacis*' (*Patriarcha and other writings*, ed. Johann
P. Sommerville, Cambridge 1991, pp. 208–16)
[37] *Digest*, I, i 1.
[38] For the Thomist view, see J. B. Scott, *The Spanish origin of international law: Franciscus
de Vitoria and his law of nations*, Oxford 1934, p. cxi, a translation of Vitoria's
commentary on the key Thomist text, *Summa Theologiae*, IIa IIae q. cii, 3.
[39] Finch, *Description*, 3, 52; Dodderidge, *English lawyer*, 194. St German had a different
conception of 'secondary natural law'. He saw it as an exercise of reason on premises that
positive systems provide (St German, *Doctor*, 33). See above, p. 13, n. 12.

law. To Henry Finch, whose thought was close to Coke's, the common law *was* 'secondary law of nature'; the English municipal system was reason received by consent, '*dogma poleos koinon* [the common opinion of the state] generally received by the consent of all'.[40] Finch seems to have understood consent as operating in a passive way, as a shared recognition that given practices were rational. Selden shared his belief that English custom was *ius gentium*, but he held that the agreement of the people creates as much as recognises law.[41]

The best example Selden gave of what his theories meant was his famous *Mare clausum* (1635), a work that he first drafted as early as 1619.[42] It supports the King of England's claim to the 'dominium' of the Narrow Seas. Such a question, he asserted, falls under the 'permissive' (as opposed to the 'obligatory') natural law.[43] 'Permissive' natural law is 'positive' or 'civil', arising through acceptance of a shared authority, or else through 'intervenient'[44] compact or custom. The origin of private property is in just such an intervenient compact, a tacit agreement to recognise the rights of occupants. There was no need, however, for the king to occupy the Narrow Seas; it was enough to demonstrate, with evidence derived from history, that his neighbours had consented to the ownership he claimed. An antiquarian of Selden's learning had very little trouble in making a plausible case.

It is usually believed that *Mare clausum* was a riposte to *Mare liberum*, a work by the Dutch jurist Hugo Grotius (1583–1645). But Selden showed no enmity for Grotius, and did his best to emphasise their similarities. Grotius believed that property was based on occupation, and that it was impossible to occupy the sea. He was prepared, however, to admit that more circumscribed inlets could be occupied and owned. He was arguing, as Selden pointed out, against the pretensions of the Portuguese, who claimed the ownership of several oceans; the Narrow Seas off England were more like a creek or a bay.[45] Selden's true enemy, surprisingly, was a now forgotten sixteenth-century Spaniard.

[40] Finch, *Description*, 53. Burgess, *Politics*, esp. 27–57 explores this possibility. Note, however, that even in Finch, it is 'consent of all' that makes a law.

[41] There was a wider context to this important shift; Selden was probably aware that contemporary Thomists were increasingly inclined to classify *ius gentium* as part of positive law (Quentin Skinner, *The foundations of modern political thought*, 2 vols., 1978, vol. II, pp. 151–4).

[42] Selden, *Opera*, II, 1181–2.

[43] John Selden, *Mare clausum*, tr. Marchamont Nedham, 1652, pp. 8, 12.

[44] Latin 'interveniens': a very common word in Selden's works, meaning to come between, come after, or 'happen to emerge'. OED suggests (among other senses) 'that comes in as something secondary, incidental or extraneous.'

[45] Selden, *Mare clausum*, 171–2.

This was Vazquez de Menchaco, who took the frightening view that prescription was irrelevant to princes.[46] They had inherited no obligations, in relation to each other and their peoples, from tacit, intervenient agreements. The history of the seas was an irrelevance, and so, by implication, was the basis of the English constitution, in silent evolution by general consent. The results would be disastrous, for 'almost all the principal points of the intervenient law of nature, being established by long consent of persons using them, do depend upon prescription or ancient custom'.[47] He must surely have been thinking, in putting down these words, of that 'limited law of nature', the English common law.

The crown of Selden's work upon these issues, *De jure naturali et gentium iuxta disciplinam Ebraeorum* (1640) was fairly described by its title, which he carefully explained. *Ius naturale* and *ius gentium* were studied through Jewish traditions which he took to be analogous to English common law.[48] The difference between them was purely one of scope: all universal rules were treated as by definition natural; *ius gentium*, by contrast, was the law 'peculiar to certain peoples'.[49] *Ius gentium* was created in two ways:

> The 'ius gentium' in my title is understood as that law which was common to the Hebrews and other peoples, whether neighbours or others (not however to all men or perpetually), whether it originated from a particular command of God, or from a pact or from an intervenient custom.[50]

It is entirely possible that Selden was at heart a moral sceptic, who doubted the existence of any natural laws. Such laws, if they existed, were totally irrelevant to practical debates; as they were universal, they were by definition already a functioning part of local arrangements. The only natural law that was necessary to his intellectual structure was the one that underpinned *ius gentium*: the principle that contracts should be kept. But a reader of *De jure naturali* carries away a different impression. The natural laws in which the Jews believed were the so-called 'Precepta Noachidarum', which were known to the morally healthy of every place and time.[51] They were known, Selden reported, by the agency of an 'Intellectus Agens' (a concept that will be discussed elsewhere), which gave access to the truths that were normally said to be written in men's hearts. To con-

---

[46] Vasquez, *Illustrium controversiarum, aliarumque usu frequentium libri sex*, Frankfurt 1668 (first published 1559), Book II, Chapter ci, 16.

[47] Selden, *Mare clausum*, 170.   [48] Selden, *Opera*, I, 71.   [49] *Ibid.*, 68.

[50] *Ibid.*, 69. 'Gentium autem Jus in titulo accipitur pro eo quod sive ex singulari Numinis imperio sive ex pacto seu consuetudine interveniente, Ebraeis aliisque gentibus sive vicinis sive aliis (nec interim universis nec semper) commune habebatur.' It is hard to translate Selden without doing more than justice to the tangle of the original prose.

[51] Selden, *Opera*, I, 153–6.

ventional observers such as Hale, Selden seemed to have defended the possibility of moral knowledge.[52]

There was thus an ambiguity deep within Selden's thought. He might be understood as preaching an untrammelled sovereignty, a right of king and parliament together to make any agreements they wished. But he had approached this conclusion by conceiving of such arrangements as 'limited natural law'. Both he and his disciples continued to be constitutionalist: in every great political debate, they enquired what the common law was, not what it ought to be. Though it was made, and could be changed, in an arbitrary way, it was nonetheless in theory an expression of the principles of nature. The Almighty had created man to enter into binding obligations, and the customs and statutes of England were therefore, among other things, the will of God himself. This view of man as a contract-making animal, constructing institutions in God's sight, was central to the thought of Matthew Hale.

---

[52] Hargrave 485, 51; Nathaniel Culverwell, *An elegant and learned discourse of the light of nature*, ed. Robert A. Greene and Hugh MacCallum, Toronto 1971, pp. 68–71.

3

The rights of the Crown

Hale entered Lincoln's Inn on 18 May 1629.[1] The date is quite important; less than two months before, Charles had dissolved his parliament and imprisoned the more militant among its leadership. Hale missed, in other words, the constitutional troubles of the 1620s, the experience which must have shaped most of his older friends. Of his previous life we know little, except that his background was puritan and that he had spent time at Magdalen Hall. His contemporary biographer Gilbert Burnet (1643–1715) says that it was an accident which brought him into law. He had business with a barrister named Glanville, who was astounded by his legal grasp and persuaded him to train for the profession.[2] The name deserves a moment's pause, for John Glanville (1586–1661) was a member of a not uncommon type, a committed constitutionalist who was later to fight for the king.[3] The progression had a logic which this chapter will explore.

Hale's work can best be understood as a synthesis of Selden's thought with Coke's, but it seems at least worth mentioning his known professional friends. A surprising early patron was the enigmatic turncoat William Noy (d. 1634), a 1620s constitutionalist who became Attorney-General during an early period of King Charles' Personal Rule (1631–34). In the time at which Hale would have known him, he was a leading government hard-liner and an ally of Archbishop Laud's. Hale seems to have been insepara-ble from this pillar of the monarchist reaction, and was known, so Burnet tells us, as 'Young Noy'.[4] He was friendly, for all this, with Laud's victim the puritan martyr William Prynne, the author of *Histriomastix* (1633), the famous attack on the stage. Prynne had his ears cut off, by order of the Council, because a passage of this work had implied that the Queen of

[1] *Records of the Honourable Society of Lincoln's Inn: the Black Books*, 1898, vol. II, p. 285.
[2] Burnet, *Life*, 6.   [3] Hale, *Works*, I, 158.
[4] Burnet, *Life*, 12. Burnet's story seems to be corroborated by Hale's own occasional memories of Noy's behaviour (2 Keble 846; Hale, *Historia placitorum coronae*, ed. Sollom Emlyn, 2 vols., 1736, vol. II, p. 346). On Noy himself, see W. J. Jones, 'The great Gamaliel of the law: Mr. Attorney Noye', Huntingdon Library Quarterly, 40 (1977).

The works, in order of their composition, are 'Incepta de juribus Coronae', 'Preparatory notes touching the rights of the Crown', and finally 'Prerogativa regis'. The Incepta, as the name implies, presents a mass of relevant material in an inchoate form.[24] The manuscript volume separately includes his jottings for the Grey of Ruthin case (1640), and also some matter connected with his argument for the defence of Laud (1644). The 'Preparatory notes', despite its humble title, is actually a polished piece of work; it has a connected argument, unfinished but divided into chapters, which must have been intended as a draft.[25] A deleted phrase at the very end refers to 'the late King Charles', but the bulk of the volume was clearly composed before the regicide. 'Prerogativa regis', which was written after 1661, can be read in a modern edition, splendidly edited by Mr Yale.[26] It follows the earlier work in its argument's structure, but covers rather less of the same ground. What matters, for our purposes, is that he was very consistent, over twenty years of political upheavals, in a particular approach to the main constitutional questions of his time.

The very idea of a treatise about the royal power was something largely new, both in conception and in execution. The previous authority was William Staunford's book *An exposition of the king's prerogative collected out of the great abridgement of Justice Fitzherbert* (1567). As the title indicated, this was a very unambitious work, which listed a number of practical points but imposed no kind of intellectual order. Staunford himself was keen to stress, no doubt for basically prudential reasons, that the account he gave was not exhaustive.[27] Hale's work was very different. He organised the law, which had previously been scattered through an enormous range of difficult sources, and made a tabular analysis. Needless to say, this would have been anathema to Coke.

Coke's law had an inner coherence which only a professional could hope to apprehend. He appears to have believed that its inter-connections were so complicated as to defeat any analysis, at least in a form that could be grasped by laymen. The law was known by long habituation, and not the exertions of an untrained mind, so reader's aids like indices were pointless.[28] The statutes could be organised, but the chaos of reason was

---

[24] Lincoln's Inn, Hargrave 5.   [25] Lincoln's Inn, Miscellaneous 48.

[26] D. E. C. Yale (ed.) *Hale's prerogatives of the king,* Selden Society 1975. Yale's useful introduction (pp. xxiii–xxvi) gives a summary of the evidence for the dating of these works. They are briefly (but very competently) discussed in Ulrike Krautheim, *Die Souveränitätskonzeption in den englischen Verfassungskonflikten des 17. Jahrhunderts,* Frankfurt 1977, pp. 420–7.

[27] William Staunford, *An exposition of the king's prerogative collected out of the great abridgement of Justice Fitzherbert,* 1567, fos. 30, 85.

[28] Coke, *First institutes,* 395a.

sacred. Hale's taxonomic feat, precursor of his staggering achievement, *The analysis of the law* (published 1713),[29] depended on rejection of this doctrine. His primary distinction (the *Analysis* was later to declare) was not between the common law and statute, but between the laws of persons and of things.[30] It was a mark of Coke's great influence that this should seem a rather daring move.

Hale's definition of prerogative was also revolutionary in spirit. A prerogative, in the *Exposition*'s words, was a 'privilege or pre-eminence that any person hath before another';[31] it was a legal right, like the rights, for example, of peers, that happened to be given to the king. Hale's topic was rather differently conceived, as 'iura summi imperii', the rights of a supreme power. A supreme power was to be known from the fact that it acknowledged no superior.[32] He admitted, rather strikingly, that there was a presumption in favour of the king:

the rights and empire of a king over his people are prima facie jura summi imperii in as much as in ordinary presumption the manner of the acquisition of a kingdom is by the voluntary translation of the same rights from the commonalty unto him or otherwise by conquest, either of which transfer a pure and absolute empire into the prince.[33]

These were, however, alienable powers, which could be limited or given back by subsequent concessions to the subject. The initially absolute 'empire' of the prince was also a right to diminish the rights of the Crown.

One of the rights the prince could give away was that of arbitrary legislation. Hale managed, all his life, to combine the view that the king had 'summum imperium' with the view that English laws were contracts between the people and the Crown. The tension was resolved by understanding such agreements as a kind of royal action needing parliament's consent.[34] The king had conceded a veto, but he was sovereign in the sense that he, and he alone, could properly be said to legislate. This theory was compatible with a perfectly plausible reading of recent 'absolutist' speculation. The Incepta shows a knowledge of Jean Bodin's *Republic* (first Latin edition 1586) and Hugo Grotius' *De jure belli et pacis* (1625).[35] Though both of these writers maintained that a sovereign *qua* sovereign could make new laws at will, both also believed that princes were morally

---

[29] It may be relevant to this achievement that a very much briefer analysis attributed to Noy is printed in William Noy, *The grounds and maxims and also an analysis of the English laws*, 1794, pp. xxi-vii.
[30] Hale, *The analysis of the law*, 1713, Preface.   [31] Staunford, *Exposition*, 5.
[32] Lincoln's Inn, Hargrave 5, 1.
[33] *Ibid.*, 2.   [34] Hale, *Prerogatives*, 171.
[35] Hargrave 5, 12–13 (Grotius); *ibid.*, 3, 10 (Bodin).

(though not legally) bound by their ancestors' contractual undertakings. Neither was very lucid on the subject of a legislative veto which happened to have been *contractually* conceded, but the intended meaning of Hale's authorities is fortunately of no importance here.[36]

It is Grotius, rather than Bodin, who provides the most illuminating backdrop to Hale's political attitudes in 1642. Grotius resembled Selden in stressing the variety of possible constitutional arrangements. Sovereignty could be vested in one person or in many, and be enjoyed indefinitely, or during a fixed term; it could be shared between a king and a representative assembly; it could also be received upon conditions, and forfeited when they were violated. The sovereign was obliged by God to keep his promises, including his concessions to the subject. This did not mean, however, that the subject was entitled to resist, on occasions when those promises were broken.[37]

The merit of this theory was its casuistic force. Hale's English mentor offered little guidance on the morally preferable standpoint in 1642: the law was a contract, his *Table talk* implied, to which the prince and people were the parties; if they then disagreed about the terms, they had no option but to fight it out.[38] In Grotius, by contrast, was the germ of a workable rule. In every state, he taught, there was *summum imperium* somewhere. The subject was bound to his sovereign by conquest or consent, however many promises the sovereign chose to break. The sovereign's power could never be resisted, except in the unusual case where the subject's death would otherwise result.[39]

There were those among the parliament's supporters who probably expected to be murdered by their king, or at least by the crypto-papists in his train. More moderate parliamentarians, whose fears were not quite so inflamed, could draw upon another Grotian point. It was wrong to take up arms against a sovereign who was 'limited' (a king who had chosen by contract to set bounds upon his power). It was possible, however, that sovereignty was 'mixed': that it was placed, by English law, in the Houses as well as the king. Where sovereignty was mixed, and one of the partners encroached upon another, the other was permitted to resist.[40] There was a

---

[36] On royal promises, as opposed to laws, see Jean Bodin, *On sovereignty: four chapters from the Six books of the Commonwealth*, ed. and tr. Julian H. Franklin, Cambridge 1992, pp. 35–6; Grotius, *De jure belli*, I, iii, 16. Grotius, *De jure belli*, I, iii, 18 appears to rule out concession of a veto, but the argument he uses could have been shrugged aside by English readers; it was obviously intended to apply to institutions like the parlements of France.

[37] Hugo Grotius, *De jure belli ac pacis libri tres*, Latin and English edn, tr. Francis W. Kelsey, Oxford 1925, Book I, Chapter iii, 7–24.

[38] Tuck, 'Ancient law', 137–161.   [39] Grotius, *De jure belli*, I, iv, 7.   [40] *Ibid.*, 13

very formidable book, the *Treatise of monarchy* (1643) by Philip Hunton, which opted for precisely this approach.[41]

From a Grotian perspective, the question was quite simple. If sovereignty was vested in the king, whatever limitations he accepted, then rebellion was almost invariably wrong; if it was vested in the king and parliament together, and the king had encroached (or appeared to encroach) on the latter, then the Houses were entitled to resist his aggression by force. It is likely (though not certain) that Hale accepted this analysis. He seems to have studied Grotius with some care, and he cited (on an unrelated matter) the chapter on sovereign power.[42] He avoided Philip Hunton's stance, and showed himself hostile (as we shall see) to the *Answer to the nineteen propositions* (1642), where the king himself accepted that his monarchy was mixed.[43]

One point on which Grotius and Selden were agreed was that sovereignty could be acquired by conquest.[44] A sovereign, who acknowledged no superior, could not be arraigned in a court. Differences between two such powers could be settled only by appeal to the outcome of a battle, which might also be seen as the verdict that God had providentially ordained. It followed, Hale said, that 'conquest ... is the supreme trial between such as have no subjection one to the other: and the title is therefore good because [in words attributed to Gentili (1552–1608)] "the outcome of war condemned the cause of the vanquished and pronounced it unjust"'.[45] Hale thought that every adult was naturally a sovereign, so conquest was one model for foundation of the state: 'the original of government is either *ab interno*, by consent, or simple agreement, or *ab externo* by force and power, though that have something of consent too'.[46]

Hale accepted, all his life, that conquest was a possibility: that legitimate authority could be founded in military power.[47] But in practice, he believed, there was always 'something of consent' involved. A conquest, when completed, amounted to a pact, depending upon the surrender of the vanquished: 'an express dedition, or which is equivalent, a tacit by

---

[41] Grotius is nowhere cited in Hunton's work, so there is no conclusive evidence of a relationship. If Hunton drew on the Dutchman, he had a strong motive to conceal the fact. Grotius believed that conquest was a legitimate source of sovereignty (a point discussed below), but Hunton denied this. He asserted, against the royalist Henry Ferne, that every kind of monarchy was founded in consent (Hunton, *Treatise of monarchy*, 1643, pp. 20–2).

[42] Lincoln's Inn, Hargrave 5, 12–13.   [43] Lincoln's Inn, Misc. 48, 93.

[44] Grotius, *De jure belli*, I, iii, 8.

[45] 'Belli exitus damnavit ac iniustum pronunciavit victi causam'. Lincoln's Inn, Hargrave 5, 12.

[46] Lincoln's Inn, Misc. 48, 1.

[47] Hale, *History of the common law of England*, ed. C. M. Gray, Chicago 1971, p. 49.

continuance of time and subjection'.[48] There was no power, it followed, that was not contractual in basis; to understand the nature of a given sovereign's power, it was necessary to know the contract's terms. So far as England was concerned, he showed it was not possible for William to have been a conqueror. William had claimed, under existing law, to inherit the rights of the Crown, and had defeated Harold, a similar claimant. His 'conquest' was a 'victoria in regem':

si victoria sit in regem it alters not the property or laws of the people. Thus the conquest of William the Conqueror. It left all the rights of the subject of right untouched. And therefore divers recoveries were in writs of mortdancestor after the coming in of the Conqueror [that is property rights at common law persisted].[49]

In a country such as England, where the original contract had been lost, the custom of the nation could be taken as a guide:

if the beginning or compact appear not extant, then that, which hath been the constant usage of a kingdom or commonwealth, is to be the rule by which to judge; because it carryeth in itself, as well an evidence of what the pact shall be presumed to have been, as also a power introductive of a right.[50]

An 'introductive' power, in the works of common lawyers, was that enjoyed by innovative statutes, in contrast to the numerous Acts that were 'declarative' of common law. 'Prerogativa regis' put the same point in a revealing way: 'custom and usage hath not only a kind of declarative evidence what the pact was in case there were any, but if it be constant and immemorial, it hath a kind of introductive or institutive power.'[51] He was attributing to common law (which is immemorial by definition) the power to make the English constitution. It was conceptually equivalent to an enormous statute, on which the king and people had tacitly agreed.

Hale was aware, of course, that custom is in practice mutable. It might

---

[48] Lincoln's Inn, Misc. 48, 3. Hale could perfectly well have used these grounds to dispense with the whole idea of *ius conquestus*. Philip Hunton took this step (*Treatise of monarchy*, 1643, pp. 20–2), as did the presbyterian Stephen Marshall (*A copy of a letter*, 1643, p. 7), and Sommerville finds earlier examples ('History and theory', 254). His curious failure to do so is a mark of his great loyalty to Grotian/Seldenian patterns of thought.

[49] Lincoln's Inn, Hargrave 5, 15. See also Misc. 48, 4v.; and Hale, *Prerogatives*, 8 and n.

[50] Lincoln's Inn, Misc. 48, 3.

[51] Hale, *Prerogatives*, 7. Compare Hooker, 'Kings which were first instituted by agreement and composition made with them over whom they reign, how far their power may lawfully extend, the articles of compact between them must show: not the articles of compact at the first beginning, which for the most part are either worn clean out of knowledge, or else known unto very few, but whatsoever hath been after in free and voluntary manner condescended unto, whether by express consent, whereof positive laws are witnesses, or else by silent allowance famously notified through custom reaching beyond the memory of man.' *Laws of ecclesiastical polity*, ed. Keble, Oxford 1835, Book VIII, Chapter ii, 11, cited in Johann Somerville, *Politics and ideology*, 64. Book VIII was first printed in 1648.

for instance happen that a king whose powers had once been absolute was limited by the usage of his times, although there was no evidence of any explicit concessions on his part. His lawyers might rely on the very well-known maxim that 'nullum tempus occurrit regi' (that the passage of time leaves the rights of the Crown unaffected).[52] Hale was untroubled by this argument: 'although nullum tempus occurrit regi; yet inasmuch as this might have a foundation upon the original institution of the government or the concession of the prince, it shall be presumed to rise upon this ground . . .[53] There were two ways, in other words, of claiming a legitimating basis for the mutations evident in English political life. The first was frankly fictional; it involved the imputation of contemporary ideas to the contract which founded the state. This was what common lawyers did every time they said a modern rule was 'immemorial'. It involved the kind of manoeuvres familiar from a reading of Coke's works, presupposing, in various ways, that a perfect legal system would answer the expectations of the judge. Such methods were alluring, but dangerous when misused. A much more promising route, so far as constitutionalists were concerned, was concentration on the king's 'concessions', conceived as modifications of the contract. This was the route, in practice, that Hale took.

The role of parliament within Hale's thought was as the only place where the fundamental contract could be altered. 'Parliament' was the name he gave to every recorded assembly that had legitimately made or modified the law. Hale can quite fairly be exonerated, along with most of his contemporaries, from the charge of historical blindness on this point. He believed that legitimate constitutional change had been frequent in the nation's history, and that such change could only be accomplished by means of royal and popular consent. He deduced from these assumptions that there had always been an institution where the nation gathered or was represented, an institution that was charged with considering the country's needs, and with altering, if necessary, the legal basis of the government.

There were good philological reasons, as every antiquarian was aware, for treating 'baronial' councils as just like parliaments. A reader of Camden (1551–1623) or Spelman (?1564–1641)[54] would have known that the English word 'baron' came from the Latin 'vir', and that its German counterpart was 'Freiherr'. John Lilburne, no great scholar, knew that the freemen of medieval London were sometimes known as barons;[55] and

---

[52] For an example, see Elizabeth Read Foster (ed.), *Proceedings in parliament 1610*, Yale 1966, vol. II, p. 200.

[53] Lincoln's Inn, Hargrave 5, 9.

[54] Spelman, *Archaeologus*, 1626, title Baro; Camden, *Britannia*, ed. Gibson, 1722, pp. clxxvi, 122–3 and in T. Hearn (ed.), *A collection of curious discourses*, 1720, p. 207.

[55] John Lilburne, *London's liberty in chains discovered*, 1646, p. 2.

every common lawyer was aware that 'baro' in Law French meant simply 'man' or 'husband'. It was therefore entirely reasonable to interpret a council of barons as a gathering of the free. Sir Robert Cotton (1571–1631) had explained, in 1621, that the Conqueror's men 'were styled barones regis, the King's immediate free-holders, for the word baro then imported no more.'[56] The 'freeholdings' enjoyed by William's army were then co-extensive with England itself. John Selden's learned friend Sir Roger Twysden (1597–1672), writing in 1643–44, claimed that the 'barons' of the Norman kings were nothing but the 'commons' of the realm:

Henry I affirms his father did amend his laws 'consilio baronum suorum'.[57] Hoveden relates the manner of doing it; and where he saith 'precatui baronum tandem acquievit'[58] the ... chronicle of Lichfield affirms it to have been done 'ad precem communitatis Anglorum', which denotes the 'commons' passed in Hoveden under the name of 'baronum'.[59]

Selden taught Hale a theory which accounted for the origins of separate Houses of Commons and Lords. All tenants in chief had been barons, with seats in parliament, till some time early in the reign of John. But by the thirteenth century, their numbers were unmanageably large, and poverty cheapened the honour. The greater barons 'foreseeing, it seems, how their dignity and power might suffer much diminution ... procured ... a law in some of those parliaments that preceded the Great Charter by which themselves only should hereafter be called barons, and the rest tenants in chief only, or knights ...'[60] Hale agreed that the barons were tenants in chief and that Magna Carta 'put a difference between the majores barones and the minores, which before it seems were summoned promiscuously, and so made the tenants by knights service like to our House of Commons at this day'.[61] There was no need, in other words, for a Norman House of Commons. Baronial councils, of which there were plenty, had the same representative function. Hale made no claim to detailed historical knowledge:

such have been the varieties of rights of government within this realm, so many vicissitudes of gain and loss between the King's prerogative and the subject's liberty, such incertainty and obscurity in the relations of historians, such brevity and darkness in the records extant of passages of ancient times, especially before the beginning of Henry III, that we can but guess what was anciently the right or form of parliament.[62]

---

[56] *Cottoni posthuma: divers choice pieces of that renowned antiquary Sir Robert Cotton,* 1672, p. 344.
[57] 'By the advice of his barons'.   [58] 'At last he assented to the prayer of his barons'.
[59] 'At the entreaty of the commonalty of England'. Twysden, *Certain considerations on the government of England,* ed. J. M. Kemble, Camden Society 1849, p. 123.
[60] Selden, *Opera,* III, 738–9.   [61] Lincoln's Inn, Hargrave 5, 246 (reverse vol., 16)
[62] *Ibid.,* 245 (reverse vol., 15).

Whatever the form, it was only the function which mattered. It was enough to know that there was an assembly where contracts could be made and modified.

Hale had been taught by Selden to regard parliamentary statute as the paradigm of law. All valid legal principles were either statute made by parliament, or custom, which was tantamount to statute. This view was well adapted to the needs of the 1620s and 1630s, when the threat to legal values came from the king's appeals outside the common law. In the notorious Ship Money case, he had claimed a right, by natural law, to raise an emergency tax, and also a right to be the judge of the existence of emergencies. By 1642, the poles of the debate had been reversed; it was the rebel Houses who proclaimed that an emergency existed. The parliamentarian view was best explained by Henry Parker's *Observations on some of his Majesty's late Answers and Expresses* (1642), which appealed to the people's natural right of preserving themselves from attack.[63] At the start of civil war, as royalists insisted, it was the king who took his stand on the high ground of 'known laws'. As Dudley Digges (1613–43) had forcibly expressed it, 'this is Ship Money again: [Parker claims that] in every man's lands and goods the state hath an interest paramount, in cases of public extremity, by virtue of which it may justly seize and use the same for its own necessary preservation . . .'[64]

This was probably much how Hale saw it. He was certainly at one with the opposition of the 1630s in distrusting all appeals to supposedly general ideas: 'arguments drawn from speculations, convenience or inconvenience, or such ingredients, which the fancy of the arguer would conceive fittest for the original institution of a commonwealth, though not appearing, are frivolous and idle.'[65] It was therefore interesting, but not surprising, that he came to several royalist conclusions. At the heart of the parliament's programme was replacement of the 'evil counsellors' who had misled the king; Hale thought the historical evidence 'concludes nothing against the power of the king to choose his own counsellors though it is safest and best to take the parliamentary advice in his choice in such cases'.[66] Parliament distinguished between the king's natural and his political capacity; Hale

---

[63] On which see Michael J. Mendle, 'The Ship Money case, *The case of Ship Mony*, and the origins of Henry Parker's parliamentary absolutism', *Historical Journal*, 32 (1989), 513–36.

[64] Dudley Digges, *An answer to a printed book entitled Observations on some of his Majesty's late Answers and Expresses*, Oxford 1642, p. 96. For another good example of the same line of thought, see *A letter from a grave gentleman, once a member of this House of Commons, to his friend remaining a member of the same House in London*, Oxford 1643.

[65] Lincoln's Inn, Misc. 48, 4.   [66] Lincoln's Inn, Misc. 48, 86.

associated this belief with the rebellion of the Despencers.[67] Parliament claimed that the coronation oath to choose 'leges quas vulgus elegerit' bound the king to agree to the bills that it proposed;[68] Hale gave the phrase its usual royalist sense,[69] but in any case he saw the coronation as a ceremonial 'solemnity', confirming a status the monarch already enjoyed.[70] He admitted that there might be certain states where 'by the original institution or pact, whereby the government was settled, there was reserved unto the people, a power to alter or resume the government thus transferred or any part thereof [e.g. the militia], either upon pleasure, or upon breach of some trust.'[71] But constitutional royalists were happy to acknowledge such a possibility; if the 'resumption' of prerogatives was merely a possible feature of the law, then it was clearly not a natural right.

In strictly legal terms, the royalists had an overwhelming case. But there was an insidious argument, which nullified appeals to the 'known laws', enabling the most legalistic to fight for parliament. The known laws could be sidestepped by claiming that the Houses were the supreme interpreters of law, including the questions at issue in their quarrel with the king. Hale totally rejected this position, advancing instead a quite new and original theory of the way that parliament should be conceived. He rejected, in so doing, an almost inescapable conception of its role. It was generally taken for granted, even by those who saw the institution as primarily a legislature along modern lines, that parliament was a special kind of court. The English constitution was most naturally described by listing and describing 'jurisdictions', beginning with the parliament, and descending to tribunals with much more specialised authority. Coke's *Fourth institutes* (printed 1644) was no more than a successor, in this respect, to such Elizabethan works as Lambarde's *Archeion* (first printed 1635), Crompton's *Jurisdiction of courts* (reprinted 1637), and Thomas Smith's *De republica Anglorum* (reprinted 1635).

Though parliament as a legislating body was arguably becoming ineffective, it was rising in importance as a court. The 1620s saw the revival of impeachment (the criminal jurisdiction of the Lords, examining charges presented by the Commons), and also of civil proceedings before the Upper

---

[67] Hale, *Prerogatives*, 85 (this was, admittedly, the Restoration version); Husbands, *An exact collection of all remonstrances, declarations, votes, orders, ordinances, proclamations, petitions, messages, answers, and other remarkable passages between the King's most excellent Majesty and his high court of parliament*, printed Edward Husbands, 1643, p. 370 for the same point in a royal proclamation.

[68] Husbands, *Exact collection*, 269. A much-debated phrase, meaning either 'the laws which the populace will choose' or 'the laws they have chosen'.

[69] Lincoln's Inn, Misc. 48, 36. 'Nota elegerit not the future tense'.

[70] Lincoln's Inn, Hargrave 5, 35–6; Misc. 48, 35. Coke, *Seventh reports*, Calvin's case, 10b, makes the same point.

[71] Lincoln's Inn, Misc. 48, 2.

House. This was of great significance in 1642. As the supreme interpreter of an omni-competent law, the Houses claimed to differentiate between King Charles' legal and his merely personal will.[72] The courts had a right to strike down royal patents, which could be extended to include a right, as a court which was also a council,[73] to preserve 'the public peace and safety of the kingdom':[74]

what they do herein hath the stamp of royal authority, although his Majesty seduced by evil counsel do in his own person oppose or interrupt the same, for the king's supreme power and royal pleasure is exercised and declared in this high court of law and counsel after a more eminent and obligatory manner than it can be by any personal act or resolution of his own.[75]

The king was ill-advised, in policy and law; he listened to 'evil counsel', and not to the Highest Court. There was a blur, in other words, between counsel and council (words then interchangeably spelt), statecraft and institutions, advice and jurisdiction. The right to advise was confused with the right to administer, and then with the right to judge. The king could veto laws, but he could not veto judgements. The militia ordinance of the two Houses, by which they raised the troops to fight their sovereign, was asserted not to be a law at all. It was no 'Act of parliament, or law; 'tis but an occasional supply of co-ordination of government (in case of one part's refusal) lest the whole should ruin'.[76] For the presbyterian clergyman Charles Herle (1598–1659), the conservative parliamentarian who was author of these words, the Houses could declare the law, although they could not make it; their political position, in 1642, was based upon their status as the ultimate court of appeal:

his Majesty often professeth himself no lawyer, therefore in law he judgeth not, but by his courts, in the meanest of which the sentence passed stands good in law, though the king by proclamation or in person should oppose it: whereas there is nothing more frequent or proper to parliaments, than to reverse any of [the courts'] judgements.[77]

It was probably this type of argument which elicited the king's remarkable statement, in the *Answer to the nineteen propositions*, that he was no more than another 'estate' of the realm. In showing he was part of parlia-

[72] On the growing impersonality of the concept of the king, with reference to the events of 1642, see also Conrad Russell, *The fall of the British monarchies*, Oxford 1991, pp. 505–8.
[73] The importance of the idea that the Houses were a council is well discussed in Michael J. Mendle, 'The great council of parliament and the first ordinances: the constitutional theory of the civil war', *Journal of British Studies*, 31 (1992), 133–62.
[74] Husbands, *Exact collection*, 304.   [75] *Ibid.*
[76] Herle, *A fuller answer to a treatise written by Dr Ferne*, 1642, p. 9.
[77] *Ibid.*, 15. For an official parallel see Husbands, *Exact collection*, 206–7, and note the denial (p. 207) that 'we go about to introduce a new law.'

ment, in the same sense as the Houses who had defied his will, he made sure of a veto on its judicial acts.

From Hale's Grotian perspective, of course, this was an admission that monarchy was mixed, and therefore that resistance was allowed. It was not surprising, then, that he rejected, as a 'great mistake', the view that the king was himself an estate of the realm.[78] His own response to these parliamentarian claims was based in a profoundly royalist view of the institutions of medieval England. He saw the constitution as based upon 'councils' not courts; councils that were in essence the royal tools in administering the kingdom. He distinguished five quite separable bodies (although their membership might overlap): the private council (privy council), the legal council (effectively, the courts), the ecclesiastical council (convocation), the great council (of peers), and the common council (parliament).[79] The judicial operations of the Lords had nothing to do with the House of Lords as such; in so far as the Lords was a court, it was functioning as the royal 'legal council'. This brilliant historical idea was to be taken further in a much later work.[80] The important point, for present purposes, is that neither of the Houses had any intrinsic authority in law; their only jurisdiction, in the strict sense of the term, was over their own members.

An obviously related misconception was the idea, which meant so much to Coke, of a merely 'declarative law'. Coke's work blurred the distinction between statutes and judgements, politics and law, because he saw lawyers as ideal politicians, the spokesmen of reason itself. But declaration, as Hale pointed out, was really tantamount to legislation:

every declaration be it of fact or law doth therefore bind, either by cause that it is true, and agreeing to the matter declared, and then the declaration binds not by the authority of the declaration, but of the thing, and consequently the declaration of a falsehood by the king binds not ... or else the declaration binds in respect of some power or authority that the declarer hath to bind, and so the declaration a law; and to make it so it must necessarily be, that the custom of the kingdom must give a legislative power to him, that it gives a declarative power to, vizt. that this that is now declared shall be by all men submitted unto as a truth, which is nothing but a law.[81]

This greatly clarified the situation. If a parliamentary ordinance was valid, it must be based in legislative power, so the Houses were unmasked as claimants to complete supremacy. The 'Incepta' (the first of these

---

[78] Lincoln's Inn, Misc. 48, 93. He may have been influenced, too, by Selden's rather different opinion that 'the King is not one of the three estates as some would have it ... for then if two agree, the third is involved'. Selden, *Talk*, 64. This seems to rest, however, on the view that sovereignty is invariably unitary, not 'mixed'.

[79] Lincoln's Inn, Hargrave 5, 195; Misc. 48, 86.   [80] See below, pp. 114–17.

[81] Lincoln's Inn, Hargrave 5, 102–3.

works), in the form that Hale first wrote it, contained a definitive verdict on 'laws' that were made without the king's consent. The manuscript that now survives has been oddly but carefully censored. An unknown hand (presumably the author's) has removed some two thirds of the page, leaving only a strip by the margin. It is obvious from the context that all the missing passages are royalist at least in implication. At one point, for example, he discusses the validity of ordinances made by king and Lords (invalid), and also by king and Commons (none in the records, perhaps because the records were kept by the clerk of the Lords). Discussion of the final permutation, the ordinances passed without the king, has suffered from the usual censorship. The marginal fragment begins, suggestively enough, with the following guillotined phrases:

> Touching ordinance ... [by Lords and Commons] ...
> I cannot find any effect ...[82]

Another passage starts:

> As without his cons ...
> No being, so wit ...

and includes, a little later

> necessity of ...
> kinge's consent in the ...
> the libty of the kinge ... [83]

Such quotations yield some teasing textual puzzles, but no conclusive evidence at all. The most interesting follows a passage concerning the royal power to levy troops:

> Touching a defensive war against a foreign invasion
> or for the repression of a rebellion generally it is
> true that such a case ought to be of necessity and
> not of fear or suspicion only. And such case[s] of
> necessity enable the King, as the person fittest to be
> trusted, and most concerned, to command those
> things for an extraordinary, which may seem to
> carry a power of imposing. This necessity doth in
> some cases dispense with private property in the
> actions of a private man. ...[84]
> The King may in case ...
> kingdom in case and [illegible: acc..?] ...
> a [illegible: casual ?] necessity eith ...
> compel men to be ar ...
> to attend the necessary ...
> or rebellion ...[85]

---

[82] Ibid., 107.   [83] Ibid., 105.   [84] Ibid., 132.   [85] Ibid., 133.

This passage leaves open, of course, the question whether the phrase 'defensive war' could be said to describe the actions of the king (it may be worth remembering that he was engaged in such a war in Ireland, at least in the crucial summer of 1642). But the content of the censored passages is not, in fact, of practical importance. Whatever the legality of the things the Houses did, Hale certainly regarded them as futile.

These manuscripts suggest an attitude of wearily conservative disdain, based on an understanding of English constitutional history. Relations between king and subject, prerogative and liberty, had been characterised in all ages by great 'vicissitudes of gain and loss'. Extremes were self-correcting, and rebellion was in general a mistake: 'the King's powers have had their full and wane, and commonly the overacting of them caused a subsequent ebb'.[86] In the 'Preparatory notes', his slightly later work, a similar thought was expressed:

as on the one side the extending of the regal power beyond the bounds of law and custom, and the misapplying it, is the greatest enemy to itself, so on the other side the best means to remedy such excesses is by convincing the judgement of the prince if it may be, or by denying supplies. An application of active force or over-rigid remedies endangers all, and at the best provides but a temporary and uncertain relief to the subject.[87]

Though the law was just a contract reflecting the relative strength of the two parties, its conditions fluctuated around a mean: there was a natural English constitution, from which the English frequently departed, but to which they would eventually return. This confidence in law's resilience, an inheritance from the thought of Edward Coke, was to guide his political conduct in the difficult years ahead.

---

[86] *Ibid.*, 76. Metaphors of inundation were popular with all shades of opinion, but compare the following: 'as the overflowing of waters do many times make the river to lose his proper channel, so in times past ecclesiastical persons seeking to extend their liberties beyond their true bounds, either lost or enjoyed not that which of right belonged to them'. Coke, *Second institutes*, 4.

[87] Lincoln's Inn, Misc. 48, 68.

4

Interregnum

The Republic was a failure because common law survived. It failed in an obvious sense, when the heir of the king was restored, but this was only the sequel, and perhaps the consequence, of a rather more subtle defeat. Intellectually, it was doomed, to put the matter simply, because it made its claims in legal terms. The 'Common-Wealth' (a very frequent spelling) chose to present itself as instrumental, as a means for the promotion of the English public good. But the English conceived of this good as the protection of their liberties, the rights and property that they enjoyed by the authority of common law. Another way to put this point might be to say that common law was the science that defined the common weal, and therefore dictated the structure of the English Common-Wealth. Among the clear prescriptions of this science (in both the senses of the word 'prescription') were prerogative rights of the Crown, rights often abused, to be sure, but instituted for the people's sake. The Rump (and still more the Protectors) were thus forced to behave like a king.

A truly republican theory, like that which James Harrington (1611–77) favoured, would need to cast some doubt on these assumptions. It would need in fact to show, like that author's *Oceana* (1656) and the literature it spawned, that the English constitution was outmoded: that the rights of the Crown guaranteed by common law were no longer appropriate to the country's social state. As it was, the Common-Wealth was based upon a simple contradiction. The Republic appealed to law, but the law recommended monarchical rule; to acknowledge legal values was to damn the new regime. To perpetuate those values, by continuing to operate the system, was thus to promote Restoration; it was to be loyal to standards that only a kingdom could meet.

The crucial decisions were taken in the course of a matter of weeks. King Charles was executed on 30 January 1649. He was tried and condemned as a 'Man of Blood', a felon, and a traitor, but no one had deprived him of his Crown. The Rump was not a radical or even perhaps a republican assembly, and it found itself running a kingless but still a monarchical state. Its first constitutional step, in a bill rushed through on the day that Charles was killed, was to prevent his heir claiming the throne: it published an 'Act prohibiting the proclaiming of any person to be king of England or Ireland or the dominions thereof', at least 'without the free consent of the people in parliament first had and signified by a special Act or Ordinance for that purpose'.[1] On 7 February, it resolved to abolish the 'office' of a king, but postponed the evil moment of a full-scale parliamentary debate.[2]

A rather more urgent constitutional need was to gain co-operation from the bench. The parliament therefore engaged (on 8 February) 'to maintain the fundamental laws of this nation for the good of the people'.[3] This was at best a rather vague commitment, in the absence of agreement on the nature of the fundamental laws. In a printed declaration (of 10 February) the wording was much more precise:

they are fully resolved to maintain and shall and will uphold, preserve, and keep the fundamental laws of this nation, for and concerning the preservation of the lives, properties and liberties of the people with all things incident thereunto; with the alterations touching kings and House of Lords, already resolved in this present parliament, for the good of the people, and what shall be further necessary for the perfecting thereof.[4]

They were promising, in fact, to respect individual rights, while retaining unlimited scope for further constitutional alterations. The printed declaration, addressed to the public at large, was bolder than the message to the judges. This pattern was repeated throughout the next ten years. The Rump's extreme conservatism in dealing with the courts began with an unquestioning acceptance of the legality of their proceedings. In 1461, when the Yorkists were 'restored', a statute confirmed the decisions of the previous three reigns.[5] In the 'first year of liberty restored'[6] the Rump passed no such measure. The status of the courts, though open to some doubt, was considerably less dubious than that of the regime. Its leaders must have hoped, if they gave the matter thought, for an aura of legality that only the bench could provide. They contented themselves, at all events, with an 'Act for better settling of proceedings in courts of justice',[7]

[1] British Library, Thomason tracts, E1060(2); *Commons Journal*, vol. VI, p. 125.
[2] *Commons Journal*, VI, 133.
[3] *Commons Journal*, VI, 135. On the role of the bench in this period, see also Stephen F. Black, 'Coram Protectore: The judges of Westminster Hall under the Protectorate of Oliver Cromwell', *American Journal of Legal History*, 20 (1976) and 'The courts and judges of Westminster Hall during the Great Rebellion, 1640–60', *Journal of Legal History*, 7 (1986).
[4] British Library, Thomason tracts, E1060(4).
[5] *The statutes of the realm*, 11 vols., 1963, vol. II, p. 380.
[6] The phrase on the Great Seal.
[7] C. H. Firth and R. S. Rait, *Acts and ordinances of the interregnum 1642–60*, 1911, vol. II, pp. 6–9.

which passed into law on 17 February. The 'better settling of proceedings', a trivial adjustment, inserted 'the Keepers of the liberties of England, by authority of parliament' wherever, in a document, there had previously been mention of the king.

'The Keepers of the liberties', a most suggestive title, epitomised the problems that the legal system raised. The Common-Wealth existed to secure the subject's rights. Among these rights, which were liberties rather than freedom, was property dependent on the powers of the church or the Crown. 'The king' as a legal expression was a part of great swathes of the law. He was needed for everyday practice: for the issue of writs, the granting of patents and pardons, the reception of fines and escheats.[8] A tyrant like Charles Stuart, who defeated the purpose of laws, discredited personal kingship and had to be removed. It was quite another thing, in the absence of pressing incentives, to undertake wholesale revision of the monarch's legitimate powers. The obvious way to proceed, the line of least resistance, was to alter the names on the writs. 'The Commonwealth would not put the executive power out of their hands', as the republican Harry Vane (1613–62) recalled: 'for this reason they set up those shadows, the Keepers of the liberties of England, as an executive power to distinguish it from the legislative'.[9] 'The Keepers of the liberties of England, by authority of parliament', a ludicrously cumbersome expression,[10] was the home for the rights of the king.

Exactly a month later, on 17 March, the so-called 'Kingly Office' had its end. The 'Act for the abolishing the Kingly Office' had the restricted purpose of putting an end to *personal* monarchy:

Whereas it is and hath been found by experience, that the office of a king in this nation and Ireland, and to have the power thereof in any single person, is unnecessary, burthensome, and dangerous to the liberty, safety, and public interest of the people of this nation ... and that, for the most part, use hath been made of the regal power and prerogative to oppress, and impoverish, and enslave the subject; and that usually and naturally any one person in such power, makes it his interest to encroach upon the just freedom and liberty of the people, and to promote the setting up of their own will and power above the laws, that so they might enslave these kingdoms to their own lust; be it therefore enacted and ordained by this present parliament, and by authority of the same, that the office of a king in this nation, shall not henceforth reside in, or be exercised by, any one single person.[11]

---

[8] See the report of the great pardons case, Custodes v. Riccaby, in Folger Shakespeare Library MS V.b.6, fo. 45.

[9] Burton, *Diary*, III, 178.

[10] In *The jovial crew, or the devil turned ranter*, 1651, p. 11, a constable has an unfortunate slip of the tongue: 'I charge you my friends in the king's name, *cry mercy in the name of the Keepers of the liberties* ...' (original emphasis).

[11] Firth and Rait, *Acts and ordinances*, II, 19.

The burden of this sentence, as a careful reading shows, was that there were great dangers in a single person's rule. The 'regal power' itself, which monarchs had misused, was not so much abolished as transferred.

The Commonwealth's supporters, a miscellaneous group, defended it in many different ways. It presented itself to the courts as a 'common law republic', as an interpretation of existing constitutional arrangements, with all the legal sanction such arrangements could provide. This view was made explicit, on 20 March, by the charge at the York Assizes, the work of one Serjeant Thorpe (1595–1665). Thorpe set out to explain 'the style and title of our commissions, under which we are now to act, being changed from Carolus Rex Angliae to Custodes libertatis Angliae authoritate parliamento'.[12] The rule of a 'single person' had led to repeated abuses, so the people had resolved to do without one. It was nonetheless unnecessary to change the Treason Act. 'The name and word king' applied to 'the supreme authority', whatever that happened to be, because 'it was frequently used to set forth the public interest of the people', as in the phrase 'the king's peace'.[13] A perfect legality beckoned, a realised common law, shorn of the casual tyrannies of actual Stuart kings.

It can be seen, with hindsight, that this was at least compatible with Coke. Coke's law was based on 'reason', which promoted the general good. The 'honour' of the king, as Ellesmere had complained, was preferred to his personal 'profit'; he was always presumed to be guided by the thought of 'common weal'. His role was thus exhausted by the law's view of the good. Thorpe drew a submerged implication: when kings turned into tyrants, converting 'the people's rem publicam' into 'the governor's rem privatam', they defeated the purpose of kingship, and lost their right to claim obedience.[14] The Stuarts were removed in the name of the common law values for the sake of which their 'office' was ordained.

The process was concluded, though not before 19 May, by an 'Act declaring and constituting the people of England to be a Commonwealth and free-state'. The measure's ambiguous wording, as much 'declarative' as 'introductive', could easily suggest that there had been no legal change.[15] The official explanation was at pains to encourage this view. It

---

12 *The Harleian miscellany*, ed. J. Malham, 12 vols., 1808–11, vol. VI, p. 106. This was called to my attention by M. A. Judson's Whiggishly-entitled *From tradition to political reality: a study of the ideas set forth in support of the Commonwealth government in England 1649–53*, Hamden, Connecticut, 1980, p. 44.

13 *Harleian miscellany*, VI, 114.   14 *Ibid.*, 108.

15 'Be it declared and enacted by this present parliament and by the authority of the same, that the people of England, and of all the dominions and territories thereunto belonging, are and shall be and are hereby constituted, made, established, and confirmed to be a Commonwealth and free-state. And shall from henceforth be governed as a Commonwealth and free-state by the supreme authority of this nation, the representatives o̍ ᵗʰᵉ people in Parliament, and by such as they shall appoint and constitute as officers and

asserted 'the clear consistency of [the law practised in the courts] with the present government of a republic, upon some easy alterations of form only, leaving entire the substance; the name of a king being used in them for form only . . .'[16] A rather later essay corroborates this claim. It was written in May 1660, on the eve of the royal return, and contained a dispiriting picture of affairs in church and state. There was, the author acknowledged, an exception to the rule: 'the fragment or broken piece of our old government that seems yet left us in form of administration of justice in the courts of justice which by divine providence hath kept somewhat of the resemble of former government.'[17] This grudgingly favourable verdict was that of Matthew Hale.

Retrospectively, at least, Hale trusted the resilience of existing English law. His most complacent statement was buried in a short undated work, the 'Observations moral and political' on his version of *The life and death of T. Pomponius Atticus* (1677). This curious little book, a translation from the Latin writer Nepos, had an obvious significance for Hale. Its subject Atticus, a learned and virtuous Roman, was neutral in his country's civil wars. Most of the 'Observations' were prompted by this fact. Hale defended his forerunner's conduct (and presumably also his own) by appealing to historical experience. This taught, he improbably claimed, that 'factions in a state never long hold their ground'.

A 'faction', on Hale's definition, involved a departure from law: 'established government, or the adherence to it, was no faction'.[18] It was factious, he strongly implied, to have obeyed King Charles in his excesses:

when any person entrusted by the sovereign power with a particular power or authority shall endeavour by force or fraud to extend the power wherewith he is entrusted beyond the bounds of it. . . . [such people] are no more excused from a faction by their authority that they had, than if they were without any such authority; because herein they act beyond the bounds and without the warrant of that authority, and consequently as private persons.[19]

A slightly later passage explains the republic's collapse:

Factions in a state never long hold their ground. But if they are not suppressed by the natural power of the state wherein they arise, yet by the same like means whereby at any time they obtain, they are commonly broken and dissolved; and by the same artifices whereby they gain the saddle, they are commonly unhorsed, either by the adverse party, or by some distemper rising in their own party . . . when one faction hath suppressed another, the victorious party fall into divisions

ministers under them for the good of the people, and that without any king or House of Lords.' (Firth and Rait, *Acts and ordinances*, II, 122).
[16] *A declaration of the parliament of England, expressing the grounds of their late proceedings, and of settling the present government in the way of a free state*, 1649, p. 24.
[17] Lambeth 3475, 309.   [18] Hale, *Atticus*, 64.   [19] *Ibid.*, 64–66.

among themselves, some thinking they have too small a share in the acquest, and others too much, and so weaken their party, and render it less and narrower.[20]

The Army's internal divisions, Hale noted at the time, were the cause of the king's restoration.[21] With the benefit of hindsight, a comforting conclusion could be reached. Factious tyranny, factious rebellion were equally destined to fail. Political action was pointless, when a virtuous passivity sufficed.

Hale's *History of the common law of England*, the greatest of his Restoration works, explained the basis of his confidence. The kingdom's 'constitution' was the English common law, which was also its 'temperament' or its 'complexion'. The 'constitution' of the land (in this sense, a medical term) was its natural state of health:

the common municipal law of England is . . . by a long experience and use . . . as it were incorporated into [the English nation's] very temperament, and, in a manner, become the complexion and constitution of the English commonwealth.

Insomuch that even as in the natural body the due temperament and constitution does by degrees work out those accidental diseases which sometimes happen, and do reduce the body to its just state and constitution, so when at any time through errors, distempers, or inequities of men or times, the peace of the kingdom, and right order of government, have received interruption, the common law has wasted and wrought out those distempers, and reduced the kingdom to its just state and temperament, as our present (and former) times can easily witness.[22]

The body's 'constitution' is presented both as cause and as effect, as normative and descriptive, as an underlying condition and as its super-structural expression. A reciprocal relation is implied: the legal moulds the social, to the point where common law is the 'complexion and constitution of the commonwealth', and the social reinforces the grip of common law.

If the law was to 'waste out distempers', then it had to be applied. To operate the system was to help restore the king. Whatever precisely his motives, Hale never stopped work as a lawyer, not even in the early months of 1649; some time in March, for instance, he prepared a marriage settlement for General Cromwell's son.[23] He had 'declared and promised', by the terms of the so-called Engagement, to be 'true and faithful to the Commonwealth of England as it is now established, without a king or House of Lords'.[24] Up until January 1654 he was one of the leading barristers in court of King's (re-named the 'Upper') Bench; from 1654 until

---

[20] *Ibid.*, 97–8.   [21] Williams, *Memoirs*, 49–50.

[22] Hale, *The history of the common law of England*, ed. Gray, Chicago 1971, p. 30. An earlier draft of this passage (Clark Library, identifiable as Selden–Hale Additional MS 1, fo. 6) omitted the words 'and former'.

[23] F. A. Inderwick, *The interregnum (AD 1648–1660): Studies of the commonwealth: legislative, social and legal*, 1891, p. 215.

[24] Kenyon, *Stuart constitution*, 307; Cobbett, *State trials*, V, 211.

Cromwell's death in September 1658 he was a Justice of the Common Bench; in the period just before the restoration he reverted to 'chamber practice', writing legal opinions but staying out of court.[25] He kept the title 'serjeant' which Cromwell had conferred.[26]

This was collaboration of an important kind, but such assistance hampered the Republic, and probably hastened its ultimate collapse. To secure co-operation from lawyers such as Hale the government was forced to acquiesce, for a whole range of practical purposes, in the legal profession's conception of the English polity. The legal history of the interregnum was the history of the common law's survival, both as the guarantee of private rights and as the natural language of English political thought. These survivals were inter-connected, as the *History of the common law* implied, if only because some property rights were highly politically charged. The bishops might have vanished, but tithes were still enforced;[27] their Lordships' House was abolished, but its membership was treated with respect; and reform of the court system, perhaps the most persistent of the radical demands, was repeatedly and skilfully averted.[28] These were not insignificant successes, and in each of them Hale played at least a part.

One way in which he strengthened common law was by helping to replace the bishops' courts. In Eeles v. Lambert (1648), for instance, one of the points at issue was the power of common law in the enforcement of a legacy (this was previously a function of the English canon law).[29] For any disciple of Selden's the matter was simple. Hale showed, on behalf of his client, that the common law had once had jurisdiction, and that the authority of canon law (in this or any other legal question) was still 'supported' by the secular system. He therefore saw no reason why common law should not resume the functions it had merely delegated.[30] Similar reasoning could be applied to any function of the canon law's, but its greatest political relevance was to the collection of tithes. For Selden, in his *History of tithes* (1618), the tithe was a secular right; for others, especially the clergy, the payment of tithes was a duty that God had ordained; at the radical end of the spectrum, it was a hated clerical

---

[25] F. J. Routlege (ed.), *Calendar of the Clarendon State Papers preserved in the Bodleian Library*, vol. IV, Oxford 1932, p. 160.

[26] *Ibid.*

[27] See the complaint about enforcement of tithes in John Jones' anti-lawyer tract, *The cry of blood*, 1651, p. 67.

[28] For specialised studies of law reform, see Stuart E. Prall, *The agitation for law reform in the puritan revolution 1640–60*, The Hague, 1966; Donald Veall, *The popular movement for law reform 1640–60*, Oxford 1970; Nancy Matthews, *William Sheppard: Cromwell's law reformer*, Cambridge 1984. The best single discussion is A. B. Worden, *The Rump parliament*, Cambridge 1974, pp. 105–18.

[29] For the complex details of the case, see Style 37–8, 54–6, 73–4; Aleyn 38–42.

[30] Aleyn 40. For the later influence of this view see Hardres 65.

imposition. The interest of Harwood v. Paty (1649), another leading case involving Hale, is that the law came down on Selden's side.[31]

Hale's client was a parson's creditor, who sought to recover the money he was owed by confiscation of the cleric's tithes. In the days when there were bishops, there was a legal process which would have met his needs; he could have applied to the bishop, who would have 'sequestered' the income until the debt in question was paid off. One solution would have been to give the bishop's function to the sheriff, who would 'levy the debt of the clergy as the bishops use to do'.[32] The sheriff would collect the tithes, and pay them over to the creditor. Hale's client was not content with this solution; he wanted to collect the tithes themselves, without resort to such official meddling. There was a writ at common law, known as an 'elegit', which answered very neatly to his purpose; it gave the creditor practical control of half his debtor's land. Hale therefore successfully argued that tithes were something like real property: he asserted that 'the tithes may be said to be tenements, and the parson hath a freehold in them'.[33] On one possible reading, of course, this argument was anti-clerical, treating tithes like any other legal right ('the court clearly held, with Mr Selden, that tithes are not due jure divino').[34] On another, it entrenched them legally, regarding them with just the same respect as any layman's property in land.

The most striking aspect of these leading cases, one of them very highly politically charged, is that no one appears to have worried about usurping parliamentary power. The common law was following its own logic, without much regard for the fragile regimes which technically controlled the English state. A promising intellectual strategy, for radicals opposed to those regimes, was to frame their subversive arguments in strictly legal form. A naive version of this strategy, applied to the law of England as a whole, can be found in a number of John Lilburne's (c. 1614–57) works, but Hale was faced with similar points in a curious local dispute. The issue was the franchise. The London corporation (the Mayor and Aldermen), were chosen by the livery company members (something over 10,000 adult males), but a radical faction of Londoners, with Lilburne's friend John Wildman (1623–93) at the fore, thought every freeman should enjoy a vote. In December 1650, for reasons now unclear, the authorities conceded an organised public debate. There is a pamphlet record, composed from the Leveller perspective, entitled *London's liberties*, but sub-titled, more tellingly, *A learned argument of law and reason* (1651).

---

[31] The main question, in technical terms, was whether tithes could be made extendible on an elegit by equitable interpretation of Westminster II.
[32] Style 169. [33] Style 161. [34] Style 169.

The significant sub-title was the heart of the radical case. Wildman believed, as might have been expected, 'that all just subjection unto governors ought to proceed from consent of parties'. He emphasised, however, his willingness to waive this argument.[35] His claims were essentially legal, and they were surprisingly strong, for the franchise confined to the liverymen was less than two centuries old. In earlier times, by contrast, all freemen had the vote. They held this right by common law, confirmed in a grant of King John's, and also, as a consequence, by the highest authority known to English law. No right could be more heavily entrenched, 'according to the principles of the gentlemen of the long robe',[36] because it was confirmed, among the other 'liberties of London', in Magna Carta itself: 'if I should believe Sir Edward Coke ... I must then say, that an act of parliament made contrary to that part of the great charter that was declarative of common law was null of itself ...'[37] This was a mild distortion of a passage in the *Second institutes*, though arguably faithful to the spirit of Coke's thought.[38] But Wildman clearly grasped the lesson that Coke taught in Bonham's case: that 'reason' was subversive, not just of kings, but of parliament itself: 'a statute made against that part of the great charter which is declarative of the common law is null of itself; for the common law, being right reason, it cannot be supposed without a contradiction that parliaments should of right have power to make a law against right.'[39]

The City had retained three different lawyers to justify its constitutional form. One of the three was almost unreported; the other two, Hale and John Maynard (1602–90), were rather unhappily yoked. John Maynard was ubiquitous for more than forty years (he lived to greet William III), and his argument was suited to a survivor's needs. His instinct was to ridicule the Leveller's known views. He therefore hastened to point out that 'there [are] but few governments but are established without assent.'[40] He went on to attack, with more panache than wisdom, the radical appeal to Magna Carta. The supposedly sacred status of this law could not be reconciled with the fact that 'we all know that there were bishops and

---

[35] *London's liberties, or a learned argument of law and reason*, 1651, p. 7.
[36] *Ibid.*, 24.
[37] *Ibid.*
[38] The reference appears to be to Coke, *Second institutes*, 187: 'all statutes made contrary to Magna Charta, which is lex terrae, from the making thereof until 42 Edward III are declared and enacted to be void, and therefore if this act of Westminster I [3 Edward I] concerning the extra-judicial commandment of the king be against Magna Charta, it is void ...' Wildman's interpretation of these words can probably be traced to Nicholas Fuller, *The argument in the case of Thomas Lad*, 1607, p. 5.
[39] *London's liberties*, 8.   [40] *Ibid.*, 13.

kings by the common law and Magna Carta, and yet they are changed and justly changed by the parliament'.[41] The frankness of his words must have delighted Wildman, who seized on the remarks about consent: 'in the time of the King it had been for his interest to have said that we ought to be subject to the son and heir of a conqueror, because such.'[42] In Hale's more subtle mind, with its complicated feelings about conquest, this must have struck a chord. We find, at all events, that he took a most conciliatory line.

His argument is clearest from Wildman's brief reply:

[Hale] was pleased to confess very ingenuously that I waived those arguments that might reduce government to an uncertainty, or to the first principles of general common right. But, saith Mr Hales, if that principle be allowed amongst a free people, that subjection to their governors ought to be by mere consent; saith he, we must consider there is a personal and a virtual assent, and it shall be conceived to be a virtual assent, where there hath been an usage time out of mind for the people to be subject to any form of government.[43]

Hale rebutted the radical case with the weapons that Wildman had chosen; he acknowledged the Leveller's claim to be talking about common law. As a matter of law (as opposed to political theory) there was a right for freemen to be governed by consent. The relatively narrow disagreement was concerned with this great principle's fulfilment. Hale was happy to agree, in spite of his royalist outlook, that agreement of the governed was the basis of government power. But consent was often evidenced by usage, and continual civic practice, a symptom of consent, outweighed the scattered precedents against it.[44] Like a number of moderate speakers in the earlier Putney debates,[45] Hale saw an absurd implication in the principles that Wildman had advanced: 'will there not be the same reason for apprentices and foreigners to plead for votes in your election?'[46]

At a theoretical level, the difference from Maynard was marked, but on points of legal substance they had almost identical views. They distinguished between 'virtual' and personal assent, and construed the London charter by the practice of their time. They ignored the many precedents against them, and feared the legal chaos that a radical triumph implied. Hale differed from Maynard, however, in seeing the advantage in placing a positive stress upon consent. The personal/virtual distinction was the key to a conservative position, a position that focussed on usage as the sign of the popular will. This could equally be turned, as Hale was quite aware, to defending institutions like the king and House of Lords.

---

[41] *Ibid.*, 14. The noted royalist author, David Jenkins, had quoted Magna Carta and 42 Edward III (see n. 38 above) in defence of the position of the bishops (Jenkins, *Lex terrae*, 1647, p. 34).
[42] *Ibid.*, 23.   [43] *Ibid.*, 33.   [44] *Ibid.*, 20.
[45] Woodhouse, *Puritanism and liberty*, 65, 80, 82.
[46] *London's liberties*, 20.

Although their House of parliament was gone, the Lords had a plausible claim to other rights. They were sheltered, for example, from imprisonment for debt. The privilege was tested, in the course of 1650, in suits against the Earl and Countess Rivers (the Countess, a little confusingly, was a peer in her own right). It might be thought (and had indeed been said)[47] that the privilege was founded on the duties they performed in parliament. This was the view, it seems, of the great Chief Justice Rolle, who inclined to the position that 'the dignity of their persons was in respect of their voice in parliament'.[48] Hale argued (quoting Coke) that the right was unconnected with their parliamentary votes; it was theirs on account of their 'station', and the wealth they were deemed to possess.[49] To the opposing counsel, the privilege was intrinsically unlawful: 'the king could not create a Countess for life in derogation and to take away the liberty and benefit of particular men. For the king could not grant such a privilege to any as not to be arrested unless it were in case of public service.'[50] Hale accepted the force of this reasoning, but nullified its practical effect:

I agree that the king cannot grant such an exception as to be free from arrest nor to imprison. But when the king creates a court, then the law gives power to arrest as a consequent. So here the king does not give any privilege to be exempt from arrest, but only confers this honour which he may do, and then the privilege to be free from arrest is but a consequent of that honour, and to which the privilege is annexed by custom.[51]

This argument was a long way from Coke, or from any legal theory that stressed the rationality of law. The king was obliged to act lawfully, but custom had arbitrary power.

The matter was finally dropped, on the death of the Countess of Rivers, but the story had an interesting postscript. As the years went by, the peerage maintained its position.[52] In Trinity 1655, when Hale had become a judge in Common Bench, a youthful peer had business that required him to visit the court. The judges treated him with great respect; he was

placed in the middle of the bar between the two eldest serjeants, the ushers gave notice to the judges of the court of his coming, who put off their caps and bow to him, at his coming and departing, and all the time he is there all pleadings cease, and the three prothonotaries sit with their round caps off.[53]

---

[47] *The privileges and practice of parliaments in England*, 1628, p. 36.
[48] 'Le dignity de leur persons fuit in respect de leur voice in parliament.' British Library, Hargrave 42, 133. See also Folger Shakespeare Library, V.b.6, fo. 4, 5.
[49] British Library, Lansdowne 1066, fo. 158.   [50] British Library, Hargrave 42, 147v.
[51] British Library, Hargrave 42, 148.
[52] In 1656, a peer pleaded his freedom from arrest before Chief Justice Glyn (Style 454). The most notable exception to this rule was an untraced occasion when a peer was burned on the hand for manslaughter (Bridgeman O., 251; Hale, *Historia*, II, 377).
[53] British Library, Hargrave 49, fo. 34.

In Easter 1657, the courts went further still, this time in Upper Bench. The Earl of Leicester quarrelled with his parish minister, and brought an action of scandalum magnatum (a statutory remedy for slander, restricted to great officers and peers).[54] Chief Justice Glyn (no royalist) apparently loved a lord. He explained that the action was a right 'not given them in respect of their peerage or as they are lords of the parliament, but as they are men of great influence and alliance . . .'[55] He did not consider the view that their 'influence and alliance' was itself not unconnected with their seats in parliament. He explained that he neither affirmed nor denied that noblemen had special legal rights, but he was clearly signalling a shift in the burden of proof.[56]

The more that the nobility were favoured by the courts, the stranger it seemed, to a logical mind, that they should be kept out of parliament. The 1657 constitution, the Humble Petition and Advice, set up a second chamber, the so-called Other House. It was natural to suggest, in fulfilment of the spirit of this clearly reactionary move, that the lords should be allowed to take their seats. In Richard Cromwell's parliament, in 1659, a member made a speech to this effect: '[the Other House is] the old House, they have only changed the names. Though new Members they are the old House. I move that you would transact with them as another House of parliament, and add the old lords to the new House.'[57] The speaker, Edward Fowell, was not a politician of much weight. The fact of his proposal, which was generally ignored, was nonetheless significant, if just as a straw in the wind. In respecting the rights of the peerage, and treating the Protector as a king, the courts had helped maintain such expectations.

An advocate like Hale, whatever his political intentions, might have voiced the same opinions for the sake of his client alone. There is evidence, however, that his actions were intended to assist the Stuart cause. Hale's 'On the amendment of laws', an essay of the early Restoration, had a welcoming approach to legal change:[58] 'he that thinks a state can be exactly steered by the same laws in every kind, as it was 2 or 300 years since, may as well imagine, that the clothes that fitted him when he was a child should serve him when he is grown a man.'[59] Reform should,

---

[54] On scandalum magnatum, Lassiter, 'Defamation of peers: the rise and decline of the action of scandalum magnatum 1497–1773', *American Journal of Legal History*, 22 (1978), 216–36. On Leicester v. Malpas: British Library, Additional MSS 35, 972, fo. 30–1; Lansdowne 1109, 120v., 122v.–23; Folger Shakespeare Library, V.b.6, fo. 113–113v.

[55] Folger V.b.6, 113.   [56] *Ibid.*   [57] Burton, *Diary*, III, 533.

[58] His son-in-law, Edward Stephens, described it as 'digested in August 1665' (Lambeth 3479, 207).

[59] Hargrave, *A collection of tracts relating to the law of England*, 1787, p. 269. The comparison to clothes was probably commonplace. It also occurs in Charles James Cocke, *England's compleat law-judge and lawyer*, 1656, sig. B2v.

however, be gradual, and suited to English conditions, both in political and social terms: 'that is in truth perfect that is perfect in relation to its use and end'.[60] The adaptation of the laws of England was not a matter for the layman's mind, still less for those who 'think the laws are foolish, because if they were reasonable things, they must understand them without study'.[61]

Usurpers were the first to alter laws, 'principally to engage the generality of men in the acting under new laws, and holding their interest and proprieties under them, and thereby they may be engaged in a common defence against the true and just power'.[62] The defence of the existing legal system, and of the property it recognised, was therefore a way of resisting usurping regimes. The interregnum years, which Hale's essay explicitly cited, were a time for opposing reform. The government 'was then fixed upon a tottering and unwarrantable basis', and so 'that which wise and honest men do now desire, they did then industriously decline'.[63] The so-called Hale Commission, of 1652, was a perfect illustration of this point.

The Commission was set up, in response to some military pressure, to act alongside parliament's committee on the law. It was 'to take into consideration what inconveniences there are in the law; and how the mischiefs which grow from delays, the chargeableness and irregularities in the proceedings in the law may be prevented, and the speediest way to reform the same, and to present their opinions to such committee as the parliament shall appoint.'[64] It met three times a week, from January to July, and a volume of minutes survives.[65]

At the start of its proceedings, to judge by this difficult source, Hale was easily the most important figure. On 23 January, when the Commission met for the first time, he was at once elected to the chair. The Independent clergyman, Hugh Peter (1598–1660), the most obvious puritan hothead in a generally moderate group, had a root and branch suggestion for reform. He demanded, the minutes record, that all but freehold tenures be abolished, adding somewhat portentously that 'in Oldenburgh for 1700 miles [there are] but 5 lawyers.'[66] His target was the 'copyhold', a kind of 'servile' tenure, a relic, at least in theory, of a time when some of the English were unfree. Hale responded with a lecture on the ways in which land could be held, and much of the rest of the meeting was taken up with a complicated discussion, dominated by the chairman, of the problems

---

[60] Hargrave, *Collection*, 258.   [61] *Ibid.*, 261.   [62] *Ibid.*, 263.   [63] *Ibid.*, 274.

[64] *Commons Journal*, VII, 58.

[65] For a general account see Mary Cotterell, 'Interregnum law reform: the Hale Commission of 1652', *English Historical Review*, 83 (1968), 689–704.

[66] British Library, Additional MSS 35,863, fo. 3.

raised by bankrupt copyholders. At the end of this first session, the Commission instructed Hale to draw up a bill embodying its conclusions, being careful to safeguard the rights of manorial lords. A radical demand, the abolition of a class of tenures, resulted in proposals for a rather unremarkable reform.

In setting the tone of debate, there is no doubt that Hale was most successful; in directing the outcome, however, his touch was less assured.[67] He was re-elected chairman for a second two-week term (thereafter, the chair rotated every fortnight) but was never more than *primus inter pares*. At times he was politically obtuse, as in standing up for benefit of clergy; a sincerely committed reformer would hardly have defended this abuse, still less have remarked, to shore up this position, that "'tis in the parent's power to breed his child to read'.[68] In April, he went out of London, while significant business was done; in later months, when several important battles had been lost, he became an infrequent attender. In the middle of the summer, in his absence, some dangerous proposals were approved. Hale would never have agreed, to give the most striking example, that a judge should be elected, still less that he be chosen to serve a four-year term.[69] He would also have been unhappy (though precedents existed) that difficult points in the statutes should be taken to the Speaker of the House.[70]

The decisive reverse, if there was one, was probably the register for land. This would have had legal authority as a record of property transfers, with scope for retrospective registration.[71] Hale was prepared to contemplate a register for future title deeds (so long as the system was voluntary, and existing claims were in no way disadvantaged) but said that 'to look back is dangerous. For if claim be put to my land I shall sue him'.[72] The certainty of extensive litigation was probably the cause of his dismay. No royalist could welcome such a prospect, at a time when so much property had recently been wrested from their hands, and when so many royalists had excluded themselves (by not taking the Engagement) from making any use of republican courts. The register would have created a propertied class, 'acting under new laws, and holding their interest and proprieties under them', with an interest in the Commonwealth's survival.[73]

---

[67] The Commission's final recommendations survive in Walter Scott (ed.), *A collection of scarce and valuable tracts* ('Somers' tracts'), 1811, vol. VI, pp. 177–245.

[68] British Library, Add. 35,863, 7.   [69] *Ibid.*, 83.   [70] *Ibid.*, 83v.

[71] *Ibid.*, 51v., 71v.–72v.

[72] *Ibid.*, 72v.

[73] Hale's contributions are found at Add. 35,863, 51v., 71v–2v. He later missed three meetings in a row (24/5, 26/5, 2/6) that were largely concerned with the register for land. For a full statement of his private views, see the anonymously published tract, a little misleadingly entitled *A treatise showing how useful the enrolling and registering of all*

Perhaps the best clue to his motives was another conservative stand. It was indefensibly absurd, as every reformer agreed, that so much petty business should pass through London courts. A suit for forty shillings was a matter for a national jurisdiction, at enormous inconvenience for everyone concerned. There were radical dreams, on the Leveller fringe, of total decentralisation, but even sober spirits had plans for county courts.[74] After the restoration, they included Matthew Hale, the author of a draft reforming bill. He would have raised the threshold (to £5), and provided for qualified judges to sit in county courts.[75] No reader of the minutes could guess he held such views, for he gave no indication, in resisting proposals for change, that local justice had the slightest merit. He emphasised instead, through a welter of detailed objections, his fear of malign fragmentation in the business of the law.[76]

A last emblematic example from this phase of Hale's career was his attitude towards the court of probate. The existing 'prerogative court', which handled significant wills, was an obviously anomalous tribunal. It was really an Archbishop's court, with civilian procedures, as probate had been dealt with by English canon law. It thus incurred suspicion on two related grounds, and puritans and legalists were united in scorning its work. The Commission took some evidence from a learned civilian named Walker. They first resolved, however, that the court was an encumbrance to the nation: 'the manner of probate of wills and granting letters of administration and of appeals thereupon as the same are now in use are an inconvenience in the law; and a charge to the people, and fit to be taken away.'[77]

The question was pre-judged, but Walker had a grilling to endure. For Matthew Hale, the leader of his critics, the court gave two grounds for complaint: that the validity of wills was really a question of fact, and therefore the proper concern of a common law jury; and that granting of costs was 'coercion', and went beyond the power of a church court: 'coercion was only excommunication ... Your power hath the effect to make a church authority, but when it comes to require payment the power ceases.'[78] Behind these cryptic minutes there lurked a vital point. Coercive power, as the old church courts enjoyed it, was based on a spiritual

---

conveyances of land may be, 1694 (written, to judge by a reference to the Great Fire, in 1666). The authenticity of this pamphlet has been doubted, but its manner is highly characteristic. As Roger North explained, Hale 'wrote a treatise, not so much against the thing (for he wishes it could be), as against the manner of doing it, of which he is not satisfied ...' (North, *Life of Guilford*, 110) Hale's papers contain two draft Acts for county registers, one of them in his hand (Lambeth 3475, 172–81; 225–8).

74 Veall, *Law reform*, 168–78.   75 Lambeth 3475, 210, 288–8v., 229v.
76 Add. 35,863, 50–51v.
77 Add. 35,863, 37v; the whole episode occupies fos. 37v–43.   78 Add. 35,863, 42.

sanction. The granting of costs was a power over property rights, which ought to be derived from common law. Dr Walker quite rightly protested that 'I can have costs without common law' and that 'this trial of jury hath been overruled by decree in chancery without a jury uncontrollably', but his audience was too prejudiced to care.[79]

This squabble over probate, which Hale so decisively won, was a typical common law triumph.[80] As the guarantors of property, the common lawyers strengthened their position, extending the range of their system into areas undreamed of before. The rights of the propertied English were defined by their unwritten law, a law that defended the clergyman's tithes and the freedom of peers from arrest. To protect such legal details, in Hale's retrospective view, was to save the 'constitution' of the realm. It is hard to disagree. The language of property rights, in a context such as Hale's, was profoundly constitutive of political debate. The law defined the liberties that 'the Keepers' aspired to protect, and thus defined the purpose of the nascent republican state. It also gave a blueprint, as Cromwell's time would show, for a steady drift towards a restoration.

[79] Add. 35,863, 43.
[80] The practical upshot was less satisfactory. Responsibility for probate was consigned to the Hale commissioners themselves, but no new legal framework was provided (for the details, see Worden, *Rump*, 318–20). There is no evidence that Hale himself played any part in running the new court, though some of his fellow commissioners continued to do so till the king's return.

5

Protectorate

Hale was consistently a royalist, in the sense that he was anxious to be governed by a king, but he made do, for several years, with serving a Lord Protector. In early 1654, when Hale was first appointed to the bench, Oliver Cromwell must have seemed the saviour of the law. The Rump (which was dissolved the previous April) had been relatively acceptable to lawyers: it was at least the ghost of the legitimate parliament of England; it had done its best, by the fiction of the Keepers, to preserve the essence of the constitution; and was unenthusiastic, in the absence of military pressure, about the projected reform of the courts.[1] Its successor, from June to December, was a body that the army had created. This was a 'supreme power',[2] a nominated puritan assembly, self-styled a parliament. The body was internally divided, especially on law reform and tithes, but the greater part was radical in outlook. Their initial reforming proposals were borrowed from the Hale Commission's work, but there was also some support, at least in later months, for replacing existing arrangements with a simplified biblical code.[3] Conservatives could reasonably believe that 'propriety was struck at', and the lawyers were exultant when the parliament collapsed.[4] At this propitious moment, the army, led by Cromwell, were faced with the task of governing the country. They would have been fools not to cement their temporary alliance with the law.

An eighteenth-century version of events, not in itself at all incredible, had Cromwell personally seek Hale out. His message, at least as reported, was uncharacteristically clear:

since he had got the possession of the government, he was resolved to keep it, and would not be argued out of it; that however it was his desire to rule according to the laws of the land, for which purpose he had pitched on him as a proper person

---

[1] For a balanced discussion of the Rump's attitudes, see A. B. Worden, *The rump parliament*, Cambridge 1974, esp. pp. 115–8.

[2] Austin Woolrych, *Commonwealth to protectorate*, Oxford 1982, p. 144.

[3] *Ibid.*, 264–73.

[4] *Ibid.*, 270; Veall, *Law reform*, 88.

to be engaged in the administration of justice, yet if they would not permit him to govern by red gowns, he was resolved to govern by red coats.[5]

Wherever this story is drawn from, it surely embodies a truth. A new dictator had to choose between legal and non-legal values, between governing as a despot and governing as a king. The latter course, which was Cromwell's, involved a kind of contract with the lawyers.[6] His power was both limited and buttressed by the legitimation derived from common law.

The Instrument of Government, by which he was to rule, was drawn up by his colleagues in the army. Its status was uncertain, but its content was a partial Restoration. It laid down, to begin with, 'that the supreme legislative authority of the commonwealth ... shall be and reside in a single person, the style of which person shall be "the Lord Protector"'. This flatly contradicted the Act abolishing the 'Kingly Office', which had spoken of the abuses of a single person's rule. The Protector's role was meant to be familiar; he had replaced the 'Keepers', who had replaced the king, and writs and other documents were issued in his name.[7] Chief Justice Rolle believed, and said so from the bench, that 'by the Protector's death (as in former times by death of the king) the judges' commissions determine'.[8] Thus Cromwell had supplanted the monarchy's republican supplanters; to 'govern by red gowns' he needed to act as inheritor (and therefore as preserver) of existing royal power.

In historical perspective, his claims were nothing new. *De facto*, he was king, though he used another title; like many an English monarch, he had usurped the Crown. There was a better claimant, but the same could be said of many undoubted kings: of William I; of William's three successors; of Edward III (who usurped upon his father); of all the Lancastrians; of Richard III, and perhaps even Henry VII. The law of usurpation, developed in order to cope with the Wars of the Roses, was surprisingly clearcut. As Brooke's *Abridgement* noted, 'where the usurping king grants a pardon or patent of being a denizen, and things of that kind, which are judicial, and does not go about to diminish the Crown, this will bind the true king when he returns, as happened between Henry VI and

---

[5] Matthew Hale, *Historia placitorum coronae*, ed. Sollom Emlyn, 1736, vol. I, p. ii.

[6] For an expression of this view from a radical perspective, see *The memoirs of Edmund Ludlow*, ed. C. H. Firth, 2 vols., Oxford 1894, vol. I, p. 365.

[7] For proofs of this, see Hardres 1–165 *passim*. Hardres' Exchequer reports reached their final form after the Restoration, so there may of course have been some retrospective tinkering. But there seems no doubt, for example, that a defendant pleaded 'that the Protector and all his predecessors, Kings and Queens of England, had time of mind had a court of record in such a place ...' (Hardres 6).

[8] 'Per mort del Protector (comme in former times per mort del roy) le commissions des judges determine'. Folger Shakespeare Library, V.b.6, fo. 55v.

Edward IV.'⁹ The servants of such kings, who followed them to battle, were protected by a very well-known law. This was the much-discussed '*de facto* Act', a statute of Henry VII, which provided 'that no person going with the King to the wars should be attaint of treason'.¹⁰ It was invoked, in the early 1640s, as a powerful argument for royalism, a cast-iron legal excuse, if one were needed, for enlisting and for fighting under Charles.¹¹

A purely legitimist theory, such as the Jacobites were to uphold, was alien to this intellectual world. The concept of allegiance, as understood by Coke, was admirably suited to a usurper's needs. This was not at all surprising, in a servant of Elizabeth and James, for both could be regarded as usurpers by their more disaffected papist subjects. The basis of his theory, that 'protectio trahit subjectionem, et subjectio protectionem',¹² generated a 'local allegiance', which was owed to whoever kept order in a given place and time, and also a 'natural allegiance', which was local allegiance at birth.¹³ A local allegiance was binding for the purposes of normal social life; it was treason to kill a usurper, except on explicit instructions from whoever was legitimately king.¹⁴

If usurpers respected the limits of their office, their acts had legal force. There was no shame, it followed, in serving a usurper, and no expectation, at least from the legal profession, of a self-sacrificing loyalty. As a die-hard republican put it, 'the long robe will sit and do justice, though a tyrant¹⁵ be on the throne. The judges sat under Richard III, while he suffered them to judge by law'.¹⁶ He referred, it should be noted, to the period of Oliver's rule. Hale's manuscripts on the prerogative, the work of the mid-1640s, also allowed great scope to the usurper. Substantively, his views were much like Coke's, but they were rationalised in different ways. He treated allegiance, in line with his general presumptions, as the fruit of contractual consent. Allegiance could not be transferred, unless both prince and subject had consented, so the king could not give it away; King John was

---

⁹ 'ou le roy usurper grant pardon ou patent destre denizen, et huiusmodi, que sont judicials, et ne va in diminishing del Crowne, ceo liera le droit roy quant il fait regresse, ut inter roy Henry VI et roy Edward IV'. Brooke, *La graunde abridgement*, 1573, title prerogative, no. 34.

¹⁰ G. R. Elton, *The Tudor constitution: documents and commentary*, 2nd edn, Cambridge 1982, pp. 4–5. The Act refers to a king 'for the time being', apparently 'a common Tudor phrase which means no more than "at the time in question"'(Elton, *Constitution*, 2). In Stuart times, following Bacon (*Works*, VI, 159), it was thought to make an implicit *de jure*/*de facto* distinction.

¹¹ Husbands, *Exact collection*, 724–5; Francis Quarles, *The loyal convert*, Oxford 1643, p. 7.

¹² 'Protection results in subjection, and subjection in protection'.

¹³ Coke, *Seventh reports*, 5b.

¹⁴ Hale, *Historia placitorum coronae*, ed. Sollom Emlyn vol. I, p. 103; Coke, *Third institutes*, p. 7.

¹⁵ In the then current sense of 'usurper'.   ¹⁶ Burton, *Diary*, III, p. 129.

not entitled to give England to the pope.[17] He could not even abdicate without the realm's consent. Hale rather daringly discussed the two medieval cases, and distinguished between them on characteristic grounds. Edward II had resigned the throne when there was no parliament sitting, in contrast to Richard II, who abdicated at a parliament.[18] The latter act was probably quite valid, the former was certainly not. The king was condemned to be king, and the subject condemned to be subject, unless the situation was altered by consent.

A subject usurping the Crown (such as Oliver Cromwell or Henry IV) could do nothing to change his allegiance to the *de jure* king. He was bound, like other subjects, by a contractual duty to the previous regime. He was nonetheless allowed by law to make a subsidiary contract with the people, creating rights good against all but the genuine prince. His position was thus analogous to that of a man who had forcibly seized another's property: he had a possessory right to the Crown.

An usurper is a king de facto, and regularly hath the consent of the generality of his subjects, either by a tacit submission, or which was ever most usual by an express acknowledgment or perfection in parliament. Therefore in relation between him and the people he is king; for so they have submitted. But in relation to him that hath the true title, he is an intruder.[19]

Coke had explained the concept of allegiance by positing a principle which 'reason' might suggest: that protection is rewarded by subjection. It was characteristic of Hale that he saw every form of allegiance as based on the people's consent. In another place, he spelt out the presumption this involved:

although the rightful heir, or inheritor of the crown, hath an unresumable right, yet the usurper hath no other right but immediately from the people; that so long as, de facto, he continues king, he hath the right of a king, as against this or that particular man or society, but not against the whole people: that so long as he continues in possession, though by power, so long, by judgement of law, he continues king; because in judgement of law, he hath so long an influence from the major, at least most powerful, part of the people.[20]

The people could never disown the rightful heir, but they could formalise the situation. The appropriate place to do so was of course a parliament.

In January 1654, when Hale was appointed a judge, a parliament was promised in September. The appointment was one of the signals of Protectoral commitment to the law, and of a change in attitudes towards the royalists. It was discussed in council on 19 January, along with abolition of the Engagement (an important result of refusal to engage was exclusion

---

[17] Lincoln's Inn, Hargrave 5, 37.   [18] *Ibid.*, 72.   [19] *Ibid.*, 39.
[20] Lincoln's Inn, Hargrave 9, 86.

from the benefit of access to the courts).[21] No doubt the council was aware that the judge replaced by Hale was famous for vindictiveness towards the cavaliers.[22] There is therefore plenty of reason to believe (as Burnet rather anxiously assures us) that Hale was encouraged to take up the post by impeccably royalist friends.[23]

Hale symbolised, in other words, a newly conciliatory line, but he may have been intended for quite another use. At about this time, in the early months of 1654, the government was taking constitutional advice, possibly with a view to making Oliver a titular king. John Selden and Oliver St John were certainly consulted,[24] while Hale was excused the spring circuit on the grounds of 'some especial occasions for the public wherein he is to be employed'.[25] In April Sir Edward Nicholas, the exiled royalist secretary of state, reported an intriguing rumour:

Cromwell's council sent to the judges to consider and deliver their opinions whether the kingdoms, by the fundamental laws of the kingdom, could be governed by the power and authority that was incident to a Protector by the laws of the land. And Mr Hale and the most of the rest of the judges answered that the three kingdoms could not by the fundamental laws or by the constitution of the government of the three kingdoms be governed by a less power and authority than that due to the title or person of a king or emperor. It is easy to guess the meaning of that question, and what the solution of it signifies.[26]

This entirely believable story can be taken in two ways. To Nicholas, in exile, the question clearly seemed a childish ruse, an obvious preliminary to seizure of the crown. But an equally plausible reading would adopt just the opposite line: that it was a request, on Cromwell's part, to have his cake and eat it, to be a mere 'Protector' while sticking to the law. Commitment to the law, unluckily for Oliver's peace of mind, suggested usurpation of the throne.

That autumn, Hale made his views publicly known. He voiced them in the most appropriate setting, the Protectorate's long-promised parliament, the place, so Selden taught, where the nation had always arrived at its settlements with kings. This parliament, the Instrument's creation, was a rather irregular body (the seats had been distributed in radically new ways), but its membership was in no doubt that it deserved a parliamentary status. The first debate, which was lengthy and very confused, was about the Instrument's validity: 'whether the government by a single person and a parliament, should be approved of'. According to the diarist Guibon

[21] Public Record Office, S.P. 25/75, pp. 59, 60.
[22] S. R. Gardiner, *History of the commonwealth and protectorate*, 3 vols, 1894–1901, vol. III, p. 15.
[23] Burnet, *Life*, 22.   [24] Worden, *The rump parliament*, Cambridge 1974, p. 339.
[25] PRO, S.P. 25/75, p. 121.
[26] *The Nicholas papers*, vol. II, ed. G. F. Warner, Camden Society 1892. p. 64.

Goddard, 'much debate was about the word approving in the question, as if it were not parliamentary, nor for the honour of the House, to approve of any thing which takes not its foundation and rise from themselves.'[27] After four days of inconclusive wrangling, a degree of consensus emerged:

> they began to break the question, and to distinguish the word 'government' into the legislative power and the executive power. The first was generally thought . . . to be the right of parliament alone . . . but as to the executive part of it, that was conceived communicable, and indeed not exercisable by the parliament.[28]

It was now that Hale made a famous intervention, one that was still remembered when the issues recurred in 1659:

> those who were for the parliament alone, would have the parliament at least to have the precedency, that is, that the government should be in the parliament and a single person, limited and restrained as the parliament should think fit. Which was proposed, in effect, by Mr Justice Hale.[29]

In supporting the radical view, the view of republican members, Hale maximised his argument's appeal. But read in the light of his usurpation theory, it was actually compatible with royalist ideas. A title that parliament gave, by consenting to Oliver's rule, could not erase the duty of the people to their king. They were nonetheless entitled to make a subsidiary contract with the *de facto* holder of the crown.

Hale's proposal was never accepted, for all its notable political merits, because Cromwell lost his patience with the House. He came to parliament next day (12 September) and made a lengthy speech, enumerating his claims to recognition, including, as it happened, the judges' legal needs. The bench declared, so their employer claimed, 'that they could not administer justice to the satisfaction of their consciences, until they had received commissions from me'.[30] The upshot of this speech, imposed next day, was a rigid loyalty oath. The Recognition, as it was known, was sterner than the Engagement, because it bound members not to 'propose, or give my consent', to any alternative government. No more is heard of Hale, who presumably refused it, and the fundamental questions continued unresolved.

In the absence of authoritative guidance, the legalistic impulse, so strong in contemporary minds, suggested a simple conclusion: that Cromwell was just an intruder, who usurped the royal power. Charles R. had been replaced by Oliver P. The title of 'Protector' was an ingenious choice, suggesting an authority of a quasi-monarchical type. The earlier Protec-

---

[27] Burton, *Diary*, I, xxv.   [28] *Ibid.*, xxvi.
[29] *Ibid.*, xxxii. For 1659, Burton, *Diary*, III, 142–3.
[30] W. C. Abbott (ed.), *The writings and speeches of Oliver Cromwell*, Harvard 1945, vol. III, p. 457.

tors, in times of royal infancy and madness, had been temporary replacements for the king.[31] They were easily confused with another historical figure, the so-called 'custos regni', who was a kind of regent when the king was overseas.[32] The office was very close, in other words, to kingship, on the one hand, and the Keepers of the liberties (*custodes libertatum*) on the other.

In the spring of 1660, when pondering the status of the interregnum courts, Hale made some jotted notes about the *custos*, but otherwise we can only guess at his own view of the legal situation.[33] With a number of his colleagues, we are on stronger ground, because of their involvement in trying royalists. In April 1655, in the backwash of a cavalier revolt, an all-important precedent was set. In the truly republican period, from 1649–53, the bench was kept away from treason trials. They were mounted in High Courts of Justice, tribunals that sat without juries, erected by parliament's power. In 1655, at the time of Penruddock's rebellion, there was no parliament at hand, nor could help from such a quarter be expected. The Council was thrown back, for want of any other legal tool, on extra-parliamentary legislation. From December 1653 to September the following year, as the Instrument of Government provided, the Council had a temporary legislative power. Their existing Treason Ordinance, which stood until a parliament revoked it, was the product of this interim arrangement. Unfortunately, it declared that 'the offences herein mentioned and no other, shall be adjudged high treason within the Common-Wealth'.[34] If this measure was legally valid, then any prosecution must employ it; if it was not, then neither was the Instrument itself.

The Council's great mistake, in trying these latest royalist insurgents, was to involve the judges on assize in the south-west. The justices in question had encountered the rebels in person, and were briefly thrown in prison at the outbreak of revolt. They nonetheless objected to the government's indictment, and brought the original charges into line with common law. Penruddock's men were tried for committing a common law treason, defined by the great statute of 25 Edward III (1352).[35] This Act referred to treason as a crime against the king, but the word was deemed to cover a Protector. After gutting the indictment, implicitly rejecting the Instrument itself, the judges then stood back from the proceedings. They could not be

---

[31] J. S. Roskell, 'The office and dignity of Protector of England, with special reference to its origins', *English Historical Review* 68 (1953), 193–233.

[32] Hale knew of this distinction. He also stressed (erroneously) that a Protector was 'not regni but regis'. Hale, *Prerogatives*, 93.

[33] Lambeth 3476, 37–8.   [34] Firth and Rait, *Acts and ordinances*, II, 831.

[35] Thomas Birch (ed.), *A collection of the state papers of John Thurloe*, 1742, vol. III, p. 398 (hereafter cited as Thurloe, *State papers*).

impartial, they quite properly alleged, because of their rough treatment by the rebels.[36]

This detail of course was as nothing, compared to the importance of their presence in the court, but the propaganda triumph had many inconvenient implications. Though the balance of short-term advantage was on the protectoral side, the judges had exacted a very significant price. The precedent was followed in a later group of trials, which were based on the Henrician Treason Act. The juries were instructed, in interpreting the charge, to remember that 'Chief Magistrates' (including regnant queens) were described in the enactment by the shorthand term of 'King'.[37] In the north, where a parallel rising had even less success, a different legal tactic was adopted. The judges on assize, Baron Thorpe and Justice Newdigate, were told to use the treason ordinance. On their refusal, they were sacked (though both of them were later re-appointed). A manuscript report suggests the reason for their stand:

Something which might induce them not to proceed upon that ordinance according to their commission might be, that they only were confined to that ordinance, whereas Rolle Chief Justice who tried those who rose in the west and other judges of assize had their liberty and so tried offenders according to the Statute of 25 Edward III wherein (King) they expounded to be meant (supreme) Magistrate.[38]

The judges' terms were simple, if this was any guide. They were happy to defend the Lord Protector, so long as he confined himself to acting as a king. In defending his 'royal' position, as no doubt they were aware, they were hastening the moment when he took the royal crown.[39]

According to Chief Justice Glyn, in a treason case of January the next year, 'let the Supreme Magistrate come in by what title he will, yet he is meant within the statute'.[40] The second protectorate parliament disliked the sweeping nature of this dictum 'which all the lawyers present agreed to

---

[36] *Ibid.*, 359, 371, 378.

[37] PRO, K.B. 33, 1/1, iv, vi. This source reveals that at least one other judge took the same constitutional line. Hugh Windham tried some rebels by the force of '6 Henry VIII' (obviously a slip for 26 Henry VIII), and instructed the jury to understand 'Chief magistrate' by 'King'. This Henrician statute was normally said to have been repealed by 1 Philip and Mary, but it had the advantage of making words treasonable. Coke seems to have thought the measure had some continuing force (*Third institute*, 19).

[38] Gray's Inn, MS 33, 209.

[39] It was claimed, in Richard Cromwell's parliament, that 'the Protector is the King of England to all intents and purposes whatsoever. There is express authority in this point, in Penruddock's case, who was adjudged a traitor within the Statute of 25 Edward III, for attempting the life of the protector, because he had indeed the kingship as if it had been against a queen regnant'. Burton, *Diary*, III, 531–2. The speaker, Edward Fowell, has been quoted once before, defending the position of the Lords. He may have been eccentric, and was certainly tactlessly rash, but his strictly legal argument was hard to contradict.

[40] Gray's Inn 33, 209.

be no law. But for Turner reader of Gray's Inn, if the Protector had come in per name of the King contra, this last was delivered in private.'[41] The opinion 'delivered in private' was probably generally held, though evidence is very hard to come by. One interregnum lawyer, whose position was analogous to Hale's, left a record of his feelings on the question. Thomas Waller was a serjeant, 'called' by Richard, who kept his professional title when the exiled king returned. He continued to practise, with official acquiescence, in the court that the serjeants monopolised, the court of Common Pleas. A term later, after wider consultation, the interregnum serjeants (including Matthew Hale) were put through the formality of a repeated call. Waller seems to have resented this occasion, and privately questioned the need:

I agree that Oliver Cromwell was a wrongful usurper of sovereign authority, but still, inasmuch as he was a usurper and writs issued in his name throughout the whole kingdom, it might be questioned whether the serjeants called by him and his son Richard (who had the same authority) were not legally called as serjeants. In the first place it seems to be clearly agreed that if the Protectors had taken upon them the name and style of the King, that then the serjeants would have been properly called by their writs.[42]

These glimpses of common law thought show the pressures that legality imposed. If Cromwell's position was legal, if the source of his authority was English common law, then he was already a king. So far as the courts were concerned, he had no other claims. The Instrument of Government, implicitly rejected in the Penruddock case, was a document without a formal status. Hale's salary was paid by a republic, but this fact had little bearing on his conduct as a judge.

There was only one occasion, in all of Cromwell's time, when the lawyers were really confronted with his 'extra-legal' claims. In Cony's case, in 1655, the Instrument of Government was attacked in the name of the law. The case was for the Upper Bench, so Hale was not concerned, but it justifies digression from the facts of his legal career.[43] George Cony was a merchant, who refused to pay a custom on his goods. He assaulted some government agents, was fined, and then imprisoned for non-payment. The

---

[41] *Ibid.*

[42] 'Jeo agree que Oliver Cromwell fuit un tortious usurper de soveraigne authoritie, mes uncore, intant que fuit usurper et que breifes issue in son nosme per my et per tout le realme, poit estre question si les serjeants appel per luy et son fits Richard (que avoit semble authoritie) ne fueront loyalement call serjeants. Primo voit estre clerement agree que si les protectors avoient prise sur eux le nosme et stile del roy, que donque les serjeants avoient estre bien call per lour breifes'. Printed in J. H. Baker, *The order of serjeants at law*, Selden Society, Supplementary series, no. 5, 1984, p. 406.

[43] For what follows see Cobbett, *State trials*, V, 935–8; British Library, Lansdowne 1109, fos. 38v.-40.

basis of the fine, imposed by the commissioners of customs, was the power of an ordinance in Council. Its ultimate foundation, clause 27 of the Instrument, provided for a 'constant yearly revenue', to be raised 'by the customs, and such other ways and means as shall be agreed upon by the Lord Protector and the Council'.[44]

Chief Justice Rolle, who was fresh from the trial of Penruddock, was faced with a difficult choice. He is said to have remarked, in the spirit of the Ship Money decision, that 'something must be allowed to cases of necessity'.[45] He was not unaware, after all, that the government was taxing without popular consent. It was quite another thing to approve this situation in the country's highest court: to recognise authority not drawn from common law. By the end of Easter term, he seemed to have made up his mind, 'inclin[ing] to bail him upon the grand exception that he should be fined and imprisoned upon an ordinance never published, nor of which he never [sic] had notice'.[46] This technical objection (which would have led to chaos) was much more devastating than it seemed; a proper 'general law' (the government's description of these rules)[47] was always presumed to be known. In the course of the vacation he resigned, apparently unasked, and serjeant Glyn replaced him. Glyn had argued for the state (though 'argue' is a flattering description) that 'I shall not dispute the authority of the Protector by which this court and all others sit'.[48]

The government's first reaction to the case had been to imprison the lawyers that Cony employed. When Cony proved quite competent to represent himself, it did not intervene to stop proceedings. Next term, when the former Chief Justice had been replaced by the more pliable Glyn, it nonetheless decided to retreat. The merchant was released, and induced to abandon his action, and a moment of decision was avoided.[49] This was a desirable outcome, for Cromwell as well as the courts, because it preserved his connection with common law values. To discredit the judges, or else to provoke resignations, was to threaten the legitimacy that lawyers could provide.

After 1656, when his second parliament co-operated, the chance of such

---

[44] Kenyon, *Stuart constitution*, 311.

[45] Ludlow, *Memoirs*, 413. For an apposite discussion of Ship Money itself, see Burgess, *Ancient constitution*, 202–10, 215–20.

[46] Lansdowne 1109, 40.   [47] *Ibid.*, 40.   [48] *Ibid.*, 39.

[49] Cony's political and religious outlook was very close to Cromwell's, so close that some observers assumed the case was a collusive suit (*Swedish diplomats at Cromwell's court 1655–1656: the missions of Peter Julius Coyet and Christer Bonde*, tr. and ed. Michael Roberts, Camden Society, 4th series, XXXVI (1988), p. 79). Cony denied, quite possibly sincerely, any wish to undermine protectoral rule (Samuel Selwood, *A narrative of the proceedings of the committee for the preservation of the customs in the case of Mr George Cony, Merchant*, 1655, p. 5). It therefore seems quite likely that he was content to be released in return for abandoning his action.

embarrassments diminished. A new High Court of Justice took over treason trials, and the ordinances were ratified by parliamentary power.[50] When the government imprisoned an opponent, it did so in faraway Jersey, outside the jurisdiction of the court of Upper Bench.[51] The profession operated, thanks to Cromwell's legal tact, in a bubble of the ancient constitution. There were many grounds to hope, in the later 1650s, that the bubble would expand, and the legal view of politics would triumph.[52] The result would have been 'Hanoverian', a *de facto* hereditary monarch, respectful of the law, untainted by the popery of the more legitimate line.

The collaboration of judges, which Hale's role symbolised, was a powerful force for reaction. It pointed back to monarchy, but not perhaps to kings whose name was Stuart. On circuit in the Midlands, in 1656, Hale told the grand jury of Warwickshire to note that treasons fell within their competence: 'I shall recite the commission (treasons) and I need make no comment upon these for it recites all particularly. These offences refer principally to the Chief Magistrate but in the concernment of them much of the peace and profit of the nation is wrapped up.'[53] It seems likely the commission, whose terms do not survive, was just a summary of common law. Hale probably told himself that even usurpers deserved the law's protection against third parties like the Levellers; there was certainly no logical implication that he approved the trial of royalists. In practice, however, the Warwickshire grand jury could be excused for missing this casuistic point; the local commander, Major-General Whalley, was left entirely confident about his loyalty.[54] He had reported, during Hale's spring circuit, that 'as he is unquestionably an able, so upon good grounds I judge him a godly man ... I never knew any at his own cost more willing to serve the present government than he.'[55] Hale's cultural affinity with Whalley, the 'godliness' the General detected, is an important topic which will be discussed elsewhere; it is clear, at all events, that Hale's dedication to law looked very much like keen support for Cromwell.

At some time in the following year, his attitudes seem to have changed. According to Gilbert Burnet, whose account must be treated with care, he began to refuse to judge felons:

---

[50] Ivan Roots, 'Cromwell's Ordinances: the early legislation of the Protectorate' in G. E. Aylmer (ed.), *The interregnum: the quest for a settlement 1646–60*, 1972, pp. 161–4.

[51] Hale made notes about the liberties of Jersey, preserved in Gloucester Record Office D1086/F72. Most papers in this bundle were composed in 1658–60.

[52] Kenyon, *Constitution*, 304.

[53] Bodleian library, Rawlinson C 182, fo. 103 (a copy of a document called 'the substance of the charge of Matthew Hale ... at Warwick on Wednesday 23 July 1656').

[54] Thurloe *State papers*, V 296.

[55] *Ibid.*, IV, 686; for Whalley's praise of Hale see also *ibid.*, IV, 663.

Since he thought the sword of justice belonging only by right to the lawful prince, it seemed not warrantable to proceed to a capital punishment by an authority derived from usurpers ... at first he was of opinion, that it was as necessary, even in times of usurpation, to execute justice in [ordinary felonies], as in matters of property ...

... but having considered further of it, he came to think that it was at least better not to do it; and so, after the second or third circuit, he refused to sit any more on the crown-side, and told plainly the reason; for, in matters of blood, he was to choose always the safer side.[56]

Hale sat 'on the crown-side' (in criminal trials) at least as late as 1656, so the details of this story can be doubted.[57] The reasoning reported, though commonplace enough,[58] sits oddly with his thought on usurpation. It would have been in character, however, to develop some such scruple about his professional work. He was always extremely reluctant to punish thieves with death, so the essence of the story is easy to believe.[59] It would also explain a strange feature of his subsequent career: his unexplained confinement, for the last four of his journeys on assize, to the generally unpopular Home Circuit.[60]

By September 1658, when the Protector died, his conscientious qualms had got much worse. He rejected Richard's patent in surprisingly blunt terms: 'I do hereby declare that I never did neither do agree to accept of the same letters patents or employment. But do utterly disagree thereunto.'[61] For the following year, he took to private practice, describing himself as 'serjeant', but staying out of court. His retirement was an isolated portent, but he was eventually followed by all the republican bench. In April 1659, a coup disposed of Richard; in May, when the Rump returned, two justices (Atkyns and Archer) refused to take a re-imposed Engagement.[62] One judge remained in Upper Bench, but even this survivor was far from a Vicar of Bray; it was the Justice Newdigate who refused to try the Northern cavaliers. In late October of that year, there was another coup, and Newdigate suspended all proceedings, 'there being nobody to grant

---

[56] Burnet, *Life*, 23–4.   [57] Thurloe, *State papers*, IV, 686.

[58] See for example Hammond, *To the Rt. Hon the Lord Fairfax and his council of war, the humble address of Henry Hammond*, 1649, pp. 9–10, a line of argument discussed in Tuck, *Rights theories*, esp. 107–8.

[59] Lambeth 3506, 115–16v; Lincoln's Inn, Hargrave 11, 'De furto eiusque poena', n.p.; Maija Jansson, 'Matthew Hale on judges and judging', *Journal of Legal History* 9 (1988), 209, 211. He would not have objected, it seems, to imposing death for murder (*Historia*, I, 12–14), the penalty for murder being part of natural law.

[60] PRO, Assises 35/99/4 records some executions, presumably the other judge's work; for the unpopularity of the Home Circuit, J. S. Cockburn, *A History of the English Assizes 1558–1714*, Cambridge 1972, p. 51.

[61] Lambeth Palace, Carte Misc. 47/11.

[62] *The Clarke Papers*, vol. IV, ed. C. H. Firth, Camden Society 1901, p. 284.

new commissions (at least such as he would own)'.[63] The lawyers thus dictated, up to the very end of the Republic, the terms on which they worked the legal system.

Throughout this turbulent last phase Hale chose to be significantly passive. In Richard Cromwell's parliament he sat for the University of Oxford, but made no contribution worth attention. The constitutional debates resembled those of 1654, but he seems to have kept his own counsel, although 'Judge Hale's expedient' was cited with respect.[64] When offered re-election, this time to the Convention that in fact restored the king, he claimed to be merely resigned about the prospect: 'inasmuch as there seem to be no engagements to be prefixed to intangle the conscience, or to prevent the liberty of those that are chosen to act according to it, I shall not refuse, if freely chosen, to serve in it.'[65] In the event, in the absence of 'entanglements' to conscience, he became a most enthusiastic member, who sat on no fewer than eighty-seven committees, and was a leading figure in debate.[66]

He represented Gloucestershire, this time as a knight of the shire, with the backing of the royalist Earl of Berkeley.[67] The fact that his county and Oxford both wanted to attract his services was a mark of the prestige he had attained. The Clarendon state papers, an index of the exiled court's concerns, reveal that his behaviour was followed with some care.[68] On 1 May, he visited George Morley (a Calvinist high churchman, and the leading royal agent then in London) to ask about the morals and religion of his king. He stressed his loyal feelings, and his wish to be of use, but was anxious, so Morley reported, that Charles find a Protestant wife.[69] The questions suggested forebodings, although his protestations proved sincere; in parliament at any rate, he defended the king's constitutional right to choose himself a bride.[70] The king arrived in Dover on 29 May, but as early as 13 May Hale 'feared the detestation of the latter extreme under which we last smarted ... will carry us over to the former extreme'.[71]

These apprehensive words, expressing fears that must have been quite common, are taken from a private memorandum. This fascinating piece, a set of 'Considerations concerning the present and late occurrences, for my own use and observation', is enormously revealing of his outlook.[72] Hale

[63] Gray's Inn MS 34, p. 406.   [64] Burton, *Diary*, III, 142.

[65] Williams, *Memoirs*, 46.

[66] *Commons Journal*; B. D. Henning (ed.), *The history of parliament: the House of Commons 1660–90*, 1983, vol. II, pp. 461–2.

[67] On the previous Earl of Berkeley's electoral influence (in 1640), see W. B. Willcox, *Gloucestershire: a study in local government 1590–1640*, Yale 1940, p. 34.

[68] *Clarendon State Papers*, IV, 160, 648, 656.   [69] *Ibid.*, V, 3.

[70] *Cobbett's parliamentary history of England*, vol. IV, 1808, p. 119.

[71] Williams, *Memoirs*, 63.   [72] Printed in full, *ibid.*, 53–78.

did not doubt the royal cause was just, but he liked the way of life of its opponents:

There was in many of the suppressed party much hypocrisy and dissimulation, much violence and oppression; but there was in them – sobriety in their conversation, pretence and profession of strictness of life, prayers in their families, observation of the sabbath. These were commendable in their use, though it may be they were in order to honour and to disguise bad ends and actions.[73]

He devoted some attention, as might have been expected, to 'those persons that are of the declining party, or that were at all, in any sort, mingled with them'.[74] Such people were to avoid 'a base despondency of mind, that a man scarce dares own that which was good and well done, even in bad times'.[75]

At the time that Hale was writing, before the king's return, the 'declining party' proper was a small and unpopular group. There were plenty of future dissenters with orthodox monarchist views, who expected to be members of a purified national church. The problem, as Hale understood, was that all of them were tainted with rebellion:

this was the walk that things had in the late desolations, both in ecclesiastical and civil matters. First the animadversion began by the presbyterian interest, upon the absolute royalist and episcopal man; the independent interest that ran along in that severity, and thought the presbyterian not sufficiently contrary to the royal interest, is as severe upon the presbyterian; the anabaptists and other highflyers, think that went not high enough, but had a secret inclination to monarchy, and though in another line, fly upon the independent . . .
. . . he that acted regularly under the Protector or Commonwealth, falls generally upon the high court of justice men; he that acted under the long parliament with the same severity, inveighs against both the former; and, perchance, invites thereby the spirits of those men that acted purely upon the royal account, to fall as sharply upon all three.[76]

The obvious conclusion, for one who 'acted under the Protector', was that the real extremists should be sheltered. From April to November, when he was elevated to the bench, he acted to defend the losing party.[77] In church affairs, which are discussed elsewhere, he worked to modify the rule of bishops. He was closely involved in the bill for confirming judicial proceedings,[78] and would have spared the regicides who surrendered themselves to the king.[79] He had earlier spoken up, in the most surprising of his interventions, for the regicidal extremist Edmund Ludlow (?1617–1692), who wished to take his seat in parliament.[80]

---

[73] *Ibid.*, 62.   [74] *Ibid.*, 68.   [75] *Ibid.*, 68.   [76] *Ibid.*, 66–7.
[77] *Cobbett's parliamentary history*, IV, 77.
[78] Lambeth 3475, 292–308; Lambeth 3476, 37.
[79] *Cobbett's parliamentary history*, IV, 102.
[80] Edmund Ludlow, *A voyce from the watch-tower: part five: 1660–62*, ed. A. B. Worden, Camden Society, 4th series, XXI (1978), p. 120.

In Burnet's short biography (of 1682), this controversial phase was barely mentioned. In the early 1680s, at the high point of reaction to Exclusion, this was, no doubt, what prudence recommended. The *History of my own time* (?1724), which Burnet himself never printed, made up for this omission with an unsupported claim. He says that Hale would have preferred a conditional restoration:

[he] moved that a committee might be appointed to look into the propositions that had been made and the concessions that had been offered by the late King during the war, particularly at the treaty of Newport, that from thence they might digest such propositions as they should think fit to be sent over to the King.[81]

There were plenty of members, of course, who would have approved this suggestion, though few would have cared to give it much support.

On balance, Burnet's story seems sufficiently specific to be worthy of belief. If it is indeed authentic, then Hale saw 1660 as a moment like 1066 or 1215, a time for the social contract to be altered and renewed. In constitutional theory, the English were bound by the letter of previous pacts; in practice the terms of the contract were regularly adjusted to reflect shifts in relations between parliament and king. For much of the previous year, Hale's would have would have seemed a royalist proposal, if of a somewhat 'presbyterian' type.[82] The times had changed, however, and no ambitious person was likely to risk favour by backing such a move. Cromwell's councillor Arthur Annesley, for instance, called for 'Isle of Wight' conditions in reaction to the army's restoration of the Rump;[83] in early 1660, he was noticeably silent on the subject. Hale was rather less adroit. He was politically aligned with those who accepted the verdict of civil war, with moderate parliamentarians, rather than cavaliers. He had made a most unpromising beginning to his relations with the new regime.

---

[81] Burnet, *History of his own time*, ed. Airy, Oxford 1897, vol. I, p. 160.

[82] Ronald Hutton, *Charles the Second: King of England, Scotland, and Ireland*, Oxford 1991, 129–30.

[83] Arthur Annesley, *England's confusion*, 1659.

6

Restoration: 'the nature of laws'

For Roger North (1653–1734), who wrote in the next century, there was a guiding thread to Hale's career: '[his principles] being demagogical, could not allow much favour to one who rose a monarchist declared'.[1] His religion and his politics were very closely linked: 'if one party was a courtier and well-dressed, and the other a sort of puritan, with a black cap and plain clothes, he insensibly thought the justice of the cause with the latter.'[2] In the Convention parliament, as the previous chapter made clear, Hale was associated with a 'presbyterian' line. It was very important to North, a Jacobite High Churchman, to show that Hale stayed loyal to his party, at worst as a republican in feeling, at best as a self-righteous and legalistic prig. North had inherited the notes of his elder brother Francis (1637–85), an Anglican loyalist advocate who was often in conflict with Hale.[3] From their sectarian standpoint, Hale was a politician committed to the 'faction' that undermined the state. Their case was overstated, with the tinge of paranoia that disfigured Tory thought, but it offers an invaluable perspective. Hale tried to be the servant of the law, but the law that he believed in was highly politically charged.

Hale was an honest man, as even North admitted, and his anti-monarchical 'bias', if that was what it was, took a fairly subtle form. According to John Dryden (1631–1700), King Charles was resigned to reverses at the hands of his principled judge. He believed

that his servants were sure to be cast on any trial which was heard before him: not that he thought the judge was possibly to be bribed: but that his integrity might be too scrupulous: And that the causes of the Crown were always suspicious, when the privileges of subjects were concerned.[4]

This was a shrewd assessment, for Hale indeed gave precedence to individual rights. His most controversial judgements were unwelcome to the Crown, unless they seemed to favour (a slightly different thing) the interests

---

[1] North, *Life of the Lord Keeper Guilford*, 1742, p. 61.   [2] *Ibid.*
[3] British Library, Additional MSS 32, 518, fo. 6v.
[4] Dryden, *Essays of John Dryden*, ed. W. P. Ker, Oxford 1926, vol. II, p. 69.

of Protestant dissent. He might have been expected, as Selden's disciple and friend, to insist upon the letter of a contractual law. In fact he was inventive and pragmatic, especially when liberties seemed threatened by the state. He was willing to find a remedy where he discerned a right, thus avoiding a 'failure of justice' where law did not provide. In some respects, this brought him close to Coke, but there was also another important background, a detailed moral philosophy that he drew from Selden's thought.

His most elaborate statement of his general moral ideas was a work 'On the nature of laws'.[5] Regrettably, Hale's manuscript is lost, but some relevant pages of notes survive, composed on the autumn circuit in 1668.[6] The treatise was clearly influenced by Selden, but its argument was also shaped by a lurking awareness of Hobbes. Selden regarded law as a command, imposed on a reasonable creature, with a penalty attached. To understand a natural rule as law, it was necessary to recognise that the rule was a piece of conscious legislation, and that the legislator had the power to punish disobedience. Selden denied that animals could be said to be governed by law, on the grounds that only an intellectual being could grasp the concept of a punishment.[7] His opinions contrasted, as contemporaries understood, with those of Hugo Grotius, a man whose law of nature dispensed with the need for a God;[8] the law would still be binding, so Grotius had notoriously claimed, 'even if we granted, what cannot without the highest sin be granted, that there is no God, or that human affairs do not concern him.'[9] The effect of Selden's thought, in other words, an effect highly congenial to a thinker as pious as Hale, was to reaffirm that natural law depended on a legislating God.

On a whole range of fundamental points, beginning with his concept of a law, Hale simply agreed with his mentor:

a law I take to be a rule of moral actions, given to a being endued with understanding and will, by him that hath power and authority to give the same and exact obedience thereunto per modum imperii commanding or forbidding such actions under some penalty expressed or implicitly contained in such law.[10]

A law is a species of rule, but not all rules are laws:

almost in all kinds of natural and artificial actions, there are certain prescript rules, which are but directions to attain certain ends proposed to these actions which yet

---

[5] British Library, Hargrave MS 485.

[6] Beinecke, Osborn files, Hale, 'Notes on circuitus autumnalis [of 1668]', last three sides.

[7] Selden, *Opera*, I, 106.

[8] See Richard Cumberland's judgement to this effect, *De legibus Naturae Disquisitio philosophica*, 1672, Prolegomena, sig a2v. Cited Tuck, *Rights theories*, p. 165.

[9] Grotius, *De jure belli ac pacis*, ed. W. Whewell, Cambridge 1853, p. xlvi (Prolegomena, 11). 'Etiamsi daremus, quod sine summo scelere dari nequit, non esse deum, aut non curari ab eo negotia humana.'

[10] British Library, Hargrave 485, fo. 3.

are not properly and strictly laws. The prescription of the physician is not his law; for it is a rule indeed, but not juncta cum imperio.[11]

It followed that 'if atheistical persons could, as they would, exterminate the great God of heaven from having to do in this world, that, which they call reason and the law of reason, would be indeed a rule, but not truly and formally a law.'[12]

To know a rule as law was thus to recognise it as the command of a superior; to know a rule as natural law, one needed to acknowledge a legislating God. There could be no such thing as natural law without a prior natural religion. Selden needed to show that a knowledge of God was almost universally diffused. The medium, for Selden, was the 'Intellectus Agens', an Aristotelian concept that was central to Hale's thought. This much-debated entity (to which we shall return) was pictured as an intellectual light. It 'illuminated' laws by which the moral life was supposed to be governed, the laws that were said in the Bible to be written on the heart.[13] Hale saw it as 'a common principle assisting all intellective operation and deriving unto the whole intellectual nature those common notions, both speculative and moral, that are necessary for their intellective life.'[14]

Hale believed, in agreement with Selden, that the *Intellectus Agens* was the basis of all natural moral knowledge, and that the rule that contracts should be kept was much the most important natural law. The laws of particular nations, which are nothing but the contracts of their members, are ultimately based upon the will of God himself:

this faith I am bound to keep, not only by an obligation between me and the party to whom it is given, for then if I could avoid his coercion I may loosen myself again, but I am obliged hereunto by a more sovereign and uncontrollable law, the law of Almighty God, who hath given this law to me and to all mankind, that fides est servanda ... this is the great foundation of the obligation of all civil contracts made between man and man, and the root of all civil government, fides est servanda, which is the uncontrollable law of the Sovereign Lord of heaven.

And this consideration solves that common mistake, that some casuists have taken up, even upon this very consideration, who, because a man cannot oblige himself to himself, have thought no legislator is bound by his own laws.[15]

A legislator could be bound by the contracts he had made 'if such pactions can sufficiently appear, either by the pacts themselves, or by long usage interpretatively evidencing them'.[16] This familiar political theory,

---

[11] *Ibid.*, 3v. The physician was a common example. See for example William Ames, *Conscience with the power and cases thereof*, 1639, p. 7.
[12] British Library, Hargrave 485, 4. [13] Selden, *Opera*, I, 153–6.
[14] Hargrave 485, 51.
[15] *Ibid.*, 7v. [16] *Ibid.*, 8.

implicit in the manuscripts on the prerogative, was obviously threatened by the thought of Thomas Hobbes, but to understand Hale's attitude to Hobbes, it helps to link both theories with Selden's.[17] A law, in Selden's view, was an order to a reasonable being, a command or prohibition with a penalty attached. A human law (a contract) was based upon God's law of contract-keeping, enforced, in the last analysis, by punishments God might visit on the soul. It was rational, in such a situation, to prefer the threat of bodily destruction to that of unending and infinite pain.

Hobbes agreed that human law was based on contract, but disbelieved in the immortal soul.[18] The function of the sovereign in his thought, and a function of God in John Selden's, was to provide a reason why contracts should be kept. The arbitrary power of the sovereign, so far from being the antithesis of law, was in fact the precondition of any tolerable social life. Both thinkers believed that an act against natural law was an act that tended to incur the worst fate that could happen to a man. Hobbes thought this fate was bodily destruction. To undermine the sovereign, and with him all the contracts that constituted social practices, was to tend to make the world a dangerous place, and was therefore an act contrary to Hobbesian natural law.

Hale agreed that 'it is ... consonant to this law of nature to enter into societies and capitulations of peace, because this is a convenient means of self-preservation'.[19] As a believer in the immortal soul, however, he thought the body's welfare was a thing of merely secondary importance 'by how much the soul is more noble than the body, by so much the more care is to be used in preserving it from that which must annoy and hurt it.'[20] There were thinkers, as he noted, who exaggerated natural law's extent, but

others ... have made in effect self-preservation the only cardinal law of human nature & all these rules or consequences that they have observed to be conducible to that cardinal law or deducible from it, they conclude to be so many ramifications of that grand natural law.

... they have improvidently singled out this one as the only governing law of nature, which is no other but one of these excellent effects, that this excellent law produceth ... as if a man should conclude that, because architecture is a notable effect or product of geometry, therefore the building of houses should take up the whole compass design end and use of that art.[21]

It was always wrong to kill, except in reasonable self-defence.[22] There was a duty, on the other hand, to be grateful to God and to others. Gratitude 'stands as it then was, no law that I know of having made it compulsory by

[17] A more detailed discussion of this point can be found in Tuck, *Rights theories*, esp. 86–100, 125–32.
[18] Tuck, *Rights theories*, 126.   [19] Hargrave 485, 31v.   [20] *Ibid.*, 31v.
[21] *Ibid.*, 18v.
[22] *Ibid.*, 36v.

any civil action, but it was as it stood before merely as a natural law obliging *in foro interiori*.'[23]

The target of these arguments was not identified, but they tended to establish an anti-Hobbist point: that the original state of nature was not, as Hobbes had claimed, a state of war. He was ready to admit, as Hobbes had persuasively argued, that 'antecedently to civil government settled there is no external judge, but a man's self, of what is a reasonable cause to invade another man's life or to deprive him of his common interest in the things of this life, because all men as in relation to themselves are equal.'[24] But murder was still murder and God rightly punished Cain.[25] The nightmare Hobbes envisaged, in the absence of a single sovereign power, was open to empirical objection: in India, for instance, the English have no sovereign to control them, but the many English merchants live at peace. There was neither, as Hale put it, 'the superinduction of a capitulation or contract to make it perfect peace, nor any hostility between them denounced or begun'.[26] A similar example, of 'a Swiss and an Indian in the woods of America',[27] is found in the works of John Locke.

The state of nature, a state of relative peace, was also a state of trade. A natural man, it followed, was also a propertied creature.[28] This claim, if it was true, was obviously fatal to Hobbes. But rejection of Hobbesian theories, as a brief explanation will show, encouraged rejection of Selden's ideas. In Selden's *Mare clausum*, a work that Hobbes admired,[29] appropriation was the work of contract. There was no such thing, for Selden, as ownership derived from occupation. The rights of occupiers, in the peaceable natural state, were based on a prior agreement that occupation should confer a title. Hobbes also based all property in contract, but denied that any contract could be valid in the absence of a sovereign who could see to it that agreements were enforced.

Hale wanted to assert, against the Hobbesian view, that there was property without a sovereign. He may have found it difficult, however, to believe in the prior agreement that Selden was obliged to postulate. At all events, he went to the other extreme, and took the view that occupants had acquired a natural right to their possessions. Hobbes was very well known for asserting, in setting up conditions for his natural state of war, that everyone had rights to everything. Hale qualified this frightening assertion:

---

[23] *Ibid.*, 40v. Richard Cumberland's book, *De legibus naturae* (1672) erects an ethical system on this basis. The rise of gratitude, a noticeable feature of Restoration thought, would repay investigation. It was probably related to worries about Hobbes.
[24] Hargrave 485, 38v.   [25] *Ibid.*, 39.   [26] *Ibid.*, 40.
[27] Locke, *Two treatises of government*, ed. Laslett, Cambridge 1988, p. 277.
[28] For another view, see James Tully, *The Locke Newsletter*, 13 (1982), 35–54; Tully, *Discourse*, 98–9.
[29] Tuck, *Rights theories*, 119.

as before the institution of the law of property it is admitted, that all have an equal right to all things, the man that hath acquired the first possession hath somewhat superadded to that primitive right in common, that puts him in a better condition than any other, and to his interest in common there is superadded somewhat by his industry that another hath not, namely a prior possession, and the same may be said in reason of such acquisitions, that are made by art or industry, whereby the things acquired are in some kind become his effects; as by planting, semination, culture, artificial manufactures and the like.[30]

The inevitable comparison provoked by a theory of property through labour is with the later doctrines of John Locke, but the views of Locke and Hale were actually quite dissimilar. The role of labour in the passage quoted is to confer 'possession' of a thing. A thing which is 'possessed' is automatically appropriated, but nothing intrinsic to labour, the technique for acquiring possession, gives rise to the resultant 'property'.[31] In the thought of Locke, by contrast, we are said to have a 'property' in our labour, because we can be said to own our bodies (an idea of no significance to Hale). To appropriate a thing, by 'mixing' it with work, is to mingle it with something that is already ours, 'fixing a property', by consequence, in something that is naturally common. The act of mixture is the source of title.[32]

The obvious parallel with Locke is therefore extremely misleading. This is not to say, however, that the comparison is wholly fruitless. Locke was at pains to ridicule contractual theories of property, demanding an 'explicit consent of every commoner' before appropriation could take place.[33] Hale's comparable turn away from contract was clearest in his treatment of the sea. His remarks upon the subject, contained in a work on the customs, composed in early 1667, were closer to *Mare liberum* than Selden's *Mare clausum*. The former work, by Grotius, had an occupation theory. For something to be owned, it had to be possessed, and the oceans (as opposed to narrow inlets) were clearly not an object for possession. Hale seems to

---

[30] Hargrave 485, 36v.–7.

[31] A possibility worth mentioning is that Hale's use of labour may have been influenced by the common law. The ownership of chattels, in early Tudor times, was on occasion traced to 'industry'. (J. H. Baker, *The reports of Sir John Spelman*, vol. II, Selden Society 1978, p. 210). A wild beast, for instance, was owned by 'occupation', but the title thus conferred was transient: '[beasts] are in common, et occupanti conceditur: as the fowls in the air, fishes in the sea, and beasts upon the land. But when I have taken a fowl, and by my industry I have tamed it by restraining its liberty, now I have a special property in it, inasmuch as it is made obedient by my own labour' (Baker, *Spelman*, II, 211). The stress on 'my own labour' is probably an accident of phrasing. Coke reported that 'in those [beasts] which are ferae naturae, and by industry are made tame, a man hath but a qualified property in them, scil. so long as they remain tame . . .' Coke, *Seventh reports*, 17b.) This suggests the role of labour was to confer possession, as in the theory advanced by Hale.

[32] Locke, *Two treatises*, 287–9.   [33] *Ibid.*, 289.

have agreed. It was only the king, he argued, that could own the narrow seas, as only a navy could really 'possess' so much water:

the civilians tell us truly, nihil praescribitur nisi quod possidetur. The king may prescribe the propriety of the narrow seas, because he may possess them by his navies and power. A subject cannot. But a subject may possess a navigable river, or creek or arm of the sea; because these may be within the extent of his possession and acquest.[34]

Hale differed from Grotius in being convinced that private property was absolute. One reason why Grotius believed in an ownerless sea was that the sea was inexhaustible. It was wrong to exclude humanity from any effectively infinite resource. Grotius had also charitably held that the starving could not be excluded from things which they had need of to survive. These ideas were wholly alien to Hale, who saw property as naturally exclusive. A further comparison with Locke's ideas has some intrinsic interest and highlights the great oddity of the view that Hale had chosen to adopt. In the primitive natural state described by Locke, there was no such thing as 'unnecessary' riches. When individuals had met their immediate natural needs, they would stop accumulating property; the things they could not use would only rot, so the hoarding of wealth was unknown. The grosser inequalities of cultivated times were the product of conventional arrangements: a contractually created store of value (such as precious stones or gold) and contractual laws to settle disagreements. The purpose of these contracts, the preservation of oneself and others, placed limits on their scope.[35] The starving had a 'title' to the means of their support, because the right to sustenance would override particular arrangements.[36]

Hale took a rather sterner view, as his great legal textbook revealed. *Historia placitorum coronae*, his survey of criminal law, discussed a claimed 'necessity' as an excuse for theft. Though he referred to Grotius, he made little attempt at abstract argument, contenting himself with the obvious point that 'men's properties would be under a strange insecurity being laid open to other men's necessities, whereof no man can possibly judge but the party himself.'[37] In England, because of the poor law, the question would never arise: 'by the laws of this Kingdom sufficient provision is made for the supply of such necessities by collections for the poor, and by the power of the civil magistrate'.[38] This was perhaps predictable

---

[34] Hargrave, *Collection*, 32. Hale was writing this work in March 1667 (p. 232).

[35] For more detailed discussion of Locke's position, see Tully, *Discourse on property*, esp. 131–2.

[36] Locke, *Two treatises*, 170.   [37] Hale, *Historia*, I, 54.

[38] *Ibid.*, I, 54–5. This complacent attitude was the one appropriate to a legal text-book. Hale's *Discourse touching provision for the poor* (1683), was much more realistic about existing law.

enough, but it masked a more unusual legal theory: that private property
was universal, and the rights of the starving (if any) a local and contractual
innovation. A lost and hungry castaway was not allowed to steal, unless, of
course, 'the tacit consent of nations, or of some particular countries or
societies' permitted him to do so.[39]

A belief in natural property had a number of important implications. It
exalted the rights of the subject, which he enjoyed before the state existed,
rights for the sake of which, one could assume, he entered into contracts in
the first place. Political arrangements, as similarly purposeful creations,
might regulate his property but would tend to secure what he owned. The
treatise on the customs, a most revealing work, made an interesting distinction, which bears upon this point. Hale recognised three categories of
English legal right: *ius privatum*, *ius publicum*, and *ius regium*. 'Ius
privatum' he defined as 'interest of propriety or franchise'.[40] The king
himself had some such rights, which he could freely alienate to subjects; he
had a private property (in the sphere that was under discussion) in a
number of rivers and ports.

'Ius publicum', by contrast, the law which regulated *ius privatum*, was
not natural but contractually created. A so-called 'public' right, imposing
contractual limits on private interests, could not be tampered with by royal
power. This was of great importance, as Chapter 8 will show, to the
much-disputed law of dispensation. An example of *ius publicum*, in the
sphere of customs law, was 'the common interest that all persons have to
resort to or from public ports, as public sea-marts or markets'.[41] Lastly,
there was 'ius regium', 'the right of superintendency and prerogative that
the King hath for the safety of the realm, the benefit of commerce, or
security of his customs'.[42] *Ius publicum* was common law and statute; *ius
regium* was Crown prerogative. *Ius regium* could not be sold or otherwise
transferred, because it was entrusted to the king. Hale spoke of it as a

right that belongs to the King jure prerogativae, and is a distinct right from that
of propriety; for, as before I have said, though the dominion either of franchise or
propriety is lodged either by prescription or charter in a subject, yet it is charged
or affected with that ius publicum that belongs to all men; and so it is charged or
affected with that jus regium, or right of prerogative of the King, so far as the same
is by law invested in the King.[43]

An example of *ius regium*, the right to give a charter to a port, suggests the
limits upon royal power. No port could be erected if another person's
property was threatened, if it removed a privilege that a previously existing

---

[39] Hale, *Historia*, I, 55.   [40] Hargrave, *Collection*, 72.   [41] *Ibid.*, 36, 72.
[42] *Ibid.*, 72.
[43] *Ibid.*, 89.

port enjoyed.[44] Prerogative was limited, not least through its own previous creations, by the pattern of the subject's private rights.

This told the lawyers nothing they did not already know. They knew, from Edward Coke, that the functions of prerogative could not be leased or sold;[45] they knew, from countless sources, that no act of prerogative could take away the subject's property. Hale's view of property as natural, as regulated rather than created by the state, thus gave expression to ideas at least implicit in existing law. 'Ius publicum', he thought, was always instrumental: it was 'a common interest' in some collective end. 'Ius regium' was a trust, again for some national purpose, and not a transferable right. Only the subject's property was 'an interest' pure and simple, a feature of the natural state and a valuable end in itself. When philosophically articulated, these prejudices were revealed as Whig.[46]

---

[44] Ibid., 67.   [45] Coke, Seventh reports, 36; 1 Plowden 487.

[46] Locke's Two treatises of government was brilliantly abridged by Michael Oakeshott as 'a brilliant abridgement of the political habits of Englishmen' (Oakeshott, Rationalism in politics and other essays, 1962, p. 121).

7

Restoration: constitutional theory

Selden believed that the common law was nothing but a contract, an arbitrary agreement which the English people happened to have made. To know the law, on Selden's view, was to know the nation's history: to trace successive actions of the legislating 'state'. Whatever the truth of this theory, it was not of much practical use, as it yielded no presumptions what the people had agreed. The advantage of Sir Edward Coke's account, identifying common law with 'reason', was that it vindicated what every lawyer did. It explained a judicial concern that the system should be certain and consistent, for these were indications that 'reason' had been found. It justified some reference to present social needs, as there were no occasions (or so it was presumed) for which so wise a law did not provide. Where Selden's law was rigid, Coke offered a flexible tool; he looked to the needs of the present, where Selden was imprisoned by the past. The danger in Coke's theory, as the lawyers had reason to know, was that his legal rhetoric might come to be misused: that a layman's conception of reason, of eccentric political content, would replace the professional learning of the sages of the law.

The writings discussed in this chapter, Hale's late constitutional works, might seem a rather miscellaneous group. In each of them, however, a tension is displayed, between law as a parliament makes it and the same law as developed by the wisdom of the courts. The making of a law was always a matter of contract, but its 'reasonable' character, its adjustment to a situation's needs, was something only judges could ensure. The result can be presented, as the following pages will show, as an uneasy synthesis of Selden's view with Coke's. Its subtlest and most interesting expression was provoked by an assault from Thomas Hobbes.

Hobbes was convinced, as Chapter 6 explained, that property was contractually created. It belonged to the sphere of *ius gentium*, and could be nullified by natural law. His ideas can be re-cast, with very little trouble, as a claim about the range of valid contracts: that no property or liberty is valid if it tends to introduce a state of war. In a book that frightened Hale, the *Dialogue between a philosopher and a student of the common laws of England*, he applied this simple principle to English constitutional ideas. He decided not to print it (he regarded the end as 'imperfect'), but we know that he composed it after 1664, and that Hale studied it, in manuscript, at some time before February of 1673.[1] Our evidence, from a letter of John Aubrey's, is the tantalising assertion that 'Judge Hales, who is no great courtier, has read it and much dislikes it, and is his enemy. Judge Vaughan has read it and much commends it'.[2]

Hobbes' principal grievance against the common lawyers, as represented by Sir Edward Coke, was that they had usurped the sovereign's power. He gladly agreed, to begin with, that '*nihil quod est rationi contrarium est licitum*; that is to say, nothing is law that is against reason: and that reason is the life of the law, nay the common law itself is nothing but reason',[3] but he objected to the claim that lawyers possessed the authority by which this reason was identified:

that the reason which is the life of the law should not be natural but artificial I cannot conceive. . . . I grant you that the knowledge of law is an art, but not that any art of one man or of many how wise soever they be, or the work of one and more artificers, how perfect soever it be, is law. It is not wisdom but authority that makes a law . . . That the law hath been fined by grave and learned men, meaning the professors of the law is manifestly untrue, for all the laws of England have been made by the kings of England, consulting with the nobility and commons in parliament, of which not one in twenty was a learned lawyer.[4]

If reason was correctly glossed, however, he was happy with the essence of Coke's theory: 'he makes the common law and the law of reason to be all one, as indeed they are, when by it is meant the king's reason'.[5] In practice, Hobbes seems to have thought, the judges did make laws by precedent, which was 'tacitly confirmed (because not disapproved) by the sovereign legislator'.[6] But at all events, there was no call for any skill unique to professional lawyers. To know the common law, in the world that Hobbes imagined, was not to have mastered the lawyer's mode of thought, but to have access to the king's instructions. There was no need for 'artificial' reason, or any of the rituals of the Inns:

if I pretend within a month or two to make myself able to perform the office of a judge, you are not to think it arrogance; for you are to allow to me, as well as to other men, my pretence to reason, which is the common law (remember this that I may need not again to put you in mind, that reason is the common law) and for

---

[1] Its modern editor suggests that it may in fact be finished as it stands (Thomas Hobbes, *A dialogue between a philosopher and a student of the common laws of England*, ed. Joseph Cropsey, Chicago 1971, pp. 2–8).
[2] *Aubrey's Brief lives*, I, 394.   [3] Hobbes, *Dialogue*, 54.   [4] *Ibid.*, 55.
[5] *Ibid.*, 143.
[6] *Ibid.*, 142.

statute law, seeing it is printed, and that there be indexes to point me to every matter contained in them, I think a man may profit in them very much in two months.[7]

The law was 'natural reason', the product of an arbitrary will, deciding points on equitable grounds. The title of Hobbes' book, *A dialogue between a philosopher and a student of the common laws of England*, may well have been a parody of St German's *Dialogue betwixt a doctor of divinity and a student in the laws of England*. Both authors were concerned, from very different motives, with determining relations between equity and law. St German thought that common law incorporated equitable thinking, and was therefore immune from correction by the chancellor's decree. What he did not believe, in contrast to both Hobbes and Edward Coke, was that equity and law were co-extensive. Hobbes saw no demarcation line between the other courts and Chancery.[8] He demanded of the lawyers: 'Now seeing it is granted that equity is the same thing with the law of reason ... I would fain know to what end there should be any other court of equity at all, either before the chancellor or any other person, besides the judges of the civil or common pleas.'[9] The chancellor's authority was essentially the same as that of the judges, and his personal jurisdiction was really a court of appeal.

Hobbes presented this curious theory, with typically innocent gall, as an interpretation of existing common law. Existing laws and liberties were valid as they stood, but their implementation was subject to the needs of a Hobbesian state. The king was quite entitled, for example, to promise not to tax without consent. Hobbes was

satisfied that the kings that grant such liberties are bound to make them good, so far as it may be done without sin. But if a king find that by such a grant he be disabled to protect his subjects if he maintain his grant, he sins; and therefore may, and ought to take no notice of the said grant: for such grants as by error or false suggestion are gotten from him are, as the lawyers do confess, void and of no effect, and ought to be recalled.[10]

Magna Carta was certainly valid, and so were all subsequent statutes, but they were at the mercy of an absolutist judge.

The 'Reflections on Hobbes' *Dialogue*', Hale's manuscript response, survive in what appears to be a fragmentary form.[11] The 'Reflections' were two brief unfinished essays, which were commentaries, respectively, on the *Dialogue*'s first chapter, 'Of laws in general and the laws of reason', and

---

[7] *Ibid.*, 56.   [8] *Ibid.*, 94–5.   [9] *Ibid.*, 94.   [10] *Ibid.*, 63.

[11] Printed in Holdsworth, *History of English law*, 15 vols., 1922–65, vol. V, pp. 500–13. It is interestingly discussed in Gerald J. Postema, *Bentham and the common law tradition*, Oxford 1986, pp. 61–80, and D. E. C. Yale, 'Hale and Hobbes on law, legislation and the sovereign', *Cambridge Law Journal*, 3 (1972), 121–56.

the second, 'Of sovereign power'. From the point of view of content, or at least the content interesting to Hale,[12] they amount, however, to a full rebuttal. There is an extant draft,[13] which covers the same ground, so he probably never intended to tackle the rest of the book.

He started with analysis of 'reason', a word that he interpreted in a manner familiar from Coke. He detected three separate senses. In 'things irrational' it meant the 'congruity, connexion and fit dependence of one thing upon another';[14] there was thus a 'reason' to morality, where he found 'there is a certain reasonableness and congruity and intrinsic connexion and consequence of one thing from another antecedent to any artificial system of morals or institution of laws'.[15] Secondly, it meant a faculty, a capacity common to all, although it could be shaped by a specialised training: 'Tully that was an excellent orator, and a good moralist, was but an ordinary statesman and a worse poet'.[16] To be used to best effect, on any particular subject, it needed to be 'directed or applied and habituated by use and exercise'.[17] Lastly, it was 'taken complexedly when the reasonable faculty is in conjunction with the reasonable subject, and habituated to it by use and exercise, and it is this kind of reason or reason thus taken that denominates a man a philosopher, a politician, a physician, a lawyer ...'[18] As Chapter 1 explained, Coke's theory depends on a pun. The lawyer recapitulates the 'reason' of the law (he discovers the coherence of the system as a whole), bringing his thoughts (his reason) in line with the justification (the reason) of a rule. The legal training that Coke advocated involved habituation to an esoteric craft. In this picture of an 'artificial reason', Hale was at one with Coke, both in his stress on the need for professional training and in his vision of the judge's task. It was of prime importance 'to keep as near as may be to the certainty of the law, and the consonance of it to itself, that one age and one tribunal may speak the same things, and carry on the same thread of the law in one uniform rule as near as is possible.'[19] To decide a particular case, while preserving the system's coherence, it was necessary to see the point in the context of the whole.

The professional's advantage, as readers of Coke's works were well aware, extended even to the written law. A statute was not made in isolation; it responded to a 'mischief', which knowledge of its origins revealed, and it therefore had a 'reason' for the lawyer to detect. Hobbes thought that any layman could master statute law, but Hale agreed with Coke this was untrue:

---

[12] Richard Tuck very plausibly argues (Tuck, *Hobbes*, Oxford 1989, pp. 33–5) that the lengthy attack on the heresy law was the author's most pressing concern.
[13] Lambeth 3479, 60–6.   [14] Holdsworth, *History*, V, 500.   [15] *Ibid.*, 501.
[16] *Ibid.*, 501.
[17] *Ibid.*, 502.   [18] *Ibid.*, 501.   [19] *Ibid.*, 506.

As to exposition of Acts of parliament and written laws certainly he that hath been educated in the study of the law hath a great advantage over those that have been otherwise exercised, let them pretend to or be masters of never so much reason. For first they have not only the preamble and body and provisoes of the Acts of parliament before them, but they have a clearer evidence of what the practice or mischief was before ... [20]

All this was purest Coke, if rather less extravagantly put. The difference between them, the fruit of Selden's thought, was in Hale's greater willingness to talk about consent. The law was unpredictable (as Selden had repeatedly explained), because it was created by agreement:

if any the most refined brain under heaven would go about to enquire by speculation, or by reading of Plato or Aristotle, or by considering the laws of the Jews, or other nations, to find out how lands descend in England ... he would lose his labour ... till he acquainted himself with the laws of England, and the reason is because they are institutions introduced by the will and consent of others implicitly by custom and usage or explicitly by written laws or Acts of parliament'.[21]

There is no sense in Hale, such as we find in Coke, that artificial reason has inherent binding power. The laws were well adapted to the nation that they served, but it was not their virtues that had legislative force.

The second of these essays, concerned with 'sovereign power', applied John Selden's theory along Hale's usual lines. The 'modifications of government ... are or may be infinitely various'. It is settled in the first place by 'the original institution of the government', but 'in ancient governments ... the original instrument of that institution is hardly to be found.' In any case 'new occasions, emergencies, accidents and capitulations do necessarily occasion alterations from the first institution'.[22]

The contract could be altered in all the usual ways: by conquest, which 'commonly ends in dedition and capitulation between the conqueror and conquered'; by mutual agreement; and also by 'long custom and usage, which carries in itself a facile consent of the governors and governed, or is at least an evidence and interpretation of the original institution of the nature of the government, or of the initial pact between the governors and governed.'[23] This was the general rule, at least in 'ancient governments' 'first because the original instrument of that institution is hardly to be found and secondly because in process of time new occasions, emergencies, accidents and capitulations do necessarily occasion alterations from the first institution.'[24] The provisions of the English constitution were known through statutes and through common law. The king was in principle sovereign, as Hale's work on the prerogative had stressed, but he was limited in some respects. He could make war and peace, pardon offenders,

[20] *Ibid.*, 506.   [21] *Ibid.*, 505.   [22] *Ibid.*, 506–7.   [23] *Ibid.*, 507.
[24] *Ibid.*, 507.

and debase the coinage, and he enjoyed 'the power of making laws'.[25] This legislative power, though certainly confined to royal hands, was exercised in parliament with the Houses' 'advice and consent'.[26]

From these general assumptions, developed in the manuscripts discussed in Chapter 3, the rest of his argument flowed. He produced one quite original distinction (if C. H. McIlwain can be believed)[27] between a coercive, an 'irritative', and a merely 'directive' power.[28] The king could be directed by the force of English law, but he was immune from coercion. An example of the 'irritative' power (from the Latin 'irritare': 'to make void, render of no effect')[29] was the power of the judges to nullify a grant. More relevantly here, he denounced a string of Hobbesian opinions, especially the statement that 'the King alone is the judge of all public dangers and may appoint such remedies as he please'. The outburst is unparalleled in tone in the temperate expanses of his prose. These 'wild propositions' were '1. utterly false. 2. against all natural justice. 3. pernicious to the government. 4. destructive to the common good and safety of the government. 5. Without any shadow of law or reason to support them.'[30]

Historical experience refuted the Hobbesian claims. No government was perfect, and we must be pragmatic in our choice: 'in the estimate and measure of the goodness or convenience of government we are to weigh which answer most exigencies of human life'.[31] There had been no inconvenience in some five hundred years from the modest limitations Hobbes deplored.[32] It would be quite absurd, in misplaced deference to a speculation, to overturn a system that had served the kingdom well.

The 'Reflections' were a brilliant distillation of the legalistic politics Hale learned from Edward Coke. They drew upon the strength of Coke's account, his description of a learned judge's practice, and rejected its obvious weakness, the suggestion that the source of obligation was the 'reason' he imputed to the law. Hale reaffirmed, in principle, that legal obligation stemmed from popular consent, but he also tried to guarantee the lawyer's political role. There was a need for change, as English society altered through time, but legislation was a complex task. His real concern, like Coke's, was that the common lawyers should control it, informed, as professionals were, by accumulated knowledge from their ancient system's past: 'those amendments and supplements that through the various experiences of wise and knowing men have been applied to any law must needs be better suited to the convenience of laws than the best invention of the

---

[25] *Ibid.*, 508.   [26] *Ibid.*, 508–9.
[27] C. H. McIlwain, *Constitutionalism ancient and modern*, Cornell 1940, p. 132.
[28] Holdsworth, *History*, V, 507–8.   [29] OED on 'irritate'.
[30] Holdsworth, *History*, V, 509.
[31] *Ibid.*, 512.   [32] *Ibid.*, 512.

most pregnant wits not aided by such a series and tract of experience.'[33]
The history of the common law of England, the formal statement of his
general views, was an extended commentary upon this simple thought.

Hale's book was a work of *History* in the broadest contemporary sense,
a sort of natural history of the law. It was not a simple narrative, although
its central chapters were written in narrative form. It could equally be read
as a varied collection of essays, discussing the sources of law, its history to
the time of Henry VII, and its relationship with other systems. The last two
chapters of the printed version were a couple of case studies of its virtues,
the procedure for trial by jury and the rules for inheriting land. The work
was meant to culminate in a tabular *Analysis* of law, which follows, in the
manuscript, from the *History* we know.[34] It circulated in this form till 1713
(the date of composition is unknown, except that it post-dates the Restoration) when the earliest of its printers divided a unified text.[35] 'The best
precursor of Maitland', as it has been conventionally known, had wider
theoretical ambitions than such a reputation would suggest.

The *History* began with a distinction, explaining the phenomenon of an
'unwritten' law. The difference between written and unwritten was based
upon the manner that a law 'obtained its force':

> for although (as shall be shewn hereafter), all the laws of this kingdom have some
> monuments or memorials thereof in writing, yet all of them have not their original
> in writing; for some of those laws have obtained their force by immemorial usage
> or custom, and such laws are properly called leges non scriptae, or unwritten laws
> or customs.
>
> Those laws ... that I call leges scriptae, or written laws, are such as are usually
> called statute laws, or Acts of parliament, which are originally reduced into writing
> before they are enacted or received any binding power ...[36]

The talk about 'originals' can easily mislead, for the history of a rule had
no importance. The focus of his interest was on its 'binding power', the
reason it obliges in the present. Much of the *lex non scripta* had once been
written law, deriving from the statutes of the reigns before Richard I. All
rules that had been binding since 1189 (the 'time of memory' in legal
jargon) were fictionally deemed to have no origin at all, but some, at least,
were made in parliament. These latter principles

> are now accounted part of the lex non scripta, being as it were incorporated
> thereinto, and become part of the common law; and in truth, such statutes are not
> now pleadable as Acts of parliament (because what is before time of memory is

[33] *Ibid.*, 504.

[34] On which see John W. Cairns, 'Blackstone, an English institutist: legal literature and the
rise of the nation state', *Oxford Journal of Legal Studies*, 4 (1984), esp. pp. 341–3.

[35] See for example Cambridge University Library Add. MS 3820.

[36] Hale, *The history of the common law of England*, (ed.) C. M. Gray, Chicago 1971, p. 3.

supposed without a beginning, or at least such a beginning as the law takes notice of) but they obtain their strength by mere immemorial usage or custom.[37]

An intermediate case, suggesting what 'incorporation' meant, was that of the 'old statutes'. These were the Acts of parliament from reigns before Edward II:

many of them were made but in affirmance of the common law; and . . . the rest of them, that made a change in the common law, are yet so ancient, that they now seem to have been as it were a part of the common law, especially considering the many expositions that have been made of them in the several successions of times, whereby as they became the great subject of judicial resolutions and decisions; so those expositions and decisions, together also with those old statutes themselves, are as it were incorporated into the very common law, and become a part of it.[38]

To be 'incorporated', it seems to be implied, a statute must inform judicial thinking. The process of interpreting a statute (determining its function in a system presumed to be wise) assimilates its working to the system as a whole. With every 'exposition', the process is advanced, for judgements are the usage of the courts. *Lex scripta* is an order to the lawyers; unwritten law is what they do unasked.

A judgement is not binding as a law, except upon the litigants in question, but judgements have a certain general role, 'expounding, declaring and publishing what the law of the kingdom is'.[39] They were a kind of 'evidence'[40] (in the verbal sense of 'making-evident') of the system's particular rules. Their authority was a function of the way they made sense of the past, their 'consonancy and congruity with resolutions and decisions of former times'.[41] Hale was not a believer, in contrast to Hobbes, in quasi-legislative precedent, in decisions strictly binding in every future case. As he once explained in court, 'I always love stare decisis', a dictum that implied he had a choice.[42]

There were judgements of varying kinds. There were various questions, of course, in both custom and statute, 'where the ancient and express laws of the realm give an express decision', a rule that simply called to be applied.[43] At other times, however, 'deduction or illation' was involved. The prime consideration, in judgements of this type, was respect for the coherence of the law, especially 'the common law and custom of the realm, which is the great substratum that is to be maintained'. The next was 'authorities and decisions of former times in the same or the like cases'. If neither yielded guidance, there was 'the reason of the thing itself', but this was fairly narrowly understood.[44] There were some judicial duties that were difficult to govern by a rule, like 'the exposition of the intention of

---

[37] *Ibid.*, 4.   [38] *Ibid.*, 7–8.   [39] *Ibid.*, 45.   [40] *Ibid.*, 45.   [41] *Ibid.*, 45.
[42] Treby MS Report, Middle Temple, p. 775.   [43] Hale, *History*, 46.   [44] *Ibid.*, 46.

clauses in deeds, wills, covenants etc.', though 'former resolutions' would often be a guide.[45] He did not mean to argue, in the spirit of his predecessor Coke, for the universal competence of judges.

Hale saw the law very much as John Selden had seen it, as a record of agreements by the English. Rules taken from the civil law (a written legal system) were nonetheless a part of *lex non scripta*, because they owed their binding force to acceptance by 'usage and custom', the immemorial practice in particular 'cases and courts' (they were, in fact, a kind of *local* custom). Those rules which were more formally received, by force of parliamentary approval, were taken to be part of statute law. The limits of civilian jurisdiction, like anything else that custom and statute established, were supervised by the judges of Westminster Hall.[46]

The *History*'s great insight, and the heart of its historical account, concerned assimilation of essentially alien rules. The focus of attention, from Hale's opening sentences onwards, was with the 'obligation' that underlay the law:

whenever the laws of England, or the several capita thereof began, or from whence or whomsoever derived, or what laws of other countries contributed to the matter of our laws, yet most certainly their obligation arises not from their matter, but from their admission and reception, and authorisation in this kingdom.[47]

He had another theme, to combine with this insistence on reception, in a subtle reassertion of Coke's vision of the law. The law was constituted by a legislative power, by arbitrary popular consent. Its character, however, was that of a reasonable system, adapted by experience to English social needs. Surprisingly, perhaps, this process was not just unconscious and collective, the tacit adaptation of a customary law. This no doubt played a role, but so did more deliberate amendment, the work of kings in parliament, assisted by professional advice. On more than one occasion, as the law reports record, Hale called for legislation from the bench.[48] The common law reached the height of its perfection, as the *History* itself makes very plain, through parliamentary statutes devised by King Edward I.[49] Such statutes were 'incorporated' in the common law, for they came to bind as customs and not as external demands, as part, thanks to the judges, of a coherent whole.

Hale could have been a little more explicit, but the nature of the process can be deduced from his account of the role of a common law judge. The concern of a legal technician, in legislation and interpretation, was that the

---

[45] *Ibid.*, 46.   [46] *Ibid.*, 19.   [47] *Ibid.*, 43.
[48] A. W. B. Simpson, *A history of the common law of contract: the rise of the action of assumpsit*, Oxford 1975, pp. 602–3; 1 Ventris 412.
[49] Hale, *History*, 101–5.

law be certain and consistent. A new or foreign principle, when tacitly or formally accepted, became the object of his exposition, which tended to find it a place within the reason of the law. The object of a judgement was always to preserve the 'great substratum', so judges treated novel rules by showing how they harmonised with the mass of the existing legal system. Properly thought out laws, such as those of King Edward I, presented them with little difficulty, but even the most foolish innovations would come, eventually, to be absorbed. Every time that a judge, in his judgements, accepted a given rule as a constraint, he produced an 'evidence' of law (that is, a manifestation of the system *as a whole*) consistent with the principle in question. At first, the lawyers would be well aware of the new idea as an alien influence, as something which had altered the 'ancient common law'.[50] Over centuries, however, the most alien of notions would come to be part of the practice of the courts. Though arbitrary contract was the origin of law, professional tradition, the law as only lawyers understood it, gave it the special character identified by Coke.

The *History* thus exhibited the system as being both legally rational and popularly willed. It was binding, to be sure, because it was accepted, but its peculiar quality was developed by the thinking of the practitioners. The law was like a ship (an image drawn from Selden), or like a human body; its identity persisted, though all of its constituents were gradually replaced.[51] In Hale (though not in Selden) this image could be doubly understood: there was a continuity of legislative power, but also continuity in the intellectual methods of the lawyer. The latter point was crucially important, and explains the oddest feature of his strictly historical thought: his resolute denial of the Conquest.

The greatest treatment of this theme, where law and history meet, is J. G. A. Pocock's *The ancient constitution and the feudal law*. The key to this brilliant book was its title's seldom-quoted second part: 'a study of English historical thought in the seventeenth century'. The 'historical method', on Pocock's view, was to start from social history, 'reconstructing the institutions of society in the past and using them as a context in which and by means of which, to interpret the actions, words and thoughts of the men who lived at that time'.[52] It was here the English failed. They had no sense, with honourable exceptions, that English social life had once been feudal, or that the feudal order was an import, unknown before the year 1066. They did not (perhaps could not) take this step, because they were imprisoned in the web of a 'common law mind'. They presumed, as the lawyers had taught them, that the present had developed

---

[50] 'Ancient' was just as likely to mean 'ancien' as 'vieux'. The 'ancient common law' or the 'ancient constitution' very often meant no more than 'the law we used to have'.
[51] Hale, *History*, 40.   [52] Pocock, *Ancient constitution*, 1.

from a related past. The law's provisions might of course be changed, might even undergo complete renewal, but the changes detected were gradual, and the common law as system was immortal. This ruled out 'catastrophic' breaks, and excluded a view of the past as essentially foreign. To see their history more historically, on Pocock's definition of the term, they needed to examine it as alien: to treat medieval England as a 'society', a cultural structure with its own dynamic, created by its own imported laws. A scholar who had made this kind of breakthrough would see the Norman Conquest as it was.[53]

For Pocock, informed by this theory, Hale's views were a marvellous find. Hale was plainly a man of enormous and critical learning, ideally equipped for proper historical work. He lacked a political motive for denying the Normans their due, for he showed that 'ius conquestus' had no influence on the law. A military victory conferred no lasting rights, 'for where the title is merely force and power, his title will fail, if the conquered can with like force or power over-match his . . .'[54] The legitimate basis of a conquest was always consent of the conquered: 'though force were perhaps the occasion of this consent, yet in truth 'tis consent only that is the true proximate and fixed foundation of the victor's right.'[55] If consent was made explicit, then its terms were clearly known; if tacit, it was signalled by an enduring peace, 'a long and quiet tract of peaceable submission'.[56] In the latter case, 'by a long prescription usage and custom, the laws and rights of the conquered people were in a manner settled'.[57] If Hale really believed these assertions (which there is no reason to doubt), then the Conquest was irrelevant to Stuart political life. His treatment of the question, to which a lengthy chapter was devoted, reflected a quite motiveless obsession.

One quibble can be raised. As Hale explained his purpose, he was anxious 'to wipe off that false imputation on our laws, as if they were the fruit or effect of a conquest, or carried in them the badge of servitude to the will of the conqueror, which notion some ignorant and prejudiced persons have entertained.'[58] The allusion of this passage was not to the supporters of the king. The notion of a 'badge of servitude' (the use of Norman French in legal practice) was common in a rather different group. As the radical John Hare complained, the laws were created by conquest, yet 'we soothe and applaud ourselves in these gyves[59] and servile robes as patrician ornaments'.[60] John Milton's *The tenure of kings and magistrates* (1649) deplored his enemies' appeal to 'that old entanglement of iniquity, their

[53] *Ibid.*, 64.   [54] Hale, *History*, 51.   [55] *Ibid.*, 51.   [56] *Ibid.*, 52.
[57] *Ibid.*, 54.
[58] *Ibid.*, 48.   [59] Shackles.   [60] *Harleian miscellany*, vol. VI, p. 92.

gibberish laws, though the badge of their ancient slavery'.[61] To the Leveller William Walwyn, the common law was a 'French garb or clothing which the Conqueror and his successors, by main strength, forced our forefathers to put on'.[62] One motive for Hale's treatment of the Conquest was fear of really radical reform.[63]

This minor objection apart, the thrust of Pocock's argument is sound. Hale's eagerness to rule out talk of conquest bore no proportion to the threat that William's status posed. He found reason to insist, through arguments notably strained, that the 'similitude of the laws of England and Normandy was not by conformation of the laws of England to those of Normandy, but by conformation of the laws of Normandy to those of England'.[64] His intellectual blindness, as Pocock rightly saw, was intimately linked to his professional habits of mind. He wanted to present the law as rational and willed, as artificial reason, as well as the fruit of consent. He needed a continuous tradition, Coke's 'fining and refining by so many learned men', devoid of sudden breaks with former practice.

The presentation of an institution as reasonable and based upon consent was part of its depiction as valid common law. A 'Whig' historiography, it follows, one that sees institutions as rational and willed, has close connections with the legal spirit. Successful legal argument, in Edward Coke's account, was recapitulation of the legislator's thoughts. In showing how a law conformed to reason it offered a Whig history of the rule, the teleological story of how the rule in question came to be. Thus in setting out to characterise law, Hale gave a Whig account of the legal past. He was not 'doing history' at all, if history is defined in Pocock's terms.

The partially fictional nature of the lawyers' historical claims was illustrated by another question. Hale wrote a learned treatise on the kind of topic that Selden had once relished: the status of the Admiralty court and its Roman-based system of maritime law.[65] The work had an obvious context: a determined but doomed attempt, with a climax in the early

---

[61] Milton, *Works*, V, 3.

[62] William Walwyn, *Juries justified or a word of correction to Mr Henry Robinson*, 1651, p. 5. Pocock himself has an elegant passage on anti-constitutionalism of the left in *Ancient constitution*, 127–9. See also, of course, Christopher Hill, 'The Norman Yoke', in *Puritanism and revolution: studies in the interpretation of the English revolution of the seventeenth century*, 1958, pp. 50–122.

[63] This view of his motives is confirmed by the parallel passage in 'Prerogativa regis', where he proposed to silence 'that untrue calumny objected against our government, laws and liberties as if they were barely of Norman extraction or the product of a Norman yoke, as some inconsiderable persons have been bold to say ...' (Hale, *Prerogatives*, 10).

[64] Hale, *History*, 85.

[65] Daniel R. Coquillette, *The civilian writers of Doctors' Commons, London: Three centuries of juristic innovation in comparative, commercial and international law*, Berlin 1988. D. E. C. Yale, 'A view of the Admiralty jurisdiction: Sir Matthew Hale and the civilians', in Dafydd Jenkins (ed.), *Legal History Studies 1972*, Cardiff 1975, pp. 87–109.

1670s, to secure the jurisdiction from encroachment by King's Bench. Civilians objected, in particular, to an outrageous fiction: the location of overseas contracts on English soil, within the jurisdiction of the courts of common law. For the purposes of pleading, if not of geography, there was a place called 'Constantinople . . . at London in the parish of St. Mary-le-Bow in the ward of Cheap'. At some stage in the battle that ensued, there was a 'famous dispute . . . before his Sacred Majesty in Council', involving Sir Leoline Jenkins (1623–85), the formidable Admiralty judge.[66] His arguments were answered by 'that great good man the Lord Chief Justice Hale, who as well by law positive as other his great reasons soon put a period to that question'.[67] On that occasion, arguing to a brief, Hale doubtless saw no reason to be fair. The treatise, from the time of his retirement, has the air of a quite genuine enquiry, but it was no doubt coloured by the victory he had won.

He stressed, in the manner of Selden, that maritime law was an import, an originally alien system that was binding by consent. But Selden was a theorist, while Hale was a practising judge. The difference emerges in Hale's pragmatic streak. He was impressed, as Coke had been, with the adaptive qualities of law:

laws, where they have been long used, and are well known, and have been by long practice and experience accommodated to the country whose laws they are, even upon that very account are more eligible and to be preferred as more conducible to the good of that people (the true adequate end of laws) than a strange law though perchance in notion and speculation more methodical and polite and literate . . .[68]

Hale did not claim that the common law was always the superior of the civil. He did, however, suppose that 'in process and length of time every nation that is civilised, forms and moulds its own municipal laws with the greatest ease accommodation and convenience to itself (as every shellfish moulds and fashions its shell best for its own constitution use defence and convenience) . . .[69] One reason for suspicion of ideas from civil law was the other system's absolutist basis: the notorious principle that 'quod principi placuit legis habet vigorem'.[70] Another was a faith in jury trial as the best

---

[66] Charles Molloy, *De jure maritimo et navali, or a treatise of affairs maritime and of commerce*, 1676, Preface, n.p.

[67] *Ibid.*

[68] *Hale and Fleetwood on Admiralty jurisdiction*, ed. M. J. Prichard and D. E. C. Yale, Selden Society 1993, p. 4. For the dating of this treatise (? late 1675) see p. xviii. I regret that this edition was published just too late for me to make full use of its learned prefatory material.

[69] *Admiralty jurisdiction* 5. Compare Davies, *Irish Reports*, 6: 'like a silk-worm that formeth all her web out of her self only'.

[70] 'What pleased the prince has the force of law.' *Admiralty jurisdiction*, 7.

of all possible ways of judging fact.[71] The civilians clearly needed supervision, preferably by the courts of common law, 'substituted by the King's commission and the law of the land to keep jurisdictions as well as persons within the limits that the law prescribes'.[72]

Questions of jurisdiction quite often involved historical assertions, which might be only loosely based in fact. Sometimes a lower court was immemorially old, but was deemed to originate later than its superiors in Westminster Hall.[73] The Admiral's court could be traced to the time of King Edward III (quite comfortably within the 'time of memory'), and it seemed to have no statutory basis. Hale was 'forced for the support of this prescription to suppose' that it had a lengthy previous existence.[74] This was basically a fictional presumption, to be justified, if necessary, in essentially practical terms. In general, as would be expected, his attitude to fictions was relaxed: 'though fictions make a show of something that is not, yet there is scarce any well ordered law, nay not the civil law, but hath its fictions'.[75] The common law was justified in its claim to jurisdiction overseas, in spite of the fictional means that it chose to adopt, because it was presumed to have a remedy for wrongs: 'no man can think the common law so deficient especially our island consisting much in foreign intercourse and journeys and voyages to foreign parts as that it should be destitute of a remedy for persons injured merely upon a supposition of want of cognizance for foreign matters.'[76] The common law also enjoyed at least a concurrent power over the foreshore (the Admiralty claimed exclusive rights), 'otherwise there would ensue a failure of justice which cannot be presumed in so long a continuance of time'.[77]

The notion of 'failure of justice' deserves at least a momentary pause, as it clearly involved a survival of presumptions much like Coke's. It was mentioned in the interregnum case of Harwood v. Paty, when the law replaced the bishop's role in sequestrating tithes,[78] and it played a part in at least one of Hale's most controversial late decisions.[79] On a more philosophical level, it harmonised with his picture of natural man. A rational propertied creature, in a relatively peaceful natural state, would only make such contracts as secured what he enjoyed. A right would have priority, in purely chronological as well as conceptual terms, over the mechanisms that he meant for its support. Where rights had been infringed (the logic of this picture would suggest) there was an expectation that a remedy be found.

There was scope, in operating this presumption, for a benign development of law. Like all such tools, however, it needed to be kept in the right

---

[71] *Ibid.*, 8.   [72] *Ibid.*, 10.   [73] *Ibid.*, 14.   [74] *Ibid.*, 65.   [75] *Ibid.*, 24.
[76] *Ibid.*, 47.   [77] *Ibid.*, 103.   [78] See above, p. 65.
[79] See below, pp. 132, 134.

hands. In Skinner's case, in the later 1660s, it was deployed by laymen, with alarming implications for both parliament and courts. The case supplied the background to Hale's last important work, so it seems worth describing in detail the arguments involved. Thomas Skinner was a merchant, who had traded with the East in Cromwell's time. The agreed facts of the case were that he had been robbed, of goods, some ships, and an island, by the East India Company's local agents. He could be redressed in King's Bench for the loss of his goods and his ships but not, the judges ruled, for the Company's theft of an island outside the jurisdiction of King's Bench. Skinner therefore applied to the Lords to remedy his wrong, and the Lords imposed a fine on his opponents, against the opposition of the Commons.[80] The row began in 1667, and reached a heated climax in 1669.

A pamphlet by Lord Holles expressed their Lordships' view:

clearly by the judges own confession, part of the case was not within the power of Westminster Hall, and under favour of better judgement ... the doubt still [remains] with us, if some of the other points also, as that of the taking of the ship, a robbery committed *super altum mare*, be punishable by the law of Westminster Hall.[81]

Holles stressed that the House of Lords had no ambition to deal with any cases which could be settled at the common law. Nor did he wish to extend existing law, except where nature itself demanded redress. He wished to distinguish

between a fact not being a crime in the eye of the law, which is neither *malum in se* nor *malum prohibitum*, and when the fact itself being odious and punishable by all laws of God and man, only a circumstance, as the place where it was committed, puts it out of the power of the ordinary courts of justice ... in the second case God forbid that there should be such a failer of justice in a kingdom, that subjects should rob and worry and destroy one another though in foreign parts ...[82]

The Lords were 'the ordinary remedy in extraordinary cases',[83] an opinion that seemed innocent enough. He also asserted, however, their right to judge in any legal case, 'when some thing extraordinary ... did induce them ... of which they were the sole judges, that being the trust lodged with them by the very frame and constitution of the government'.[84] The fears that this evoked, of a steady drift to oligarchic rule, were shared, as we shall see, by Matthew Hale.

The civil judicature of the Lords, revived in 1621 with Sir Edward

---

[80] For all this, Cobbett, *State trials*, VI, 711–18; James S. Hart, *Justice upon petition: the House of Lords and the reformation of justice, 1621–1675*, 1991, pp. 243–50.
[81] Holles, *The grand question concerning the judicature of the House of Peers stated and argued*, 1669, pp. 28–9.
[82] *Ibid.*, 97–8.   [83] *Ibid.*, 99.   [84] *Ibid.*, 134.

Coke's support,[85] was a right to respond to petitions.[86] It was of some significance, in the minds of Hale and others, that their authority was not dependent on the issue of a writ from Chancery. Although they aimed to supplement the courts, rather than undermine the legal system, they were the only judges of when to use their power. The revival had alarmed Sir Robert Cotton (1589–1631), the learned patron and friend of most of the great scholars of the day. He reacted with *A brief discourse proving that the house of Commons hath equal power in matters of judicature*, which ended on a note of dark foreboding.[87] He saw a possibility, if the Lords were to capture the law, that 'monarchy again may sooner groan under the weight of an aristocracy as it once did than under a democracy which it never yet either felt or feared'.[88] In the later 1660s, such fears would strike a chord. Suspicion of the Lords was really a manifestation of the recurring English dread of any untrammelled court of equity. No one had an objection to their acting in appeals, proceeding on receipt of writs of error, as the apex of a hierarchy of courts.[89] The doubts concerned their claim to act outside the common law, providing their own remedies where the system was deemed not to do so; as a furious member put it, 'these people have a legislative conscience, pretending to a law in heaven to control the law upon earth'.[90]

The Commons case was very well expressed in a speech by Serjeant Maynard, Hale's colleague at the time of the London debate. The essential mark of common law was jury trial of fact: 'the judge may not try the fact, nor the juror the law'.[91] The Upper House, where juries were unknown,

---

[85] C. C. G. Tite, *Impeachment and parliamentary judicature in early Stuart England*, 1974, pp. 83–148 describes the sequence of events. See also J. Stoddart Flemion, 'Slow process, due process and the high court of parliament: a reinterpretation of the revival of judicature in the House of Lords in 1621', *Historical Journal*, 17 (1974), 3–16.

[86] The best guide to the issues is Hargrave's long introduction to Hale, *The jurisdiction of the Lords House or parliament considered according to ancient records*, ed. Francis Hargrave, 1794. For a helpful discussion of the Lords' constitutional position, see Henry Hallam, *The constitutional history of England*, 10th edn, 3 vols., 1886, vol. III, pp. 15–36. For a survey of the range of its activities, see James S. Hart, *Justice upon petition: the House of Lords and the reformation of justice*, 1991.

[87] *Cottoni posthuma*, 343–51. Discussed in Kevin Sharpe, *Sir Robert Cotton 1589–1631: history and politics in early modern England*, Oxford 1979, pp. 165–9.

[88] *Cottoni posthuma*, 351.

[89] Thus the Humble Petition and Advice, the conservative constitution of May 1657, provided 'that the Other House do not proceed in any civil causes, except in writs of error, in cases adjourned from inferior courts into the parliament for difficulty, in cases of petition against proceedings in courts of equity, and in cases of the privileges of their own House ... That they do not proceed in any cause, either civil or criminal, but according to the known laws of the land, and the due course and custom of parliament' (Kenyon, *Stuart constitution*, 327).

[90] Anchitell Grey, *Debates of the House of Commons from the year 1667 to the year 1694*, 10 vols., 1769, vol. I, p. 160.

[91] *Ibid.*, I, 448.

could never establish the facts of a previously undecided case. It was therefore a court of appeal, deciding points of law, when other courts had settled factual questions. To do so, it needed a writ from the king, transmitting the case in question to the Lords, and not a bare petition from a subject:

> the king is the original and fountain of all justice to his people, which is administered in several courts, one subordinate to the other, of which the Lords in parliament is or are the highest, by way of error. But though the judges in these several courts administer justice, yet the door into this court is not opened but by a key which the king sends under his seal.[92]

Hale's earliest contribution to this topic was a passage of his early 'Preparatory notes touching the rights of the Crown', his work from the 1640s on the prerogative. At some time after Skinner's case, he produced 'A discourse or history concerning the power of judicature in the king's council and in parliament'. It lacks any topical detail, but refers both to Lord Holles, and to the 'late *Animadversions*' (that is *Brief animadversions on ... the Fourth Part of the Institutes of the laws of England*, 1669), a great assault on Coke by William Prynne.[93] Both the 'Preparatory notes' and the much later 'Discourse' took the same constitutional line: that the 'king's council in parliament', a carefully chosen title, was not the House of Lords. The House of Lords proper, or 'magnum consilium', was distinguished from the 'consilium ordinarium or legale', which also included the judges and other legal servants of the Crown. Judicature in parliament was normally to be seen as the work of the *consilium legale*, though acting in conjunction with the whole of the House of peers.

There was a court that acted *with* the Lords, as opposed to a court *of* the Lords, and it drew upon the wisdom of the bench. Hale distinguished three different functions that the Upper House legitimately performed, but he stressed the vital role the judges played. First, it received petitions, transmitting them for judgement to one of the inferior jurisdictions.[94] Next, there were difficult cases, adjourned to the Council from a lower court. This function had been largely taken over by the common law judges in Exchequer Chamber (where the judiciary collectively considered most of the period's great cases), because it was usual and proper to act on the bench's advice.[95] Lastly, there were appeals by writ of error, to overturn the judgement of some inferior court. These should be issued sparingly, and again on judicial advice. The whole process 'ought to be by the assent of the judges, who are experienced in the laws, by which judgements of

---

[92] *Ibid.*, I, 458.
[93] Lincoln's Inn, Hargrave 11. The Prynne reference is Hargrave 11, p. 6.
[94] *Ibid.*, 27–31.   [95] *Ibid.*, 32–48.

that kind ought to be squared'.[96] There was no escape, in other words, from the artificial reason of the law to the merely natural reason of the layman. Hale's treatment of 'failure of justice' was thoroughly dismissive, for it threatened to unsettle all the certainty of law. The technical procedures that made property secure quite often ruled out actions to regain a person's rights. It would be quite disastrous if the victim of such rules 'should entitle himself to relief in the Lords House because he was not relievable at common law. The reason holds not, for it is not relievable at common law because it ought not to be relievable by the established laws without an act of parliament.'[97]

In 1669, when the Skinner controversy reached its peak, the parliament was paralysed by the bitter disagreement of the Houses. Eventually the king imposed a truce, but the Lords had been effectively defeated. They never renewed their claim to act as a court of first instance, and the ground of battle shifted to a new judicial power. Suspicion of the Upper House resurfaced in the famous case of Shirley v. Fagg (1675). This was an appeal by petition against a judgement in the Chancery. Sir John Fagg, the defendant, happened to be a member of the Commons, and the privilege of the Commons was the focus of the subsequent debate. It nonetheless revived the claim that justice by petition was illegal, so it renewed the passions aroused by Skinner's case. The parliament was crippled, once again, and again the king was forced to intervene to stop all further action on both sides. This time, the Lords were victors, for the appeals from Chancery continued, but perhaps the breach of privilege was the real point at stake.

In 1675–76, Hale duly returned to the question, this time with some 'Preparatory notes touching the parliamentary proceedings', whose principal novel feature was a detailed exploration of the Lords' place in appeals from Chancery.[98] A third and final manuscript, indebted to both of the former, was printed by Francis Hargrave (?1741–1821), with a preface of astounding erudition, as *The jurisdiction of the Lords House* (1796). The second and third of these works were of markedly similar structure. Both started by asserting as a basic legal truth that jurisdiction flows from royal power.[99] The King of England governed through four councils: the *consilium privatum* (privy council), the *magnum consilium* (the Lords spiritual

---

[96] *Ibid.*, 49–59.   [97] *Ibid.*, 76.

[98] The original is lost. Hargrave's transcript is Lincoln's Inn, Hargrave 6. Hale characteristically noted that the equitable side of the chancery, from which Dr Shirley had hoped to appeal, was no more than an excrescence on this system, but one which 'hath now so long obtained, and is so fitted to the disposal of lands and goods, that it must not be shaken'. (Hale, *The jurisdiction of the Lords House, or parliament, considered according to ancient records*, ed. Francis Hargrave, 1796, p. 46.)

[99] Hale, *Jurisdiction*, 1; Hargrave 6, fo. 1.

and temporal), the *commune consilium* (parliament), and what he called
the 'consilium ordinarium'.[100] The *consilium ordinarium*, as Hale very
freely admitted, was a body whose membership was rather vague, embracing the great officers of the kingdom, the judges, the officials of the
household, and of course the whole *consilium privatum*.[101] It was a

> constellation or collection of persons, fitted to advise upon several occasions, and
> when they were called together, it was styled plenum consilium. But when the
> business were of a more contracted nature, and fell more specially under the
> cognizance of some of his council, then those were called to it that were fittest to
> advise about it; as the Chancellor and the judges when the advice concerned
> matters in law . . .[102]

Thus the judges of England collectively could claim to be an embodiment
of the council, and it was in this capacity that they advised the Lords. Any
authority to judge that the Upper House enjoyed was derived from this
council's presence in its ranks.

Hale insisted that the Lords themselves were no more than a 'magnum
consilium', 'barely a council of advice and not a court of jurisdiction'.[103]
He admitted the judges appeared to have been reduced to advisers themselves, but he stressed that judicial opinions had

> been always the rules whereby the Lords do or should proceed in matters of law,
> especially between party and party; unless the case be so momentous, that they are
> not fit for the determination of judges, as in questions touching the right of
> succession to the crown . . . or the privileges of parliament . . . or the great cases
> which concern the liberties and rights of the subject, as in the case of Ship Money,
> and some others of like universal nature.[104]

These cases of transcendent consequence were a matter for the parliament
considered as a whole, for the ultimate appeal, in interpreting a law, was to
the institution that had made it. There was no point in making law if
another jurisdiction could pervert it: 'wherever the dernier resort is, there
must needs be the sovereignty'.[105] Even in an impeachment (when someone
accused by the Commons was tried before the Lords), the Lords were not
acting alone: the trial 'might be said to be done *in pleno parliamento*, both

---

[100] Hale, *Jurisdiction*, 5–13.   [101] *Ibid.*, 4–10.   [102] *Ibid.*, 6.
[103] Hargrave 6, 18–19.
[104] Hale, *Jurisdiction*, 159.
[105] *Ibid.*, 205. There is no evidence that Hale read Filmer, but the same thought appears in
The free-holders grand inquest (1648): 'if the dernier resort be to the Lords alone, then
they have the supremacy' (Sir Robert Filmer, *Patriarcha and other writings*, ed. Johann
P. Sommerville, Cambridge 1991, p. 114). The expression 'dernier resort', along with the
doctrine Hale and Filmer share, can be traced to Bodin's *Six livres de la Republique*. It is
not used, however, in either the Latin or the English versions (the ones that Hale was
likely to have read). On Bodin, Hale, and the Lords, see also Ulrike Krautheim, *Die
Souveränitätskonzeption in den englischen Verfassungskonflikten des 17. Jahrhunderts*,
Frankfurt 1977, pp. 426–7.

Houses being present; and yet the judgement itself given by the Lords, though in presence of the Commons and thus far by their tacit consent, as being the accusers and present at the judgement'.[106] The highest 'extra-ordinary court' was therefore parliament.

The highest ordinary court was indeed the House of Lords (though only when it acted on a writ), but its power must be exercised in line with common law. It could not find a remedy where

in truth there is no law already established for their relief, though it may be just and reasonable, that a law should be provided for the case or cases of like nature ...

... the House of Lords hath no jurisdiction or power of relief in such cases, for that were to give up the whole legislative power unto the House of Lords. For it is all one to make a law, and to have an authoritative power to judge according to that, which the judge thinks fit should be law, although in truth there be no law extant for it.[107]

Hale's main constitutional writings span more than thirty years, but they have a great consistency of outlook. The 'Incepta de Juribus Coronae' (1643–44), and the *Jurisdiction of the Lords House* (1676) describe a kingdom ruled through various councils. The king was in principle sovereign, though checked by historic agreements, whose content was known to the lawyers of Westminster Hall. This law was quasi-statutory in force, though some of it began as simply custom. The *History of the common law* explained, with subtlety unique in his tradition, that law with beginnings in statute would come to have a customary nature. The system developed the character described by Edward Coke, although it had its origins in contract. His synthesis was brilliantly contrived, and even, to a kindly eye, coherent. The latter quality was harshly tested by the pressures of the Restoration bench.

---

[106] Hale, *Jurisdiction*, 18. Hale's view of the king's role in this was left very obscure.
[107] *Ibid.*, 108–9.

8

Restoration: legal practice

A proper assessment of Hale as a judge would involve assessment of his whole profession, at a puzzling transitional moment in the history of the law. The law of 1642 was easily restored, but the culture of the lawyers had undergone a change. The formal part of legal education, the 'readings' and the exercises of the Inns of court, was killed by the disruption of the previous eighteen years.[1] This ritualistic process (whose details are of no importance here) was less and less connected with the student's actual needs, but it must have had some formative effects.[2] Two features seem especially important: the assumption it made that all learning was basically oral; and the way it involved the profession (through taking part in exercises at each Inn of court) in training up replacements for its ranks. A 'reading' at his Inn (a kind of lecture series on a statute) was traditionally the climax of an advocate's career, a symbol of the intimate connection between practising and passing on the law.

Hale recognised a duty to teach the law he knew. North used to see him, when he was Chief Justice,

> managing matters of law to all imaginable advantage to the students, and in that he took pleasure or rather pride. He encouraged arguing when it was to the purpose, and used to debate with the counsel; so that the court might have been taken for an academy of sciences, as well as the seat of justice.[3]

Almost the only point on which Hale and North were in complete agreement was in their advocacy of resorting to the sources of the law. North regretted that 'industry and order in the law ceased with order and peace in the state',[4] and praised the generation of 'Jones,[5] Windham, Rolls,

---

[1] Prest, *Inns*, 115–36; W. C. Richardson, *A history of the inns of court: with special reference to the period of the renaissance*, Baton Rouge 1975, pp. 167–210; Baker, *Profession*, 31–8.

[2] For some reflections on this theme see J. H. Baker, 'The Inns of court and legal doctrine', in T. M. Charles-Edwards *et al.* (eds.), *Lawyers and laymen: studies in the history of law presented to Professor Dafydd Jenkins*, pp. 274–83.

[3] Roger North, *A discourse on the study of laws*, 1824, p. 32–3. [4] *Ibid.*, 19.

[5] Probably Sir Thomas (1614–92).

Maynard, and Hales',[6] who had risen to the top of their profession by reading through and mastering every surviving Year Book of the medieval law.

Hale's only published legal work was a preface to Rolle's *Abridgement* (1668), consisting largely in advice to students. The *Abridgement* was never intended for publication, as it was just Rolle's 'commonplace', a notebook of points from his reading, alphabetically arranged by subject heading. Hale presented it as a model for the student, who might care to proceed by annotating Rolle, 'it being printed on purpose with a large margin for the addition of such cases as are here omitted'.[7] Hale practised what he preached, leaving a monumental compilation, his 'Black Book of the new law', and also a volume of 'Preparatory collections additional to my Lord Rolle's'.[8] This suggests the book was used as a companion while going through the Year Books and Reports.

Hale was prepared to contemplate 'for ordinary study' a 'complete corpus juris communis ... extracted out of the many books of our English laws'. But such a compilation would be 'a work of time', requiring 'many industrious and judicious hands and heads'.[9] Like every reform Hale envisaged, it would itself depend upon the 'reason' of the finest professional minds. For the present, there were no short cuts to learning; immersion in the sources, recapitulating Rolle, was the only way to 'artificial' reason, the grasp upon the system that professionals enjoyed. These educational ideas must have had some connection with a sense of the law as tradition, a knowledge best exhibited in action, rather than as a doctrine to be summarised in books. As Coke had much earlier put it, 'by reasoning and debating of grave learned men the darkness of ignorance is dispelled, and by the light of legal reason the right is discerned'.[10] 'Reason' was an activity, the thing that lawyers did, as much as a series of principles that they had memorised. Hale's 'strong' judicial style, his confidence manipulating law, was surely at least related to this old-fashioned view.

These general remarks are just conjectures, on a subject that eludes direct research. A question with related implications, important for an estimate of Hale, is the degree of unity on the Restoration bench. An 'artificial' reason was appropriate to a unified profession, in which a

---

[6] North, *Discourse*, 19–20.
[7] Hargrave, *Collectanea juridica*, 276–8. A remote ideological descendant, Michael Oakeshott, supplies an interesting echo: 'the solicitor can use his own (annotated) copy of Pollock on *Partnership* or Jarman on *Wills* more readily than any other. Familiarity is of the essence of tool-using; and in so far as man is a tool-using animal he is disposed to be conservative' (Oakeshott, *Rationalism in politics and other essays*, 1962, p. 179).
[8] Lincoln's Inn, Hale MS 121 (191); William Andrews Clark Memorial Library. Uncatalogued but identifiable as Selden–Hale Additional MS 2.
[9] Hargrave, *Collectanea juridica*, 276. [10] Coke, *First institutes*, 232b.

collective wisdom could fairly be invoked. The evidence is mixed, but judicial solidarity was certainly a force. The most liberal of the judges, on almost any measure, was certainly Hale himself; the most authoritarian was the peppery John Kelyng (Justice of King's Bench 1663; Chief Justice 1665–71), who had spent the best part of two decades in parliamentary gaols.[11] A symbolic treason case, that of Messenger and others, gives a flavour of their difference in approach. It concerned an apprentice disturbance with a frightening political tinge.[12] The rioters had sacked some bawdy houses, a not unusual target for such groups, but 'some of them said that unless the King would give them liberty of conscience, May Day should be a bloody Day'.[13] Worst of all, they threw some stones at Sir Philip Howard, believing him to be the Duke of York. Kelyng was thoroughly alarmed, and resolved to

make greater examples, that the people may know the law is not wanting so far to the safety of the king and his people, as to let such outrages go without capital punishment, which is at this time absolutely necessary because we ourselves have seen a rebellion raised by gathering people together on fairer pretences than this was.[14]

Hale saw the leading culprits with more sympathetic eyes, as 'but an unruly company of apprentices', and he was the only judge to oppose their condemnation for high treason.[15]

On another well-known occasion, the trial of Thomas Tonge (for planning a 'rising', encouraged by government spies), Hale was found in a minority of two. He wanted to reject some evidence secured in exchange for a promise of a pardon.[16] His attitudes were creditably constant, for he made a very similar point, eleven years before, when acting for the defence of the presbyterian royalist Christopher Love.[17] Hale was evidently relatively relaxed about the monarchy's security needs, and distaste for the government's tactics was probably connected with his feeling for dissent. It should be admitted, however, that the common law had a libertarian streak which needed no religious reinforcement. In Hopkin Huggett's case, a man was prosecuted for killing a naval officer who had press-ganged his friend. Eight out of the twelve judges inspiringly declared that

if a man be unduly arrested and restrained of his liberty by three men, although he be quiet himself, yet this is a provocation to all other men of England, not only his friends but strangers also, for common humanity sake, as my Lord Bridgeman said,

---

[11] DNB.

[12] Treated in Tim Harris, *London crowds in the reign of Charles II: propaganda and politics from the Restoration until the exclusion crisis*, Cambridge 1987, pp. 82–91.

[13] Cobbett, *State trials*, VI, 898.   [14] *Ibid.*, 897.

[15] Hale, *Historia*, I, 134. On the textual history of this passage, see P. R. Glazebrook, Introduction to his 1981 reprint in the series 'Classical English law texts'.

[16] Cobbett, *State trials*, VI, 227–8.   [17] *Ibid.*, V, 240–3.

to attempt his rescue, and if in such endeavour of rescue they kill any one, this is no murder but only manslaughter.[18]

Inevitably, Kelyng disagreed.

It is no surprise to find that the cavalier Lord Chief Justice was generally at variance with Hale, but the legal situation had unexpected quirks. Thus Kelyng took the 'Whiggish' view that Chief Justices held office for their lives, while Hale believed they could be sacked at will.[19] On occasion, the judges united to resist an outsider's demand. At a most important moment, June 1662, the king had considered suspending the new Uniformity Act. The judges refused to confirm his right to do so, a refusal they consistently sustained.[20] They were equally intransigent, in 1668, when asked about the status of some customs. The parliament had made a two year grant, expressly for the purpose of paying for the fleet. The government asked the judges if the grant was 'absolute' (if the disappointed Houses could revoke it) and if the customs granted could be farmed.[21] The former question they refused to answer; the latter one they orally denied. Their spokesmen were Twysden and Kelyng, who were neither of them noticeably hostile to the King.

They must have been reminded of a similar affair, the 'extra-judicial' opinions of 1634–35, when the judges agreed that Ship Money was legal. As Kelyng himself recorded,

our great reason was not that we doubted but that the king had a certain interest in the duty for two years, but in case we had declared a certain interest, then the king might have sold the same for what he pleased, and so disappointed the guard of the seas, which was the design of the Act. And though we could not suspect the king, yet if ill use had been made of it, the blame would have been laid on us.[22]

The government repeated its attempt, but the judges sent a note (unsigned), declining to reply, 'inasmuch as several matters depending on the same question may judicially come before us'.[23] Kelyng retained a copy, which they signed, as insurance against any future trouble.[24]

The judges were quite capable of a united front, if their collective interest was threatened. The ultimate government sanction, dismissal from the bench, was used only once in the earlier part of the reign. Our knowledge of the episode is drawn from a single source: the minutes of the Committee for Foreign Affairs.[25] This body had resolved, on 1 December

---

[18] Kelyng 60.   [19] Burnet, *Life*, 102; Middle Temple, Treby MS report, 564.
[20] George R. Abernethy Jun., 'Clarendon and the Declaration of Indulgence', *Journal of Ecclesiastical History*, 11 (1960), 62.
[21] Lincoln's Inn, Miscellaneous 501, pp. 12–13.   [22] *Ibid.*, 12.   [23] *Ibid.*, 13.
[24] *Ibid.*, 13.
[25] PRO, S.P. 104/177, fo. 101.

1672, that Hale and his colleague Archer be dismissed.[26] The latter was removed from his official duties, retaining however his salary and patent, which could not be removed without a cause.[27] (This incidentally shows that a patent 'dum se bene gesserit' was not the safeguard which is often claimed). The dismissal of Hale was delayed until after the end of the parliamentary session,[28] and in the event the government lost its nerve.

This pattern was repeated, and may suggest faintheartedness in Charles. In 1676, when Danby's cavaliers were in command, the distinguished future Whig Sir Robert Atkyns escaped from a sacking through influence at court.[29] Ellis, the replacement for Archer, was 'looked upon as a disaffected person', at least from Danby's Anglican perspective, but Danby had to be 'unmannerly' before Charles was persuaded to dismiss him.[30] A couple of years later, when further change was mooted, the government was fearful of the outcry which was likely to result: 'there being now such jealousies of an arbitrary government, people would not believe the Lord Chief Justice [Hale's successor Richard Rainsford, 'who most commonly slept on the bench'] was laid aside for his incapacity for the place.'[31] In later years the Crown became much bolder (in the next reign, of course, it made very sweeping changes) but up to Hale's retirement it was hardly to be feared.[32]

The common law remained, for Charles as for Oliver Cromwell, a way to claim prerogatives and a badge of legitimate rule. Direct intimidation of the bench was politically impracticable, and was never at all seriously attempted. It would be wrong, it follows, to attribute Hale's minority decisions to nothing but his probity and courage, and to dismiss his colleagues as supine royal tools. His motives are hard to recover, partly because the evidence is scanty, but it seems that his boldest behaviour was

---

[26] A possible reason for the sackings was concern for martial law. The committee had been told, a couple of months before, that 'Lord Chief Justice Kelyng always allowed [the judges] were to ask leave before they arrested a soldier' (PRO, S.P. 104/177, 92v). His successor was unlikely to show the same restraint. They discussed the matter again on December 15 (S.P. 104/177, 120v.), the meeting after Archer was dismissed. His successor on the bench was William Ellis, the author of the government's new Articles of War (S.P. 104/177, 91v.).

[27] Gray's Inn MS 34, p. 724; Sir T. Raymond 217.   [28] PRO, S.P. 104/177, 101.

[29] *Correspondence of Henry Hyde, Earl of Clarendon*, ed. S. W. Singer, 1828, vol. I, p. 3; *Correspondence of the family of Hatton*, ed. E. M. Thompson, Camden Society, 2 vols., 1878, vol. I, p. 132.

[30] *Hatton correspondence*, I, 132.   [31] *Ibid.*, I, 164.

[32] This is substantially the conclusion of A. L. Havighurst. 'The judiciary and politics in the reign of Charles II', *Law Quarterly Review*, 66 (1950), 62–78, supported by Howard Nenner, *By colour of law: legal culture and constitutional politics in England 1660–89*, Chicago 1977, pp. 76–7. For a highly important case study, which proves that the judges had minds of their own at the climax of the panic aroused by the Popish plot, see J. P. Kenyon, 'The acquittal of Sir George Wakeman: 18 July 1679', *Historical Journal*, 14 (1971), 693–708.

prompted by a sympathy for the sufferings of dissent. At times, as we shall see, he just applied the theory that he learned from Selden's works, treating the law as an arbitrary creation of customary and statutory consent. There were, however, at least some occasions, all of them most inadequately reported, when he claimed for himself an authority that was more reminiscent of Coke. He departed from the letter of the law in the name of various charitable presumptions about the law's respect for the subject's rights. The discussion which follows is rather episodic, but several consistent themes emerge.

One way Hale used his influence was to dampen down hostility to alien legal ideas. It is striking, in so orthodox a sage of common law, that he spent ten years presiding (Michaelmas 1660 to Easter 1671) in a newly founded equitable court. The Exchequer was mainly concerned with deciding legal questions connected with the royal revenue. The 'equitable side', by a fairly natural development, helped debtors of the Crown recover money without which (they asserted) they would be prevented or hindered from paying their debts to the king. This service was made general, in 1649, by accepting bogus claims to debtor status.[33] That the use of this fiction survived, when so much was 'restored', was surely due to Hale.

This tolerance of equity was an advance on Coke. It was Hale, in 1671, who lifted a lingering threat: the charge of 'praemunire' against equitable courts. The essence of this crime, the diversion of law suits abroad, was obviously a practice of the Roman canon law (though it could be applied, by extension, to many other clerical misdeeds). To Coke and only Coke, its meaning was considerably wider. He quarrelled with Lord Ellesmere, defensibly enough, when the latter had tried to reverse a King's Bench judgement.[34] His reaction, less defensibly, was to accuse his foe of *praemunire*, for 'proceeding', he later explained, 'by the rule of another law'.[35] In King v. Standish, some fifty-five years later, the question was revived. Kelyng recommended that: 'the opinions of all the ... judges be had in it: we know what heats there were betwixt Lord Coke and Lord Ellesmere, which we ought to avoid.'[36] In the event, the parties reappeared in front of Hale, who 'held, that this case was not within the statute [of *praemunire*] and so he said it would appear by the petition whereon the statute was

---

[33] For this, see W. H. Bryson, *The equity side of the exchequer: its jurisdiction, administration, procedures and records*, Cambridge 1975, pp. 13–27.

[34] W. J. Jones, 'Conflict or collaboration? Chancery attitudes in the reign of Elizabeth', *American Journal of Legal History*, 5 (1961), 12–54, and Jones, *The Elizabethan Court of Chancery*, 1967, paint a peaceful picture of the common law's normal relations with equity. Coke's conduct in 1616 is convincingly defended, at least from a jurisprudential standpoint, in J. H. Baker, *The legal profession and the common law*, 1986, pp. 205–29.

[35] Coke, *Third institutes*, 122.   [36] 1 Modern 61.

founded.'[37] In this he agreed with Lord Ellesmere, and indeed with common sense.[38] The matter was instantly settled, but it had genuinely been in doubt.

In Fisher v. Patten (1671), a slightly later case, a lesser jurisdiction was attacked. The palatine Duchy of Lancaster, the source of many knotty legal problems, was founded well within the time of memory. For reasons no one knew, it had an equitable court.[39] This court was theoretically illegal; no one suggested it was based on statute, and it was very far from immemorially old. Hale's argument was typically pragmatic: 'how their court of equity came to be does not plainly appear ... but [Hale] and Twysden both [agreed] it might be inconvenient to examine their power after so long continuance and practice ...'[40] The requirements of orderly justice, demanding respect for long usage, would always trump the legal rule defining 'immemorial' as 'older than 1189'.

Under Hale's guidance, then, the common law was tolerant of equitable courts. He acted with a similar restraint towards the church's system of English canon law. The issues were thoroughly aired in the revealing law suit of Manby v. Scott (1663). Dame Scott had left her husband and run up a debt with Manby, a draper, for apparel 'suitable to her station'. Scott had warned the local tradesmen that he would not pay her debts. Manby nonetheless sued Scott. Scott had a legal duty to support his errant wife.[41] The disagreement centred on the means by which he was to be compelled to do so. The traditional authority between a man and wife was the bishop of the diocese in which the couple lived. He had powers to decree a separation 'a mensa e thoro',[42] and to establish alimony for the wife's support. If Manby won his case, then the common law would in effect have usurped the bishop's role.[43]

The events to which the legal case referred had taken place in interregnum times. Under the circumstances, in the absence of the bishops and

---

[37] 1 Levinz 243. The fullest report is Middle Temple, Treby MS report, 602–3.

[38] Louis A. Knafla, *Law and politics in Jacobean England: the tracts of Lord Chancellor Ellesmere*, p. 324.

[39] This must have been quite useful, because its jurisdiction was confirmed in 1654, and Hale himself had a commission to sit there while on assize in the North-west. (Firth, *Acts and ordinances*, III, 916, 921).

[40] 2 Levinz 24. See also Middle Temple, Treby MS report, 628.

[41] The courts of the interregnum had recognised this duty, in the case of Yeane v. Browne, where it was held that 'albeit the wife be obstinate and will not cohabit with her husband, yet the law will not suffer the wife in such case to perish for want of maintenance' (Folger, V.b.6, 70).

[42] From bed and board.

[43] The existence of alimony was clearly much resented, at least among enemies of the church courts, because it was twice debated in the Convention Parliament, where a bill said to be very 'severe upon the women' reached committee (Cobbett, *Parliamentary history*, IV, 143, 145).

their courts, the common law adapted to supply the legal void. If Manby v. Scott had been discussed when it arose, the judges would no doubt have favoured Manby. Orlando Bridgeman recognised this point, in his elaborate argument for Scott:

necessity made it more excusable in those judges, if, where they found no remedy they made one; especially when there was not then nor like to be any legal parliament, consisting of a King and two Houses of parliament to have by an Act of parliament supplied the defect. It was on the same ground they allowed suits for legacies at the common law [Eeles v. Lambert]; and that upon an elegit they adjudged the sheriff might extend ecclesiastical tithes [Harwood v. Paty] which was contrary to the common law before. But the reason in both cases and so openly adjudged was because the bishops and ecclesiastical courts were taken away ... Will you allow these opinions to be law now, because they were the practice then?[44]

Like Matthew Hale on Skinner's case (but not, as we shall see, on other questions) Bridgeman refused to supplement the remedies of the existing law. If the law in some way failed, then legislation was the only cure.

Hale just ignored the interregnum judgements, presumably on Justice Bridgeman's grounds. The arguments with which he was concerned, like many others mentioned in this book, were appeals to overriding natural law. Justice Twysden thought that 'this concerns her being. In case of necessity the law would give me power over another man's goods, as if in a boat there is great danger of drowning I may justify the throwing them overboard.'[45] Twysden himself believed that alimony was not a part of English canon law.[46] Others recognised the remedy's existence, but doubted (very reasonably) that it was of practical use. The church's sanction, excommunication, was easy for a husband to ignore. Justice Tyrrell made the point that 'the process of excommunication is but a civil and not spiritual obligation and medicinalis not mortalis therefore obedience to it not always to be presumed and in what case is the wife then ...'[47]

Hale's answer was the one he learned from Selden. The canon law was part of English law, binding because the common law allowed it.

for her inconveniences the law has appointed the bishops to oversee, and whereas it is said this is not the common law I answer they are [the] jurisdiction appointed by the common law and though their coercions and proceedings are after another law yet their derivation as to their use here was from the common law.[48]

So far as the law was concerned, an excommunication was a perfectly adequate threat, which might, at least in theory, result in close confinement until the man complied: 'And concerning the amplitude of their power

[44] Bridgeman, O., 250.   [45] Lincoln's Inn, Hill MS 83, 17.   [46] *Ibid.*, 18.
[47] *Ibid.*, 40.
[48] *Ibid.*, 46.

which is not said to be able to administer a medicine for this disease I say as it is by the *brachium seculare*[49] the power of it falls as severely on them that disobey it as the common law can use when men won't pay their debts.'[50] The reality, of course, was that excommunication was an ineffective power, but this was a point of no interest to the Seldenian judge. The canon law in England was law because the English had approved it, whatever its deficiencies in meeting social needs.

Approaching such a judgement after reading Edward Coke, one is struck by the lack of assertiveness in the Restoration bench. Coke would surely have discovered some solution that satisfied the wants of the fugitive wife. His intellectual confidence was perhaps an unrepeatable extreme, which only Hale, of all these men, was likely to approach. But it was obviously of some importance that the author of the common law's most influential books was more of an activist than his successors. Coke gave the lawyers an intellectual tool, a rhetoric for expanding judicial discretion, that most of them were disinclined to use. This was nowhere more significant than in treating of the power to dispense.

Dispensation was the great constitutional issue of the period 1660–88. The king wished to protect his papist subjects from the effects of various penal laws. One way in which this end could be achieved was by suspending all the laws in question, but another, quite possibly legal, was by piecemeal dispensation (remission of the penalties that parliament imposed). The scope of the king's power of dispensation was therefore uniquely politically charged. In Thomas v. Sorrell (1674),[51] the era's best reported single suit, the question was exhaustively explored. Apart from the case's political importance, it was a test of attitudes to law, involving, as a brief account will show, a typically bold claim by Edward Coke.

The traditional distinction between acts that the king could dispense with and acts that he could not was based on an appeal to natural law: a *malum in se*, an intrinsically evil offence, was not susceptible of dispensation; a crime at municipal law (*malum prohibitum*) could be permitted by prerogative. Coke's doctrine on the subject, combining ambiguity and boldness, is to be found in his report on the famous monopolies case. The case involved a licence for the sole importation of playing cards (an import forbidden by statute), that was granted, or so Coke inferred, for a courtier's personal gain. To play at cards (the court agreed) was *malum*

---

[49] 'The secular arm', i.e. the common law.   [50] Hill MS 83, 46.
[51] The published reports give a full picture of this case. The only MS material not better reported in print is Hale's own judgement, for which see Lincoln's Inn, Miscellaneous MS 555, fos. 13v.–17 (numbered on verso). The earlier history of dispensation is usefully summarised in Carolyn A. Edie, 'Tactics and strategies: Parliament's attack on the royal dispensing power, 1597–1689', *American Journal of Legal History*, 29 (1985), 197–234.

prohibitum only, an offence with which the Crown was perfectly entitled to dispense, at least for particular purposes at particular places and times.[52] But 'when the wisdom of Parliament' (a highly significant phrase)

has made an Act to restrain pro bono publico the importation of many foreign manufactures to the intent that the subjects of the realm might apply themselves to the making of the said manufactures &c. and thereby maintain themselves and their families with the labour of their hands; now for a private gain to grant the sole importation of them to one or divers (without any limitation) notwithstanding the said Act, is a monopoly against the common law and against the end and scope of the Act itself; for this is not to maintain and increase the labours of the poor cardmakers within the realm, at whose petition the Act was made, but utterly to take away and destroy their trade and labours, and that without any reason of necessity, or inconveniency in respect of person place or time, and eo potius, because it was granted in reversion for years, as hath been said, but only for the benefit of a private man, his executors and administrators, for his particular commodity, and in prejudice of the commonwealth.[53]

This passage was ambiguous in a way completely typical of Coke. It appealed to a conception of intention, the 'end and scope of the Act', but also to the court's beliefs about the public good. For Coke himself there was no contradiction, as parliament's intentions were informed by the infinite wisdom of perfected common law. His legacy for other minds was two distinct ideas, both of them still available in 1674. Some lawyers thought that royal dispensation should not defeat the purpose of an Act,[54] but others held that Coke proposed a rule: that a law 'pro bono publico' was indispensable.[55] This gave the court discretion, through judging 'public good', to control the royal power of dispensation.

The legal core of Thomas v. Sorrell is relatively simple to describe (though numerous side issues were involved). A parliamentary statute of the reign of Edward VI forbade the sale of wine without a licence, but James I dispensed with this enactment in a patent to the Vintners Corporation. The patent allowed corporation members the right to sell wine retail in every corporate town. Justice Windham summarised the implications: 'by this means all laws might be blowed up; for as the King dispenses with this law to this corporation, so he may with another to another, and so ad infinitum; nay, it would be but making a corporation of dissenters, and then he might dispense with them too.'[56] There were thus two separate grounds on which the dispensation might be challenged: that the Act itself

---

[52] Coke, *Eleventh reports*, 88a.   [53] *Ibid.*

[54] Ireland, *Exact abridgement*, 436–7. Davies, *Perfect abridgement*, 291 is ambiguous on this point. See also, Folger, V.b.6, fo. 45.

[55] Henry Rolle, *Un Abridgement des plusieurs cases et resolutions del common ley per Henry Rolle serjeant del ley*, 1668, 2 vols. in 1, title prerogative le roy, p. 179; Hardres 110.

[56] 1 Freeman 87.

was not dispensable; and that dispensation in perpetuity, to a body with a membership of undetermined size, was really just as good as a repeal.

Both parties were agreed that selling wine was 'naturally' permitted (though drunkenness resulting was regarded as *malum in se*). It had been legal at common law until the statute of King Edward's time. This did not prove, however, that the Edwardian law could be dispensed with. The counsel opposed to the patent were keen to invoke Edward Coke. They maintained, to quote Hale's own judicial notebook, that laws were indispensable if they made for the public good: '11 Reports, monopolies case, the sole importation void 1. because contrary to the public good ...'[57] An overlapping principle, occasioning much intricate debate, was that the king could not permit a 'nuisance'. The Act of 1665 forbidding the importation of Irish cattle had declared the trade a nuisance, thus shielding the statute from the king's dispensing power. Obstruction of the highway was a nuisance, which perhaps explained another known exemption: the statutory duty to repair a public bridge was something that no monarch could dispense with.[58]

The most famous of the judgements was that of Hale's friend Vaughan. Vaughan recognised the essence of the problem, the existence of *mala prohibita* with which kings could not dispense: 'with *malum prohibitum* by statute indefinitely understood the King may dispense. But I deny the King can dispense with every *malum prohibitum* by statute, though prohibited by statute only.'[59] A crime that could not be dispensed with was a 'nuisance', but nuisances were difficult for lawyers to define. Distinctions based on 'public good' were useless, as every law was for the public good: 'as the laws of nuisances are *pro bono publico*, so are all generall penal laws; and if a nuisance cannot be dispensed with for that reason, it follows, no penal law, for the same reason, can be dispensed with.'[60] The solution he adopted, in very much his mentor Selden's spirit, was to treat the nuisance as the fruit of contract. The nuisance of importing Irish cattle had been defined by parliamentary statute (Vaughan was in the House of Commons at the time). A nuisance at the common law was also once a statutory creation, as common law was nothing but lost statute:

if by accident the records of all acts of parliament now extant, none of which is older than 9 Henry III (but new lawes were as frequent before as since) should be destroyed by fire, or other casualty, the memorials of proceeding upon them found by the records in judicial proceeding, would upon like reason be accounted common law by posterity.[61]

---

[57] Lambeth 3478, 51v. '11 Reports case de monopolies le sole importation void 1. quia contrary al bien publique'.
[58] 1 Plowden 487.   [59] Vaughan 333.   [60] Vaughan 335.   [61] Vaughan 358.

The logical conclusion of this view, which Vaughan was quite ready to press, was the elimination of the notion of *malum in se*. The common law was created by the contracts that the English people made, and its content was in principle an arbitrary affair. The only true *malum in se* was an act which was a crime by definition, like murder or adultery or theft. A murder was 'unlawful killing'; to legalise a murder was to declare (nonsensically) that 'unlawful killing is lawful', a patent contradiction that not even a god could resolve.[62] A nuisance was an act defined as harmful, and could not be permitted while the definition stood. This left a simple loophole for the king: by dispensation with the definition (itself of course a statute) he was able to dispense with nuisance status. He could thus permit a nuisance at some given place and time; a permanent nuisance, however, could never be allowed, as permanent toleration of any harmful thing would defeat the only purpose of the act which had defined that thing as harmful.

This philosophical investigation went far beyond the situation's needs. It clearly showed, however, that the Edwardian act could be dispensed with. There was after all no evidence, from common law or statute, that the selling of wine was a nuisance, in Vaughan's contractual sense. A more perplexing question, for the purposes of Thomas v. Sorrell, was that of surreptitious abrogation. The exceptional scope of the patent, (affecting every vintner, in every corporate town, forever) struck some qualified observers as amounting to repeal. In answer to this powerful objection, Vaughan focussed on the legal rights involved. The king was always able to dispense, however sweepingly he used this power, so long as only he was assignably damaged. If a subject or subjects enjoyed a determinate right, which royal dispensation would affect, then the statute could not be dispensed with.

Vaughan's ruthlessly elegant judgement, available in polished form in print, has attracted more attention than Hale's less flamboyant argument. Hale's judgement seems pedestrian beside it, but their views on dispensation were in some ways rather close.[63] Hale probably never believed that laws 'pro bono publico' had any special status; the first time he appeared in the reports, in the Easter term of 1642, he had argued that 'where the subject has an immediate interest in an Act of parliament, there the King cannot dispense with it ... but where the King is entrusted with the managing of it, and the subject only by way of consequence, there he may.'[64] In Thomas v Sorrell he thought along similar lines. The king was always able

---

[62] Vaughan 335–6; Compare Hobbes, *De cive: the Latin version*, ed. Warrender, Oxford 1985, p. 210 (xiv, 10); Grotius, *De jure belli*, I, 12–13 (I, i, 5–6).

[63] The structure of his argument is greatly clarified by his own notes (Lambeth 3478, 186) and by Lincoln's Inn, Miscellaneous 555, 13v.–17, which are summarised in what follows. See also 3 Keble 268–71.

[64] March N.R. 214; Yale Law School MSS G.R. 29/25, fo. 368 (an almost identical French version from a manuscript in Hale's own possession).

to dispense with statute law, unless one of two courses was adopted. Prerogative was limited, as the treatise upon the customs had explained, by the existence of a 'ius privatum'. If the penalty exacted by the statute was given to the subject not the king, then a kind of *ius privatum* was created; the king could not dispense with such a statute without some damage to a private right. The other possibility, as the affair of Irish cattle showed, lay in declaring an abuse a nuisance, creating a 'ius publicum' to check the royal power. A nuisance (he agreed with Vaughan) was simply the fruit of a contract defining a given phenomenon as harmful.

King Edward's act took neither of these courses, so James had been entitled to dispense. There remained the awkward question (which Vaughan had effectively ducked) of limits on the royal patent's scope. A dispensation was by definition restricted to particular occasions, 'and this', so Hale believed, 'is the very point resolved in 11 Reports case of monopolies. A grant to Darcy to have the sole importation of cards without any limitation or stint is void'.[65] It followed that 'if this grant to the vintners be no other than a dispensation grounded and bottomed on the prerogative the reasons given against it ... are never to be answered'.[66] The vintners' patent was in fact a licence. A licence draws authority from parliamentary power and not from a prerogative inherent in the king. A dispensation 'neither repeals nor suspends the law but by anticipation avoids the penalty'; a licence can relax the obligation, something that only parliament can do.[67] The power to grant a licence is inferred from the statute concerned, and the penal laws relating to the wine trade seemed to envisage licensing on an extensive scale. The patent to the vintners, so far from defeating the purpose of the Edwardian act, was actually a product of the legislative will.

Hale brilliantly escaped from a dilemma that baffled all his colleagues on the bench. The Crown had always exercised discretion in licensing departures from statutory law. There was a great temptation to see this as an extra-legal power, a natural prerogative that courts could not control. The notion of public good, the nebulous conception drawn from Coke, offered no certain standard to which they could appeal. For Vaughan and Hale, reacting to this vagueness, prerogative was limited by certain concrete rights, by *ius privatum* (property) and by *ius publicum* (the nuisance as contractually defined). For Vaughan, these were the only limitations, and

---

[65] Lambeth 3478, 179v. In 1667, when writing on the customs, Hale offered the following summary of this passage: 'in that case, the King hath regularly power by a non obstante, though not in toto to abrogate it, yet in particular cases of particular quantities, or particular persons, and for a determinate time, to dispense with this law [forbidding import of cards], and to open the ports, notwithstanding this prohibition, but not with a general dispensation'. Hargrave, *Collection*, 93.

[66] Lambeth 3478, 179v.   [67] *Ibid.*, 185v.

patents as broad as the vintners' were perfectly permissible concessions. Hale took the sterner line that dispensation must be strictly measured. His message to King Charles, in other words, was that individual papists, in particular conditions, could temporarily be excused the penalties that statute had imposed. More general relaxation of any penal law was not a dispensation but a licence, an expression not of royal but of parliamentary power.

In Thomas v. Sorrell, the law was seen as a Seldenian contract. The other side to Hale's late jurisprudence, the side that drew on Coke, was to surface for a final time in Barnardiston v. Soame (1674). This case originated in a symbolic clash, the Suffolk by-election of 1673.[68] Sir Samuel Barnardiston, the head of a family noted for puritan feeling, had stood against a courtier opponent, the picturesquely named Lord Huntingtower. The division of opinion was predictable and sharp, at least as viewed by prejudiced observers. Barnardiston attracted the dissenters and the mob, while Huntingtower won the support of the mass of the Anglican gentry.[69] Barnardiston certainly won, but the sheriff (the Soame of the case) refused to acknowledge the fact. He therefore 'returned' both candidates, and left it to the Commons to decide. The Commons chose Barnardiston and fined the meddling Soame. Barnardiston, however, felt personally aggrieved, so he sued the unfortunate sheriff in King's Bench.

To Barnardiston's supporters, the merits of the case were obvious. The double return was illegal, as parliament had found. The sheriff had been fined, but only for breaking the rules; the damage Barnardiston suffered had never been redressed. A jury then established, on rather slender grounds, that Soame's error was both conscious and malicious. The Commons were competent judges of electoral returns; the jury were competent judges of the fact of the sheriff's intent. Barnardiston was therefore wronged, and the courts were obliged to avenge him. This at least was Hale's opinion. There was no question, as he stressed, of dictating to the House: 'C. J. Hale said twice to the bar, take notice we meddle not with the privilege of Parliament, we only pursue them, they have determined the right, we give damages for the wrong.'[70] This view in fact prevailed, by three votes against one.

Just after Hale retired (succeeded by his colleague Justice Rainsford,

---

[68] Cobbett, *State trials*, VI, 1063–120 includes almost all the important material. It can be interestingly supplemented by Gray's Inn MS 34, 771–2, by some 'General Considerations' of Francis North's (British Library, Additional MS 32, 519, fo. 133–5), and the account in Roger North, *Examen, or an enquiry into the credit and veracity of a pretended complete history*, 1740, pp. 516–26.

[69] *Calendar of State Papers Domestic*, Charles II, 1672–73, 597, 608; Ashcraft, *Revolutionary politics and Locke's two treatises of government*, Princeton 1986, p. 171.

[70] Gray's Inn MS 34, 772.

who cast the vote for Soame), the matter was argued again, this time by all the judges in the court of Exchequer Chamber. This stage of the debate was very much better reported, and the recorded arguments reveal what was really at stake. On one side were believers in the wisdom of the law, and its duty to adapt to new conditions.[71] There was a remedy at hand, the 'action on the case'. According to Sir Robert Atkyns, 'nothing is more frequent than actions upon the case, where an injury is done, and damage sustained'.[72] Inevitably, he referred to Coke, quoting the view that 'no wrong or injury, either public or private, can be done, but it shall be reformed or punished in one court or another, by due course of law', as well as the pithier dictum 'a failure of justice is abhorred in law'.[73] He needed, however, to answer an objection: it was not clear that damage was sustained, except through the loss of the honour attached to a knight of the shire.

This honour was a recent thing, as antiquarians knew, but Atkyns was untroubled by the fact. He was aware, and said so, that parliament itself was not immutable in form. Before de Montfort's time, the Commons left no trace. Nonetheless,

we must not be governed by historians in matters of law; and therefore, notwithstanding this observation of Sir Robert Cotton's and Mr Prynne's, we must presume that the House of Commons, and elections of knights of the shire, are as ancient as the common law and have been from time immemorial; because we find no written law that does first begin any such institution.[74]

The history the lawyers believed, the history found in Coke, was acknowledged as a kind of legal fiction. They looked, as a profession, to the present not the past: 'the common law does comply with, and conform to, the general opinion and genius of the Kingdom, and values, what they generally esteem and value, and disesteems what they value not.'[75] The obvious riposte, at least to modern eyes, is that of Francis North:

the laws are fitted to the genius of the nation; but when that genius changes, the parliament only is entrusted to judge of it, and by changing the law to make it suitable to it. But if the judges shall say it is common law, because it suits with the genius of the nation, they may take upon them to change the whole as well as any part of it, the consequence whereof may easily be seen; I wish we had not found it by sad experience.[76]

It might have been expected, from what is known about Hale's jurisprudence, that he would be found in support of Francis North. Hale's

---

[71] For an eighteenth-century controversy along similar lines, see David Liebermann, *The province of legislation determined: legal theory in eighteenth-century Britain*, Cambridge 1989, esp. pp. 133–43.
[72] Cobbett, *State trials*, VI, 1086.   [73] *Ibid.*, 1077.   [74] *Ibid.*, 1085.
[75] *Ibid.*, 1089.
[76] *Ibid.*, 1095.

writings in general suggested that he had parted company with Coke. It was certainly desirable that judges be consulted in the making of the law, but law was essentially contract, and the source of obligation was consent. If a grievance had no remedy in the existing law, then that was just the litigant's misfortune. As his work about the House of Lords had put it, 'it is not relievable at common law because it ought not to be relievable by the established laws without an act of parliament'.[77] In Barnardiston v. Soame, he appeared to relapse from this view, finding a novel remedy where he discerned a right. The judgement is hard to account for without reference to some extra-legal motives.

The only judges who agreed with Hale were Sir Robert Atkyns and Sir William Ellis (the two, by no coincidence, that Danby wished to sack). Atkyns at least was influenced by his general political outlook; he had defiantly remarked that 'there is a design to model the parliament to the humour of the court'.[78] Hale's views are very much harder to make out. Judicial activism, to give his style an uncontentious name, was not automatically Whig, and a rhetoric like Coke's, presenting all legal authority as deriving from the wisdom of the judge, could equally be turned to serve an absolutist king. But when Hale appeared to strain against the letter of the law the usual beneficiaries were opponents of the Anglican regime.

A comparable example of his Whiggish tendencies was the Exchequer case of Wagstaffe and others (1665).[79] The plaintiffs were all members of a jury. They had tried and acquitted some Quakers, in the face of Justice Kelyng's plain instructions, had been fined, and then imprisoned for non-payment. They appealed to the Exchequer for their fines to be removed. The crime of which the Quakers were accused was attending a conventicle, in breach of the previous year's Conventicles Act. They were said to be notorious as Quakers, and some of them had also carried Bibles, but the meeting had been silent, so the evidence against them was at best extremely slight. They could hardly have been guilty of sedition, a fact of great significance to Hale. We know this from a letter of September 1664, reporting that 'at Exeter the Quakers were through [Hale's] means found not guilty, because no sedition appeared under the exercise of religion, and the Act is not against religious meetings, but seditious conventicles.'[80] This incident must have been known to Wagstaffe and his friends, so it was not surprising that they went to Hale's court, the Exchequer, for relief. Hale

---

[77] Lincoln's Inn, Hargrave 11, 76.   [78] Cobbett, *State trials*, VI, 1079.

[79] For useful manuscript accounts, see Lincoln's Inn, Miscellaneous 499, 158; British Library, Lansdowne 1109, 180–1.

[80] H. P. to John Knowles, 30 September 1664. PRO, S.P. 29/102, no. 137. A private letter intercepted by the authorities. Both sender and receiver appear to have been Quakers themselves.

wanted to excuse them of their fine, by the common law writ of *certioriari*, on the grounds that he could see 'no other course for [them] to be discharged'.[81] The judges of his own court were divided, and the matter went against him when referred to the bench as a whole.

In *Historia placitorum coronae*, his criminal law textbook, this stance received an interesting defence. The fining of juries, in civil and criminal cases, was seen as a worrying trend. There were precedents, from the early 1660s, when Hale released such fines. It was a practice, he believed, 'of very ill consequence, for the privilege of an Englishman is, that his life shall not be drawn into danger without due presentment or indictment'.[82] He was backed, or so he claimed, 'by the advice of most of the judges of England'.[83] If so, he was deserted, when it came to Wagstaffe's case, for the judges held, with 'only one dissenting',[84] that he was not entitled to overturn the fine.

Hale's account was a little misleading, for the matter that was actually at issue was the right of the Exchequer to remit the penalty. Plenty of his contemporaries were uneasy about fining trial juries, and Kelyng was later rebuked in parliament for similar behaviour in an unconnected case.[85] The right of juries to ignore instructions was established, five years later, by the influence of Vaughan.[86] What marked Hale out, as in Barnardiston, was willingness to innovate when property or liberty was threatened. He would supply a remedy, enhancing the machinery of law, whenever folk were manifestly wronged. The law was not a list of remedies, as much in its practice and history would seem to suggest, but a reasonable system whose justice would not fail.

A presumption in favour of rights, as Chapter 6 suggested, harmonised very neatly with Hale's view of the natural state. The contracts which ended this phase would presumably secure the goods which natural man enjoyed. It is therefore no surprise to learn, from North and Burnet's *Life*, that Hale refused to bastardise the children of a marriage between Quakers.[87] He could have learned from Selden that marriage was not naturally a matter for the Church. Selden had shown, as his avid reader Milton had expressed it, that 'the clergy insinuated that marriage was not

---

81 Hardres 409, corroborated Lansdowne 1109, 180v.–181. The authority on *certioriari*, Edith G. Henderson, *Foundations of English administrative law: certioriari and mandamus in the seventeenth century*, Cambridge, Mass. 1963, makes no mention of its use in the Exchequer.

82 Hale, *Historia*, 160–1.   83 *Ibid.*, 158–60.   84 *Ibid.*, 160.

85 Grey, *Debates*, I, 67.

86 Thomas Andrew Green, *Verdict according to conscience: perspectives on the English trial jury 1200–1800*, Chicago 1985, pp. 200–64; Barbara Shapiro, *'Beyond reasonable doubt' and 'probable cause'*, Berkeley 1991, pp. 54–9; Vaughan 135–58.

87 Burnet, *Life*, 84.

holy without their benediction'.[88] Hale seems to have agreed, for he
declared that 'marriage and succession' should be respected as a 'right of
nature'.[89] But Selden also showed that natural right was shaped through
municipal law. There seemed to be no reason, in a nation such as England,
why forms of legal marriage (like the service in the Book of Common
Prayer) should not be defined by the state. Hale nonetheless preferred to
privilege his own conception of the natural.

The most that can be said, in conclusion to this survey of Hale's judicial
work, is that his sympathy towards dissent was consistent with some other
attitudes. A high view of the judge's role, as charged with maintaining
coherence in the system, could be harnessed for a variety of ends. When
combined with a sense that property was natural, and with a firm presumption that the law would give a remedy for wrongs, it obviously helped
defend a persecuted group. But a theory worth considering is that Hale's
tenderness for nonconformists was neither the cause nor the effect of these
features of his later jurisprudence: that his activism took a Whiggish form
because legal rights and puritan religion were both of them expressions of
God's will. In the first half of this book, the content of Hale's law has been
examined; to go a little deeper, and understand its purpose in his eyes, we
must now turn to his religious life.

---

[88] John Milton, *Complete works*, Columbia 1931, vol. VI, p. 72. Selden's shocking views are
set out in *De jure naturali*, Book V, and *Uxor Ebraica* (1640).
[89] Burnet, *Life*, 138.

Part II

RELIGION

9

Hale's 'puritanism'

Hale struck his own contemporaries as 'godly', on excellent, if superficial, grounds; he spoke deliberately and dressed in black. There are hints that the more rigorous had doubts, but competent observers were won over. Thus Major-General Whalley said, in 1656, that 'as he is an able, so upon good grounds I judge him a godly man', and Richard Baxter stressed, with the same implicit criticism in mind, that so far from being a 'righteous moral man', he was a paragon of true religion.[1] His sympathy with puritans undoubtedly ran deep; he was prepared to see religious feeling where others saw 'enthusiasts' and knaves, their cloak of irrationalist folly concealing seditious intent. Intellectually, however, he had much more in common with a very different group, with 'moral men' of younger generations who were hostile to subjective validations of the faith.

The problem Hale exemplifies is that of 'latitudinarian' religion. Most Restoration Anglicans had broken with the orthodoxy of the recent past, and were happy to associate all Calvinist beliefs with the supposed excesses of an antinomian fringe.[2] Such attitudes were not at all surprising in high episcopalians on the church's Laudian wing. The latitudinarians, by contrast, arrived at the same convictions by a rather different route.[3] They shared the anti-Calvinism of the heirs of Laud, and their suspicion of

[1] Thurloe *State papers*, IV, 686; Baxter, *Reliquiae Baxterianae*, 1696, Part III, p. 47. For some good examples of the phrase 'moral man', see J. Sears McGee, *The godly man in Stuart England: Anglicans, puritans and the two tables, 1620–1670*, New Haven 1976, pp. 251–2.

[2] For the relative homogeneity of Restoration Anglican beliefs, see John Spurr, *The Restoration Church of England 1646–1689*, Yale 1991, esp. pp. 29–104.

[3] Spurr has gone so far as to deny that 'latitudinarians' are usefully distinguished from their brethren: 'Latitudinarianism and the Restoration Church', *Historical Journal* 31, (1988), 61–2. This seems an overstatement; for a flavour of the difference, compare the attitudes towards dissent outlined in his own excellent 'Schism and the Restoration Church' (*Journal of Ecclesiastical History*, 41 (1990), 408–24) and John Marshall, 'The ecclesiology of the Latitude-men 1660–89: Stillingfleet, Tillotson and "Hobbism"', *Journal of Ecclesiastical History*, 36 (1985), 407–27. For a useful recent survey of latitudinarian writers, see Isabel Rivers, *Reason, grace and sentiment: a study of the language of religion and ethics in England*, Cambridge 1991, vol. I, pp. 25–88.

enthusiasts, but not their sacramental piety, still less their emphasis on rule by bishops, except as a convenient means of governing the church. They favoured 'comprehension' of dissenters, the dilution of Anglican practice to re-admit the nonconformist godly to the fold, but not the toleration of dissent. Hale's friends among this group were its most distinguished spokesmen: John Wilkins (1614–72), the Bishop of Chester, Wilkins' son-in-law, the future Archbishop Tillotson (1630–94), and Edward Stillingfleet (1635–99).[4] Each of these could be quoted out of context to suggest an almost deist attitude, a Christianity divorced from dogma and hardly more than ethical in content. They nonetheless believed their faith to be at least continuous with the historic mainstream of Protestant English belief. Hale offers a case study in an almost unaccountable transition.

Hale's education, it is clear, was puritan by any contemporary standards. It displeased the bigoted Tory mind of Anthony a Wood, and embarrassed the frankly Whiggish Gilbert Burnet. He was brought up, Wood noted with distaste, 'under severe puritans and under a puritanical discipline'.[5] His guardian Anthony Kingscot revealed the nature of his influence (also, admittedly, its limitations) by a denunciation of his son, who had joined 'the Popish army [that is the royalists], the enemies of God, his Church and this nation'.[6] According to Burnet, who spoke with almost tortured indirectness: 'being inclined to the way of those then called puritans, [he] put [Hale] to some schools that were taught by those of that party'.[7] Wood's bluntness has the relish of prejudice confirmed: Hale was entrusted to the 'scandalous vicar', a Mr Staunton, instead of Wotton's public grammar school.[8] He proceeded to Magdalen Hall, where his tutor was one Obadiah Sedgwick (?1600–58), then at the start of a career as a leading 'presbyterian' divine.[9] Sedgwick became the chaplain to England's leading general of the time, the very devoutly puritan Lord Vere.[10] Hale

---

[4] Burnet, *Life*, 74. Burnet also mentions Thomas Barlow (1607–91), the Bishop of Lincoln, probably on the strength of a letter now at Lambeth (Lambeth 3513, 128).

[5] Wood, *Athenae Oxonienses*, 3rd edn, 1813, vol. III p. 1091.

[6] H. P. R. Finberg, *Gloucestershire studies*, Leicester 1957, p. 164.

[7] Burnet, *Life*, 5.   [8] Wood, *Athenae*, III, 1091.

[9] Sedgwick was prominent enough for an unusually venomous article in Wood's high Anglican reference work *Athenae Oxonienses*. He preached a number of sermons to the Long Parliament, including two calls for religious persecution (*An ark against a deluge*, 1644; *The nature and danger of heresies*, 1647), which stamp him in a broad sense as 'presbyterian'. His theologically substantial works, which were posthumously printed, have no particular similarity to Hale's. For a marked difference see his idiosyncratic discussion (*The bowels of tender mercy sealed*, 1661, pp. 170–3) of the covenant of works.

[10] Burnet, *Life*, 5, 9. For Vere's religion, see Keith L. Sprunger, *The learned Doctor William Ames: Dutch backgrounds of English and American puritanism*, Urbana 1972, pp. 30–2.

nearly followed Sedgwick into a soldier's life (he was a most enthusiastic fencer) before instead deciding to enter Lincoln's Inn.[11]

All of these names and places had vaguely puritan associations. It is fair to add, however, that Hale himself made light of their effects. He made the conventional claim, in an Augustinian Christian of this time, that his childhood and young manhood had been 'full of lusts and sins'. He came to religion, he tells us, when he was twenty-five or twenty-six (in 1635–36).[12] In Burnet's edifying version, which may perhaps be doubted, the transition was dramatically abrupt:

> he did not at first break off from keeping too much company with some vain people, till a sad accident drove him from it, for he with some other young students, being invited to be merry out of town, one of the company called for so much wine, that notwithstanding all that Mr Hale could do to prevent it, he went on in his excess till he fell down as dead before them ... this did particularly affect Mr Hale, who thereupon went into another room, and shutting the door, fell on his knees and prayed earnestly to God, both for his friend, that he might be restored to life again; and that himself might be forgiven, for giving such countenance to such excess ...[13]

After the friend recovered, Hale abandoned his frivolous ways, and applied himself to a religious life. This is the only evidence of anything approaching a classic evangelical conversion, an event, if it occurred, that nowhere rates a mention in his writings. He never seems to have been very wicked, in thought, or word, or deed; though he harboured an attraction to the theatre, he had been spared, as he confessed, from any 'great transgressions'.[14] Perhaps as a result, he differed from most puritans in taking no great interest in himself, either as chief of sinners, or as a rescued saint. God's goodness to mankind, as opposed to particular men, was always his main focus of attention.

One of the great advantages in studying Hale's thought is that he summarised his starting point. *A discourse of the knowledge of God and of ourselves*,[15] published by Richard Baxter in 1688, was written, Baxter tells us, when Hale was about thirty or thirty-one (1639–41).[16] Baxter had read

[11] Burnet, *Life*, 5, 9. This story seems implausible but Burnet had no reason to invent it. The dates fit very well. Vere went back to the wars, after several seasons of absence, in 1629, recruiting several promising young men, including Thomas Fairfax, Philip Skippon and Jacob Astley (See D. N. B. under Vere). Hale entered Lincoln's Inn in April of that year.

[12] Lambeth 3500, 240.   [13] Burnet, *Life*, 8–9.

[14] *Ibid.*, 6; Hale, *A discourse of the knowledge of God and of ourselves*, 1688, sig. a3v; Lambeth 3500, 240.

[15] A title recalling the first sentence of Calvin's *Institutes*: 'true and substantial wisdom consists of two parts: the knowledge of God, and the knowledge of ourselves.' Jean Calvin, *Institutes of the Christian religion*, tr. John Allen, 2 vols., Philadelphia 1935, p. 46.

[16] Hale, *Discourse*, sig.a2.

the manuscript while Hale was still alive, and he discussed the contents with its author, admiring, in particular, the knowledge of the schoolmen it displayed. Hale answered, in effect, that everything he wrote was learned at Oxford. He mentioned Scotus, Suarez, and Aquinas, as well as several other names which Baxter then unluckily forgot.[17] The treatise was composed at the start of his career in legal practice, after a lengthy period immersed in the study of law.[18] Some passages show traces of Selden's influence, but this was less pervasive than it afterwards became.

Like many similar works, the *Discourse* is divided into two. It treats of nature before grace, of reason before scripture's revelation. To begin with, it proves the existence of God and the need for some kind of religion, without more than bare reference to specifically Christian beliefs. Its topic, the knowledge of God, demanded a treatment of knowledge, so it starts with a discussion of the ways in which God might be known. Epistemologically speaking, Hale took a traditional view. The soul was quite incapable of knowing any object 'till the object be some way applied to it'. There were three types of knowledge.[19] A supernatural knowledge, consisting in some 'principles of truth', was given at creation. These principles were 'not essential to the soul but a habit or quality, which God put into his understanding, and therefore though his knowledge decayed by his Fall, yet his soul continued the same.'[20] An artificial knowledge was 'derived from man to man', whether by speech or writing. It was by artificial means that 'the relics of the knowledge of God in Adam were derived to his posterity, though still it grew for the most part of men weaker and corrupter.'[21] The moral law of nature was a supernatural code, but it was handed down, like any other knowledge, 'by writing, speech, and other signs that are agreed to communicate intelligence from the understanding of one man to the understanding of another'.[22] It was revealed and not innate, an unearned grace and not a human virtue, transmitted, if at all, by fallible because linguistic means.

The final category was natural knowledge, derived, he thought, from 'simple apprehensions'. These were, of course, sensations, in keeping with the then old-fashioned tag that 'nil in intellectu nisi prius in sensu'. They were 'let into the phantasy and so shown to the understanding without either affirming or denying anything concerning it'.[23] 'Phantasy' was a most important concept, referring to a faculty that humans and animals shared. Because it lacked any capacity for making or joining abstractions, it dealt exclusively in sense impressions. In a later work, Hale set this out at

---

[17] *Ibid.*, sig.a3v.
[18] *Ibid.*, sig.a2. Hale was actually called to the bar in 1636, but perhaps he regarded his practice as starting at some later date.
[19] *Ibid.*, 2.   [20] *Ibid.*   [21] *Ibid.*   [22] *Ibid.*   [23] *Ibid.*

length;[24] the *Discourse* hurried on to the category of 'complex apprehensions', which combined two simpler elements, either by affirmation or negation. They could be merely objects that might appear to sense, like 'man', for example, or 'redness', or else they could be objects 'that do not immediately fall within our senses', as in the statement 'the spirit is a substance'. Such statements 'though originally derived from the sense, yet they are refined by the help of discourse'.[25] 'This 'discourse', 'rational discourse', was

a faculty or power put into man, whereby he is beyond all other visible creatures; and whereby all his actions, whether civil or religious, are and ought to be guided. This is that power, whereby we may improve even sensible objects, apprehensions and observations; to attain more sublime and high discoveries, and rise from effects to their causes, till at last we attain to the first cause of all things.[26]

Hale never ceased to be convinced that attention to the natural world was meant to be religious, both in its general character and in its intellectual implications. It was a way, the only 'natural' way, that God had intended his creature to discover the divine. The natural religion, in the absence of innate religious feeling, was knowledge of the deity as a scientific cause.

Later in life, Hale was obsessed with imaginary atheist threats, and devoted some hundreds of pages to pointing out the evidence for God. At this earlier stage, his proof seems quite perfunctory at best, resting in the absurdity of an infinite succession. He would have learned, at Oxford, that an actually infinite number of things could never co-exist; infinities could only be potential (arrived at, in the mind, by indefinite multiplication or division of an existing quantity). It was common, among Hale's contemporaries, to extend this thought to infinite 'successions'. This proved the universe had a beginning (or at least it had not always been in motion). An infinite chain of motions was inconceivable, so there had to be a first efficient cause. Aquinas had believed that an infinite succession could exist, and therefore that creation was a doctrine known by faith, but 'almost all the moderns' disagreed.[27] Hale's later works went into elaborate detail about the paradoxical results (if there had been an infinite number of weeks, there had been seven infinities of days) but his argument in the *Discourse* was simplicity itself:

In every successive motion it is necessary to arrive to some beginning of it, and it is impossible it should be eternal: as in [the] case of the motion of the sun, which is successive, it cannot in reason be, but there must be a time or instant, wherein it either was not, or did not move; for otherwise the revolutions would be actually infinite in number; and yet that infinite number of revolutions be still augmented

---

[24] Lambeth 3504, 102   [25] Hale, *Discourse*, 3.   [26] *Ibid.*
[27] This at least was the view of Ruvio (*In octo libros Aristotelis de physico commentarium*, Cologne 1629, p. 527), in a passage respectfully cited by Hale (Lambeth 3489, 20).

by daily new revolutions ... Therefore of necessity it had a beginning. If it had a beginning of its motion, it could not have it from itself, for why did it not then move sooner?[28]

At this stage, it seems clear, the existence of a First Cause was too obvious, in Hale's eyes, to merit any serious discussion. He must have been familiar with the main scholastic proofs, but made use of only one of them, in a form that was very naive. The topic was dismissed in just three pages.

After he had established that the First Cause exists, Hale gave it all the qualities of the usual Christian God. As a being which existed prior to time and space, it could not be restricted in spatial or temporal ways. It was very important to Hale that time was not an absolute but only a 'relational' idea, 'nothing else but that conception whereby we measure successive motion: were there no successive motion in the world, it would be impossible that there should be any of those affections of time, and consequently time is not any thing real, but a relation to motion.'[29] A being that was uncaused was exempt from circumscription and exclusion, and was therefore necessarily unique; to co-exist with something else was in some sense to be bounded by that thing. The First Cause was undivided, unlimited and omnipotent, it being 'not possibly imaginable, that the production of new effects should exclude or straiten that indivisible extent, which that being had before those effects were produced.'[30] Because God was not subject to or diminished by time and space, he was present in all his fullness throughout the universe, 'tota in toto et tota in qualibet parte'.[31] This was a common formula, not least in Hale's own writings, for discussing the soul's relation to the body, and an interesting analogy is called to the reader's mind.

Because God pre-existed, Hale's argument went on, he must be both simple and perfect. A mixture is the product of a mixer, and nothing is more perfect than its cause. The First Cause includes all conceivable perfection, because it causes everything we do or can conceive.[32] It is interesting to note that he argues from existence to perfection, and never the other way round. An 'ontological' argument, one showing that the concept of a God entails that that God is, was never a component of his armoury of proofs, a fact of some importance when he came to read Descartes.[33] The notion of the deity's perfection, which showed that he was free and intellectual and good, was not a way of showing that he actually exists.

The last of God's perfections was his justice, 'for justice is nothing else

[28] Hale, *Discourse*, 6.   [29] *Ibid.*, 8.   [30] *Ibid.*, 10.   [31] *Ibid.*, 11.
[32] *Ibid.*, 13.
[33] See below, p. 199.

but goodness in a rational being endued with will'.[34] This, too, could be deduced from pre-existence, for reasons that determined the shape of much of the rest of Hale's thought. God could not but be just, as

nothing can be said unjust which is not contrary to the prohibition of some law, given by something that can exact obedience to it. Nothing can give the first being a law or rule but his own will and consequently he can do nothing but what is most just, because it is impossible that any thing else can be a rule of justice but himself.[35]

Whatever God wills for his creatures is therefore to be looked upon as just. But beings to which freedom has been granted must be controlled by threat of punishment. The right of legislation, as Hale carefully explained, depended on the power of enforcement:

There can be nothing imaginably unjust without these two considerations 1. A law commanding or forbidding a thing under a pain: whatsoever falls not within the command or prohibition is permitted and cannot be unjust. 2. A power to exact an obedience to that law, and to inflict the punishment that follows upon the breach of the law. Otherwise the law were ridiculous and vain.[36]

Hale was consistent on this point, both in his legal and religious works.[37] An obligation to obey a law depends upon the power to enforce it. If human laws were taken in themselves, they had no permanently binding power. 'The power of society ... is but a thing extrinsecal, I may avoid their power, and then I am absolved; and if external power were enough to denominate my disobedience injustice, then if I could procure a power to overmatch theirs, their obedience to their own law were injustice.'[38] A human law was binding (here Selden's influence can be presumed) because a person promised to obey it. Such promises were then enforced by God's irresistible power.[39] This theory has been discussed before, in the context of political debates. Its presence here, at some time in the later 1630s, gives powerful support to earlier claims about Seldenian influence on the thought of Thomas Hobbes.

Hale seems to have been nervous about the implications of his voluntarist ideas, because he qualified his bold assertions. He conceded, for example, that 'were there no precise law given to rational creatures ... a conformity in the actions of rational creatures to the similar actions of the first cause towards his creature would be comely and just in a rational creature.'[40] There was a kind of instinct, he went on to explain, suggesting this conformity even to primitive men:

---

[34] Hale, *Discourse*, 21. [35] *Ibid.*, 21. [36] *Ibid.*, 22–3.
[37] British Library, Hargrave 485, 3; Lambeth 3492, 305.
[38] Hale, *Discourse*, 23–4. [39] *Ibid.*, 24. [40] *Ibid.*, 22.

questionless as the irrational creatures have certain instincts implanted in them by their first creation, which though they are not properly laws, but inclinations, [so] man, as he came out of the hands of his maker with the impression of his image upon him, had some conformity to the supreme justice without any reference to any command, which is not clean lost but even in men without education doth strongly manifest itself in divers particulars.[41]

Both human instinct and divine command are signs of God's intentions for his creatures. The universe is purposefully governed, by 'principle, instinct or law', so everything is carried to its appointed 'end'. The 'interruption' of these natural rules results in a 'privative' consequence. The creature's 'end' is lost, and a 'deformity, uselessness and uncomeliness' defaces the natural order.[42] Man's disregard of God's command has a similar privative punishment. But man is governed by a 'moral' law, to which his disobedience is conscious. His defeat of God's intention is not just a

privative offence ... to which a privative punishment may be answerable, but a positive rebellion, rejection, and disobedience to that duty and subjection he owes, and is enabled to perform to his maker: and therefore it is most just and rational, that there should be added, as a sanction to that law, some positive penalty to avenge such a violation.[43]

Hale surreptitiously reverts, as in his talk of the 'comeliness' of instinct, to a 'rational' foundation for God's action - but it would be pedantic to continue. It is clear, at all events that Hale regarded punishment as the divinely chosen way of influencing intellectual beings. The moral law supplied a means to guide man to his 'end', just as the instincts of the beasts directed them to theirs.

As human nature shows, this end must lie outside our present state. Unlike a brute, a human has intellect and will, the former thirsting after truth, the latter after good. The intellect can comprehend the universe itself, for it 'pares off the bulk of quantity ... and the vastest body takes up no more room than an atom'.[44] This infinite capacity is designed for an infinite knowledge, which only God's own being can provide. The will is similarly disappointed by nauseating streams of finite pleasures, when only an infinity can really satisfy.[45] It is the intellect's function to determine the genuine good, the proper object of the human will. The essence of a moral life is intellectual effort,

specificating and determining this or that to be good, and giving the degrees thereof, which is or should be the measure of the motion of the will. This is the last act of the practical understanding: for though all good be the object of the will in

---

[41] *Ibid.*, 22.   [42] *Ibid.*, 52–3.   [43] *Ibid.*, 53.   [44] *Ibid.*, 47–8.
[45] *Ibid.*, 62–7.

its latitude, yet the will fastens particularly upon that good, which by the understanding is presented to be his chiefest good.[46]

Contemporary casuists taught that moral reasoning was syllogistic.[47] The major proposition, in Hale's words, was a 'natural principle of conscience', known by reason, revelation or tradition 'from the first man to his posterity and from one man to another'.[48] The minor proposition was 'the stating of what I have done' (or else have yet to do). Comparison results in a 'conclusion either of acquittal or of condemnation, of obligation to that guilt, which ariseth upon the breach of that law, loss of my end, deformity, and liableness to the curse.'[49] Moral failure thus involved miscalculation, or else calculation's pre-emption by some hasty appetite. This intellectual failure, which among humans was the general rule, deprived them of course of their end, the enjoyment of God, and laid them under a guilt 'which is an obligation to punishment'.[50] The punishment in question was the pains of hell itself. This situation was accounted for, and the amazing remedy declared, in the pages of the Bible, the revealed word of God. Its teachings were 'above' but not at all opposed to human reason, while its general credibility was vouched for by its internal harmony, by the fulfilment of the prophecies, and by a wisdom which surpassed the mind of natural man.[51]

The first part of the *Discourse* had proved the need for truth to be revealed; the second described revelation's content. It corrects the understandable impression, the fruit of a cursory reading of his general presumptions about law, that he was just an advocate of a purely prudential religion, a matter of successful calculation of where the balance of advantage lies. Though he laid much stress on intellectual error, he also found a vital role for the help that the spirit must give. The intellect was capable of apprehending truth, in the religious sphere just as elsewhere, but a firm and lasting grip on the biblical doctrines demanded the assistance of God's power.

Faith and reason differ as much as knowledge and opinion, faith creating 'another kind of impression upon the soul'[52] even in points discoverable by purely natural means. There might be 'probable grounds' for trusting holy writ, grounds even amounting to a 'firm conclusion', but they are nothing more than preparation for 'that high and noble assent'.[53] The

---

[46] *Ibid.*, 58–9.
[47] H. R. McAdoo, *The structure of Caroline moral theology*, 1949, p. 66. The most likely single source for Hale's own thinking is William Ames, *Conscience with the power and cases thereof*, 1639 (first Latin publication 1622). Hale's later works use terminology (Synderesis/Syneidesis/Crisis) that had also been favoured by Ames (Lambeth 3507, 5v.-6)
[48] Hale, *Discourse*, 55.   [49] *Ibid.*, 55.   [50] *Ibid.*, 42.   [51] *Ibid.*, 100–13.
[52] *Ibid.*, 239.
[53] *Ibid.*, 100.

distinction was slight but important, and its subsequent erosion (most notably, as we shall see, by William Chillingworth) was an important symptom of Calvinist decline. Without divine assistance, we cannot make the slightest move towards God, whatever we are capable of knowing. In principle knowledge is passive, while faith is a variety of act, as Hale was very careful to explain:

> It is true that knowledge is that which precedes all the works of grace in the soul: but in this, the soul is not so much active as passive ... the first motion of the soul to union is not that faith of assent, which differs not from knowledge, but the faith of recumbency or adherence [that is, an act of trust]. And this priority of the act of faith is not in time, for life is wrought all at once in the soul, but in nature and actual operation ...[54]

The somewhat obscure distinction between priority of time and of 'actual operation' was a mark of the importance he attached to distinguishing an act of faith from the conclusion of a train of thought.

Another way to put this crucial point was to say the spirit acts upon the will: 'as the death and disability was in both faculties [of intellect and will], so the life is conveyed into both universally'.[55] This influence was not confined to the moment of conversion, but persisted through the course of Christian life, so that 'all those actions which are pleasing to God are wrought by the spirit of Christ, by which they were at first animated'.[56] At every stage, from 'preparation' on, the same force was at work. The spirit moves upon the heart to soften its hardness, and 'strive with' its lusts, and 'open' it for Christ;[57] it is the holy spirit that gives life to the words of the preacher, which 'for the most part die and lose their efficacy before they come at the spirit of a man'.[58] The hearing of God's message is the start of a gradual process, a 'sanctification' by spiritual means of the believer's life: '"that which is born of the spirit is spirit". That abideth in him and will by degrees, like a living spring, work out that mud, that our flesh and corruption cast into us.'[59]

The greatest good is liveliness of the spirit; there is a possibility of a 'dead and unacceptable obedience', unmotivated by true love of God.[60] A rational calculator, concerned above all to avoid damnation, is guilty of a merely 'servile' fear.[61] This language could be dangerous, as various extremists were to show, but the pre-war Hale was untroubled. The 'liveliness' of which he spoke was not 'enthusiastic', an uncontrollable external force, but the animating feature of normal Christian life. The elect were 'conformed' to the image of Christ by means of the spirit's direction, but the substance of the 'image' was dutiful performance of the dictates of

[54] *Ibid.*, 264.   [55] *Ibid.*, 242.   [56] *Ibid.*, 242.   [57] *Ibid.*, 388.
[58] *Ibid.*, 389.
[59] *Ibid.*, 271.   [60] *Ibid.*, 396.   [61] *Ibid.*, 253.

natural law. The image was frequently pictured as an impress on the soul, an idea that harmonised neatly with the Calvinist conception of sacraments as 'seals': 'God intending to re-instamp his image upon man, did send his son, the image of the invisible God, as a soul into the world, to imprint upon his followers the image of God, which consisted in righteousness and true holiness.'[62] The place of works in Calvinist religion could hardly be more accurately put. They may not be the cause of grace (though they are, in part, its purpose), but they have a certain sacramental function: they both constitute and signify the 'calling' of the elect.[63]

The motions of the spirit have a further most important characteristic. They are by nature 'secret'. Because they are in part mysterious, the individual conscience should be treated with respect, although its prompt-ings seem irrational. The burden of proof is always on those who ignore it, not those who are too scrupulous in trying to attend to its commands. Hale gave the examples of usury, 'stage-plays', long hair, and gaming.[64] He refrained from mentioning more controversial scruples, about kneeling at communion, for instance, where the same consideration might apply. He respected one such scruple all his life, by bowing at every description of God in the course of common prayer. He thus escaped idolatry towards the name of Jesus, while sticking to the letter of the law.[65]

These typically puritan instincts were backed by a theology of typically puritan form. God dealt with man by covenant, in Adam and in Christ. The covenant with Adam promised eternal life if he could be obedient to the law. Adam was quite entitled to make this contract bind on his descendants; potential beneficiaries of arrangements of this sort were bound to bear the pains of non-performance.[66] God did not will the Fall, though he of course foresaw it; the agent of temptation was the serpent, which managed to corrupt its prey by its superior powers of understand-ing. The root of moral failure was in an intellectual mistake.[67]

The eating of the apple brought death into the world, darkening the human intellect, and causing sensual appetites to dominate the will. The fact that Adam was deceived could not excuse or palliate his sin. In falling, he had lost all claim on God, and so had his descendants after him. God nonetheless decided to rescue a proportion of these traitors from the miserable fate that they deservedly incurred.[68] He had made them as 'vessels of honour', but 'men made themselves all vessels of dishonour'.[69] If

---

[62] *Ibid.*, 444.
[63] On this see John S. Coolidge, *The Pauline Renaissance in England: Puritanism and the Bible*, Oxford 1970, pp. 126–7.
[64] Hale, *Discourse*, 371.   [65] Hale, *Works*, I, 104.   [66] Hale, *Discourse*, 162.
[67] *Ibid.*, 164–5.   [68] *Ibid.*, 169, 172–5.   [69] *Ibid.*, 172–3.

mercy is granted to some, the others have no cause for a complaint, for all that many are called and few are chosen: 'they are continued to be but what they made themselves, and what they most freely desire still to be'.[70] When Christ agreed with God (by a covenant in heaven) to sacrifice his life for sinful men, the sacrifice's benefits went just to the elect.[71] A great theological crux, at the time that Hale was writing, was whether Christ intended that all men should be saved (the thesis, in the jargon of these questions, of 'hypothetical universalism'). If the 'effectual' sacrifice was narrower in scope than the intention, then it seemed the will of God had been frustrated. Hale's statements on this topic, sufficiently carefully read, show he approached this question from the rigorous 'high Calvinist' perspective. The texts supporting 'the universality of an intended redemption' appear as difficulties to be explained away.[72]

As Richard Baxter tells us, Hale later 'somewhat altered his opinion touching some points in controversy, especially between the Remonstrants and Contra-Remonstrants' (that is, he moved from Calvinist towards Arminian thought).[73] This seems a fair assessment, though his earlier position contained the germ of later and more liberal ideas.[74] Arminians are often loosely said to have believed in freedom of will.[75] A better definition, for present purposes, is 'the belief that God's foreknowledge was somehow prior to predestination'.[76] This was, at all events, the view that Hale was anxious to reject.

The argument he used, though probably conventional enough, could well have been drawn from a great theological text-book, the *Medulla theologiae* (1627) by the notable puritan exile William Ames (1576–1633). It was wrong of the Arminians to distinguish between God's will and his foreknowledge 'though in our apprehensions there is a difference', because knowledge, in the usual human sense, was actually inconsistent with God's nature. This was entailed, as he and Ames made clear, by an epistemology that traced all forms of knowledge to 'impressions' on the sense:

this prescience is not an objective impression of the things themselves, upon the divine understanding, for that were to suppose a kind of passibility, which is

70 *Ibid.*, 172–3.   71 *Ibid.*, 227–30.   72 *Ibid.*, 230.   73 *Ibid.*, sig.av.

74 This chapter has no direct concern with the vigorous debate about the influence of Calvinism (See esp. Peter White, *Predestination, policy and polemic*, Cambridge 1992; Nicholas Tyacke, *Anti-Calvinists: the rise of English Arminianism c. 1590–1640*, Oxford 1987; and Peter Lake, 'Calvinism and the English church, 1570–1635', *Past and Present*, 114, 1987). It is clear that Hale himself emerged from an entirely Calvinist milieu.

75 An accessible guide to these issues is Dewey D. Wallace, *Puritans and predestination: grace in English Protestant theology, 1525–1695*, Chapel Hill 1982.

76 Thus Samuel Ward referred to 'the Arminians' "predestination from faith foreseen"' (cited Tyacke, *Anti-Calvinists*, 50).

incompatible to the divine perfection, and supposeth a kind of priority in the nature of the object to the power, and a kind of dependence of the act upon it.[77]

The main objection to Arminianism, the source of the horror it provoked in orthodox Calvinist minds, was the clear implication that 'God must take up new counsels upon the vision, or at least prevision, of the actions of men';[78] it rescued the deity's goodness, but only by subjecting him to a mere creature's will. This robbed the doctrine of predestination of all the comfort that it could bestow. As Obadiah Sedgwick was later to complain, 'to speak plainly, according to the Arminian doctrine, all the stability and state of a sinner's salvation is made to depend upon the will of a sinner ... if the covenant of grace had no surer foundation than a man's will, it may quickly cease to be an everlasting covenant'.[79] This was an especial disaster, because the doctrine's function was to comfort, to assert that God's love for his chosen was utterly unalterable by any human act. In its 'highest' respectable version, as William Perkins (1558–1602) explained it, God willed the fate of every particular soul before he willed creation and the Fall. No shadow of condition crossed election, which was the end to which all else was just a subordinate means. A corollary of this claim, which Perkins heroically faced, was that the same was true of reprobation. The purpose of the history of the world was that some should be vessels of honour, and others should be damned, and all this without reference to any human sin.

Hale's theory was nothing like this. He believed, to recapitulate, that God made 'all [men] vessels of honour, and men made themselves all vessels of dishonour'.[80] He was therefore an 'infra-lapsarian'; he thought predestination depended on a knowledge of the Fall. Before the Fall, God willed (conditionally) that everyone be saved; after the sin of Adam he willed (without condition) that some be rescued from their fallen state. After the Fall he might be Calvinist; before, he was Arminian in behaviour. The eating of the apple, which doomed the non-elect (Hale never speaks, of course, of reprobation) was envisaged not as pre-destined but foreknown:

God did foresee the Fall of man in the counsel of his prescience, but did not fore-appoint it in the counsel of his pre-determination: the rule of nature is, that whatsoever is, while it is, is necessarily. And because all things, before they are, are

---

[77] Hale, *Discourse*, 135. For the same point see Ames, *The marrow of theology*, tr. from the third Latin edn and ed. by John D. Eusden, Boston 1968, pp. 95–6.

[78] Hale, *Discourse*, 140.

[79] Obadiah Sedgwick, *The bowels of tender mercy sealed in the everlasting covenant*, 1661, p. 158.

[80] Hale, *Discourse*, 172–3.

present with God as if they were, and in the same degree as if they were, therefore it was in the same degree of foreknowledge, as if it had been necessary.[81]

He was making a distinction which he previously dissolved, between predestination and foreknowledge. The blatant inconsistency was a pointer to a weakness of his stance. If election had some reference to the Fall, it might also have some reference to subsequent events.

A consistently Arminian position must have been very tempting to a man like Matthew Hale. He lacked the usual motives for remaining orthodox, as he had little sense of being 'chosen', still less of being a brand plucked out of the fire. He was silent on 'assurance of salvation', the believer's certainty that he was saved, a doctrine of vital importance to logical extremists cast in the Perkins mould.[82] Denial of conditional election was not the heart of his religious life, and his predestinarian attitudes had the character of abstract speculations. It was hardly surprising that later in life he came to see such points as barren quibbles, born of presumptuous logic in questions that defeated human minds.

In practice Hale was sure, whatever his more voluntarist statements might suggest, that the standards of God were in some sense analogous to man's. He denied that God would ever be responsible for sin, for though

it is impossible that the laws, which God gives to man, do bind the law-giver, yet this is inconsistent with his purity, truth and justice: ... with his purity, for certainly there is an intrinsic justice and holiness in the law of God, whereof he cannot cause the violation; inconsistent with his truth: the will of his counsel never crosseth the will of his command; inconsistent with his justice, to require an obedience to that law, whereof he doth necessitate the breach; and in this case, predeterminating the action by way of necessitating the will, and to pre-determine the obliquity, differs little.[83]

It is very important to grasp that this was an orthodox view. The Calvinists in general were not determinist; they recognised a very clear distinction between voluntary and necessary causation (they denied, in contemporary terms, that they were 'Stoics'). The human will was free, as even Perkins held, to choose between courses of action; it was naturally incapable, however, of accomplishing anything good.[84] The question of 'good' deeds, the deeds worked by the spirit, will be considered later; in deeds that were either evil or indifferent, the position was perfectly clear. Every event was willed by God, but he willed necessary events to happen necessarily, and voluntary events to happen voluntarily. It was the freedom of the will, as

[81] *Ibid.*, 163–4.   [82] A silence particularly noticeable at Hale, *Discourse*, 300.
[83] *Ibid.*, 140.
[84] Perkins, *Reformed Catholic*, pp. 11–13. *The judgement of the synod holden at Dort concerning the five Articles*, 1619, p. 91.

respectable opinion agreed, which exonerated God from accusations that he had caused humanity to sin.[85]

Hale treated God's respect for human freedom as a mark of his consistency and power:

> we may observe the reason why Almighty God in all times hath used rational ways for the reducing men to the obedience of his will, not but that he could, if he pleased, force the wills of all mankind to what dispositions or actions he pleased; but that were to infringe that law, which he at first planted in voluntary agents.[86]

In this insistence upon 'rational ways', we see the germ of Hale's more liberal thought. God dealt with human beings by presenting them with objects of aversion and desire. This occasioned 'convictions of the understanding', and 'the act of the rational appetite or will following that conviction, if not perturbed'.[87] The possible perturbing influences were 'the passions or affections, partly managed by the command of the will, partly by the temper and constitution of the body'.[88]

In the ordinary course of events, the process was assisted by God's power; men were the undeserving beneficiaries, even in the absence of a saving faith, of a certain amount of supernatural aid. These 'ordinary supplies' could be withdrawn, without a violation of the freedom of the will, 'for they are extrinsecal to his nature, and therefore not due to him'.[89] This explained how everything was predetermined, and yet no blame attached to God for being the author of sin. It was the will's consent, not the 'external action', that made a particular human impulse sinful, and God respected the freedom of the will.

> if one man had an exact knowledge of the frame temper and constitution of another man; and had power to apply his object so exactly to his understanding and affections as to meet with them exactly; and could discover the motions of the soul upon that object proposed, and could apply to every opposition a suitable answer or qualification, this man might easily predetermine what the other should do, and yet, in drawing out that action, no way injure his liberty.[90]

God did not need to influence the will, because he acted on the 'understanding', bearing always in mind the 'affections' that influenced particular men.[91]

To show what this could mean, Hale considered a classic example, the 'hardening' by God of Pharoah's heart.[92] Calvin had taken 'hardening'

---

[85] Perkins, *Works*, I, 15; *The Westminster confession of faith*, ed. S. W. Carruthers, Presbyterian Historical Society of England: Extra publications, no. 2, Manchester n.d., pp. 94–5; *Synod at Dort*, 87–91.

[86] Hale, *Discourse*, 131. [87] *Ibid.*, 137. [88] *Ibid.*, 137.

[89] *Ibid.*, 132–3, 141–2.

[90] *Ibid.*, 138. [91] *Ibid.*, 138.

[92] Exodus iv 21; vii 13; ix 12; x 1, 20, 27; xi 10; xiv 8. The Arminian Thomas Jackson, who was also writing in the 1630s, devoted a great deal of energy to these texts (Tyacke, *Anti-Calvinists*, 142).

literally, to imply that God had made his creature sin.[93] In Hale's account, the tyrant's heart was hardened by giving him a 'rational occasion' to deny the Israelites their liberty 'for then he should lose their work, which was beneficial to him. Moses to confirm his embassage casts down his rod, it becomes a serpent; the magicians that were of a contrary counsel to Moses do the like. This object hardens the heart of Pharoah.'[94] God led the Egyptian king to a false but certainly rational conclusion, without directly meddling with his will. The episode was only one in an astonishing chain of apparently random events. The enslavement of Joseph, his unjust imprisonment by Potiphar, his consequent meeting with Pharoah's butler, his successful interpretation of the butler's and then of Pharoah's dreams, the famine he predicted, his family's migration into Egypt, the exposure of Moses in the bulrushes, the discovery of Moses by the daughter of Pharoah, and countless other 'tumultuary and disorderly passages' had all of them contributed to the successful outcome of God's plan.[95] The effect, a little oddly, was of a vision of history as a vast providential machine, continually adjusted for smooth working by *ad hoc* interference with the human intellect. An object of desire was not strictly speaking a 'cause' of the sin that resulted, but in practice the will was determined just the same.

God's influence on the elect was of a different nature. The Almighty saved and sanctified his chosen by acting on the human will, not just the intellect.[96] Salvation was not achieved through 'rational ways', but by God's work *in* man: 'there is some kind of motion in us, which though it be the work of our Creator in the first giving of it, and again his work in reviving, quickening and enabling it, yet he is pleased to require it from us and to expect it of us'.[97] From an absolute perspective, this motion was a gift, though the gift took the form of the virtues of faith and hope and love.[98] It involved, at all events, immediate exertion of God's power. God's dealings with the unregenerate were mediated by the world's ingenious design, by strategic arrangement of 'objects', and by assistance to the

---

[93] Calvin, *Institutes*, I, 255–6, 337–8. Strictly speaking, of course, God was the cause of Pharoah's act, but not of its sinful aspect. To say that this was *tantamount* to making God 'Author of sin' was to take up an Arminian position.

[94] Hale, *Discourse*, 132.   [95] *Ibid.*, 128–9.

[96] *Ibid.*, 242. John von Rohr, *The covenant of grace in puritan thought*, American Academy of Religion, Studies in religion, no. 45, 1986, pp. 68–71 discusses the respective roles of intellect and will, and notes an increasing 'tendency to give the intellect a position higher than the will' in the puritan thought he surveys. R. T. Kendall's profound exploration of the logic of the theology involved stresses that 'English Calvinists' saw faith as an act of the will (*Calvin and English Calvinism to 1649*, Oxford 1979). Perhaps there is no real contradiction; Hale's thought could be interpreted in support of either view. Although the role of intellect occupies much more space, the indispensable first step, the 'faith of adherence', appears to be a voluntary motion.

[97] Hale, *Discourse*, 243.   [98] *Ibid.*

intellect. The human will was in effect diminished to the endpoint of an intellectual process, or else a merely brutal appetite. The latter was connected, in at least a quasi-necessary way, with the apparent good that called it forth; the former was wholly dependent on assistance provided by God.

Hale's later 'latitudinarianism' involved the extension of the 'rational' sphere to cover God's approach to his elect. The role of will was minimised, and faith became no more than a 'faith of assent'. The disturbing idea of a merely 'servile' virtue was dropped from Hale's conceptual repertoire; religion consisted in knowledge of supernatural rewards and pains. God's 'rational ways' consisted, after all, in the cunning presentation of objects of aversion and desire. Nothing could be more obvious than the breach with the younger, more Calvinistic Hale; the explanations for that breach, and the hidden continuities with an orthodox Protestant past, are topics for subsequent chapters to explore.

❧ 10 ❧

Hale's 'latitudinarianism'

One part of Hale's residual puritanism was strict observance of the sabbath day. Between the evening sermon and his supper, he meditated on the Christian faith, 'and having a very ready hand at writing, he usually wrote his thoughts'.[1] The bulk of the Hale papers now at Lambeth are products of this pious exercise. A few of them were read within his household, and published as a collection, the *Contemplations moral and divine* (1676), but most are quite unpublishable in their present form. The ten parts and five volumes of 'De Deo', which he worked on intermittently from 1662 to 1667, exemplify the method's obvious faults. This uncompleted monster of a work collapses into essays (many themselves unfinished) on an encyclopaedic range of topics. He was attempting a compendium of all the arguments for God's existence, beginning with 'the voice of metaphysics', then proceeding through physics and ethics to providence and conscience and the Bible. Its most important purpose, by the author's own account, was

(1) To keep my thoughts fixed.
(2) To keep them from being wholly lost.
(3) That I might in after time when perchance my understanding were better informed see my former mistakes.[2]

These works exist to register opinion, and they certainly give the impression of a man who is thinking aloud. They have many of the qualities of an actual train of thought, being very repetitious, and painfully long-winded in making the simplest of points. With the restraint appropriate in a man who was himself the author of approaching 150 printed works, Baxter conceded Hale could be too 'copious'.[3] A convenient result, so far as the historian is concerned, is that every idea of importance is stated a number of times. Hale was also conscientiously exhaustive whenever he examined rival views, and readable simplicities never disguise his thought. A better

---

[1] Hale, *Discourse*, A3v.   [2] Lambeth Palace Library, MS 3493 (Fairhurst MSS), fo. ii.
[3] Hale, *Works*, I, 107.

156

source could hardly be invented for exploring the internal logic of his latitudinarian beliefs.

The individual pieces range in length from approaching a million words ('De Deo') to fragments of a paragraph or less. It should be confessed at the outset that many shorter essays are impossible to date, but this is not a serious handicap. The purpose of this chapter is not to establish a chronology in the development of Hale's ideas; it is concerned with continuities, with Hale's ability to feel that he had barely altered his position. It seems certain, however, that virtually all of these works were written in his final twenty years. The earliest datable item (apart, that is, from the *Discourse*) is a piece 'on the chief end of man', which he composed in 1651.[4] We know he turned, during the interregnum, to 'studies now more easy grateful and seasonable for me'.[5] A trickle of other short essays became a steady flow at approximately the time the king returned. He hoarded many trivial scraps of paper, and even put them into vellum bindings, so it seems fairly unlikely that much has been weeded or lost.

These writings give unusually free access to a mind of unusual acuteness, at a time of rapid change in English thought. As a source, they are, however, more treacherous than they seem. These were not private papers, if 'private' means that they were meant for none but their author's attention. It is true they are carelessly written, much more so than *The primitive origination of mankind* (1677), the only one he took steps to have published. There are many signs, however, that a modest circulation was envisaged, though perhaps only after his death. The treatises that might unsettle faith, his elaborate discussions of the soul, were composed in a simplified Latin in order to deter the ignorant.[6] He would hardly have gone to this trouble if he had not imagined some kind of readership. He remained on friendly terms with Edward Stephens, the son-in-law who printed the *Contemplations moral and divine*.[7] He even sent 'De Deo' to John Wilkins, who showed it to John Tillotson, another of Hale's liberal clerical friends. He had concealed his authorship, but the two of them admired it, in spite of its unfinished state, and easily guessed who was responsible.[8] There was a sense, it followed, in which these writings must be seen as public, in spite of their blatant shortcomings of structure and style.

The issue of 'public' intentions is actually of very great importance in making an assessment of Hale's religious thought. We know from Richard Baxter that Hale was obsessed, at the end of his life, by detailed specu-

---

[4] Lambeth 3481.   [5] Lambeth 3512, 148v.   [6] Lambeth 3492, 106.
[7] Richard Baxter (ed.), *The judgement of the late Sir Matthew Hale of the nature of true religion*, 1684, Preface.
[8] Burnet, *Life*, 50–1.

lations about liberty and grace. Baxter himself wrote much about these issues, and had enormous reverence for Hale, but was shocked at this unhealthy fascination, especially in a man so close to death: 'I took the boldness to tell him that I thought more practical writings were more suitable to his case, who was going from this contentious world'.[9] Hale's writings sometimes touch upon these questions, but not in a way to suggest any burning concern, and he uses the Arminian controversy as one of his examples of a sterile scholastic dispute.[10] The predestinarian issue had never been resolved, nor had it ceased to trouble Hale himself, but it ceased to be an aspect of religion which ought to be considered by any pious mind.

There was a gap, in other words, between Hale's presentation of religion and his private theological ideas. His writings were intended to encourage piety, and he had come to feel, along with many others of his time, that speculations of this kind were something of a dangerous distraction.[11] As the previous chapter noted, Hale showed very little anxiety about his prospects in the afterlife. He was not, in R. T. Kendall's useful phrase, an 'experimental predestinarian', someone for whom the fear of reprobation, and that fear's resolution by 'assurance', was at the heart of Protestant religion.[12] Whatever the truth about predestination, the doctrine was far from essential to proclamation of the Christian faith.

Hale never thought that human minds could encompass the truth about God. Such expressions as God's 'will' and 'knowledge' were always analogical at best.[13] He remained a Trinitarian, believing Jesus Christ was God incarnate, and that only God's own sacrifice could atone for human sin.[14] But abstract theological enquiries were losing their previous function in

---

[9] Hale, *Works*, I, 108.   [10] *Ibid.*, 292, 299.

[11] A modern Calvinist writer, Alan C. Clifford, has presented even Tillotson, who is normally considered the archetypal lukewarm rationalist, as essentially quite orthodox in spirit. His case is not wholly persuasive, but it is interesting that it can be made at all (Alan C. Clifford, *Atonement and justification: English evangelical theology: an evaluation*, Oxford 1990).

[12] Kendall, *English Calvinists*, esp. 8–9.   [13] Lambeth 3492, 214v.

[14] Hale, *Discourse*, 461–72; Lambeth 3498, 309 (undated, but highly liberal in its attitude towards original sin). The latter piece was an essay 'touching punishments the relaxation, remission, and translation of them in order to the disputes between us and the Socinians'. Socinians denied the need for atonement (and therefore for a sacrifice that only God incarnate could provide), because they envisaged sin as creating a variety of debt. Hale saw it, following Grotius, as a punishment intrinsic to God's law. A debt could be forgiven, but God could not, consistent with his justice, permit a breach of law to go unpunished. A belief in incarnation was therefore entailed by Hale's theory that legislation involved the creation of sanctions. For a later expression of this general view, see his friend Edward Stillingfleet's, *A discourse concerning the doctrine of Christ's satisfaction*, 1696. On latitudinarians and the Trinity, see Isabel Rivers, *Reason, grace and sentiment: a study of the language of religion and ethics in England, 1660–1780*, Cambridge 1991, vol. I, p. 48.

approaching the divine. The Atonement was an interesting truth, vouched for by holy writ, and a striking testimony to God's transcendent goodness; it was not, from the human point of view, the essence of Christ's work. Christ's nature was of secondary concern, compared to his role as the bringer of ethical truth.

The *Discourse* itself had suggested a useful ambiguity in Christian experience of God: 'there is some kind of motion in us, which though it be the work of the Creator in the first giving of it, and again his work in quickening reviving and enabling of it, yet he is pleased to require it of us and to expect it of us'.[15] At the time of the *Discourse*, it still seemed important to see this motion as an unearned gift, as well as a duty God imposed on man; in the papers now at Lambeth, the latter aspect is predominant, almost to the exclusion of the former. The covenant of grace is treated as an offer of salvation on 'condition' of 'evangelical obedience', by which he meant an effort to obey the law of Christ.[16] Religion is depicted as a simple moral law, 're-published' and greatly clarified by Christ, but known to the virtuous heathens, who believed it and were saved. The purpose of this chapter is to show how these virtually deist beliefs could nonetheless be experienced as an orthodox Protestant faith.

One major intellectual influence was obviously the figure of John Selden. Selden was often felt to be only very dubiously Christian, but Hale defended his sincerity, assuring Richard Baxter that 'Selden was an earnest professor of the Christian faith, and so angry an adversary to Hobbes that he hath rated him out of the room'.[17] Hale's mentor certainly strikes the modern reader as highly secular in thought and deed: an irreverent anti-clerical gifted with pungent wit, who lived in a scandalous *ménage à trois* with the Earl and the Countess of Kent. In fact, as a previous chapter attempted to explain, his moral philosophy was based on a clearly theological position. God was the linch-pin of his legal thought, because human laws were contracts, and God alone could see to it that contractual agreements were kept.

Considered as a Christian theologian, his major contribution was his re-evaluation of the Jews. *De jure naturali et gentium juxta disciplinam Ebraeorum*, the most elaborate of all his efforts, considered the relationship between Jewish and natural law. Most puritans felt deep respect for every Old Testament practice. Although the ceremonial law had of course been abrogated, Jewish arrangements might be normative as God's own

---

[15] Hale, *Discourse*, 243.
[16] Hale, *Works*, I, 256, 292. Compare Hale, *Discourse*, 294. On the rise of explicit talk about 'conditions', see C. F. Allison, *The rise of moralism: the proclamation of the Gospel from Hooker to Baxter*, 1966.
[17] Baxter, *Reliquiae*, III, 48.

proclamation of natural moral rules. This was the possibility that Selden's work effectively denied. A natural law, he thought, was known to everybody who was in moral health; the Jewish law, by contrast, the law declared specifically to a single race, was really just a local or 'civil' law system. Not even the command to keep the sabbath had any power over Christian folk. The liberating character of Selden's masterpiece can be seen from an enthusiastic letter that the future Cambridge Platonist Ralph Cudworth (1617–88) had felt inspired to send him in 1643:

> under the Christian state, there is scarce any thing of ius divinum besides the universal and catholic law of nature, excepting only the *nomos tes pisteos*, the law of faith. The sabbath I have long satisfied myself in, which I think never a jot the more moral ... because it hath a place in the Jewish decalogue and you have already taught the world what the ius gentium of religion is [he means the law that binds upon the Gentiles], in your incomparable discourse, upon the precepts of Noah ...[18]

God was certainly the author of much of Jewish law, but only as the monarch that the Hebrews had happened to choose; he acted in precisely the same way, by virtue of a contract with his people, as any human governor making locally authoritative rules.

If Selden's full significance is to be understood, he must be seen from a Calvinist perspective. The people of Israel, in Calvinist eyes, were the 'type' of the community of faith, prefiguring in many ways the institutions of the Christian church. Its members could hope for salvation by virtue of the atoning work of Christ, as they were included in the scope of the 'covenant of grace'.[19] For Calvin and for Calvinists, the laws that God made for the Jews had set them apart as his church; Selden believed, by contrast, that the Jews were no more than God's state. Their peculiar relationship with God, initially established by a contract, was just another political arrangement. But to deny, as Selden did, that Jewish law was ever 'ius divinum', any more than Babylonian or even common law, was to break down the barrier dividing grace and works. There was salvation, Selden thought, outside the Jewish state, the Biblical example being the Gentile Job.[20] The implication, for a Calvinist, was that there was salvation outside the Christian church. The *Table talk* made this idea explicit:

> [the Jews] held that themselves should have the chief place of happiness in the other world, but the Gentiles that were good men should likewise have their portion of bliss there too. Now by Christ the partition wall is broken down and the gentiles that believe in him are admitted to the same place of bliss as the Jews. And

---

[18] Bodleian Library, MSS Selden supra 109, fo. 270.
[19] Calvin, *Institutes of the Christian Religion*, tr. John Allen, vol. I, pp. 465–88.
[20] Selden, *Opera*, I, 747–50.

why should not that portion of happiness still remain to them who do not believe in Christ, so they be morally good.[21]

The intended effect of this teaching was probably to undermine the basis of clerical power. If even the most minimal of Christian dogmatic beliefs was not a precondition for salvation, then particular forms of church government were surely indifferent things. He went out of his way to discredit the Laudian theory that episcopal succession was essential to the church.[22] To be out of communion with bishops was not fatal to the soul, so excommunication had no intrinsic force. The secular authorities might choose (as the people of England had done) to punish excommunicates with various civil pains, but this was a matter determined by secular law. The massive *De synedriis*, his last, unfinished work, expanded on a crucial fact uncovered by *De jure naturali*.[23] Expulsion from the synagogue was compatible with access to the Temple. This showed that biblical 'excommunication' was actually a civil penalty (expulsion from the day to day society of Jews) as opposed to a spiritual sanction. Presbyterians and Laudians and papists were equally mistaken in assigning the clergy such power.

The specifically Christian revelation was much reduced in content and importance. The church's primary duty was to reinforce the teachings that were known through natural law. As Selden once complained: 'the things between God and men are but a few, and those forsooth we must be told often of, but the things between man and man are many, those I hear not of above twice a year ...'[24] It may seem rather puzzling that such an attitude appealed to a pious sabbatarian like Hale. The priorities of Selden, so frankly secular, appear as an open departure from any traditional faith. But seen from another angle, his writings satisfied a puritan need by heightening the significance of ordinary life. The law of the Jews was established by God, but the laws that were made by the English played precisely the same role: they were in fact a duty, religious in authority and content, that a people could establish for itself. As the Scottish presbyterian Robert Baillie reported from the Westminster Assembly, 'this man is the head of the Erastians; his glory is in the Jewish learning; he avows every where that the Jewish state and church was all one, and that so in England it must be, that the parliament is the church.'[25] In attacking *ius divinum*, he seemed to raise all other laws to the level of a known divine command. Selden himself was probably aware that this sacralisation of secular things

[21] Selden, *Table talk*, 123. [22] Selden, *Opera*, II, 440, 1130. [23] *Ibid.*, I, 5, 488.
[24] Selden, *Table talk*, 106.
[25] *Letters and journals of Robert Baillie*, ed. D. Laing, Edinburgh 1861, vol. II, pp. 265–6. There is a helpful discussion of Erastianism as a religious theory in William M. Lamont, *Godly rule: politics and religion 1603–60*, 1969, pp. 106–31.

was a covert means to secularise the sacred, but Hale was not equipped by temperament to recognise this hazard in his mentor's attractive ideas.

Between the *Discourse* and the later papers, Hale felt a rather different influence. The minimal religion of William Chillingworth emerged from controversy about the 'rule of faith'.[26] His book *The religion of Protestants a safe way to salvation* (1638) was aimed against the arguments of a Jesuit called Knott, who had ably expounded the problems raised by appeals to the Bible alone. Knott stressed the need for some authority to give infallible interpretations, not least by defining the boundaries of the canon of scripture itself. The answer that Chillingworth gave had numerous disturbing implications: he denied the possibility of infallible knowledge of Christ. No conceivable chain of reasoning was stronger than the weakest of its links, and papists could give no infallible grounds for the infallibility they claimed for the Roman church. Religious truth could not be proved with the exactness known in mathematics but believers could become at least 'morally certain' that the Bible was indeed the word of God. This purely 'moral' certainty, compelled by the book's historical credentials, was nothing but a rational conviction, analogous to belief in Julius Caesar, or in a town that we have never seen.

Knott had additionally pointed out that the Bible was a most uncertain rule. A generalised assent that the scriptures were the standard of the truth had been no help to Protestants in their bitter internal debates. The answer to this damaging objection was to minimise the doctrines that were necessary to faith. Not only were they very 'plain and easy', but they were all available in the Gospel according to Luke.[27] God has less interest in correct beliefs than in the effort to discover them: 'I am fully assured that God does not, and therefore that man ought not to require any more of any man than this, to believe the Scriptures to be God's word, to endeavour to find the true sense of it, and to live according to it.'[28] God's purpose for his creatures is that they should be purely rational. He therefore 'desires only that we believe the conclusion, as much as the premises deserve, that the strength of our faith be equal or proportionable to the credibility of our motives to it.'[29] It was a deplorable error to hold 'that it is in vain to believe the Gospel of Christ with such a kind or degree of assent, as they yield to other matters of tradition'.[30] Of course this was exactly what most of his English contemporaries (including the young Hale) had always found it natural to assume. He was reducing faith to the fruit of a specialised branch of historical knowledge.

[26] On Chillingworth see Robert R. Orr, *Reason and authority: the thought of William Chillingworth*, Oxford 1967; Robert Martin Krapp, *Liberal Anglicanism 1636–47: an historical essay*, Ridgefield, Conn., 1944.
[27] Chillingworth, *Religion*, 212. [28] *Ibid.*, 376. [29] *Ibid.*, 36. [30] *Ibid.*, 37.

For Chillingworth, this was an easy step, as his own preferred religion was that of his godfather Laud. An unmediated personal experience of grace had little part in his religious life. He had briefly been a papist, and approved of the Laudian emphasis on ritual, so his religious sympathies were more complex than they seem. The minimum conditions for salvation were liberal by almost any standards, but it was still desirable that high church attitudes should be adopted, including, for example, the notion that the clergy were sacrificing priests.[31] A most important influence was Grotius, who combined very similar rationalist ideas with a great admiration for the ways of the Laudian church.[32] It was easy for a puritan, however, to overlook this side of Chillingworth. In a reader like John Tillotson, whose famous book *The rule of faith* (1666) restated Chillingworthian ideas, the upshot was an ethical religion: a minimalist theology, indifferent to the church's sacraments, reducing Christianity to the vehicle of some 'plain and easy' truths.

Hale came to feel, as Chillingworth had done, that knowledge of Christ was like knowledge of Julius Caesar;[33] that God's expectations of man were proportioned to what his creature could reasonably know; and that the essential content of the Bible, once it had been established as the morally certain truth, was a perfectly unambiguous ethical message, quite readily accessible to even the simplest of minds. One way to examine this shift is to look at his treatment of knowledge in relation to saving faith. According to the *Discourse*, faith is a kind of knowledge, and knowledge of the deity is bound to engender love.[34] 'It is true', Hale admits, 'that education, instruction and discipline may make us know these truths speculatively, and yet our soul [be] not affected with them: but the conviction, which is wrought with the power of the spirit, is not so thin and jejune a union of these truths to the understanding but deeper and more radicated . . .'[35] This 'deeper and more radicated' knowledge, surpassing a mere speculative assent, involves a literal union with Christ, a union with an atoning saviour, not with the truths that he was born to bring. This union results in a double imputation: Christ bears the consequences of the sins of the elect, while they receive the benefit of his unspotted and transcendent merits.[36]

The same cluster of themes can be detected in a manuscript probably

---

[31] *Ibid.*, Preface.
[32] Trevor-Roper, *Catholics, Anglicans, and Puritans: seventeenth century essays*, 1987, p. 98n.; Baxter, *The Grotian religion discovered*, 1658, for a perceptive contemporary attack.
[33] Lambeth 3485, 10v. On the varieties of certainty, see Barbara J. Shapiro, *Probability and certainty in seventeenth century England*, Princeton 1983. On Hale, see esp. pp. 180–93.
[34] Hale, *Discourse*, 240   [35] *Ibid.*, 240.   [36] *Ibid.*, 268–9.

dating from the 1650s.[37] Some kinds of knowledge are inadequate, for the devils themselves of course 'believe and tremble' (James ii 19).[38] Hale also quite flatly denied, against the spirit of his later thought, that mere self-preservation can motivate true faith: if I do anything that is good upon this account only to save my own soul it is plain I love my own soul better than I love God.'[39] The essence of Christ's mission, in this piece, is to save the sinner by imputed merit,[40] a process which involves 'a union of concretion, a kind of incorporation of the believer into Christ'.[41]

Though knowledge alone may be powerless to cause this saving union with Christ, it is enough to justify the Almighty in damning those who make no act of faith. One of Hale's favourite texts, at every stage of his development, was St Paul's alarming claim (Romans i 20) that 'the invisible things of him are clearly seen, being understood by the things that are made, even his eternal power and Godhead, so that they are without excuse'.[42] As Hale once frankly put it 'though the light of nature do not afford sufficient to save a man, yet the sin against that light will be sufficient to condemn a man.'[43] An essay of the early 1660s, headed 'reason not a sufficient guide in matters of faith', explored this unattractive paradox. He stressed that 'the very proposing of the gospel is so rational that the non-submission to it is a thing deserving to render vengeance to them that obey not the gospel.'[44] However, mere 'proposal' of the truth created 'assent' and not faith: 'though truth proposed under natural demonstrations may create and justly challenge an assent for the very devils themselves convinced by the evidence they saw acknowledged him to be the Christ yet that assent is but preparatory to a supernatural faith expressed by reception of Christ ...'[45] Hale envisaged this 'proposal' taking Chillingworthian form; he likened purely rational conviction to knowledge of the existence of Julius Caesar.[46] The new idea of moral certainty was still to be distinguished from a proper saving faith. This apparently unchanged view was subverted by a liberal concession. It was intimately connected, like a great deal else in his development, with a sense of the regularity with which God could be expected to behave: 'the submission to the gospel upon rational grounds is never deserted by God but he affords his spirit to produce either concomitantly or subsequently grace to produce supernatural faith and conversion ...'[47] Human beings

---

[37] Lambeth 3483. The reverse end of the volume is occupied by a false start at a sequel to Lambeth 3481, a treatise written in 1651.
[38] Lambeth 3483, 3   [39] *Ibid.*, 89v.   [40] *Ibid.*, 34v., 67.   [41] *Ibid.*, 99.
[42] Hale, *Discourse*, 118, 229.
[43] Lambeth 3480, 235v. These words were probably written in 1657; at all events, he uses '1657 circumvolutions' of the sun as a figure plucked out of the air (fo. 227v.).
[44] Lambeth 3506, 104.   [45] *Ibid.*, 103v.   [46] *Ibid.*, 104v.   [47] *Ibid.*, 104.

would always be saved if they reasoned correctly, although they could never be saved by reason alone.

At the liberal extreme in Hale's late writings is an undated essay of 'the triumph of faith over the world'. Faith is a mere species of knowledge 'but some things are of such a nature as being once truly and firmly believed or known, carry a man out to action, and such are especially the knowledge or belief of such things as are the object of our fears or of our hopes.'[48] This was actually compatible with a point to be found in the *Discourse*; a knowledge of God, once achieved, would naturally result in strict obedience to his law.[49] But the *Discourse* had stressed that such knowledge was not to be arrived at in purely rational ways. His piece on the triumph of faith now abandoned this view. The method by which the world was overcome was by 'rectifying our judgements and removing those mistakes that are in us concerning the world and our own condition'.[50] He was unmoved by the thought of the trembling devils:

to say this is but a historical faith, and that the devils have as much, they believe and tremble, and they do as fully assent to divine truths as any can do, yet it avails them not, concludes nothing; the reason is evident, because the salvation which is to be obtained the faith which is the instrument to attain it, concerns them not . . .[51]

There was a close connection between changes in the character and changes in the object of a truly Christian faith. Instead of uniting himself to an atoning saviour, so as to gain the benefit of an imputed grace, the believer was now envisaged as assenting to some 'truths'. To believe in Jesus Christ was really to have faith that Christ was the authorised teacher of natural law. Hale's most considered summary of his later religious ideas was a short general 'Discourse of religion', which he sent to Richard Baxter as a kind of legacy.[52] This last word on the subject stressed that 'religion' in some form was almost universal, 'so appropriate to the humane nature that there are scarce any sort of men, but have some religion'.[53] A mark of God's great goodness was provision 'in all ages and among all nations' of 'some means and helps to discover unto them, though in different degrees, some principal sentiments of true religion'.[54]

These means and helps were very various: they included the voice of conscience, the works of nature and of providence, and also those 'men in all ages, of great wisdom, observation, and learning, which did instruct the more ignorant in this great concernment, the rudiments of natural

---

[48] Hale, *Works*, II, 110.   [49] Hale, *Discourse*, 240.   [50] Hale, *Works*, II, 112.
[51] *Ibid.* 111. Contrast (about the devils) the non-puritan Calvinist Daniel Featley, *Clavis mystica: a key opening divers difficult and mysterious texts of Scripture*, 1636, p. 343; Sedgwick, *Bowels*, 406.
[52] Hale, *Judgement*, Preface.   [53] Hale, *Works*, I, 288.   [54] *Ibid.*, 288.

religion'.[55] In spite of all these helps, the truth was very easily corrupted, so God had devised a 'more fixed and permanent means' by which to achieve the same ends.[56] This means was intended for all, whatever their natural talents, so 'there is not nor indeed may not be any great difficulty in the attaining of a true saving knowledge of the Christian religion'.[57] Hale presupposed, in fact, that the Bible's useful content must be intuitively plausible. A reader armed with such a principle was bound to discover a message that accorded with the moral ideas he brought to the Biblical text.

Hale thought there were 'agenda' and 'credenda', things to be done and things to be believed, but the latter boiled down to believing that Christ was sent by God. This was shown clearly by another piece, 'A brief abstract of the Christian religion', described by Richard Baxter as 'one of his later writings'.[58] Its most interesting feature was its frank degradation of belief to nothing but a motive for good works:

if those to whom this message of the Gospel of Christ should be published, should yet not believe the same, nor yet believe that Jesus was the true Messias, or that his doctrine was the true and real message of Almighty God to the world it could never be expected that they would obey this heavenly command, nor return to God, or the duty they owed him; he did therefore require of all persons that were of understanding, to whom the Gospel should be published, that they should believe it to be true . . .[59]

If, as Hale claimed, the function of credenda was merely to give credibility to Jesus Christ's account of natural law; and if the same 'natural religion' was available in substance to all men at all times, then it was only reasonable to suppose that virtuous pagans could be saved. The biblical example, for Hale as for Selden, was Job. One manuscript treats Job, in an orthodox Calvinist spirit, as profiting from the covenant of God with Abraham (and therefore from the covenant of grace):

this rescue of Job from the idolatrous practices of the times and place wherein he lived as likewise of his four friends we attribute it to the grace and goodness of God who although he made not that special covenant with the descendant of Nahor as he did with Abraham in whose seed all the nations of the earth were to be blessed, yet even in the virtue of that covenant his goodness extended even to those that were not visibly parties to it.[60]

It should be noted, even here, that grace has been directed to producing a life of good works. Job's blessedness derives from the covenant of grace, but consists in a simple religion such as the light of nature might suggest.

The notion of a covenant 'of grace' is attenuated further at the end of

---

[55] *Ibid.*, 289.   [56] *Ibid.*, 288–9.   [57] *Ibid.*, 291.
[58] Printed Hale, *Discourse*, 461–72. For the date see Baxter's preface.
[59] Hale, *Works*, I, 255.   [60] Lambeth 3488, 178v.

another late work, the very wide-ranging manuscript that deals with 'the nature of laws'.[61] This also discussed the salvation of virtuous pagans:

> though the ordinary condition of covenant was faith as well as repentance to as many as were capable of it, yet tis without warrant to exclude all from that general benefit which were invincibly uncapable of performing it for how could they believe unless they had heard and therefore it seems to stand with the wisdom and goodness and intention of God that [there should be] some other method of communicating that benefit and none more probable than the sincere and industrious walking according to the natural law.[62]

The covenant of grace, at this late stage in Hale's development, had lost almost all of its meaning. Once it referred to God's free undertaking to save a number of his sinful creatures by virtue of the sacrifice of Christ. Now it referred instead to the 'conditions' (penitence and faith) that humans were expected to fulfil. The covenant of grace, unlike the former covenant of works, took a sincere endeavour for the deed (C. F. Allison has christened this the 'lowered market' doctrine), but the sincere endeavour was to be generated by the sinner.[63]

Once God had been presented as offering rewards for human effort, it was hard to resist extending the point to the moral efforts of the virtuous pagans. They were governed by the same laws as the Christians, and had at least a dim and imperfect awareness of the behaviour that God required. The doctrine of Christ was 'the most universal, perfect, effectual, explicit publication of the law of nature that ever was or can be given',[64] but it was known and 'at least in great measure' fulfilled by philosophers like Socrates and Zeno.[65] The difference between their beliefs and Christianity was one of degree, not of kind; Christians were not so much better as better informed.

Reading such passages, with their edifying praise for the plainness and simplicity of Christian theological essentials, it is hard to imagine Hale wrestling with the details of predestinarian dogma, as we know he continued to do. A religion that demands 'sincere endeavour', in accordance with the lowered market doctrine, a religion in which faith is reduced to the conclusion of a rational train of thought, seems to have parted company with the orthodox Calvinist past. In the terms of the *Discourse*, the change had been profound; 'faith of recumbency', a supernatural gift, was replaced by a 'faith of assent', the product of a natural operation. What was unchanged, as we shall see, was a sense of man's dependence upon God.

In the pages of the *Discourse*, as the previous chapter showed, God's

---

[61] Probably written in 1668. Discussed above, pp. 90–94 [62] Hargrave 485, 88v.
[63] Allison, *Rise of moralism*, 100. [64] Hargrave 485, 79. [65] *Ibid.*, 899.

influence on natural man (as opposed to the elect) was routed through the intellect alone. He could manipulate the will, however, using his detailed knowledge of his creature, by giving it an 'object' it was certain to find irresistible. The manuscript 'De Deo' expands upon this view, by speaking of a 'knowledge which some do ... call scientia conditionata'. This was 'a knowledge what a free agent would do under such and such an objective motion, though he were not predetermined by the divine will'.[66] He was aware, however, that this might turn the whole of history into no more than a well-designed machine, the Creator being 'an attendant purely' upon the doings he had fore-ordained.[67] He found this possibility abhorrent, both in the natural and the moral world, and all his later works, on science as well as religion, are concerned to depict the Almighty as more than a Clockmaker God.

The agent of involvement was the spirit, a force that he came to associate with merely natural light. An interesting transitional piece, dating from after 1655, discusses the 'invisible church' of Christ.[68] Hale thought this body probably includes the infants and virtuous pagans who have never had a chance to hear the Gospel. The means by which Christ rules this scattered group is by an 'immediate influence of grace', not just the 'light that enlightens every man that cometh into the world' (John i 9), but a 'distinguishing appropriate quality or tincture added to it more than if not different from [the natural light]'.[69] As another essay put it, with a revealingly defensive touch,

those that truly fear God have a more secret guidance from a higher wisdom than what is barely human; namely, by the spirit of truth and wisdom, that doth really and truly, but secretly, prevent and direct them. And let no man think this is a piece of fanaticism. Any man that sincerely and truly fears Almighty God, relies upon him, calls upon him for his guidance and direction, hath it as really as the son hath the counsel and direction of his father.[70]

The survival of the workings of the spirit as a central feature of Hale's religious ideas posed both a private and a public problem. He needed to find ways to reconcile this spiritual influence both with a low-key ethical religion, and also, in an age obsessed by the crimes of real or imaginary 'fanatics', with the requirements of public order.

He accomplished this, in essence, by identifying God's aid to the faithful with the ordinary promulgation of natural law. Selden's *De jure naturali* had suggested a medium by which the moral law was to be known, a medium which made available those principles traditionally said to have

---

[66] Hale, *Works*, I, 369. 'Objective' means 'pertaining to an object'.
[67] Lambeth 3492, 223v.
[68] Lambeth 3507, 117–122v. The volume is entitled 'contemplationes ... ab anno 1655'.
[69] Lambeth 3507, 119v.-120.   [70] Hale, *Works*, II, 31.

been 'written in the hearts of men'.[71] The morally healthy person partici-
pates in an 'active intellect'. The *Intellectus Agens* was a notorious Aristotelian concept, the crux of many arguments about the philosopher's
relevance to Christianity. Some held that he believed that only this shared
faculty survived the body's death; these were the 'Averroists', a few of
whom (like the famous Pomponazzi (1462–1525), a stock example of an
'atheist') secretly shared this anti-Christian view. This was a point that was
to trouble Hale, when he came to write a treatise on the soul. In Selden's
hands, however, the *Intellectus Agens* served some rather more orthodox
ends.

Selden presented his ideas, as often in his works, as the consensus among
Jewish thinkers. He identified the entity with God, or with a subordinate
'intelligence', and compared it to an intellectual sun, illuminating the
truths of natural law.[72] The most attractive feature of this hypothesis was
its account of human moral failure. The principles of morality were
eternally the same, and in a sense were 'written on the heart', but they
could only be perceived with assistance provided by God. The *Intellectus
Agens* was not a moral sense (as it were, the moral sight), but just a
precondition of the sense's exercise. God could withdraw a 'light' without
affecting man's identity. It was no more a part of the soul, as Selden
himself had explained, than the sun was a component of the eye.[73]

Hale's immediate source was Selden, but there may have been nothing
unusual about his approach.[74] The philosopher Leibniz certainly thought
(in 1685) that it was something of a commonplace:

God is the sun and the light of souls – lumen illuminans omnem hominem
venientem in hunc mundum[75] – and this opinion has not been invented only today.
In addition to the Holy Scripture and the fathers, who were always more Platonists
than Aristotelians, I recall having observed long ago that at the time of the
scholastics, several believed that God is the light of the soul and as they put it, the
intellectus agens animae rationalis. The Averroists gave this a bad turn of
meaning . . .[76]

Hale was well aware of Averroist dangers, as a subsequent chapter will
show, particularly in view of the importance of punishments God threatened to the sinner. If a collective entity was man's immortal part, then it
was wholly unacceptable; if, on the other hand, it 'assisted' or even
'advanced' him, to 'render him a more resplendent image of God than

---

[71] Selden, *Opera*, I, 157.   [72] *Ibid.*, 152–3.   [73] *Ibid.*
[74] For a contemporary influenced by Selden, see Nathaniel Culverwell, *An elegant and
learned discourse of the light of nature*, ed. Robert A. Greene and Hugh MacCallum,
Toronto 1971, esp. pp. 67–71.
[75] 'The light that enlightens every man coming into this world.'
[76] Leibniz, *Philosophical letters and papers*, tr. and ed. L. E. Loemker, 2nd edn, Dordrecht
1969, p. 321.

barely what he had by his natural constitution', then it had obvious theological uses.[77] To Averroes himself, Hale more than once reported, the active intellect was 'spiritus sanctus'.[78] He therefore took a middle path, insisting that man unaided was capable of thought but acknowledging

a divine principle or power de foris which is assisting form and oftentimes (if not always) joines itself to the human intellect (as a tree though it have a vital principle in itself yet receives influence from the sun) and it will not be of much moment if it be called the Intellectus Agens or by any other name.[79]

This power was 'the light that enlightens every man that cometh into the world' (John i 9), the spirit that 'strives' with man (Genesis vi 3), and the 'light that is the life of men' (John i 4).[80] These characteristic texts go some way to explaining the concept's importance for Hale; it enabled him to slip between talking of grace as spirit and talking of grace as the only source of intellectual light.[81]

This spirit that was light both prepared and helped the soul, 'irradiating the understanding' and 'warming and sweetly moving the will by its heat', in order that God himself should be received.[82] What had been lost since the *Discourse* was the sense that faith is an act of God *in* man, as opposed to an act *of* man, assisted and preceded by God's power. It was possible, he granted, that there might be some 'extraordinary effluxes' of God's grace (biblical prophecy and miracles were certainly examples of this type). God usually acted, however, through a 'general and common efflux of the spirit'. This was 'a common instituted order settled in the intellectual world for the common good of mankind though possibly not in the same measure nor equally received by all men and this is what is meant by that of John i 9 [the light that enlightens every man] ...'[83] The grace of God was not an extraordinary mercy, but a manifestation of a general rule.

---

[77] Add. 9001, 148; Lambeth 3500, 75.   [78] Lambeth 3500, 93v., 234.

[79] *Ibid.*, 93v.

[80] Lambeth 3498, 76v.; Lambeth 3500, 93v.

[81] Nuttall notices that 'the simile of light, with or without mention of the sun, occurs again and again in [puritan] writers, and forms the link in their thought between experience and intuitive reason'. Nuttall, *The Holy Spirit in puritan faith and experience*, Oxford 1946, p. 40. For a parallel development, in another cultural context, see Andrew C. Fix, *Prophecy and reason: the Dutch Collegiants in the early Enlightenment*, Princeton 1991, esp. pp. 185–214.

[82] Lambeth 3498, 76.

[83] *Ibid.*, 76v. Contrast, on John i 9, the opinion of Calvin himself: 'since fanatics eagerly seize upon this verse and twist it into saying that the grace of illumination is offered to all without distinction, let us remember that it is only referring to the common light of nature, a far lowlier thing than faith ... Moreover, we must remember that the light of reason which God imparted to men has been so darkened by sin that scarcely a few meagre sparks shine unquenched in this intense darkness or rather dreadful ignorance and abyss of errors'. *Calvin's commentaries: the Gospel according to St John i–x*, tr.T. H. L. Parker, ed. D. W. and T. F. Torrance, 1959, p. 15.

This new understanding of spirit remained wholly compatible with a sense of the creature's absolute dependence. He denied, against Arminians, that humans could resist the grace of God. It was possible, he continued to believe, that the deity might act upon the will. This 'irresisistible' exercise of grace, which many scriptures vouched for, was not to be regarded as a breach of the natural order. As the 'De Deo' manuscript insisted, 'an immediate bending of the soul is not to be said a violence but a result of its essential dependence'. He added, a little equivocally, that 'I do not say that it is always or that it is frequent', and he had earlier written that 'ordinarily [God] doth not'.[84]

One possible solution to this problem, consistent with the general transformation in Hale's thought, was to reduce the will, as such, to a conclusion of the intellect. The manuscript treatise concerned with the 'nature of laws' confessed attraction to the proposition that 'the understanding and will are not so much two distinct faculties but rather the will is the last act of the soul in things practical'.[85] Elsewhere he pronounced that the will was 'distinguished from [the intellect] rather notionally than really', by being the mere completion of intellection.[86] This very close connection gave the human understanding (intellect) the mastery over voluntary actions, unless it was pre-empted by a bestial appetite:

For it is a hard matter to conceive how the understanding can deliberately and plenarily conclude an object to be particularly good or evil unless the will go along with it for such a conclusion is in effect the conjunction of the act of understanding to the will and if the sensitive appetite be powerful upon the will and averse to the conclusion of the understanding it precipitates the will before the understanding hath plenarily resolved or determined a particular good nor evil.[87]

The will could not resist the intellect, and the intellect, as Hale was always sure, could not resist an intellectual light:

Almighty God doth and may convince the understanding irresistibly and by a secret and intrinsecal operation upon it neither is it any difficulty to conceive that

---

[84] Lambeth 3492, 224v ; Lambeth 3480, 183. A more compressed version of these views is Hale, *Magnetismus magnus, or metaphysical and divine contemplations of the magnet or loadstone*, 1695, pp. 136–7.

[85] Hargrave 485, 6v.

[86] Lambeth 3505, 211. A thought-provoking opportunity for comparison is the psychology of Thomas Hobbes. As Hobbes did not believe in universals, he chose to identify 'will' (a human faculty) with impulses derived from the 'imagination' (a term of art describing a faculty we share with animals). Thus *Leviathan* declared that 'imagination was the first internal beginning of all voluntary motion' (p. 118), while 'the last appetite or aversion adhering to the action, or to the omission thereof, is that we call the will; the act (not the faculty) of willing. And beasts that have deliberation, must necessarily also have will. The definition of will, given commonly by the schools, that it is a rational appetite, is not good. For if it were, there could be no voluntary act against reason ... Will therefore is the last appetite in deliberating' (pp. 127–8).

[87] Lambeth 3505, 211.

this may be. For that active part of the understanding which the philosophers call Intellectus Agens is a pure immaterial nature . . .[88]

The will would then fulfil its proper role, in longing for the object (man's chief end) that correct moral thinking presents. There was a sense, indeed, in which grace was a precondition of 'that noble power which we call liberty of will vizt. to act from an internal intellectual principle'.[89] Only a mind informed by the *Intellectus Agens* (that is, by the spirit of God) could properly claim to be free, as only such a mind could really be said to operate in an intellectual way.[90] The religion of the *Discourse* was a religion of the quickening spirit, but so was the rational creed of Hale's last years.

---

[88] Lambeth 3492, 225.   [89] Lambeth 3493, 116v.

[90] Hale was not, of course, the first to resolve the problem of 'freedom of the will' by routing the influence of grace through the intellect instead. Richard Baxter's *Catholick theology* (1675), a work that Hale greatly admired (Hale, *Works*, I, 109) repeatedly associates this view with the Franco-Scottish thinker Camero (John Cameron of Saumur). He was probably thinking especially of two of Camero's 'Theses Salmurienses':

VII Haec porro gratia non mentem modo afficit, verum etiam voluntatem idque motu proprie dicto, atque (ut loquuntur) reali. non modo enim per eam obiicitur utcumque animo species veri boni; sic enim nihil aliud promoveretur, quam ut animus id respueret. sed ita afficitur animus, ineffabili quadam spiritus sancti vi, ut quod vere bonum est pervideat primum, tum deinde amet et sectetur.

IX Caeterum haec Dei actio sic peragitur, ut quemadmodum mens et voluntas natura sua inter se sunt aptae et connexae, ut voluntas a mente pendeat. Sic mentis renovatio, voluntatis renovationem producat. (*Defensio Johannis Cameronis S. evangelii ministri* Saumur, 1624., sig. e2.)

Hale and religious dissent

The mark of true religion, Hale believed, was the way that it transfigured the duties of everyday life: 'this is the great art of Christian chymistry, to convert those acts that are materially natural or civil into acts truly and formally religious; whereby the whole course of this life is both truly and interpretatively a service to Almighty God, and an uninterrupted state of religion....'[1] Hale had been taught by Selden that obedience to local regulations was really obedience to God. God had created man as a maker of binding contracts in his sight, as a creature who was free to constitute practically all of his moral obligations. As the 'De Deo' manuscript expressed it, 'I do not violate another man's wife, his life, his goods because I have expressly or tacitly promised the contrary'.[2] If a society were to survive, the God who enforced these contracts must be preached.

One of the many puritan attitudes Hale kept from the religion of his youth was the importance he attached to sermons. He wrote a little essay on the theme 'that a preaching ministry of the Gospel must be kept up', depicting the maintenance of preachers as an essential function of any Christian state: 'the public neglect of the ordinances of Christ for the saving of souls will be a plain profession of rejection of Christ and a plain symptom of God's rejecting of the nation, a professed making way for the dominion of darkness and evil.'[3] The material needs of the preacher were a highly important religious and political constraint. As a loyal disciple of Selden, Hale denied that the clergy enjoyed a divine right to tithes, but he freely acknowledged their God-given right to the laity's support, 'which maintenance was always moulded according to different positive laws, customs and dispositions of several places and times'.[4] He was severe to radicals who objected to this levy on conscientious grounds, and spoke of their behaviour as a kind of 'sacrilege'.[5] The alternative to preaching, in purely political terms, was 'disorder in all civil offices between man and

---

[1] Hale, *Works*, II, 246.   [2] Lambeth 3492, 141.   [3] Lambeth 3506, 125.
[4] Lambeth 3479, 38. See also Lambeth 3506, 125–7; Lambeth 3497, 28v.
[5] Lambeth 3497, 28v.

man, and if there were no other reason the light of moral prudence will teach a preservation of religion.'[6]

'Religion' in this sense was a feature of every imaginable state, one which was every magistrate's legitimate concern. God must be publicly worshipped, and the authorities had both a right and duty to command the strict observance of certain outward forms: 'the enjoining of decent ceremonies is commendable in the magistrate and commendable in them that submit to it'.[7] If a patriarchal father, someone like Abraham,[8] could organise the worship of his household, then so could the Christian prince: 'it were hard and unreasonable to deny that to the magistrate which the law of God and nature allows to the father of a family, who may counsel his children to religious duties as well as will by correction and punishment be suitable to their conditions and capacities.'[9] This was the far from liberal presumption that ruled his theoretical approach to religious dissent.

Hale's sense that any society depended on acquaintance with God's punishments for sin made heresy a concern for the secular lawyer. The Commonwealth had made an Act (in the absence of church courts) 'against several atheistical blasphemous and execrable opinions, derogatory to the honour of God, and destructive to humane society'. This law had been discussed, perhaps in Hale's own presence, in the Upper Bench case of the Keepers v. Norwood and Tany (1652). The court had been asked to decide if denial of hell but not heaven was beyond the statute's scope.[10] He would certainly have approved of the Commonwealth's measure, as he showed in the case which established that blasphemy was a crime at common law. In R. v. Taylor (1676), a blasphemer of unusual thoroughness was arraigned in the court of King's Bench. He had openly proclaimed, amongst other horrible statements, that 'Christ is a whoremaster, and religion is a cheat, and profession a cloak, and all cheats, all are mine, and I am a King's son and fear neither God, devil nor man. I am Christ's younger brother (proved by three witnesses), and that Christ is a bastard, and damn all Gods of the Quakers etc.'[11]

The natural jurisdiction to cope with this offence was of course the bishop's court; Hale needed to show that King's Bench was also competent. He found that

these words, though of ecclesiastical cognisance, yet that religion is a cheat, tends to the dissolution of all government, and therefore punishable here, and so of contumelious reproaches of God or the religion established. An indictment lay for saying the Protestant religion was a fiction for taking away religion, all obligations

---

[6] Lambeth 3506, 125.   [7] *Ibid.*, 99.   [8] Genesis xviii 19.
[9] Bodleian Library, Rawlinson MSS, A 400, p.30.
[10] Gray's Inn MS 33, 123–4.   [11] 3 Keble 607.

to oaths etc., ceaseth, and Christian religion is a part of the law itself, therefore injuries to God are as punishable as to the King, or any common person.[12]

The other version of this famous judgement suggests that he decided on two grounds: first that 'to say, religion is a cheat is to dissolve all those obligations whereby the civil societies are preserved', and secondly that 'Christianity is parcel of the laws of England; and therefore to reproach the Christian religion is to speak in subversion of the law'.[13] The preservation of the Christian faith was part of the defence of common law.

For latitudinarians like Hale, believers that Christ had 'republished' natural law, the Christian faith was practically exhausted by its function in enforcing social norms. The errors that opposed it, the evils of idolatry and atheistic vice, were closely linked, as we shall see, to contemporary political disorders.[14] Like many devout believers till close to our own time, Hale doubted that anyone really thought that God did not exist.[15] Some people, however, behaved as if this were the case, or at least as if the wicked were not punished; this was 'practical atheism', based on the sinful yearning for a world without a God, amounting morally to deicide.[16] Such people were invariably keen to deny the soul's survival after death, and therefore the existence of the sanctions of natural law. Atheism was not really a speculative belief, but a depraving tendency that afflicted fallen man. It was no less universal than the moral intuitions it denied, as anyone could know by introspection: 'though it be against the very light of nature yet if any man examine himself he shall find in himself secret corrupted inclinations of his heart towards it.'[17]

Religion's other enemy, the sin of idolatrous worship, might also have a damaging effect on political life. Idolatry was worship misdirected, resulting from a pious will mistaking means for ends. It arose from man's sensual nature, with its preference for an object that could be touched and seen, and ended in full-blown polytheism: 'when once they began to worship god in a sensual and prohibited way they fell at length to terminate their worship in those very things which at first they used but as helps to their senses, and the same are now become the object of their worship.'[18] This had its analogue, of course, in the history of the Christian faith itself; in ancient times

there were certain gay and splendid entertainments to win them over to Christianity as we deal with children: they shall see fine copes and palls and gesticulations and hear delicate music and this possibly was of some use at that time. But when men are grown up into the knowledge of the truth and understand that the

---

[12] *Ibid.*   [13] 1 Ventris 293.
[14] Hale's attitude to atheism is clearest in Lambeth 3482, 44v.–53v.
[15] Lambeth 3492, 339.   [16] Hale, *Discourse*, 283.   [17] Lambeth 3482, 44v.
[18] Lambeth 3484, 59v.

business of the Christian religion is a trade for another world and find that these are but childish allurements ... they become utterly useless.[19]

The spiritual and sensual, or 'carnal', were regularly treated as inherently opposed. The good for man could not be seen or sensed, and any lower pleasure potentially distracted from this goal; most sins were a kind of idolatry, mistaking passing carnal goods for the chief end of man. Church music, for example, though it seemed just a harmless adornment, was dangerous to the extent that it was beautiful. Beauty was to be feared, for 'anything of rareness and curiosity doth affect the senses too strongly and carries the heart after the ear or eye'.[20]

It was idolatry, of course, that puritans detected in the disputed ceremonies enforced by the Anglican church. Conformists defended these practices as things that were 'indifferent' in themselves. Hale recognised a possibility that something much more sinister might grow from such a root: 'the practice itself it may be was at first looked upon as a thing indifferent yet succession of time hath given it another title. And so the latter generation taking up as necessary what the former successions of ages hath [sic] practised they multiply superstitions.'[21] In the modern world, however, the prime example of idolatry was the fruit of a religion that was consciously corrupt. There was no point in arguing with papist clergymen, because their 'religion of interest' was not sincerely held. It was the consequence of 'politic design or contrivance to support the dignity power wealth splendour and magnificence of their ecclesiastical state or church as they call it.'[22] The Roman Catholic faith was just a tissue of absurdities, abuses whose one common feature was promotion of clerical power.[23] Some opinions, he reluctantly admitted, might not have been invented for pure gain, 'but here hath been the art of it: the politicians of the Roman clergy have taken up such as might be serviceable for the ends of that ecclesiastical state'.[24] On assumptions such as Hale's about the very nature of religion, there was obviously no question of tolerating atheists or papists. These were not the kind of doctrines that a reasonable person might erroneously hold: atheism, strictly speaking, was not an intellectual position, but an unnatural impulse that subverted civil life; the popery of educated men was just a vulgar fraud upon the faithful, as well as a conspiracy against the English state. Behind the one lurked anarchy; behind the other the tyranny of the pope.

Hale's attitudes to both these social dangers are known from various writings of the Restoration years. He thought the needs of church and state

---

[19] Lambeth 3497, 41.   [20] Lambeth 3507, 115.   [21] Lambeth 3491, 16–16v.
[22] Lambeth 3496, 38.
[23] *Ibid.*, 38–219; Lambeth 3498, 279–91.   [24] Lambeth 3496, 106.

were quite inextricably intertwined, a fact which gave the magistrate an interest in suppressing religious dissent:

the reasonableness and indeed necessity of this coercion in matters of religion is apparent for the concerns of religion and the civil state are so twisted one with another that confusion and disorder an[d] anarchy in the former must of necessity introduce confusion and dissolution of the latter.[25]

The history of the civil war and interregnum years had given empirical backing to this authoritarian assumption. In times when order was enforced there had been very little heresy, which prompted the sad conclusion that 'much of that religion which seemed to prevail in many men in the former and more sober times was in truth either forced or feigned for temporal advantage'.[26] At first 'the only party that visibly appeared were some that desired some reformation in church matters', generally known as presbyterians. They soon acquired a rival, in the shape of the independents, who 'much despised the former as not arrived to a just measure of reformation'. These were in turn out-flanked by 'a kind of lay party which as much undervalued the independent and indeed the ministry in general', before some sort of logical conclusion was reached by the Quaker beliefs.[27]

Hale was particularly alarmed by appeals to divine inspiration, entitling the Quakers and others to disrupt the public services in church: 'he that today pretends an inspiration or a divine impulse to disturb a minister in his sermon tomorrow may pretend another inspiration to take away his goods or his life'.[28] The climax of religious and political disorder was made more horrible by just such claims: 'breaking down all the most sacred and solemn and awful protections of religion liberty property and authority, and all this without any seeming reluctance, nay printing upon it and coining it with the pretence of religion of the impulse of God himself.'[29] The experience of these radical excesses left Hale profoundly sceptical about institutional change. He defended the rule of bishops, on the grounds that he defended other parts of English law: that it was 'most prudential and suited to our civil constitution'.[30] Like other constitutional arrangements, it had been vindicated by the failure of experiments with change: any one that 'hath but strictly observed the walk of things in these late times' would conclude that 'the kingdom will soon cast off' attempts to govern the church in other ways.[31] The presbyterian discipline by elders was viewed with a particular distaste. Hale saw it with a lawyer's eye, as an imperialistic jurisdiction, which 'will consequentially if not immediately draw the decision of all causes to their consistories the consequence

---

[25] Lambeth 3496, 10.   [26] Lambeth 3507, 77v.   [27] Lambeth 3485, 126v.
[28] Lambeth 3497, 26.
[29] Lambeth 3507, 77v.   [30] Lambeth 3497, 52.   [31] Lambeth 3498, 275.

whereof must of necessity be a perfect subjection of all civil rights and government to the ecclesiastical.'[32] Even this was preferable to congregationalism, which tended to dissolve the primary social unit, creating 'disunions in families the husband of one church, the wife of another, the child of a third, the servant of a fourth.'[33] and leading observers to conclude that 'all religion is but a notion and cast off all'.[34]

In 1660, then, Hale was what Richard Baxter called a 'moderate episcopal man'. He had been a friend of the great Archbishop Ussher (1581–1656), a figure that most puritans admired, who was author of 'Ussher's Reduction', a famous scheme to compromise with puritan objections to the English episcopal frame. He was in touch, in 1659, with Ussher's chaplain and biographer, who wrote to him, as to a kindred spirit, lamenting 'a dying nation and a forsaken church'.[35] He could write of a course of action to be taken 'if I can gain a moderate episcopacy settled',[36] and he favoured the appointment of leading 'presbyterians' like Baxter to the episcopal bench of a broad-based church.[37] He was therefore a natural supporter of the 'Worcester House Declaration' (25 October 1660), which would have modified the rule of bishops to conform with various presbyterian scruples. He would have been closely involved in the bill to make this compromise a law, if the king had not removed him from the Commons by giving him an office as a judge.[38]

Hale's own proposals for a settlement were contained in a modest essay, 'Touching church government', composed in the aftermath of restoration. They are notable, if anything, for their pragmatic tone. He assumed like many others, including probably Clarendon himself, that Anglican ceremonial could not be re-imposed: 'the impressions of the presbyterian ministers have now prevailed these 18 years and although they could never carry on all their presbytery yet they have much possessed the minds of their hearers with an opinion against these ceremonies.'[39] The *Book of Common Prayer* was orthodox, except under 'a very hard uncharitable and strained construction',[40] and Hale certainly preferred it to the parliamentarian *Directory for the public worship of God* (1644), dismissively referred to as 'the late essays of some of the presbyterian judgement'.[41] The

---

[32] Lambeth 3507, 154.
[33] *Ibid.*, 151 (foliation confused: 151 follows 142). In 1646 Thomas Edwards told the story of 'one Mr Y, who related that in his family there were but four persons, himself, his wife, a man and a maidservant, and, saith he, we are of several churches and ways'. Cited in Murray Tolmie, *The triumph of the saints: the separate churches of London 1616–49*, Cambridge 1977, p. 133.
[34] Lambeth 3507, 151v.
[35] Samuel Parr to Hale, Camberwell, 14 July 1659. Lambeth 3513, 114.
[36] Lambeth 3507, 136v.   [37] Hale, *Works*, I, 94–5.
[38] Henning, *House of Commons*, II, 462.
[39] Lambeth 3507, 167.   [40] Lambeth 3506, 99–100.   [41] Lambeth 3497, 42r.

revisions he proposed were nonetheless designed to meet traditional moderate puritan objections. He envisaged the abolition of the surplice, which had 'too much assimilation to Romish clergy', and 'carries some resemblance of legal priesthood'.[42] The placing of the table at communion altarwise and the practice of bowing towards it came in for rather harsher criticism. They were 'not only unfit to be enjoined but fit to be inhibited, giving offence to many that are well persuaded of other ceremonies'.[43] The singing of prayers, use of the Apocrypha ('offensive to the best'), bowing at the name of Jesus, kneeling at communion, and the sign of the cross were all to be abolished or at least made optional.[44] It need not be assumed that he shared or even sympathised with all of the puritan scruples; he disliked bowing at the name of Jesus,[45] but he found the act of kneeling rather helpful,[46] so he was doing more than list his own liturgical hates.

These objections all arose from prayer book rubrics; so far as the text was concerned, Hale's major substantial proposal concerned the role of baptism in transmitting saving grace. The claim that 'this child is regenerate', which usurped a decision for God, was to be dropped from the baptismal service.[47] Otherwise, he objected to praying for 'others departed in the Christian faith'[48] and to the implication that episcopal rule in the church was a 'great marvel',[49] which seemed to differentiate the bishops from other ordained ministers having a cure of souls. In another concession to presbyterian theories, the dean and chapter of each diocese were to become a college, elected by their fellow presbyters. They would assist the bishop in everything he did, including, crucially, in excommunication and ordaining.[50]

In reading these proposals, one is struck by Hale's aloofness from bitter theological debates. His strongest personal feelings, as might have been expected in Selden's spiritual heir, seem to have been reserved for points at which the rule of common law was threatened. Thus he characteristically stressed that powers of jurisdiction (that is, in this context, of excommunication) were not intrinsic to the bishop's role. The only abuse he described that prompted him to show much indignation was the practice, denounced as 'illusory and vain', of convocation making laws without a parliament.[51] In one rather striking respect, he was actually more conservative than Anglicans like Stillingfleet or Ussher. Notable by its absence from his scheme is any plan to disendow or divide the ancient sees, whose wealth he considered a useful means of 'keeping up the honour of religion'.[52]

[42] Lambeth 3507, 164. [43] *Ibid.*, 165. [44] *Ibid.*, 165–6.
[45] Hale, *Works*, I, 104.
[46] Lambeth 3507, 165. [47] *Ibid.*, 166. [48] *Ibid.*, 166. [49] *Ibid.*, 166.
[50] *Ibid.*, 172.
[51] *Ibid.*, 166v. Opposite fo. 155. [52] Hale, *Works*, I, 101.

Hale wanted to accommodate the godly, by doing away with the features they were known to find objectionable in the English church. He thought he was dealing with people who agreed with him on all essential points, but who gave a religious significance to things that were 'indifferent' in themselves. The question of religious 'toleration', of allowing heretics to persist in error, did not at this moment arise. A sadly undated later manuscript gave an interesting taxonomy of the forms of religious dissent.[53] Only the Anabaptists and the very few Socinians in England disagreed with the English church on points of doctrine. All other disagreements were over ceremonies and government. Of the nonconformist groupings only the Brownists,[54] Quakers, and some Baptists would actually 'unchurch' the church of England: deny, in other words, that a sincere believer could be saved within its ranks. Hale wanted to 'give satisfaction' to the mass of remaining dissenters, the various presbyterians and congregationalists, ideally by allowing them a place within a comprehensive church.[55]

This would obviously prove impossible, if they were inflexibly wedded to their incompatible theories about the church's form. In fact, he argued, probably correctly, that strict ecclesiologies found little dissenting support. The Genevan and Scottish model, with its role for the lay elders in maintaining discipline, had seldom had much influence on English 'presbyterian' ideas: 'as to the point of formal excommunication and authoritative ordination they most commonly reserve it to the *consensus presbyterorum*'.[56] The congregationalists gave the powers of discipline and ordination to the congregation taken as a whole, but this was probably just a reaction against the threat of a minister's absolute rule.[57] The idea that 'every presbyter was to be *de jure* a bishop in his own congregation' was never popular among the English, although strict congregationalists did better 'by the favour of the later end of the late troubles'.[58]

Hale had convinced himself, in other words, that the only real divisions among English Protestants were based on particular conscientious scruples, arising from objections to various features of the liturgy. Hale's views about the conscience in relation to the state were reasonably clear. There was no such thing, of course, as a legal right to obey one's private conscience, unless perhaps the founding civil contract included an explicit conscience clause. This was improbable, to say the least, if only because 'the supposition of such a condition doth utterly enervate all the power of

[53] Bodleian Library, Rawlinson MSS A 400, pp. 32–7.
[54] Rigid separatists, defined by their total rejection of any non-congregational church, as opposed to 'non-separating congregationalists' (the type found in New England, whose English leader was the great John Owen).
[55] Rawlinson A 400, 35.   [56] *Ibid.*, 35–6.   [57] *Ibid.*, 36.   [58] *Ibid.*

[the] magistrate, for it sets up in every particular subject a tribunal superior to that of the magistrate ...'[59] No one could claim exemption from the magistrate's commands on the grounds they believed those commands to be morally wrong. Conscience must be obeyed, in preference to any human power, but the government was perfectly entitled to punish sincere objectors to its will.

Hale disapproved of any institution, like presbyterian synods or the Roman Catholic church, which asserted a claim upon conscience (in things indifferent) potentially in conflict with the state's. His theory precluded creation of such institutions, by limiting the force of private vows:

determination of a thing indifferent by the vow of a subject unless tacitly or expressly assented to by the supreme power may be rescinded by the supreme power and the reason is ... the subject as to this thing indifferent is not purely sui juris nor civilly master of his own will as in reference to the supreme magistrate unto whom he hath tacitly or expressly transferred his will as to this matter by an obligation precedent to his vow ...[60]

This was a point of some significance, for a high proportion of the English nation, including Hale and even Charles II, had taken the 'Solemn League and Covenant', a promise amongst other things to 'endeavour the extirpation' of the existing government of the church.[61] Whatever the king's own position, this explained why other Englishmen were entitled to regard this oath as null.

So far as things indifferent were concerned, the magistrate's power was quite unlimited. He did have a duty, however, to consider the likely results of his arrangements. He should avoid imposing laws that were bound to offend against the subject's conscience. It was 'a breach of the law of charity' to give someone an unnecessary order that he could not conscientiously obey. There might even be a duty to retract a command of this type.[62] The magistrate should also bear in mind that something like a surplice, though harmless in itself, might tend to lead a simple mind astray. A biblical example that godly writers gave was the destruction of the brazen serpent (2 Kings xviii 4), an object made by Moses without the least idolatrous intent.[63] The serpent was destroyed by Hezekiah because the Israelites had worshipped it. Hale agreed with the puritan writers that

[59] Lambeth 3507, 32.
[60] *Ibid.*, 28. For a similar use of the phrase 'sui juris', by the conformist casuist Sanderson, see McAdoo, *Moral theology*, 85–6. Compare also Hobbes, *Leviathan*, 366: 'the law is the public conscience, by which he hath already undertaken to be guided'.
[61] Kenyon, *Stuart constitution*, 240. It was necessary to take this oath to practise in the parliamentarian courts.
[62] Lambeth 3507, 36v.
[63] Cobbett, *State trials*, II, 84. A point rebutted in Francis Mason, *Of the authority of the Church in making canons and constitutions in things indifferent*, 2nd edn, Oxford 1634, p.39.

if in truth [the serpent] did seduce the people to idolatry and Hezekiah had been told of it but believed it not it had been a sin at least of ignorance if he continued it. But if it had seduced the people to idolatry and Hezekiah had not known or been acquainted of it then it had been no sin in Hezekiah to have continued it . . .[64]

Hale further agreed that some aspects of Anglican practice, like the treatment of a table as an altar, were helpful to the papists in perverting English minds.[65] It was, by implication, 'a sin at least of ignorance' that parliament 'continued' the abuse.

Faced with a puritan, in other words, who believed that a thing indifferent was wrong, Hale was inclined to change the rules to suit the puritan. Faced with more radical dissent, involving denial of truths that the church upheld, he was much more authoritarian. The magistrate too had a conscience, which might instruct him to enforce his own religious tastes, but there were anyway at least four cases in which he was always entitled to ignore the subject's views. He could employ coercion to uphold the laws of nature, to keep the public peace, to punish 'injuries to the civil interest' (Hale's example was refusal to pay tithes), and to 'punish the neglect of a moral action which might advance the knowledge of a better persuasion in the party'.[66] This final category seems flexible, but would obviously cover attendance at Anglican Mattins.

There was indeed a duty to educate the heretic out of his heresy. Someone afflicted with an 'erroneous conscience' was necessarily condemned to sin, either against his conscience or the truth, 'and therefore there is no way of extricating such an erroneous conscience from sin but first by rectifying and convincing the mistake of his conscience for till that [be] done he is under a necessity of sinning.'[67] On these assumptions it was difficult to resist the paternalist case for religious coercion, particularly as error appealed so powerfully to carnal man. Hale considered the optimistic view that a general toleration would lead to the final victory of truth, but concluded that bad religion would tend to drive out good:

Thou shalt not tempt the Lord thy God. God Almighty hath given the children of men reason and prudence and it is to be employed as well in matter relating to religion as in civil concerns. It were a wildness to expect that the corrupt religions should not more probably infect our weak and corrupted nature rather than to think a true religion should not receive corruption . . .[68]

This was the side of Hale that had noted the triumph of atheism in the absence of the king's authority, and that reportedly described the Test Act

---

[64] Lambeth 3507, 23v.   [65] *Ibid.*, 165.   [66] Lambeth 3498, 269.
[67] Lambeth 3507, 22.
[68] British Library, Stowe MS 163, fo. 154.

(1673), which he may have helped to draft, as 'the best Act ever was made'.[69]

Hale conceded that capital punishment was rarely an appropriate response to errors on points of theology alone; there was certainly never a reason to kill to enforce a particular theory about the sacraments.[70] He also acknowledged some practical grounds for avoiding persecution:

> sometimes when a distemper grows too patent a liberal concession gives it bounds when granted before it is asked which when men know their strength and begin to demand know no other bounds than their own desires. And this I must confess carries more weight than forty other little reasons besides multitudo dissidentium dissidentibus libertatem quasi cogit.[71]

Even in such an unfortunate situation (the situation, surely, of Restoration times), it was wise to keep some powers in reserve. He thought that 'some laws may secure even when they may not be fit to be at all times severely pressed'.[72]

Hale's position is rather confusing, perhaps because its author was confused. On the one hand he believed that some form of religious coercion, including imposition of 'decent' ceremonial in worship, was both the right and duty of the civil magistrate. As the history of the civil wars had shown, religious diversity ended in social collapse. The plea of conscience was untestable, and in any case inherently subversive. Hale was notable, however, for his kindness to dissenters he encountered, including the Baptist John Bunyan, who would have been excluded from any national church.[73] For all his suspicion of Quakers and their claims to inner light, he greatly admired their 'exquisite righteousness'.[74] He even showed some sympathy, if Fox's *Journal* is to be believed, for the sufferings of the movement's founding father. A brilliant Quaker barrister named Corbett had managed to secure the old enthusiast's release. Hale was urged to re-imprison him, as 'a dangerous man to set at liberty', but 'Judge Hale said he had heard some such reports of me, but he had heard also many good reports of me'.[75]

One explanation of Hale's attitudes was a profound ambivalence about the spirit's role in human life. In the *Discourse*, it may be remembered, he

---

[69] Burnet, *History*, II, 16n. There is an undated 'Act for suppression of popery' among Hale's papers (Lambeth 3475, 277), containing a suggested oath against transubstantiation identical with the Test Act's.

[70] Lambeth 3496, 11.

[71] 'A multitude of dissenters as it were compels a liberty for dissenters'. Lambeth 3498, 275.

[72] *Ibid.*, 276v.

[73] See John Bunyan, *Grace abounding to the chief of sinners*, ed. Roger Sharrock, Oxford 1986, pp. 129–33.

[74] Lambeth 3509, 59.

[75] John L. Nicholls (ed.), *The journal of George Fox*, Cambridge 1952, p. 705.

showed a great respect for private conscience, however irrational its promptings might seem. The revolution years made Hale and other Englishmen suspicious of claims to special revelation; appeals to inspiration from the spirit, as various antinomians had shown, were an implicit threat to social peace. The result (to some extent perhaps the purpose) of the shift away from Calvinist ideas was to re-define the spiritual to exclude the socially dysfunctional. Hale's behaviour clearly showed a certain unease about this implication, which surfaced on an intellectual level in the fact that he 'had great distaste' for two famous attacks on nonconformity.[76]

Samuel Parker was nearly a deist, but also a profoundly authoritarian man. His indifference to religious forms was such that he could have held office in anyone's church, and he was in fact to prosper in that of James II. His *Discourse of ecclesiastical polity* (1670), the book of which Hale so much disapproved, based an intolerant argument on the premise that 'the essence of divine worship consists in nothing else but a grateful sense and temper of mind towards the divine goodness.'[77] It was beyond the power of earthly monarchs to stop their subjects feeling gratitude, but the sentiment's outward expression was a matter for the state. The most minimal of natural religions proved the ideal foundation for justifying repression of dissent.

The second book that Hale disliked was Simon Patrick's *A friendly debate between a conformist and a nonconformist* (1668), a highly unfriendly assault on puritan conceptions of the 'spirit'. The conformist prefers to take 'reason' as his guide, and derides every claim to subjective experience of God: 'whatever you feel it is not proof of the truth of the thing, but only of the truth of your belief'.[78] A most important element in Patrick's attack upon puritan religion was a sneer at all the tactics that were likely to encourage an 'enthusiastic' faith. There was no place for eloquence in the pulpit, as the best form of preaching was an unadorned presentation of the facts. He jeered at puritan metaphors, even when drawn from impeccably biblical sources, in ways as offensive to modern ideas about metaphorical language as to puritan ideas about the Bible. Patrick set out, in other words, to discredit the means of expressing traditional puritan psychology. Statements of orthodox Calvinist belief were not so much mistaken as unintelligible; he referred to Richard Baxter's non-Calvinist theology of

---

[76] Hale, *Works*, I, 111. On this general theme see John Marshall, 'The ecclesiology of the Latitude-men 1660–89: Stillingfleet, Tillotson, and "Hobbism"', *Journal of Ecclesiastical History*, 36 (1985, 407–27); Richard Ashcraft, 'Latitudinarianism and toleration: historical myth versus polititical history', in Ashcraft, Perez Zagorin and Richard Kroll (eds.), *Philosophy, science and religion in England 1640–1700*, Cambridge 1992, pp. 151–77.

[77] Samuel Parker, *A discourse of ecclesiastical polity*, 1670, p. 98.

[78] Simon Patrick, *A friendly debate between a conformist and a nonconformist*, 1669, 133.

grace by recalling 'what a noise and clutter there was, when Mr Baxter began to write more intelligibly about some weighty things in Christianity than others did'.[79]

The tone of Patrick's book moved Hale to deplore the 'rendering of religion itself and scripture expressions to be ridiculous and pieces of railery'.[80] This was, he thought, a new development, though religious disagreements had often thrown up scurrilous invectives of the type of the puritan Marprelate tracts. An example of the change in attitudes was the case of Jonson's play *The Alchemist* (first performed 1610), in which Jonson

> brings in Ananias in derision of the persons then called puritans with many of their phrases in use among them taken out of the scriptures with a design to render that sort of persons ridiculous ... But although those persons were not in very good esteem among the great ones and gallants yet the play was disliked and indeed abhorred by cause it seemed to reproach religion itself ... [81]

This is a very interesting statement, not so much for what it tells us about Jonson (*The Alchemist* was a wildly popular play), as for the light it sheds on Hale himself. To regard an attack upon puritans as 'reproaching religion itself' was to accept that serious piety was likely to be puritan in form. The same implied identity was found in a letter written to his son, warning him of the jibe that piety involved 'mere empty fancies and imagination wherein lies puritanism'.[82] This attitude was nowhere more apparent than in his admiration for his dissenting neighbour Richard Baxter.

The two men met in 1667, when Hale moved to a house in the Middlesex village of Acton, where Baxter was already resident.[83] The meeting was arranged by Serjeant Fountain (1600–71), a man much of Hale's type: a former royalist, interregnum judge, and sympathiser with the nonconformists. The two men evidently felt an immediate intellectual sympathy, but Baxter's touching record of their friendship is nonetheless a potentially treacherous source. Hale consulted Baxter on predestination,[84] signed himself as 'one that loves and honours you and remains your very affectionate and faithful friend',[85] and remembered the dissenter in his will,[86] but their relationship was characterised by reticence on a number of sensitive topics. In general they avoided politics; Hale revealed he would like to revise the existing Act of Uniformity, but seems to have given no details of what he would prefer.[87] Baxter was later quite surprised to

---

[79] Simon Patrick, *A continuation of the friendly debate*, 1669, p. 112.
[80] Hale, *Works*, I, 326.
[81] *Ibid.*   [82] Lambeth 3516, 21.   [83] Heward, *Hale*, 94.
[84] Hale, *Works*, I, 109.
[85] Lambeth 3499, 77   [86] Hale *Works*, I, 113.   [87] Hale, *Judgement, Preface.*

discover that Hale was a writer of 'practical' works, so it seems their theological discussions were conducted on a rather abstract plane. Their relations, though certainly close, left plenty of room for such misunderstandings.

One influence on their friendship was probably the state of Acton's church. Throughout the interregnum, the ministers of Acton were congregationalists, including the famous preacher Philip Nye (?1596–1672).[88] When Baxter and Hale were parishioners, the incumbent was a royalist absentee, and the resident Anglican clergyman was 'a weak, dull young man that spent most of his time in alehouses'.[89] As a 'presbyterian' conservative, committed to the ideal of a national church, Baxter could hope for no better pastoral field. He set himself to supplement the inadequacies of the Anglicans, preaching sermons to his local followers, but also attending parish services.[90] Hale not only condoned but encouraged his neighbour's unofficial ministry:

When the people crowded in and out of my house to hear, he openly showed me so great respect before them at the door, and never spoke a word against it, as was no small encouragement to the common people to go on; though the other sort muttered that a judge should seem so far to countenance that which they took to be against the law . . .[91]

When Baxter was arrested, in 1669, Hale may well have been responsible for securing the preacher's release. Advised by Serjeant Fountain, Baxter applied for his release to the judges in the court of Common Pleas. They went out of their way to be helpful, not least in consenting to hear the case at all (it would have been more natural to apply to the court of King's Bench, where the violently prejudiced Kelyng was Chief Justice). Hale had encouraged them to sympathise by mentioning the affair at their communal table.[92] Baxter's account downplays the tone of exasperation in their judgements, but they nonetheless applied themselves to finding some flaws in the warrant that justified setting him free.[93] On another occasion, at Baxter's request, Hale himself found a technical reason for letting a minister go.[94]

His attitude was no doubt based in the sense (which Baxter shared) that Baxter was a mainstream Anglican, excluded by a freak of politics from his proper role inside the national church. In fact their priorities subtly

---

[88] *Baxter, Reliquiae Baxterianae*, ed. Sylvester, 1696, Part III, p. 46; *Calamy revised: being a revision of Edmund Calamy's account of the ministers and others ejected and silenced 1660–62*, ed. A. G. Matthews, Oxford 1934, p. 182.

[89] Baxter, *Reliquiae*, III, 46.   [90] *Ibid*., 46.   [91] *Ibid*., 47.   [92] *Ibid*., 59.

[93] *Ibid*. A more balanced account is Bodleian Library MSS, Rawlinson C 719, pp. 37–45. See also the references in Rawlinson C 719, 82–3, and Middle Temple, Treby MS Reports, 490.

[94] Baxter, *Richard Baxter's penitent confession*, 1691, p. 38.

diverged. Baxter refrained from communion at Acton, where the rector was 'commonly reputed a swearer', to avoid 'an offence to the congregational brethren'.[95] His obligation to preserve the cohesion of the godly took precedence over his loyalty to the parish. Both wanted 'comprehension', the enlargement of the church to include the moderate mass of the dissenters, but they understood this programme in rather different ways. Hale wanted to strengthen the church by making it easier for puritans to conform; Baxter wished to transform it, in line with his own ecclesiological theories. An illustration of the difference, showing the gulf between a man like Baxter and even sympathetic Anglicans, was Hale's draft comprehension bill of 1668.[96]

The main source on this episode is Baxter's *Reliquiae Baxterianae* (1695). He says he received an approach, in January 1668, from an intermediary of Lord Keeper Bridgeman, enquiring about the terms on which the 'presbyterians' might be 'comprehended'.[97] Along with Thomas Manton (1620–77) and William Bates (1625–99), two other leading moderate dissenters, he had talks with John Wilkins, the rationalist Bishop of Chester, and Bridgeman's chaplain Hezekiah Burton (d. 1681). He described the negotiations in some detail, reproducing the various documents on which their discussions were based. After a certain amount of difficulty, the parties were agreed on every point, and

> it was agreed, that the papers should all be delivered to the Lord Chief Baron, to draw them up into an act. And because I lived near him, he was pleased to show me the copy of his draft, which was done according to all our sense; but secretly, lest the noise of a prepared Act should be displeasing to the parliament.[98]

In February, when parliament re-assembled, the mood was so obviously hostile to dissent that it was pointless to bring in the bill. The interest of this abortive scheme lies in Baxter's recollection of events.

It is plain from the *Reliquiae* that Hale was allowed some freedom in his draft; Baxter was gratified to find that its contents were 'according to all

---

[95] Baxter, *Reliquiae*, III, 46–7. This undermines his earlier claim that 'when I was there, there remained but two women in all the town and parish whom [Nye and his successor] had admitted to the sacrament ... this rigour made the people speak hardly of them' (*Reliquiae*, III, 46).

[96] This appears to have been quite distinct from the scheme (or possibly schemes) that was mooted the previous summer (passingly mentioned in Paul Seaward, *The cavalier parliament and the reconstruction of the old regime, 1661–1667*, Cambridge 1989, pp. 318–19; Ronald Hutton, *The Restoration: a political history of England and Wales 1658–1667*, Oxford 1985, p. 279). Even in early 1668, there appear to have been other moves afoot (see Newton E. Key, 'Comprehension and the breakdown of consensus in Restoration Herefordshire', in Tim Harris, Paul Seaward and Mark Goldie (eds.), *The politics of religion in Restoration England*, 1990, pp. 196–8). The relationship between these various projects deserves some more detailed research.

[97] Baxter, *Reliquiae*, III, 23.   [98] *Ibid.*, 35.

our sense', so there must have been a possibility of at least some variation from the terms that the clerics agreed. Elsewhere in his writings, however, he implied he had a veto on Hale's work. In the *Additional notes on the life and death of Sir Matthew Hale* (1682), his story was as follows: 'After some days conference we came to agreement in all things, as to the necessary terms. And because Dr Wilkins and I had special intimacy with Judge Hale, we desired him to draw it up in the form of an Act, which he willingly did, and we agreed to every word.'[99] In *Richard Baxter's penitent confession* (1691), Hale's role was almost equally reduced: 'Dr Wilkins and Dr Hezekiah Burton were appointed to treat with us of the terms: we came to an agreement to a word: we gave it Judge Hale to draw up in form of an Act to be offered to the parliament.'[100]

One seventeenth-century writer was sufficiently annoyed by Baxter's claims to ask Hezekiah Burton for his version of events.[101] Burton confirmed that Bridgeman had tried to arrange a comprehension bill, but denied that the subsequent talks bore any fruit. Bridgeman made simultaneous approaches to Baxter and his friends, the measure's intended beneficiaries, and to the great John Owen, the leader of the congregationalists. The stricter 'independents' could not be comprehended in the church, but could hope for a degree of toleration. Owen accepted Bridgeman's terms but Baxter responded by wrangling over details. Bridgeman seems to have thought this ungrateful, and complained that

these men (meaning the independents) from whom I expected the least compliance, thankfully accepted the terms proposed; but the others (presbyterians, Mr Baxter and his brethren) whom I believed most ready to promote such a peaceable design will never agree in any thing; and I will never have more to do with them.[102]

This version of the story is taken from William Sherlock's (1640–1707) *Vindication of the rights of ecclesiastical authority* (1685), a work (as its title implies) that is hardly an unbiased source. But Sherlock's account is supported by a document containing the provisions of Hale's draft.[103]

This manuscript was owned by Thomas Barlow (the Calvinist Bishop of Lincoln), who was himself involved, the previous summer, in an unsuccessful comprehension scheme.[104] Barlow prefaced his copy by writing 'it is generally said (and believed) that the following draft for comprehension was contrived and formed by Matthew Hale Chief Baron of the

[99] Hale, *Works*, I, 103.
[100] Baxter, *Richard Baxter's penitent confession*, 1691, pp. 38–9.
[101] Sherlock, *A vindication of the rights of ecclesiastical authority*, 1685, pp. 185–8. As Burton died in 1681, the question cannot have been prompted by the *Additional Notes* (1682); no doubt the claim is found elsewhere in Baxter's voluminous writings.
[102] Sherlock, *Vindication*, 188.
[103] It is bound with some relevant pamphlets in Bodleian Library, B.14.15.Linc.
[104] Hutton, *Restoration*, 279.

Exchequer'.[105] The document is not itself the bill prepared by Hale (it is not in legal form) but could easily be a close paraphrase. It is certainly the product of the specific talks described by Baxter; it contains, for example, the words 'take thou legal authority', which resolved a long debate about the reception of those ministers who had never been episcopally ordained.[106] The proposals for 'indulgence' to those who were still excluded from the church were exactly as Baxter recorded in his *Reliquiae*, but the bill for comprehension diverged from Baxter's wishes on three important points.

The most obvious of these was the oath that the ministers swore. The presbyterians proposed that the newly comprehended ministers should 'assent' to the 36 Articles (the doctrinal ones that were generally accepted) and should 'hold that the doctrine, worship and government there established do contain all things absolutely necessary to salvation'.[107] There was a fine distinction between 'assent' and 'consent', to which Baxter and others attached significance. Hale adopted the oath that Wilkins had suggested,[108] which required them to 'profess and declare that I do *approve* the doctrine worship and government established in the church of England as concerning all things necessary to salvation. And that I will not endeavour my self, or by any other directly or indirectly to bring in any doctrine contrary to that which is so established ...'[109] 'Approval' was a strong word, connoting an emphatic approbation, derived from trial by experience; in the negotiations, Baxter had raised objections to this oath, which would, he thought, 'on many accounts be scrupled'.[110]

A second, related divergence was in the policy to be adopted towards ministers who took the oath but still refused to read the liturgy. Baxter would have allowed them to preach and catechise, but Hale made no mention of this.[111] Baxter presumably supposed that his more scrupulous colleagues would form a kind of puritan penumbra, like the many preaching 'lecturers' who escaped the demands of conformity in the church of pre-war times. Puritanism before the wars was part emancipated from the parish by 'sermon-gadding' and private exercises,[112] but comprehension, on Hale's terms, would have tended, at the very least, to do away with such activities. Hale's bill conceded everything that the presbyterian spokesmen had demanded, abolishing or making optional all features of the prayer book to which puritans were accustomed to object. But the

---

[105] B.14.15.Linc., p. 8.   [106] B.14.15.Linc., 9; Baxter, *Reliquiae*, III, 34.
[107] Baxter, *Reliquiae*, III, 27 (paginated as 35).
[108] *Ibid.*, 25.   [109] B.14.15.Linc., 9. My emphasis.
[110] *Reliquiae* III, 29 (paginated as 37). See OED: 'Approve'.
[111] Baxter, *Reliquiae*, III, 35.
[112] Patrick Collinson, *The religion of Protestants: the Church in English society 1559–1625*, Oxford 1982, pp. 242–83.

purpose of the exercise was uniformity, in a deeper sense than the church had ever known.

Lastly, and most importantly for Baxter, there was no mention in Hale's bill of a highly authoritarian suggestion. Baxter had hoped to re-define the category of 'scandalous' offenders (parishioners to whom a minister could summarily refuse communion): 'those who are proved to deride or scorn at Christianity, or the holy Scriptures, or the life of reward and punishment, or the serious practice of a godly life, and strict obedience to God's commands, shall be numbered with the scandalous sinners.'[113] He had earlier proposed that each diocese should register the godly, but Wilkins had persuaded him to abandon the idea.[114] As William Lamont has shown, the absence of parochial 'discipline' (that is the right of ministers to control their flocks by excommunication) was the heart of his objections to the government of the church.[115] What Baxter failed to grasp was that his fellow countrymen would never allow the ministers such power. The most persuasive argument for bishops, so far as the mass of the English were concerned, was that they were far preferable to 11,000 presbyterian popes. As a loyal disciple of Selden's, Hale himself was committed to thinking that excommunication was a part of the secular law. He was unlikely to agree that every parish clergyman should use it to punish non-puritans at will.

The point about this episode is not that Baxter falsified events; though he no doubt exasperated Bridgeman, he may easily have carried Wilkins with him, and have glimpsed what seemed a very helpful bill. The letter of Hale's proposals was very generous, but their spirit was alien to a mind like Baxter's. Baxter was theocratic in his sense of the minister's authority, while Hale was an erastian common lawyer.[116] Hale was also more deeply committed to the principle of uniformity. His comprehensive church would have curbed any possible threat from the puritan clergy, giving them what they claimed to want and obliging them to let the matter rest. This would have left them with their proper role as preachers of a minimal religion that reinforced existing social norms. His arrangements were designed, in other words, to help the tender conscience with its scruples; they were of no assistance to those with a detailed programe for another kind of church.

There was no room, in the state that Hale envisaged, for more than one religion, or more than one source of legal authority. Baxter's ecclesiology, claiming coercive power for clergymen, distinct from that approved by common law, could not be made the basis for a uniform religious settle-

---

[113] Baxter, *Reliquiae*, III, 28 (paginated as 36).   [114] *Ibid.*, 34.

[115] Lamont, *Richard Baxter and the millennium: protestant imperialism and the English*, 1979, p. 217; Lamont, *Godly rule*, 149–53.

[116] The fullest statement of his views is Hale, *Prerogatives*, 145–68.

ment, nor could it, in the long term, enjoy a toleration outside the national church. In theory, it followed, Hale should have been happy to persecute his friend, still more to suppress the Quakers, whose mad pretence of 'inner light' subverted every kind of social order.

An accident of temperament and background had given Hale a sympathy with claims to subjective experience of God. Although his own religion was a 'republication' of principles declared in natural law, he was still convinced that this rationalistic faith was a religion of the quickening spirit. When Baxter read the *Contemplations moral and divine* (1676), the edifying essays that were printed without Hale's consent, he recognised this quality in his friend's religious thought, and wrote him a moving letter that touched upon this point:

when I heard ignorant men talk of the witness of the spirit enthusiastically, it kept me from considering that which I am fully convinced of, that the regenerating, illuminating, quickening spirit, disposing the soul with filial affections to God, is Christ's great agent in the world, and his witness and ours, and the mark and grace of God upon us. Experimental knowledge only maketh truly wise. Only the living know what life is, and only the seeing know what life and sight are.[117]

'Experimental knowledge' remained a central feature of Hale's religious life, preventing Christianity from being subsumed in Seldenian natural law. It must have been this, if anything, which let him sympathise with Fox or Bunyan, or with the Quakers he set free on the grounds their gatherings were not 'seditious'.[118] He evidently felt that nonconformists looked like serious Christians, rather more so, perhaps, than the bishops and their friends. Though he deplored Quaker absurdities such as refusal to remove their hats, 'take away but these and the like affected superadditions, these men are as other men, some indeed very sober honest just and plain hearted men, and sound in most if not all the important doctrines and practices of Christianity'.[119] His behaviour makes no intellectual sense, unless his latitudinarianism is seen as a development of puritan ideas. The duties of natural law were a mode in which a Calvinist religion was expressed. The same could be said, as we shall see, for the 'scientific' writings to which he increasingly turned.

---

[117] Baxter to Hale, 2 May 1676, *Bulletin of the John Rylands Library* (1940), p. 174. Compare 'he that sees the sun, knows it is bright and light; he that tastes honey, knows it is sweet', and other examples collected in Nuttall, *Holy Spirit*, 39.
[118] See above, p. 133.   [119] Lambeth 3485, 123.

Part III

NATURAL PHILOSOPHY

Natural motions

Hale thought that God created man with natural philosophy in mind: 'he was made to be the Spectator of the great work[s] of God, to consider and observe them, to glorify and serve the God that made them; and he is accordingly furnished with an intellective faculty answerable to his condition.'[1] As an intellectual being, 'the common high priest of the inanimate and irrational world', he was placed on earth to 'gather up as it were the admirable works of the glorious God, and in their behalf to present the praises, suffrages, and acclamations of the whole creation'.[2] A contemplation of the universe, in a spirit combining gratitude and awe, was the original natural religion.

The purpose of Hale's 'scientific' writings was always, in a characteristic phrase, to 'carry up' the human mind to God; they both proved the Creator's existence and constituted, in themselves, a pious exercise. The philosopher had the privilege and duty of experiencing the order of things as the product of God's will. The physical laws of nature were really divine commands, upheld by the Almighty like 'a law of Justinian and Trajan.'[3] A mark of his omnipotence and wisdom, as Hale's earliest work, the *Discourse* had explained, was his action in accordance with a number of self-imposed rules.[4] Even 'necessary' relations, correctly understood, were voluntarily created and sustained:

we may justly admire the wisdom of God, that while he intends a purpose above the conception or drift of a natural agent, he bringeth it about without the violation of the rules or laws, which he hath appointed to be constant in nature, and may most justly conclude, that the law of necessity in the natural agents, is but the effect of that very counsel, that hath predetermined his own purposes by them; and they are all of a piece, all laid at the same time ... And hence it is, that those effects, which are produced naturally by natural causes, we do and may call natural and necessary; and yet it excludes not the counsel of the divine will in the

---

[1] Hale, *Primitive origination*, 327.   [2] *Ibid.*, 372.   [3] *Ibid.*, 346.
[4] On the *Discourse*, see pp. 141–55 above.

production of it: for it is the same counsel, that hath made this necessary connection between the cause and the effect, that did predetermine the effect to be produced.[5]

Hale was and remained committed to seeing apparent 'necessity' as willed, and apparently autonomous connections as utterly dependent on God's power.

The philosophy best suited to Hale's Christian devotional needs was that of 'the great priest of nature',[6] the pagan Aristotle. The reason was epitomised in an argument used by the *Discourse*. There are no recorded instances of spontaneously generating humans (in contrast, he believed, to worms or mice), a fact that suggests the species was created. It might, however, be replied that spontaneous generation only occurs to satisfy a need. There is no need at present for any fresh supply of human beings, and it is axiomatic that 'nature doth nothing in vain'. Hale took this teleological assertion to be itself an argument for God:

if nature doth nothing in vain, it is plain that whatever is so called nature is in truth the First Cause, though miscalled nature; for not to do anything in vain, is an act of a voluntary and rational agent; a mere natural agent cannot but work uniformly, whether in vain or not in vain, when the matter is uniformly disposed.[7]

This assumption was the root of his entire approach to natural science. The Aristotelian system placed heavy explanatory weight on final causes, but Hale rejected the idea of teleological principles in nature.[8] He wished to keep the substance of the Aristotelian theory, but to replace the final cause with a divine intention, supernaturally effected by means of a physical 'law'. This brought him into conflict with various purely mechanistic theories, which accounted for every phenomenon in terms of efficient causation, exerted by the motions of merely material things.

For many of Hale's contemporaries, including Robert Boyle (1627–91), such theories were partly a strategy for proving there must be a God. Boyle tried to account for natural events in terms of the size, shape and motion of the atoms of which nature was composed. A machine composed of millions of microscopic parts, devoid of any organising form or final cause, was obviously the product of intelligent design. Hale owned and cited *The*

---

[5] Hale, *Discourse*, 130–1.   [6] Lambeth 3500, 49.   [7] Hale, *Discourse*, 5.
[8] There are four Aristotelian causes (efficient, formal, material, final), dismissed by Hale as follows: 'when we are considering of the dependence of causes we speak not so much of final causes for that hath still a reference to the efficient, nor to [sic] formal causes for that is in truth nothing but the effect itself, nor to the material cause for that in material things whereof we now speak is not so much a cause as at most a subject upon which the efficient works' (Lambeth 3484, 22).

origin of forms and qualities (1666), the clearest exposition of this general approach.[9] His disagreement with Boyle's line of thought was based on his conception of the natural philosopher's role. Boyle had firmly mechanistic views about what constitutes an explanation, opposing the use of 'nature', souls, or forms, or even of God-given natural laws. His *Free enquiry into the vulgarly received notion of nature* (first drafted 1666; completed 1682) was not a book that Hale could have consulted, but it gives a useful basis for comparing their ideas.[10] The work continually recurs to the image of a watch, a phenomenon that must be understood in terms of the machinery inside.

> We shall not easily look on [other] accounts, as meriting the name of explications. For to explicate[11] a phenomenon, it is not enough to ascribe it to one general efficient, but we must intelligibly show the particular manner, how that general cause produces the proposed effect. He must be a very dull enquirer, who, demanding an account of the phenomena of a watch, shall rest satisfied with being told, that it is an engine made by a watch-maker . . .[12]

The key word in this passage is the word 'intelligibly'. To understand a thing, for Boyle, was to apprehend it as a mechanism. This actually excluded grasping it as something that obeyed the 'law' of God. The mechanism's individual parts were of course created and sustained by God, and they were also given 'determinate motions' (the heavenly bodies, for instance, move at a 'determinate celerity' on given heavenly 'lines')[13], but talk of laws was strictly speaking nonsense:

> it is intelligible to me, that God should at the beginning impress determinate motions upon the parts of matter, and guide them, as he thought requisite, for the primordial constitution of things; and that ever since he should, by his ordinary and general concourse, maintain those powers [deriving of course from size and shape alone[14]], which he gave the parts of matter, to transmit their motions thus and thus to one another. But I cannot conceive how a body devoid of understanding and sense, properly so called, can moderate and determinate its own motions, especially so, as to make them conformable to laws that it had no knowledge or apprehension.[15]

---

[9] In 1668, when Hale made a list of his books, he also possessed a copy of the *Sceptical chymist* (1661) and most of the available experimental works (Beinecke, Osborn files, Hale, 'Catalogus librorum meorum').

[10] On this see J. E. McGuire's highly stimulating 'Boyle's conception of nature' (*Journal of the History of Ideas* 33 (1972), 523–42), though McGuire seems over-generous in his picture of Boyle as a sceptic, anticipating Hume, about the very notion of causation.

[11] A word that retained connotations of its literal sense of 'unfold'.

[12] Boyle, *Works*, IV, 418.

[13] *Ibid.*, 380.

[14] The choice of the word 'powers' is most unfortunate, because it implies what Boyle was always very anxious to deny: that there are active 'qualities' implanted in mere particles of matter.

[15] Boyle, *Works*, IV, 367.

God's interference with the natural order, so far as human minds could understand it, was restricted to his merely 'general concourse' (the scholastic phrase for sustaining it in being). Hale wanted to make the universe understood as more than a machine upheld by God; he wanted to present it in addition as depending for particular operations on continuing exertion of an Almighty will. It was intrinsic to his view of the natural philosopher's task that the world should be interpreted in ways that left a space for God's command.

His 'natural philosophy', to a very large extent, explores the failures of the mechanists. The elimination of the final causes had left a wide range of phenomena that matter and motion alone were hard pressed to explain, including gravity and magnetism, to say nothing of the various forms of life. A handful of the chapters in 'De Deo' (1662–?66) show signs of sympathy with this approach, and he continued writing in this spirit until his death in 1676. Most of these works or passages of works are studded with contemporary citations, which make it clear he did his best to master the main contributions to Europe-wide debates. He took an interest 'in my youth' in such philosophical questions,[16] but everything he wrote upon the subject dates from his last twelve years. The corpus will be treated as a whole, taking the clearest statement of any particular point, a procedure which seems licensed by Hale's own attitude.

Hale's longest and most carefully written work, which touches on virtually all of his principal themes, is *The primitive origination of mankind, considered and examined according to the light of nature* (1677). Like the 'De Deo' manuscript, it was written, so he tells us, at 'leisure and broken times, and with great intervals'. He composed it 'some years since', and illness had prevented him from attempting a thorough revision of his thoughts.[17] It cites from a number of books that were published in the later 1660s, but there are just two references (which might have been inserted in the course of an inadequate revision) to material that was printed after 1669.[18] Hale's decision to publish the treatise, which he must have taken just before he died, suggests that his thought did not develop much between the later 1660s and his death, a suggestion that his manuscripts confirm. An absence of contradiction is as hard as any negative to prove, but there was only one significant question (admittedly a point of great importance) on which he demonstrably changed his mind.[19]

---

[16] Hale, *Observations*, To the reader, sig. A3.   [17] Hale, *Primitive origination*, Preface.

[18] A paragraph in Hale, *Primitive origination*, 121 (quoted below, pp. 205–6) makes an implicit reference to More, *Enchiridion metaphysicum* (1671). There are also explicit citations (pp. 191, 192) to John Ray, *Observations topographical, moral and physiological made in a journey through part of the Low Countries, Germany, Italy, and France*, 1673.

[19] See below, pp. 225–9.

The *Primitive origination*'s fault, as the author himself had candidly confessed, is the disjointed nature it shares with all his works of any length. Its argument never achieves momentum, and most of its individual points are amplified in Hale's unpublished papers, but it has one useful feature that later writings do not duplicate. It gives an account of his attitude to the great disturbing force in contemporary science, the mechanistic system of Descartes (1596–1650).

In the *Discourse*, it will be remembered, there was just one formal argument to prove the existence of God. He asserted that the world had been created, on the grounds of an Aristotelian view about infinity. An 'actual infinity', including an actually infinite 'succession', was a natural impossibility. The later works expand upon this point.[20] Nothing that can be counted can be truly infinite; it is characteristic of numbers that they can be increased by adding one. The material world is a 'quantum', divisible into numerable parts, and therefore essentially finite.[21] A succession of natural motions (of circuits of the heavens, for example) was also a variety of quantum: 'in all successions of what kind of nature so ever there is such a distinction and division that doth of necessity reduce them under number'.[22] It followed there was no such thing as an infinite succession, and therefore that the First Cause must exist. All this was brought in question by Descartes.

Descartes had made impossible the argument from an infinite succession. He had replaced the infinite, the source of so much intellectual trouble, with the idea of the 'indefinite', and depicted the physical universe as indefinitely large.[23] He neglected the physical proofs for the existence of the deity, resorting instead (Hale disapprovingly noted) to the questionable subtleties of an argument from the idea of God. The dangers of relying on such uncertain grounds were shown by his immediate refutation at the hands of the great atomist Gassendi (1592–1655).[24] The universe itself was turned into a great machine, while magnets, gravity and animal life (all of them to be treated in Hale's works) were given mechanistic explanations.

Hale's answer to this challenge was to place the French philosopher in a long line of thinkers carried away by an *a priori* theory. The paracelsan 'chemists' held, on very inadequate grounds, that the fundamental elements were mercury, sulphur and salt:

their evidence that they are so [is], because they find by their solutions by fire, some things which they call by these names, to be that whereinto bodies are dissolved; when, for ought can be evidently made out, many of these are not so much really in the constitution of the bodies themselves, as the very alterations and changes of

---

[20] Lambeth 3491, entitled 'De Deo: Vox Metaphysicae', esp. fos. 62–71.
[21] Lambeth 3491, 65.
[22] *Ibid.*, 71.   [23] Descartes, *Principles*, 13–14.   [24] Lambeth 3489, fo. 4.

them by the force and energy of that active element [i.e. fire], or at least, though after their solution they assume the shapes of salt, sulphur and mercury, yet there are even in these consistences very various contextures, differing extremely in each body ... though they seem to assume some analogy of shape ...[25]

The belief in no more than three elements was more of a presupposition than an outcome of disinterested research. Even the greatest of philosophers was open to the charge of dogmatism. The Aristotelian principles of matter and form were arguably little more than intellectual tools: 'it is very difficult to conceive that any such thing should be as matter, undetermined by form'.[26] A number of so-called 'substantial forms' might well be no more than 'modifications [arrangements] of matter', while others were perhaps 'some middle nature' that escaped classification within existing scholastic terminology, 'neither bodies nor accidents, but powers of a different nature from bodies, accidents, or qualities, or substances, though not so adequate to our perception'. The Aristotelian 'hypothesis' therefore 'seemed, for the most part, to be a kind of artificial contrivance, not wholly taken from the nature of things, but fitted to give some kind of conception of them'.[27]

The atomism of Democritus was another example of dubious presuppositions, a theory 'not only perfectly inevident to our sense, but altogether improbable'.[28] As another work of Hale's was to point out, the universe has many soft compressible components, which it is perverse to explain as the product of hard if microscopic atoms: 'to suppose the first constituent minute particles of air or water are hard, or of any other nature than the whole body, is a precarious, inevident, and unreasonable supposition'.[29] In its atheistic form the theory was simply absurd. A stable cosmic order had somehow coalesced from the random conjunction of atoms in a void. Lucretius had shored up the theory, at least in its application to the biological world, by admitting the existence of certain 'moleculae seminales ... to keep the world and its integrals from an infinitude and extendlessness of excursions every minute into new figures and animals', but these intermediate entities were themselves 'made up merely by chance, and by the contexture of those atoms which have neither qualities nor energy, nor anything else besides their small and imperceptible moles to make them operative, and that local motion [sic] which they there have; but they teach us not from where they have it.'[30]

The theory of Descartes gave 'some correctives' to these mad ideas, but the spirit of the systems was the same. Hale often bracketed the Frenchman's thought with that of Democritus and Epicurus. Cartesians thought

[25] Hale, *Primitive origination*, 9.　　　[26] *Ibid.*, 9–10.　　　[27] *Ibid.*, 10　　　[28] *Ibid.*
[29] Hale, *Observations*, 94.　　　[30] Hale, *Primitive origination*, 10.

the universe was full (they identified matter with space, so there could be no question of a void), and composed of fundamental particles of basically spherical form. These particles once came in a variety of shapes, but had gradually been worn down into spheres. Their continual collisions had had the effect of knocking their corners away. The resultant, still more microscopic debris made up the Cartesian 'materia subtilis', which occupied all spaces between the little spheres. This sea of subtle matter, pervading all the chinks of matter proper, was continually invoked (as we shall see) to explain away the problems raised by commitment to a mechanistic theory. Hale saw the new philosophy as a plenist atomism, barely to be distinguished from the vacuist atomism of the Greeks, and he scorned the role attributed to 'materia subtilis':

what colour of evidence have we of the various configurations of his atoms, the grinding of them round by their mutual attritions, the coalition of the globular atoms into the heavenly bodies, the filling of the chinks and interstices by the ramenta of the greater, whereby a materia subtilis is diffused through the universe, which is invisible [and] performs most of the motions that we see in things . . .?[31]

The Christian scientist had an advantage in giving an account of the physical world, because the 'Mosaic hypothesis' was set out in the pages of the Bible. The opening verses of Genesis i are seldom read as theoretical physics, even (a little oddly) by the most literal-minded of believers. It therefore seems worth printing the 'hypothesis' in full:

1 In the beginning God created the heaven and the earth.
2 And the earth was without form and darkness was upon the face of the deep. And the spirit of God moved upon the face of the waters.
3 And God said, Let there be light; and there was light.
4 And God saw the light, that it was good: and God divided the light from the darkness.
5 And God called the light day, and the darkness he called night. And the evening and the morning were the first day.
6 And God said, Let there be a firmament in the midst of the waters, and let it divide the waters from the waters.
7 And God made the firmament, and divided the waters which were under the firmament from the waters which were above the firmament: and it was so.
8 And God called the firmament heaven. And the evening and the morning were the second day.
9 And God said, Let the waters under the heaven be gathered together in one place, and let the dry land appear: and it was so.
10 And God called the dry land earth; and the gathering together of the waters called he seas: and God saw that it was good.

The story of creation confirmed Hale's instinctive beliefs about the roles of matter, God and motion in shaping the visible world. He inherited from

[31] *Ibid.*, 10.

the Aristotelian system the sense that matter in itself was utterly formless and passive. The world had

these deficiencies in it, in and for some time after its production:
1. It was without form and order.
2. It was without light.
3. It was without activity, life or motion: and
4. All the superficies which it had bore the greatest analogy to water, though in that confused abyss there was a confused mixture of other matter.[32]

The spirit that moved on the face of the waters set in train the transformation of this mass:

1. It derived into it motive powers or energies, whereby the parts of it were agitated or moved, or at least rendered more obsequious to the agitation or motion of that active nature which was afterwards created, namely light or fire.
2. It did gradually digest and separate its parts, whereby they became more capable of disposition and order, according to their several designed and destined places, positions, and uses.
3. It did transfuse into this stupid, dead and unactive moles certain activity and vital influence, whereby it did in general affect that which Aristotle calls the common life of bodies, namely motion; and the several parts thereof were impregnated with several kinds of vital influence.[33]

These were not in fact original ideas. An almost identical theory, treating 'spirit' as a moulding influence and 'light' as a means of softening intractable matter, can be found in a work by Jan Comenius (1592–1670), a treatise called *Natural philosophie reformed by divine light* (1651), to which Hale made occasional allusions.[34] The source of their appeal is fairly clear. They offered a way of understanding 'spirit' as equivalent to Aristotelian 'form', and treating the organising force as having a quasi-material existence. Thus an undated essay 'Concerning the works of God' distinguished *creatio prima*, 'the production of a being from not being', from *creatio secunda*, 'the production of a being out of such a being, and in such a method or way as exceeds all created power'.[35] There were two essential elements in the process of creation:

1. The common mass of matter; and
2. The common spirit of material beings.
As the former is the materia prima of bodies, so the latter may possibly be the materia prima, as I may call it, of substantial forms; and these lay confusedly mixed together, so that neither was the matter purely informis, for that were to suppose such ... a subsistence of matter, or corporeal moles, as is without any kind of form; nor is it on the other side imaginable that the spiritus universi, as I

---

[32] *Ibid.*, 292.   [33] *Ibid.*, 293.
[34] Lambeth 3492, 205v.; Lambeth 3499, 112; Lambeth 3504, 240.
[35] Hale, *Works*, I, 373.

may call it, was distinct complete or subsisting without matter; but they were both mingled indistinctly together.[36]

This 'spirit of material beings' was the spirit that moved on the waters in Genesis i.

Hale differed from his atomist opponents in insisting on an active principle (apart, that is, from the motion the Almighty originally gave) in a naturally passive material world. He never made it wholly clear, however, whether this 'spirit' was a quasi-material 'substance', or a label for the various manifestations of the unmediated will of God. His position was defined with reference to Cartesians on the one hand, and on the other to an Englishman who set himself to refuting Cartesian physics, the famous 'Cambridge Platonist' Henry More (1614–87).[37] More was concerned, like Hale, to use the failures of the mechanists to point to the existence of a non-material force. He was a great admirer of Descartes, whose system he regarded as a supreme achievement of the human intellect. Its manifest absurdities, in spite of the ingenuity its author lavished on his theories, were a sign of the wrongheadedness of a strict mechanistic approach.[38]

At the end of the 1640s More had a correspondence with his hero, in which he praised the new philosophy, but objected, amongst other things, to two Cartesian claims: that spirit is not spatially located, and that animals are nothing but machines.[39] His later objections were succinctly put in the preface of *Enchiridion Metaphysicum* (1671), which summarises what he saw as a hopelessly contradictory position:

That God is a being absolutely perfect; but that matter (in virtue of its own form and considered in itself) necessarily comes to exist. That God indeed is; but that he is nowhere, whether in the world, or outside it. That matter is not moved by itself, but by God; that God however does not impinge on *any* part of matter, nor on the whole, nor has he ever impinged in such a way that he could transmit motion to matter. That matter, however modified, cannot think; but this principle is taken so far that all brute animals are simply machines, and there is no more sense in an apparelled horse than in his saddle-brasses. That there is a mind or immortal soul in, or at least at, the human body, but only through its operations, not its essence. That there is a divine providence, but the ends of things [final causes] are not to be searched after.[40]

---

[36] *Ibid.*

[37] For an introduction to More, see Sarah Hutton (ed.), *Henry More (1614–1687): tercentenary studies*, Dordrecht 1991; A. Rupert Hall, *Henry More: magic, religion and experiment*, Oxford 1990.

[38] More, *The immortality of the soul, so far forth as it is demonstrable by the light of nature and of reason*, 1659, sig. B4 + 3v. The point is emphasised by Alan Gabbey, 'Henry More and the limits of mechanism', in Hutton, *Tercentenary studies*, 19–32.

[39] Descartes, *Correspondance avec Arnaud et Morus*, Latin and French edn, Paris 1953, 97–9, 105–7.

[40] 'Deum Ens absolute perfectum esse; et tamen Materiam ex propria sua idea et in se consideratam necessario exsistere. Esse quidem Deum; sed Deum nusquam esse, aut in

The real heart of all of More's objections was his belief that intellect is 'extended', on the grounds that to exist at all is to exist in space. Cartesians believed that everything was intellect or 'extension' (the categories were mutually exclusive), that extension was synonymous with matter, and therefore that the human mind and God were incapable of physical location. More favoured an alternative classification, distinguishing matter and spirit. Both the spiritual and material were extended, but matter was 'discerpible' (a stronger term than 'divisible': it has physically separable parts) and impenetrable (only one piece of matter at a time could occupy a given spatial point), while spirit was penetrable (a number of spiritual substances could share a given point) and indiscerpible. A spirit also had the power of originating motion, unlike merely material things which could only transmit an impulse they had themselves received. As spirit was extended, there were none of the difficulties that vexed Descartes in explaining how the soul could move the body.[41] The apparently purposeful motions for which the Cartesian theory so obviously failed to account could also be traced to an impulse that a spiritual substance supplied. This was not God himself, but another ubiquitous force, which More described as the 'Hylarchic Spirit'. This was the efficient cause of every motion that Aristotelians explained in teleological ways. It was the grand omission that made a nonsense of Cartesian physics, and of any other mechanistic system;[42] it did not occur to More that he had given the machine an additional, flexible part.

More was at one with Hale in pointing to the inadequacy of atomist and Cartesian explanations. Both wanted to use phenomena for which the mechanists could not account as visible arguments for God's existence. The problem with More's theories, from Hale's theological standpoint, was that they naturalised God's operations. Hale believed in a God that stood outside a finite universe, that caused particular motions (chiefly those once explained through final causes) by issuing commands. The Cambridge Platonist's Hylarchic Spirit, which performed a similar function in

Mundo, aut extra Mundum. Materiam a seipsa non moueri, sed a Deo; Deum tamen nec ulli quidem parti Materiae nec toti adesse, vel unquam adfuisse, quo Motum Materiae impertiret. Materiam cogitare non posse qualitercunque modificatam; id vero eousque verum esse, ut omnia Bruta Animalia purae putae sint Machinae, nec equo phalerato plus sensus insit quam suis ephippis. Mentem animamve immortalem humano corpori inesse, vel adesse; sed per operationes solummodo, non per essentiam. Esse quidem divinam providentiam; et tamen rerum fines non esse inquirendos.' More, *Enchiridion metaphysicum sive de rebus incorporeis succincta et luculenta dissertatio*, 1671, sig. A3 + 1.

[41] Or so at least More seems to have believed; in fact there is no reason why a penetrable spirit should move anything at all. The ability of matter to move matter is intrinsically connected with the property of resisting penetration. Hobbes understood this point, and insisted that anything moving 'body' is body. Most of his Restoration critics missed it.

[42] More's *Enchiridion metaphysicum* is largely taken up with illustrations of this point.

More's physics, was extended in infinite space. More came to believe, in other words, that the universe had an inhabitant who was ubiquitous and purposeful, the cause of every motion that mechanistic physics was unable to explain. As Hale reasonably complained, More gave an account of everything and nothing: 'it would be a pitiful refuge for a man pretending to philosophy, to give this general solution to all phenomena of nature, that this is so, because the Spirit of nature thus orders it.'[43] He was criticising More's Hylarchic Spirit on precisely the grounds that Boyle attacked the use of natural 'laws'.

Hale thought that the purpose of science was to 'carry the mind up to God', and not to a 'spiritual' creature, however exalted. He made notes on *Enchiridion Metaphysicum* (1671), which show that he strongly disagreed with More's belief that space is infinite.[44] If any quantity were infinite, then of course his argument for the creation, the absurdity of an infinite succession, was robbed of all its force. But he also disagreed with More's idea that space itself was a kind of spiritual substance. The *Discourse* held that space and time were purely 'relational' things, and his later works were loyal to this view. As the *Primitive origination* put it, 'duration without a thing that dureth and space without a thing that is extended in it is the veriest the absolutest nothing that can be'.[45] His comments on the *Enchiridion* explain how we arrive at such ideas. Our notion of an empty space, 'antecedent to any body or spatiatum really existing with it or in it' comes from our picturing a phantom body, an 'imaginary spatiatum', 'and then by cause the nimbleness of our intellective faculty substitutes this imaginary spatiatum and knits it to space we presently think that space devoid of any spatiatum is really and actually extended.'[46] More held (against Descartes) that space can be imagined without matter, though it is quite impossible to imagine a form of matter without space. Our conception of matter involves a conception of a substance that is penetrable, eternal, self-subsistent and infinitely extended: in fact of a spirit like God.

Part of the *Primitive origination* discusses this ingenious argument:[47]

A late excellent author hath used a very incongruous medium to prove ... the existence of God, because there was really a space before the world was created; whereas first of all, there could be no space without a body, and secondly, if there could be such a space, it were of a divisible existence, which could hold no proportion with the indivisible nature of the glorious God, space being quid

---

[43] Hale, *Observations*, 35.   [44] Lambeth 3498, 1–33.
[45] Hale, *Primitive origination*, 118.
[46] Lambeth 3498, 3.
[47] The view that space is God, or at least has all the properties of God, is a doctrine of the *Enchiridion metaphysicum* (1671), though More has earlier passages which hint at some such view (Hall, *More*, 188–9; 207–8).

extensum, and divisible, but the essence of God purely spiritual and indivisible, and equally immense, whether there were a world or no world, space or no space.[48]

Space and time were 'modes of being'; there might be entities which were non-spatial and non-temporal. Even in the material world, he interestingly but puzzlingly suggested, a 'permanent being' like gold might have 'another kind of duration'.[49] God's manner of existing is different again. He 'co-exists' (Hale's word) with the created world, but the world does not affect his mode of being. It is made of 'divisible body', but he of course is indivisible; it experiences 'time or successive duration', but he has 'indivisible duration'.[50] A 'spirit', as defined by More, cannot possibly be God; if divisible space is infinite, 'why may we not rather suppose matter eternal and the material world eternal and also immense and infinite?'.[51]

The problem with the mechanists was their attempt to do without a God, except as an ingenious designer. More's deep dislike of mechanistic science induced him to make an equally damaging error. Because he assumed an identity between atheist and materialist ideas (a belief that was clearly encouraged by reading Thomas Hobbes) he thought an argument for 'spiritual substance' amounted to a proof that God exists. In showing that nature is not a machine, he presented it as a vegetable instead. He then increasingly implied that the vegetable was God.[52] Hale clearly wanted to avoid More's ultra-vitalist aproach to nature, but the notion of 'spiritual substance' acquired a place in his philosophy. The compromise he sought, preserving an ambiguity between mechanist and vitalist approaches, led him towards 'Helmontian' ideas.

The works of John Baptist van Helmont consist in a succession of short tracts.[53] They first became available to the general learned world in the Latin edition of 1648; an English version followed in 1662. Helmontian science dispensed with the Aristotelian forms and final causes. Helmont was categorical that 'the form of the thing composed cannot be the cause of the thing produced, but rather the last perfect act of generation'.[54] He saw a need, however, for some internal organising force in a range of the

---

[48] Hale, *Primitive origination*, 121.   [49] *Ibid.*, 119.   [50] Lambeth 3482, 94.
[51] Lambeth 3498, 4.
[52] More's vitalism became more pronounced in the course of the 1660s. On the *Enchiridion metaphysicum*'s innovations, see Gabbey, 'Limits of mechanism', 25, and Hall, *More*, 208.
[53] Hale's explicit references are always to two essays, referred to as 'De fermentis' (*Oriatrike*, 27) and De origine formarum (*Oriatrike*, 128), which are summarised in the following paragraphs.
[54] Helmont, *Oriatrike, or physick refined*, 1662, p. 28. On Helmont see Walter Pagel, *Joan Baptista Van Helmont*, Cambridge 1982, Allan G. Debus, *The chemical philosophy: paracelsian medicine and science in the sixteenth and seventeenth centuries*, 2 vols., New York 1977.

phenomena of nature, including fires and magnets and every living thing.[55] This 'inward and essential'[56] cause was what he called a ferment: 'the ferment is a formal created being, which is neither a substance nor an accident, but a neutral thing framed from the beginning of the world in the places of its own monarchy, in the manner of light, fire, the magnall or sheath of the air, forms etc . . .'[57] A substance is entirely self-subsistent; an accident is something that can only exist by inhering in a substance. A ferment inhabits some matter, but is more than just a property of its material base. In Helmont's terminology, which is frequently borrowed by Hale, it is a 'vis' or 'virtus', while the 'place of its own monarchy' is a 'hypostasis'. A fire, which subsists in its fuel, and dies when the fuel gives out, is something entirely different from heat in something hot.

The distinguishing mark of a ferment was its ability to replicate, transmitting the vis or virtus to separate stocks of the hypostasis. Helmont was not, however, a believer in sharp distinctions, in any branch of his philosophy. He placed these 'neutral creatures' along a continuous spectrum, with self-subsistent angels at one end, and at the other accidents like heat. Somewhere between these two extremes were light, fire, magnetism, and the 'souls' that lived in animals and plants, as well as the so-called 'Archeus', an organising spirit for the whole of the visible world. The appeal of Helmontian thought lay in its imprecision. The ferments might be understood as non-material substance, just like the examples of 'spirit' in the writings of a vitalist like More. But they could equally be seen as essentially nothing but 'motions', as a curious class of activity in merely material things.

This was how Thomas Willis (1621–75) appears to have used the idea.[58] Willis, the greatest doctor of Restoration times, was probably an atomist at heart, but he used the Helmontian ferment to label operations that no one understood. He thought that the soul of an animal was a ferment of some kind, a complex mechanical motion which might even be responsible for thought. Willis was Hale's own doctor, and an influence on his attitudes towards the whole complex of issues surrounding the 'animal soul'.[59] One side of Helmont's theory was thus compatible with mechanism. But Helmont was also an alchemist with a credulous or even fraudulent streak. He exasperated Robert Boyle, who greatly admired his experimental work, by claiming to have found the Alkahest, the paracelsan universal solvent.[60]

---

[55] Helmont, *Oriatrike*, 29.   [56] *Ibid.*, 29.   [57] *Ibid.*, 31.
[58] On Willis see Hansruedi Isler, *Thomas Willis MD, 1621–75*, 1968; R. G. Frank, *The Oxford physiologists*, Berkeley 1980, p. 166.
[59] Hale, *Works*, I, 99; Isler, *Willis*, 172–9.
[60] Boyle, *The works of the Honourable Robert Boyle*, ed. Thomas Birch, 5 vols., 1744, vol. I, pp. 307, 313–15.

He also believed in 'weapon-salve', a means of curing wounds applied to the instrument responsible. The world-soul, or Archeus, was another concept drawn from alchemy, totally incompatible with mechanistic thought.

Though Hale was not much interested in alchemical ideas, he was drawn to Helmont's notion that matter was 'inhabited' by a non-material force. The latter's alien paracelsan side could anyway be overlooked for the sake of his helpful suggestion that ferments were God's laws. As Robert Boyle had put it, in the course of the *Free enquiry*'s attack on such ideas, 'the famous Helmont ... will have every body ... to act that, which it is commanded to act'.[61] Hale strongly approved of this general approach. His nearest thing to a pure theoretical statement was the opening chapters of his final book. The *Observations touching the principles of natural motions* (1677) was one of a series of pamphlets to be discussed at length in the next chapter. Its most important feature, for present purposes, was its general account of his views on 'natural motions'. Though God of course supported every motion 'by way of concurrence and concomitance' (what Boyle referred to as his 'general concourse') he also acted 'by causality'. Hale therefore assumed that 'those created beings that seem to have the immediate principle of motions in themselves, have that principle from his fiat and institution'.[62] Such principles were numerous, including: 'the motions of augmentation and conformation of vegetables, the motions of ascent and calefaction in fire, the motions of attraction and aversation in magnetical bodies, and the very motion of descent in physical bodies.'[63] Hale gave a summary of Helmont's theory, which offered a middle way between

two extremes in the modern philosophy: some are so wholly intent upon vital and plastic principles that they contend even almost against all mechanical motions of bodies ... others are so greatly taken up with the thoughts of matter and mechanical motions, that they wholly exterminate any intrinsic principles of motion and resolve them wholly into matter and its modifications, and mechanism and mechanical motions.[64]

The ferment's intellectual charm was that it made a choice unnecessary. Hale was sure that a ferment would count, unlike an act of More's Hylarchic Spirit, as a genuine scientific explanation. He could ignore the question of whether the explanation that he gave was mechanist or vitalist in form. He had fulfilled the philosopher's principal duty, using the fabric of the world to 'carry up' the human mind to God.

---

[61] Boyle, *Works*, IV, 367.   [62] Hale, *Observations*, 3.   [63] *Ibid.*, 6.
[64] *Ibid.*, 21.

The Torricellian experiment

Hale's 'scientific' interests covered a baffling range, but he published only three polemical works. An *essay touching the gravitation or non-gravitation of fluids* (1673) was followed by *Difficiles nugae, or Observations touching the Torricellian experiment* (1674; second edition with 'Occasional additions' 1675) and *Observations touching the principles of natural motions* (1677). All three were in some way concerned with a single much-discussed phenomenon:

a glass tube of three foot or more long, closed at one end, and then filled with mercury or quicksilver, and then the open end stopped with the finger, and inverted into a vessel of restagnant[1] mercury; and when the end is sufficiently immersed, then the finger nimbly removed, so that no air get in, the mercury will subside in the tube to the height of 29 ins. and half an inch, or near thereabouts, but infallibly between 27 and 30 ins, leaving the residue of the upper end of the tube emptied of the mercury.[2]

This 'Torricellian experiment' raised questions of the highest interest for the interpretation of natural events. Some believed that the column of metal was supported by the weight of air upon the open vessel; others believed the same phenomenon was explained by the abhorrence of a vacuum. Some thought that the space at the top of the tube was empty, others that it was occupied by something that had filtered through the mercury or glass, others again that it contained a vapour drawn out of the metal itself. Cartesians, atomists and Aristotelians had all advanced accounts of what occurred, depending on the presence or absence of vacuums and the explanatory validity of teleological principles in nature. The 'trifling and ludicrous experiment' as Hale mock-modestly presented it, was actually a crucial test for competing cosmological ideas.

If the pamphlets are taken together, they constitute Hale's chosen public statement of the correct approach to the natural world. The enemy, here as

---

[1] 'Overflowing'.

[2] Hale, *Difficiles nugae, or Observations touching the Torricellian experiment*, 1674, pp. 1–2. In general, see Schaffer and Shapin, *Leviathan and the air-pump*, Princeton 1985.

elsewhere, was any purely mechanistic theory, presuming to account for the workings of nature without some reference to the 'laws' of God:

> I confess I am none of these adepts in philosophy, that can tell us how to solve all the effects in nature, without recourse to the infinite wisdom, power and goodness of the glorious God, who certainly knew better how to frame the world, and fix the laws of nature, than the wisest of men or angels.[3]

Hale's target was a tendency, the 'general mode and fashion' of the ancient atomist philosophy, especially in its recent 'restitution' by the modern atomism of Gassendi and Descartes.[4] Unlike the empirically minded Aristotle, these modern thinkers hawked 'hypotheses'; with astonishing presumption, they played at being God, 'telling us not so much what the truth is, as what he thinks he could have made it if he had had the handling of it'.[5] A prime example of this kind of error, with all the implausibility that tended to result, was Robert Boyle's 'elatery' of the air.

Boyle tried to explain the support for the column of metal in terms of a column of air of equivalent weight, pressing upon the mercury exposed to the atmosphere. The air had an intrinsic 'elatery' or spring, deriving from the spring-like form of some or all of its component parts: 'our air either consists of, or else abounds with, parts of such a nature, that in case they be bent or compressed by the weight of the incumbent part of the atmosphere, or by any other body, they do endeavour, as much as in them lieth, to free themselves from that pressure . . .'[6] Not all of the supporters of this theory were committed to believing in a vacuum, but they all denied, in this particular case, that abhorrence of a vacuum was involved. In Boyle's key work, the *New experiments physico-mechanical touching the spring of the air* (1660; second edition 1662), he confined himself to asserting that there was no air in the tube. The question of whether a space could be totally empty he took to be merely metaphysical.[7] Hale was, of course, a plenist, but he recognised that plenism was quite compatible with Boyle's solution.[8]

Hale's great dislike of Boyle's suggested spring was really based in a teleological outlook. He believed that the air had weight, that it could be

---

[3] Hale, *Difficiles nugae*, 55.   [4] Hale, *Observations*, To the reader.

[5] *Ibid.*, sig. A4v; Hale, *Difficiles nugae*, 5. This is not quite the caricature it seems, but a perfectly accurate paraphrase of the hypothetical method commended by Descartes. Descartes, *Principles*, 105–6, 180.

[6] Boyle, *New experiments physico-mechanical touching the spring of the air*, 2nd edn, Oxford 1662, pp. 12.

[7] *Ibid.*, 61, 127; Boyle, *Works*, IV, 406.

[8] Hale, *Difficiles nugae*, 279–80, refers to Gaspar Schott, *Technica curiosa sive mirabilia artis*, Würzburg 1664, pp. 306–8. Schott was a plenist, who refers to *horror vacui* in explaining cupping glasses. For the purposes of the Torricellian problem, he was nonetheless a follower of Boyle.

mechanically compressed, and even that it might have springy parts. Boyle's friend John Wallis (1617–1703), the Oxford mathematician, was convinced that he conceded 'what is contended for, that the air hath a gravity and a spring, and that by these the phenomena may be solved'.[9] What Wallis overlooked was a fundamental difference in their concept of the spring. As Hale himself explained,

herein we do not considerably differ, only they say that this elasticity is of a vast and almost unlimited nature, that scarce hath any bounds to it; we say that it hath more contracted and determined bounds of its elasticity, and those are such as every portion of free air obtains in a common and usual state of the temperament of the weather.[10]

Hale thought, in other words, that atmospheric pressure would be nil so long as the air was in its usual state. A pressure in a gas was an impulse to revert to its 'natural' volume, the volume God created it to fill, in response to some compression by artificial means. The elatery of air, which had no reference to a natural state, was barely comprehensible to someone of Aristotelian habits of mind. Hale saw no reason for the atmosphere to press upon the earth which it surrounded; it was simply maintaining the station to which it was appointed by God's power:

the proceeding of this sovereign architect in the frame of this great building of the universe not being like to the architecture of men, who begin at the bottom, but he began at the roof, and builded downwards, and in that process, suspended the inferior parts of the world upon the superior. But this kind of reasoning, I know, is not grateful to the palate of the present philosophers.[11]

It was not surprising, then, that the opening shot in Hale's campaign was a work concerned with atmospheric pressure, the *Essay touching the gravitation or non-gravitation of fluids* (1673).[12] Experience suggested that the cumulative weight of a sea of air (which Hale agreed must be considerable) had no perceptible effect on human and animal life. Whatever the explanation, it was probably analogous to a rather similar phenomenon: 'a flounder should at land be pressed to death by the weight of a gallon of water in a bucket laid upon him; and yet should not be damnified by the weight of two, or three, or ten ton of water in the bottom of the sea.'[13] This striking fact appeared to show that pressure was uniform in even the

---

[9] Oldenburg, *Correspondence*, XI, 37.   [10] Hale, *Difficiles nugae*, 181.

[11] *Ibid.*, 57.

[12] The *Essay* in particular called forth two printed replies: John Wallis, *A discourse of gravity and gravitation grounded on experimental observations presented to the Royal Society November 12 1674*, 1675; and Thomas Hobbes, *Decameron physiologicum*, 1678, Chapter viii, printed in *The English works of Thomas Hobbes*, ed. William Molesworth, 1845, vol. VII, pp. 138–54.

[13] Hale, *Essay*, 46.

deepest container of any particular homogeneous fluid. The drops of water filling up a bucket seemed to exert no pressure on each other, but their cumulative weight pressed on the bottom. Descartes himself believed in this 'non-gravitation' within water, and his proposed solution for this non-mechanistic effect was one of the very lamest in his system.[14]

This was just the kind of problem that excited Henry More, who discussed it in *Enchiridion metaphysicum* (1671), which had recently been published when Hale wrote. Having shown that the French philosopher had failed to explain what occurs, he attributed the fluid's 'non-gravitation' to the agency of his Hylarchic Spirit.[15] Hale criticised this all-too-effective device, the '*principium hylarchicum*, under whose regiment the various appearances of things are managed, of which we cannot find any ready sufficient natural solution', on characteristically theological grounds:

most certainly the ever-glorious and most wise God is the author of nature, and of all the laws thereof; they are his institutions by which he orders and regulates the motions and appearances in nature. And he supports them as a universal cause, by the constant influence of his power and goodness; and all their appearances are nevertheless ordinarily regular according to his instituted laws of nature. And as it far more advanceth the honour and skill of an excellent artist, that hath so framed and ordered an automaton, that it may be regularly guided to its end ... so it far more advanceth the glory of the divine wisdom, in that he hath settled such a regular order in things of nature, that may regularly conduct them to their designed end, than if the glorious God, or any intelligent power by him substituted, should by immediate and identical interposition produce every phenomenon in nature ....[16]

There are similar statements to be found, often in opposition to More's thought, in almost all Hale's scientific writings. They express an expectation about God rooted in latitudinarianism, but they function as an axiom of a natural philosophical position.

The basis of the *Essay's* argument is a careful initial distinction. Gravity was defined as an 'intrinsical quality of heavy bodies, whereby they tend downwards to, or towards, the centre of the earth';[17] Hale was primarily concerned with 'gravitation', which was 'nothing else but motion, or at least *conatus* or *nisus ad motum*'.[18] He tries to show why particles of water do not attempt to move with respect to each other, although they have the 'quality' of tending towards the centre of the earth. It is clear that he was hopelessly confused, in ways that defy reconstruction, about the whole idea of 'gravitation'.

---

[14] Descartes, *Principles*, 193. Aptly described by Hale as 'obscure and scarce intelligible' (*Essay*, 39).
[15] More, *Enchiridion metaphysicum*, 152.   [16] Hale, *Essay*, 43–4.   [17] *Ibid.*, 9.
[18] *Ibid.*, 11.

The first of his solutions depends on an analogy with the structures of solider things. The constituents of a single piece of metal do not move or seek to move towards each other, but the lump as a whole still gravitates on whatever is beneath.[19] The atmosphere resembled a heap of 'solid bodies in contiguity and not in continuity', whose structure nonetheless precluded them from any significant mutual gravitation.[20] A number of bricks can be removed from a given pyramid's base without the whole of the pyramid collapsing.[21] Hale placed a hollow eggshell at the heart of a pile of wheat, where it survived undamaged.[22] Hale showed himself aware, in one of his manuscript drafts, of an obvious objection to this theory:

no one column of this air doth gravitate upon any one portion of its base. This indeed may seem a paradox for it may be said that if the whole weight must gravitate somewhere suppose that B should not sustain his third part of the weight yet at least it must be sustained by A and C and then the whole weight impendent upon the whole will be a moiety upon A and a moiety upon B which will be unreasonable. And again if A and C be so kind as to bear the part of B yet B will recompense them by bearing the share of their third parts and so the business will be as broad as long as each basis will one way or another bear his full proportion of weight vizt a third part.
I confess the inference is hard . . .[23]

It was possible, however, that the atmosphere was actually self-supporting, having no need at any point to rest upon the earth. He sometimes visualised the air as an enormous arch, or rather a series of concentric arches, composed of 'interwoven filaments'.[24] The reader was asked to imagine that the inmost core of the earth was made of wax. The decapitated wedge shapes which formed its rocky shell would stop the structure from collapsing inwards.[25] The line of argument could be extended to explain the lack of atmospheric pressure.[26] This last idea was stolen from the *Dialogus physicus* (1661), the Hobbesian contribution to this topic, but Hale ungratefully disguised his source.[27]

Though Hale seemed pleased with this hypothesis, which he certainly never formally rejected, he preferred to concentrate upon another.[28] Instead of the fluid's constituent parts moving towards the centre of the earth, in a way that might create an arch-like structure, they gravitated randomly in every direction at once.[29] The effect of all these contradictory motions, including motions of 'direct ascent', was that they cancelled one another out.[30] This was a 'natural' theory (the other was, he said,

[19] *Ibid.*, 15.   [20] *Ibid.*, 19–28.   [21] *Ibid.*, 20–4.   [22] *Ibid.*, 24–5.
[23] Lambeth 3511, 34.
[24] Hale, *Difficiles nugae*, 50.   [25] Hale, *Essay*, 15–18.   [26] *Ibid.*, 18.
[27] Hobbes, *Dialogus physicus*, tr. Simon Schaffer in Schaffer and Shapin, *Air-pump*, 376–7.
[28] Hale, *Essay*, 58.   [29] *Ibid.*, 11.   [30] *Ibid.*, 67.

'mechanical'), because the random movement of the parts was intrinsic to the nature of a fluid.[31] Hobbes wittily summarised the implications:

the endeavour being, as he saith, intrinsical, and every way, must needs drive the water perpetually outward; that is to say, as to this question, upwards; and seeing the same endeavour in one individual body cannot be more ways at once than one, it will carry on perpetually and without limit; and so we shall never more have rain.[32]

The point of these fallacious arguments was to refute the elatery of air.[33] In *Difficiles nugae* (1674; supplemented by 'Occasional additions' 1675) Hale proceeded to give his own account of what really supported the column in the tube. The real philosophical issue, as Henry More, for one, was well aware, was the role of teleological explanation. More produced a brief pamphlet of commentary, *Remarks upon two late ingenious discourses* (1676), which tried to claim Hale's writings as allies for his vitalist crusade. Boyle's theory, he pronounced, was 'against more solid and searching reason, that enquires after the final causes of things.'[34] In spite of Hale's dissent from More's idea of a Hylarchic Spirit, the judge at least rejected the 'monstrous spring of the air'.[35] In fact Hale was endeavouring to steer his customary middle path, guided by a respect for Aristotle. The most important influence on his work, surprisingly in so stern a Protestant, was a pair of Aristotelian Jesuits.

As Hale interpreted the situation, there were three principal accounts of what was in the space above the mercury in the tube. Boyle's party believed it was nothing but a vacuum, or at least that whatever remained had no explanatory significance. Another group thought it was ether, 'strained' through the glass by the weight of falling metal.[36] The final possibility, to be found in the works of the Jesuits Fabri (1607–88) and Linus (1595–1675) was that it was a vapour extracted from the mercury itself.[37] Fabri believed this vapour was previously dissolved within the liquid, but Linus preferred to regard it as a microscopic quantity of metal, in enormously dilated vaporous form. Hale's version of this theory drew heavily on the ideas of both.[38]

---

[31] *Ibid.*, 52.   [32] Hobbes, *Works*, VII, 142.   [33] Hale, *Essay*, 87–8.
[34] More, *Remarks upon two ingenious discourses*, 1677, Preface.
[35] *Conway Letters: The correspondence of Anne Viscountess Conway, Henry More, and their friends*, ed. M. Nicholson, New Haven 1930, p. 423
[36] Hale, *Difficiles nugae*, 124. The Hobbesian variant on this theory claimed that the space was occupied by air (admittedly of a type that was very refined), which passed through the descending mercury.
[37] Linus, *De inseparabilitate corporum*, 1661, pp. 34, 37–43; Fabri, *Dialogi phisici*, Lyons 1665, p. 208. Hale's explicit references are all to the work of the same title published in 1669, which amplifies the earlier discussion and is barely intelligible without it.
[38] Hale, *Difficiles nugae*, 8.

All three of them had trouble grasping the Boylean concept of the 'spring', in part because of a literal understanding of the role that was said to be played by the 'column of air'. The column of air counterbalanced the mercury supported in the tube; it weighed the same, in other words, as 29 inches of metal. This was a testable hypothesis; the apparatus could be covered up, so that the column's influence was excluded.[39] The spring of the portion of air shut off from the weight of the column was nonetheless sufficient (on Boyle's hypothesis) to support the mercury to the same level. When this postulated spring was combined with the weight of the column, it would surely, on Boyle's argument, support double the amount of mercury.[40] They evidently saw the spring of air as a kind of uncaused motion, a propensity to expand in all directions, quite unrelated to the weight that was pressing down upon the air concerned. It was no wonder they dismissed the concept with a mixture of incomprehension and contempt.

Fabri's main contribution lay in proving, to Hale's satisfaction, that there was a vapour dissolved within the metal. Fabri had shown that mercury was 'embased' by frequent use, and that shaken up with water it would produce a gas, so the theory was supported by a number of experimental details.[41] Hale seems to have believed that every liquid included such vaporous parts; he was unmoved by Pascal's demonstration that a column of wine (an obviously spirituous substance) behaved identically to a column of water.[42] Boyle himself had observed the formation of numerous bubbles in water placed inside his vacuum pump.[43]

The little book by Linus which was the dominant influence on Hale was *De inseparabilitate corporum*, published in 1661 and answered by Boyle the next year.[44] It used some Aristotelian arguments that even Hale was disinclined to stress. He discounted, for example, the alleged impossibility of an empty space transmitting light and sound.[45] But the principal message of Linus' book was his claim that the column of metal was held in place by a 'funiculus',[46] a fragment of the liquid that was forcibly dilated to fill up the vacant space. His argument was simple, depending largely on a single datum. If the usual procedure is followed, but the tube of mercury is open-ended, the top end being stoppered with a finger, the finger will

[39] Fabri, *Dialogi* (1665), 201; Linus, *De inseparabilitate*, 20–1.

[40] Hale, *Difficiles nugae*, 187–94.

[41] *Ibid.*, 135–6; Fabri, *Dialogi* (1669), 497; *Dialogi* (1665) sig. Ddv., Dd3v.

[42] Hale, *Difficiles nugae*, 'Occasional additions', p. 40. Linus, by contrast, accepted Pascal's argument, *De inseparabilitate*, 34–5.

[43] Hale, *Difficiles nugae*, 145.

[44] On Linus in general, see C. Reilly, *Francis Line, S.J.: an exiled English scientist, 1595–1675*, Rome 1969.

[45] Hale, *Difficiles nugae*, 118.   [46] Literally 'a little piece of rope'.

experience a 'pull', apparently from the mercury that is trying to descend. Linus interpreted this pull as the impulse of the vapour to contract to its natural state.[47]

Hale thought that the space was occupied by vapour dissolved in the metal, and not a fragment of the mercury, but otherwise he followed Linus' theory. The novel feature of his final pamphlet, the *Observations touching the principles of natural motions and especially of rarefaction and condensation* (1677) was his detailed defence of the Jesuit's claim that matter could condense and rarefy.[48] Hale rightly saw this point as central to the difference between the Aristotelian approach and its more mechanistic enemies. Rarefaction occurs 'when the same body or at least portion of material substance takes up a greater external dimension'.[49] The atomists thought this reflected a greater dilution of matter with the vacuum; in the Cartesian theory, the rarefying presence was *materia subtilis*. Both sects agreed that 'the first material principles of bodies are certain minute corpuscles or atoms', each of which occupied a constant volume.[50]

Hale thought this unquestioned assumption was most implausible: 'to suppose that the first constituent particles of air or water are hard or of any other nature than the whole body is a precarious, inevident and unreasonable supposition'; he therefore preferred to assume that compressible things were made up of compressible parts.[51] He regarded rarity and density in things that expand and contract as 'but natural affections, or rather passions, qualities or modes of such bodies arising from their very texture and make, and are as naturally belonging to them as heat or cold, humidity or driness, smoothness or roughness, or other tangible qualities to other bodies that are more gross and corporeal.'[52] He was therefore very willing to believe that the urge of a funiculus to revert to its natural size could sustain some particular weight of mercury.

The objections to Linus' book with which Hale would have been familiar were contained in the published response of Robert Boyle. Boyle objected to the notion of a self-contracting gas, announcing that 'I am not very forward to allow acting for ends to bodies inanimate, and consequently devoid of knowledge'.[53] He also wished to know how the gas was attached to the finger on which it allegedly pulled. Hale's answer to this question (in *Difficiles nugae*) summed up his attitude to Boyle's ideas. The question was

as if a man should ask, how doth the stone understand that he must descend, when yet all the men in the world can never give any satisfactory reason for its motion to the earth, more than to the moon, but only nature that is the principium motus or

[47] Linus, *De inseparabilitate*, 24–8; Fabri, *Dialogi* (1665), 191.
[48] Linus, *De inseparabilitate*, 164.
[49] Hale, *Observations*, 39.   [50] *Ibid.*, 58.   [51] *Ibid.*, 94.   [52] *Ibid.*, 88.
[53] Boyle, *New experiments, A defence against Francis Linus*, p. 34.

quietus, or rather the God of nature, whose standing and statuminated law nature is, hath so ordered it, and ordered so in the best way for the use beauty and accommodation of the universe.[54]

There came a point when the philosopher could do no more than trace the execution of God's will. To arrive at the great original of motion was indeed the purpose of philosophy. Nothing attached the vapour to the finger, but this was no objection to the theory that Linus advanced: 'what are the hooks or grappers, whereby the humane soul and body, yea the souls and bodies of animals are knit together, whereby the blood and spirits are colligated, whereby the loadstone attracts the iron notwithstanding an interposed plate of glass or body of impervious brass ...?'[55] The examples must have been familiar, because these problems were the subject matter of Hale's unpublished scientific works.

[54] Hale, *Difficiles nugae*, 238.   [55] *Ibid.*, 248.

The soul

John Baptist van Helmont created for Hale the basis of a Christian natural science, a means of re-describing various natural events as motions in obedience to God's will. The Helmontian ferments were ranged along a spectrum, from life in all its forms, through such phenomena as fires and magnets, to mere propensities like gravitation; they spanned the 'qualitative' gap between the falling stone and human minds. Hale never quite decided if a ferment was a kind of spiritual substance, or just an unexplained activity. The concept's ambiguity was the feature which made it so useful, but there was an evident danger in blurring the distinction that separated matter from immaterial things. In giving religious importance to trivial natural events, Hale tended to naturalise God's interventions. His talk of a spectrum of ferments brought even man's immortal part to the edge of the natural sphere, at a time when Christianity was being reduced to a message about the existence of a 'future state'. His 'biological' treatises merged seamlessly with writings about the human soul. They were more than a support for his religion; they constituted a theology.

The continuities within Hale's thought can be seen from the closing pages of *The primitive origination of mankind*. At the conclusion of his book, Hale turned to 'a farther enquiry touching the end of the formation of Man, so far as the same may be collected by natural light and ratiocination'.[1] He promised to pursue this in a sequel, which would treat 'that vital immortal beam of light, life, and immortality, that seminal principle of eternal life, the soul, irradiated and influenced by the sacred spirit of life and love ...'.[2] A number of versions of such a work survive, in various stages of polish and completeness.[3] They give a biological account of the spiritual life of the Christian, dealing with 'generation' in animals and

---

[1] Hale, *Primitive origination*, 358.   [2] *Ibid.*, 380.

[3] Lambeth 3490, Lambeth 3500, Lambeth 3504, and the various false starts preserved in Lambeth 3499. In September 1676 he began yet another attempt upon the subject (Lambeth 3504, 298v.). For the date of the three main versions, see n. 51 below.

plants as a means of approaching human reproduction, and culminating in remarks on the 're-generation' of the soul.

A treatise of this kind depends upon one obvious assumption: that plants have a vital principle that is at least analogous to man's, belonging to a class of entities perhaps better described as 'anima' than 'soul'. Hale used the existence of 'anima' to meet a wide variety of needs. It was the purposeful internal agent that superintended the growth of living things (and therefore incompatible with the Cartesian picture of animals as nothing but machines); a non-material substance (and therefore incompatible with Hobbes); and a basis of identity that could be rewarded or punished after death. He had inherited the view that anima had three varieties, each of them having 'faculties' denied to more primitive things: the vegetable (augmentation and nutrition), the animal or 'sensitive' (perception, imagination, locomotion), and the intellectual (intellect and will). Like most of his generation, he was shocked by the Cartesian assertion that only the last of these categories existed. He drew on Gassendi's discussion of the soul, which pointed out that 'anima' conflated two separate ideas, conveyed in Greek by *psyche* (the principle of life) and *nous* (the intellect).[4] Descartes, it might be said, had surrendered the concept of *psyche* in order to safeguard *nous*, while Hobbes dispensed with both; Gassendi believed in both *psyche* and *nous*, but saw them, controversially, as wholly independent entities.

It is very important to understand that Hale was never a 'biologist', someone who saw his object of attention as the study of a quality called 'life'. The concept of 'anima' covered a part of the longer series of Helmontian ferments, entities which disclosed themselves in some kind of impulse to motion. The souls of animals and plants were considered less as constituting life than as bundles of abilities without a discernible mechanistic cause. Hale drew attention to the fact that metals must be nearly vegetable, because they have been known to grow in places underground.[5] He also quoted Aristotle's very suggestive phrase that motion was 'vita quaedam quae omnibus inest'.[6] A motion was a simple kind of life, and the spectrum was graded too finely to allow for sharp distinctions between organic and non-living things. One illustration of this attitude was Hale's discussion of magnetic force.

It is no surprise that magnets were of interest to Hale. No serious anti-mechanist could afford to ignore an apparent case of action at a

[4] Gassendi, *Opera omnia*, Lyons 1658, vol. II, p. 237. On Gassendi see Margaret J. Osler, 'Baptising Epicurean atomism: Pierre Gassendi on the immortality of the soul', in *Religion, science and worldview: essays in honour of Richard S. Westfall*, Cambridge 1985, pp. 163–83.
[5] Lambeth 3504, 209v.   [6] Hale, *Observations*, 2.

distance. The mysterious powers of magnets, what was more, had long been traced to possession of a soul. Hale mentioned this had been the view of Thales, cited by Aristotle in an early passage of *De anima*.[7] A principal aim of Gilbert's *De magnete* (1601) the classic modern study of the problem, was to show that the earth was a magnet, possessing 'anima', in spite of being found below the moon.[8] A further advantage of magnets, from the standpoint of a dabbler in these questions, was that an individual could easily conduct his own research. The equipment necessary was neither cumbersome nor over-expensive, the effects involved were highly entertaining, and the literature encouraged the duplication of experiments.[9]

Hale's major intellectual spur was probably the Cartesian explanation. Descartes attributed the magnet's power, which was an obvious problem for his system, to invisible screw-shaped particles passing through special grooves.[10] There was also a brilliant Hobbesian conjecture that some kind of vibration was involved, but Hale was as always reluctant to give any space to the atheist's ideas.[11] He concentrated fire on the 'Epicurean or Cartesian philosophy', which attributed not just magnetism but even sentience to 'matter and its various modifications'. It had ignored an 'internal active principle', and was open to several practical objections.[12] A lump of iron wholly surrounded with gold, the densest (and therefore least porous) of known bodies, was still affected by the magnet's power.[13] Hale was sure he could propose a less implausible hypothesis.

The property of loadstones that most interested Hale was the way they could communicate their powers. A magnet had a capacity to 'generate' another, impressing its north/south axis (Hale called this its 'verticity') on a previously lifeless stock of iron.[14] Hale set out to discover whether this generation created what he called a 'specifical form' or only 'a magnetical quality as fire [infuses] heat into water', whether, in fact, the magnet was a ferment.[15] The evidence strongly suggested that it was. The magnetic poles of a given stone could always be reversed, if brought in contact with a stronger magnet, but they subsequently tended to revert to their previous state.[16] This showed that the poles were intrinsic, and not a removable

---

[7] Aristotle, *De anima*, tr. J. A. Smith, Oxford 1931, Book I, Chapter 2; Lambeth 3501, 1.
[8] Gilbert, *De magnete*, tr. Fleury Mottelay pp. 24–6.
[9] Mark Ridley, *A short treatise of magnetical bodies and motions*, 1613, sig. A3.
[10] Descartes, *Principles*, 243. Discussed by Hale, Lambeth 3501, 35–6; 3502, 80–2.
[11] Hobbes, *The English works of Thomas Hobbes*, ed. Molesworth, vol. I, p. 527.
[12] Lambeth 3502, 80.   [13] *Ibid.*, 81–2.
[14] Lambeth 3501, 32. Hale treats the magnet in the MS volumes Lambeth 3501–3; Lambeth 3503, a work of edification entitled *Magnetismus magnus*, was published in 1695. Lambeth 3501 cannot be earlier than 1672, because it refers (fo. 62) to George Sinclair's work on coal mines published in that year.
[15] Lambeth 3501, 4–5.   [16] Lambeth 3502, 18–19.

quality like heat. The motion caused by magnets was not mechanical; the magnet did not move 'as the bellows drawn up attracts the ashes', but 'by an inward principle without any external or mechanical motion'. It resembled the 'vital attractive power of the root of a vegetable' (which presumably 'attracts' its nutrients).[17]

This last analogy made clear the general trend of Hale's philosophy. The magnet was a ferment, a 'self-moving compositum' consisting of a 'substratum or hypostasis corporea which seems but a dull stupid unactive nature' and a '*vis* or *virtus essentialis* which is the active principle of all its motions and operations'.[18] To call it an 'essential form' was to miss its 'inward virtue power and energy', though the pagan Aristotle could not know this, in the absence of biblical truth.[19] The whole discussion's purpose was to show that 'active principles' must be explained as motions in obedience to God's law. The tendency of heavy things to fall, the simplest and most common of all such principles, could have no other type of explanation. The centre of the earth was just a 'mathematical point' and 'hath not therefore in itself any physical attraction', but the 'institution and law of nature (which is no other than the ordination of Almighty God)' ensured that it attracted matter downwards.[20] A ferment was a symptom of God's omnipotent command over the universe, enabling Hale to integrate a semi-devotional feeling with his 'scientific' thought. The same ideas could be applied to other 'self-moving *composita*': plants, animals, and men.

From a mere biological standpoint, Hale was writing at a most propitious moment, because of impressive advances that his medical contemporaries had made. The greatest of these, of course, was William Harvey, but he also read the extant works of Glisson, Wharton, Lower and Thomas Willis.[21] He consulted both Glisson and Willis about his last disease.[22] He rated Harvey above Aristotle (the highest compliment that he could pay) as a writer about physiology, and he was strongly influenced by both of the doctor's great works.[23] The circulation of the blood encouraged a mechanistic understanding of the way in which the human body worked. Hale noticed that Harvey had greatly affected Descartes, and probably saw the Cartesian beast-machine as an over-reaction to Harvey's observations.[24] The balance was redressed in his second great work, *Exercitationes de generatione animalium* (1651). This came to the conclusion (which Hale was to reject) that the male contributed nothing to the nascent embryo. Its importance for Hale and for others was its defence of 'epigenesis', the view that organic material is in continuous development,

[17] *Ibid.*, 86.   [18] *Ibid.*, 84.   [19] *Ibid.*, 85.   [20] Lambeth 3501, 90.
[21] Lambeth 3504, 96; 3499, 121v.
[22] Hale, *Works*, I, 92, 107.   [23] Lambeth 3504, 138.   [24] *Ibid.*, 94.

as opposed to 'preformation', the view that any organism's parts exist in miniature within the seed.[25] Only a preformationist account could lend some plausibility to the theory that all brutes were just machines. The epigenetic principle went naturally with belief in *psyche*, as it enhanced the miracle of apparently purposeful growth.

What Hale found most impressive was the unvarying sequence of given cycles of development: the fact that organisms of one kind never gave birth to offspring of another, and that minute and homogeneous seeds were somehow impelled to repeat their parent's story. Plants and animals were similar to magnets, not machines; they were evidently guided by some internal organising force, which they were able to communicate to stocks of suitable material. The anima contained in living things explained why an acorn would always grow into an oak tree, why children resembled their parents, and why the best-fed sheep never grew to an elephant's size.[26] As in his legal thought, he showed an interest in identity, stressing that organisms could persist when all of their constituents were in perpetual flux.[27]

These views faced an empirical objection, based on the overwhelming evidence for creatures that appeared not to need an inherited soul: 'imperfect' living things, the products of spontaneous generation. Hale was by no means credulous; he knew Francesco Redi's *De insectis* (1668), which had discredited many alleged examples, and he consistently denied that anything more impressive than a mouse had ever just spontaneously assembled.[28] The inconceivability of humans generating in this way was always one of his arguments for an omnipotent and wise creator. He bowed to the facts, however, and offered an explanation along his usual lines, avoiding mechanistic explanations but also emphasising the law-like regularity with which God operates. God's edict to the universe created active powers, 'which in some things are called substantial forms, in things endued with life are called souls'.[29] Subsequent alterations to these rules suggested an inadequate design:

it far more advanceth the wisdom of God so to frame the universe and the several parts thereof in such number weight and measure and to furnish them with stocks of active powers virtues and energies appropriate to them that may under him so

---

[25] Hale often referred to Kenelm Digby's so-called *History of bodies* (*Two treatises in the one of which the nature of bodies, in the other the nature of man's soul is looked into*, Paris 1644) which contained a naively mechanistic account (pp. 217–18) of the development of a bean. He also cited (Lambeth 3504, 26) the attack upon it in Nathaniel Highmore's *History of generation* (1651), a vernacular popularisation of Harvey's work, and must have known the similar criticisms in Robert Sharrock's *History of vegetables* (1660), which he cites at Lambeth 3504, 81.

[26] Lambeth 3500, 38; Lambeth 3499, 106–7.   [27] Lambeth 3500, 38; Lambeth 3509, 41.

[28] Lambeth 3504, 209; Hale, *Discourse*, 5.   [29] Lambeth 3500, 59.

regularly and orderly exert their operation and motions suitable to the ends of their general offices ranks and natures than if he should by his immediate supreme efficiency be the only immediate identical and identifical cause of all their motions and operations.[30]

Hale's most developed treatment of this question, composed in 1671–72, was a typical modification of Helmontian ideas. Helmont believed, in essence, that a plant was a ferment plus water. The ferment was envisaged, at least for the purposes of this account, as surviving undetectably in apparently barren ground.[31] Hale found this theory somewhat unconvincing, but commented that the undetectable ferment was at least no more absurd than Cartesian *materia subtilis*.[32] His view was complicated, but seems, at all events, to be rather more reductionist than Helmont's. He held that the world breeds minerals, which themselves then spread 'effluvia' in the surface of the earth. Combined with water and the sun and 'vapours' from the air, they in some sense 'accommodate' the soil for production of vegetable life.[33] The other precondition for spontaneous (that is, seedless) generation was the presence of some decomposed dead plants. The remaining scattered particles, decayed into material based on sulphur, salt and oil, had a 'vis' or 'disposition', which they retained from their organic state.[34] These particles 'disposed' the soil to recreate dead plants, and turned the surface of the earth into what Hale called 'a kind of giant ferment'.[35] They needed the assistance of the 'vis animastica' created by the minerals with the help of sun, water and air.[36] It was unclear, as usual, if ferments were a kind of spiritual substance or if they were reducible to the activities of their components. This crucial ambiguity, endemic in his thought, was to be just as prominent in his work upon the higher animals.

The usual plant and animal generation was fairly well adapted to Helmontian ideas. The animal and vegetable souls resembled other ferments in being composite. The 'vis' had a 'hypostasis', composed of the spirituous parts of the blood or the sap. The enlivening *vis* was compared to the flame of a torch (an image that Gassendi had used of the animal soul), 'irradiating' the *hypostasis*.[37] It could irradiate another stock of a suitably spirituous base, much as a flame can light another fire, or a loadstone magnetise a stock of iron.[38]

Applied to the vegetable soul, this theory presents no difficulties. The vital principle of plants is seated in the sap, which normally suffuses the whole creature. Both the *hypostasis* and *vis* are easy to divide, so grafting,

---

[30] *Ibid.*, 60.   [31] Lambeth, 3504, 74.   [32] *Ibid.*, 75.   [33] *Ibid.*, 76–7.
[34] *Ibid.*, 79. Salt, sulphur and oil were the elements believed in by the chemists.
[35] *Ibid.*, 80.   [36] *Ibid.*, 79–80.   [37] Gassendi, *Opera*, II, 252.
[38] Lambeth 3500, iii; Lambeth 3504, 226.

for example, creates a new vegetable soul.[39] But the usual means of reproducing plants is by formation of some kind of seed, containing its own organising force.[40] The seed contains a small material soul, which has divided from the parent soul, creating a new individual. If it were not material, then it could not divide – an important point, as we shall see, in the interpretation of the start of human life. Animal reproduction is closely similar to that of plants, with the circulating bloodstream playing a role analogous to sap. The animal soul is based in the 'animal spirits', which develop from and are carried in the blood. Hale set great store by the famous observation that the earliest part of an embryo to develop is a tiny 'punctum saliens',[41] a primitive forerunner of the heart.[42]

The difference between animals and plants was that animal reproduction involved the combination of two seeds. Animals had two parents, each of whom gave material to form an embryo. Acceptance of this principle distinguished him from both of the observers to whom he owed the bulk of his ideas. Aristotle had taken the view that the male supplied the form and the female was the source of the material, while Harvey was led, by work dissecting deer, to conclude that the father's semen had no contact with the egg. A family resemblance with relatives on the paternal side was explained by the force of the mother's 'imagination' on the foetus being shaped within her womb.[43] Rejection of this theory, on the grounds that some resemblances were to people unknown to the mother,[44] had a corollary of great importance.

In the case of human beings, the mixture of the seeds implied that nothing except matter was involved. It was thought to be axiomatic that an immaterial or 'spiritual' thing was also indivisible by nature, and that nothing indivisible could mix.[45] The animal process of sexual reproduction could not explain transmission of the immortal soul. Hale's treatment of this problem, like many aspects of his later thought, can be approached through the ideas worked out by Henry More. Joseph Glanvill's *Lux orientalis* (1662), a popularisation of More's theories, explained the dilemma that Hale and More both faced.[46] The usual picture of the human

---

[39] Lambeth 3500, 128; Lambeth 3504, 11, 38.   [40] Lambeth 3504, 34–47.
[41] 'Jumping dot'.
[42] Lambeth 3490, 42v.–43; Lambeth 3504, 96, 110, 149, 154, 223.
[43] Lambeth 3504, 163.
[44] *Ibid.*, 163, 184; Lambeth 3490, 33.   [45] Lambeth 3504, 227.
[46] Glanvill, *Lux orientalis, or an enquiry into the opinion of the eastern sages concerning the prae-existence of souls*, 1682 (1st edn 1662). See More's *Annotations* printed at the end of this edition. Hale spent four shillings, probably in late 1659, on a copy of More, 'Of the soul' – presumably *The immortality of the soul, so far forth as it is demonstrable by the light of nature*, 1659 (Gloucester Record Office, D 1086 F68).

soul was of something immaterial and simple, and present, in its fullness, in every bodily part ('tota in toto et tota in qualibet parte'). This was the understanding of Hale's own early thought: he described it as 'actus simplex' (God was 'actus simplicissimus') an entity whose matter was indistinguishable from its form.[47] More's great objection to this theory was based on his view that spirit is extended. It was spread out, like body, across three-dimensional space; the notion of an omnipresent substance, 'tota in toto et tota in qualibet parte', was just an unintelligible 'jingle'.[48] But although it was located (indeed, in the case of God, it was *location*) it was entirely 'indiscerpible'.

This raised a knotty problem in giving an account of life's transmission. So far as human beings were concerned, in Glanvill's presentation of the question, there were two schools of thought. The 'traductionist' view (that the soul was passed down) clearly involved division of some kind. The 'infusionist' alternative (that the soul was inserted by God) could hardly account for the fact of original sin. It was unthinkable, of course, that souls should be created with this taint; if the new soul was innocent, and only the body inherited sin, then God was manifestly most unjust to place it in this doomed receptacle.[49] Augustine was committed, on very much these grounds, to supporting the traductionist position.[50]

The difficulty with infusionism was created by assuming that every soul was an *ad hoc* creation. This was objectionable on general grounds (as Augustine characteristically complained, it subjected the Almighty to every adulterer's whim), as well as implicating God in defiling his innocent creature. More's answer was to break the link between divine creation and infusion, by postulating a separate 'world' of pre-existing souls. These souls were automatically combined with nascent bodies, so God was not responsible for putting them in vessels that were damaged by the Fall. Those who were virtuous in their fleshly lives were promoted at death to more 'aetherial' vehicles, subsisting far above the atmosphere; the wicked were punished with grosser 'aerial' bodies, which hovered near the earth. The world would end in a great conflagration, in which these aerial beings would be consumed by fire. Hale was much too conservative to accept these extraordinary doctrines unamended, but his own preferred solution had a number of similar points.

He was obviously torn between Augustine and the Platonists, because he demonstrably changed his mind. His three completed treatments of the topic were composed in the nine-year period from 1664–73. The earliest of

---

[47] Hale, *Discourse*, 41. [48] More, *Immortality*, 73. [49] Glanvill, *Lux*, 1–16.
[50] Migne, *Patrologiae cursus completus*, Paris 1845, vol. XLIV, pp. 475–548.

the three (if the date of the many works cited is a guide)[51] rejected infusionist theories for the sake of original sin:

the propagation of original sin from Adam seems not in any way to be consistent (saving God's justice) with this hypothesis; nor, perhaps, does it leave room for explanation of the eternal penalty for an erring soul in the body, a soul which was pure and unsullied in its creation, and then was thrust down into a polluted and contaminated body where it might be hardly possible not to sin.[52]

Hale was clearly very struck by this objection, and came to the verge of concluding that the immortal human soul was in fact a material thing. He dismissed one obvious counter-argument, on the grounds that a material thing could last indefinitely, if God were to support it by his power.[53] He also refrained from asserting that matter cannot think. In the end he avoided the logic of his theory only by dint of re-defining 'spirit'. The properties of non-material substance have never been made clear to human minds, but they probably differ as much as those of matter. The human anima, at all events, is spirit of the very basest sort. Even if not divisible, it is 'extendible', present throughout the space that a given human body occupies, and expanding (or contracting) as its vehicle grows (or shrinks). He could think of no reason why such an extendible thing should not in addition be able to divide.[54]

One powerful objection to the idea that human souls divide was the thought of the parent diminishing each time it emitted a seed. Hale replied that there are some material things (the sun and magnets were the best examples) that pour out 'radiation' all the time. The soul has the same capacity, without diminishing in any way, to radiate and communicate its 'vis'. The male and female seeds are both 'irradiated' by the anima of the bodies that produced them. When the two seeds meet and mix, the radiation becomes so intense that it can recreate the parent souls. The analogy Hale drew was with a burning glass, which produces a fire by combining the rays of the sun.[55]

This account of reproduction was the logical conclusion of Hale's Helmontian thought. The immortal intellectual soul, the criterion of

---

[51] The three are Lambeth 3504 ('De generatione vegetabilium et animalium'), finished March 1672; Lambeth 3500 ('Tentamina de anima et eius immortalitate'), finished August 1673; and Lambeth 3490, which is undated but incorporates a reference to Thomas Willis, *Cerebri anatome* (1664) at fo. 47. Lambeth 3500 and 3504 both refer to numerous later works. Lambeth 3504 also devotes a chapter (fos. 246–59) to exploring and refuting views much like those of Lambeth 3490.

[52] 'propagatio originalis peccati ab Adamo nullo modo videtur cum hac hypothesi salva justitia divina conciliari; nec forsan explicabilem relinquit, poenam aeternam animae in corpore peccatricis, quae pura et intaminata in sua creatione extiterit, et demum in corpus pollutum et contaminatum ubi non peccare vix possibile sit detrusa' (Lambeth 3490, 50).

[53] Lambeth 3490, 58v.–60.   [54] *Ibid.*, 62v.   [55] *Ibid.*, 64.

human identity as the object of God's law, was treated as a form of radiation, differing more in degree than kind from lesser natural creatures such as magnets. He later discussed these points with Richard Baxter, who reached a rather similar conclusion, though by a different route.[56] Baxter recalled that 'he and I did think that the notion of immateriality had little satisfactory to acquaint us with the nature of a spirit'[57] In stressing the failings of mechanistic theories, and postulating ferments on a graduated scale, Hale blurred the line distinguishing the soul from other, purely natural entities. The lowest form of spirit was very like the highest form of matter. *Psyche*, to use Gassendi's word, had come to be identified with *nous*, the animal soul with the immortal mind; biology had merged with theological ideas.

At some stage in the next few years, however, Hale seems to have reverted to an orthodox approach. His extremely elaborate treatise, 'De generatione vegetabilium et animalium', was definitely finished in March 1672. It contains a very careful exposition of the 'superstitiosa opinio' that matter could form an intellectual soul.[58] He ruled out the traduction of the soul on the grounds that immaterial things are indivisible, and denied there was any comparison with the lighting of a torch. Setting light to an inflammable material gives a new 'habitus' or disposition to particles already in existence; the generation of the soul, by contrast, involves creating something wholly new.[59] If the soul could be transmitted like the anima of animals or plants, then every aborted foetus would have to be regarded as immortal.[60]

Instead he adopted a view much like Gassendi's, distinguishing the sensitive from the intellectual soul. There was a seamless quality in the development of human bodies, which made it clear that the same force had been at work throughout. This principle, the animal soul, was passed down from one human to another; the intellect, however, was infused, though he showed himself uncertain when or how. He retained a certain hankering for his earlier, Helmontian ideas, and he emphasised the closeness of the link between the souls. At times he implied that the two made up a ferment: material 'hypostasis' and immaterial 'vis': 'if the intellectual soul be *quid spirituale* destitute of all matter and of all corporiety though never so subtle and highly rectified but yet the sentient and vital soul be somewhat that is distinct from the intellectual in which

---

[56] Baxter enormously admired the work of Francis Glisson, author of *Tractatus de natura substantiae energetica*, 1672. On which see John C. Henry, 'Medicine and pneumatology: Henry More, Richard Baxter, and Francis Glisson's treatise on the energetic nature of substance', *Medical History*, 31 (1987), 15–40.

[57] Hale, *Works*, I, 99. Baxter's views are set out in his *The reasons of the Christian religion*, 1667, pp. 492–600.

[58] Lambeth 3504, 259.   [59] *Ibid.*, 226.   [60] Lambeth 3500, 95.

nevertheless it lives as it were in its house.'[61] They had a bond so strong that it survived the body, with the result that both of them enjoyed immortal life:

the vis unitiva of the intellective soul is so potent and vigorous and the hypostasis so pure and congenerous[62] that the vinculum between this vis intellectiva and its proper hypostasis though material is not broken nor can be broken by the occision of the body the dissipation of the animal spirits and the extinction of the sentient principle.[63]

Underlying this intimate union was the intellect's need of a vehicle of some kind. Hale solved the problem of divine unfairness by agreeing with More and Origen that the soul had an existence before it was infused. Insertion even in a sinful body represented a kind of 'advancement', as only in a body was it capable of thought. Hale had been taught at Oxford that 'nil in intellectu nisi prius in sensu', and he was loyal to this principle. The intellect needed perception (a faculty assigned to the sensitive soul) because its potential for thought was not matched by a 'stock of intelligibles', material with which it could actually think.[64] As common experience showed (he instanced drunkenness and epilepsy), disorders of the body can inhibit intellectual operations. The intellectual and the sensitive were related like the lutanist and the lute.[65]

The Christian faith, in Hale's interpretation, depicted human beings in three quite different states: the union between soul and body, their later separation after death, and the reunion with a 'spiritual body' at the final resurrection of the dead. About the last he was a little vague, but he felt the need for a detailed account of the disembodied self, largely so as to prove it was susceptible of punishment. He therefore held the separated soul to have a memory of its former life, partly because a memory of sin would constitute a kind of punishment, and partly because 'it is essential to that which is properly a punishment of any reasonable nature that it should have as well a sense and memory of its former fault as of its present pain'.[66] It also retained moral 'habitus', acquired in the course of its sojourn in the body, which helped to determine its happiness between bodily death and bodily resurrection. A soul whose lower instincts obtained habitual pre-dominance, 'that in this life transformed itself in effect into a brutal nature' would find 'conversing with a pure and holy God, with holy angels, and blessed souls' a natural punishment.[67] An important advantage of this way of thinking was in avoiding 'the inconvenience of Plato's commonwealth: he that is but *modice bonus* shall enjoy a common and equal share of

[61] Lambeth 3499, 44.
[62] 'Of the same kind as another, akin in nature or character' (OED).
[63] Lambeth 3500, 129.   [64] *Ibid.*, 185.   [65] Lambeth 3399, 85; Lambeth 3499, 14.
[66] Lambeth 3500, 68, 188–9.   [67] *Ibid.*, 206.

happiness with him that is *apprime bonus* and he that is *modice malus* ...
will share the equal misery with the *valde mali*.'[68] He had evidently
relinquished any Augustinian sense that everyone deserves to go to hell.[69]

The choice between traduction and infusion, as it appeared to men like
More and Hale, had much to do with attitudes to the natural depravity of
man. More's position implied that the human soul, as such, had not
directly suffered from the Fall; it was union with a corrupt and 'brutal'
nature that explained man's undoubted propensity for sin. Belief in inherited guilt (as opposed to a propensity for committing wicked acts) was not
a part of his theology.[70] Hale seems to have thought (at the time of his
traductionist discussion) that inherited sin depends upon an immaterial
soul.[71] Nothing material could transmit an obligation to a punishment; I
can no more inherit guilt from Adam by such means than from the clay of
which Adam was formed.[72] Hale's subsequent switch to infusionist ideas
involved him in abandoning a great deal more than a mere biological
theory.

There was thus a very intimate connection between Hale's late psychology and his liberal theological position. The survey of the latter offered in
Chapter 10 depicted a shift in the way that he understood grace, diminishing its nature to little more than intellectual light. This obviously fitted
very well with increasingly 'Platonist' views of the human condition. The
problem faced by an infused (and therefore essentially blameless) intellect,
the part of man that alone was properly 'moral', was its embroilment with
a carnal nature. This accounted for biblical language depicting the flesh as
warring with the spirit, and for the will's enslavement to transitory brutish
satisfactions. One way to make this picture plausible was to show that
spirit and flesh, the intellectual and the sensitive, were genuinely rival
principles. The writers Hale normally cited as believers in a separate
animal soul were Willis and Gassendi, who shared a generous estimate of
its capacities: Gassendi showed great interest in the extensive reasoning
powers of beasts, but denied their material faculties were capable of
intellective (that is, strictly abstract) thought; Willis went rather further,

---

[68] Lambeth 3499, 86.

[69] There is an interesting discussion of differential rewards in Emma Disley, 'Degrees of
glory: Protestant doctrine and the concept of rewards hereafter', *Journal of Theological
Studies*, NS, 42 (1991), 77–105. Disley shows that many quite orthodox Protestants were
happy to speak of differential rewards, because they related them to sanctification;
justification remained the work of God alone. Hale's ideas seem more frankly pelagian, as
there could be no question, in this context, of a justification/sanctification distinction.

[70] He once defined original sin as 'that over-proportioned proneness and almost irresistible
proclivity to evil' (*The Cambridge Platonists*, ed. C. A. Patrides, Cambridge 1969, p. 38.
Patrides quotes this as a rare exception to the Platonists' unwillingness to mention the
phenomenon at all.)

[71] See quotation above, p. 226.   [72] Lambeth 3490, 58.

and held there was no philosophical bar to material things achieving intellection.[73]

Here theological psychology could intersect with anti-Cartesian views.
There was an important contemporary debate about the rationality of
brutes. At Cambridge University, as early as 1614, the topic was chosen for
debate to entertain the king; at Oxford in the 1650s, it was being used for
routine disputations.[74] The Cartesian beast-machine intensified discussion
on the question, but the arguments went back to the translation, in the late
sixteenth century, of the great ancient sceptic Sextus Empiricus. Sextus
gave several instances of rational behaviour in brutes. Hale cited him to
this effect, and he evidently influenced Gassendi, the source of Hale's conviction that humans have two souls.[75] One of Henry More's complaints, in
his published correspondence with Descartes, concerned the reduction of
animals to machines, and he too gave examples of intelligent animal acts.[76]

The Cartesian account of perception reduced this sensitive capacity to
impulses that strike the pineal gland. Hale ridiculed the theory, but this
was only the start of his objections.[77] He stressed that an object of desire
was not the appetite's efficient cause, and that even beasts were capable of
a genuine choice between goods: 'The object has not touched the animal;
moreover, a natural motion, which they classify as something caused by
matter, is not mechanical without a contact. This motion, however, is only
directed to an object [objectivus] or moral.'[78] The 'knowledge' of the
phantasy was attained by the medium of sense. In the *Discourse*, it will be
remembered, all knowledge was derived from images 'let into the phantasy
and shown to the intellect', and every proposition was based on simple or
complex 'apprehensions', combined with the help of a process of 'rational
discourse'.[79] His definition of 'imagination' (phantasy), given in 1671–72,
was strongly reminiscent of this passage. Imagination can perform three
functions:

1. Simple apprehension of an object, which happens through the making of sensible images from objects perceived by sense. 2. The putting together of images
which they call *propositio imaginativa*. 3. The putting together of propositions

[73] Isler, *Willis*, 172–9. Gassendi, *Opera*, II, 408–14.
[74] Costello, *The scholastic curriculum in early seventeenth-century Cambridge*, Harvard
1958, pp. 24–6; Webster, *The great instauration: science, medicine and reform*, 1975,
p. 135.
[75] Lambeth 3504, 100.
[76] Descartes, *Principles*, 105–7; Descartes, *Correspondance avec Arnaud et Morus*, Latin
and French edn, ed. Genevieve Lewis, Paris 1953, pp. 105–7, 145–7.
[77] Lambeth 3504, 100.
[78] 'objectum [non] tetigit animal motus autem naturalis quem affectionem materiae esse
supponunt mechanicus non est nisi contactu. hic autem motus est tantum objectivus seu
moralis' (Lambeth 3504, 99).
[79] Hale, *Discourse*, 2–3.

with a deduction or practical conclusion which they call discursus imaginativus and hence arises the appetite.[80]

Discursus imaginativus is obviously parallel to 'rational discourse' itself.

This primitive form of reasoning was known to Hale as 'ratio imaginativa', an attribute of animals, and also, in its highest form, of man. It was difficult to see how even the simplest mental operation could be accounted for by sense impressions:

It is but a folly to think that memory even of brutes themselves much less of men is by impressed characters or images rallied in the brain for let any one but think with himself what kind of image can be made of a voice or sound of a thought of a universal notion or a complex proposition or syllogism formed immediately by the understanding and that never was nor ever could be in the phantasy.[81]

The principal difference between 'ratio intellectiva' and 'ratio imaginativa' was that the former dealt in universals abstracted from the images provided by the sense:

ratio imaginativa can never reach to universals or the concepts common to diverse things, nor does it have an image [imaginem] or perception of anything unless it is composed of individual and material parts. The intellective process knows universals through abstraction. Thus every discursus intellectivus should start from some universal proposition.[82]

The God the Christians worshipped was of course an abstract thing, unlike the God of the idolators. The knowledge of natural laws, which depended upon knowledge of a legislating God, was the starting point of moral calculation. It followed that *discursus intellectivus* was necessary for humans to be good. The phantasy, by contrast, knew only the immediate gratifications presented it as sensual images, and passed as fitting 'objects' to the will. It was thus that the flesh could be said to conflict with the spirit, as phantasy attempted to debase the human will to nothing but a bestial appetite. The influence of God upon this struggle, his work 're-generating' humankind, was through the ubiquitous *Intellectus Agens*.

The *Intellectus Agens* was a disturbing presence in Hale's thought, one very often mentioned but seldom unambiguously affirmed, denied or defined. It was a spiritual entity – discussed by Aristotle in the third book

---

[80] Lambeth 3504, 113. '1. simplex objecti apprehensio quae fit per imaginum sensibilium fabricationem ex objectis a sensu perceptis 2. compositio imaginum quam propositionem imaginativam vocant. 3. compositio propositionum cum illatione sive practica conclusione quam discursum imaginativum vocant et hinc oritur appetitus.'

[81] Lambeth 3500, 107.

[82] 'ratio ... imaginativa numquam attingere potest ad universalia seu communes rerum diversarum notiones nec cuiusquam nisi corporei et singulari concreti imaginem vel perceptionem habet ... processus intellectivus universalia per abstractionem cognoscit. sic omnis discursus intellectivus sit ex aliqua propositione universali' (Lambeth 3504, 102).

of his *De anima* – in which the human race participated.[83] Extreme Aristotelians believed that this shared intellectual soul was the only immortal part of human minds. As watered down by Selden, the *Intellectus Agens* became a sort of intellectual light, illuminating for mankind the provisions of natural law. Hale used it, in his later thought, as essentially a substitute for 'grace', and his equivocations on the topic were a mark of ambiguous attitudes towards 'enthusiastic' Protestantism. Hale's earlier traductionist manuscript came close to saying that this grace helps constitute the being of the intellectual soul. It certainly 'contributes if not to the essence or existence, yet to the operations of the intellectual or rational soul'.[84] The entity was 'superinduced' on the believer's 'natural constitution', and raises him to the dignity of his pre-lapsarian state. It was this feature of mankind that it had been Christ's mission to restore, as attested by a shower of texts about life, grace and 'spiritual generation'.[85]

Hale's treatments of the theme were always very cautiously expressed, but some development can be detected. The earlier work confessed that

all these expressions may be metaphorical, and intend nothing else but the moral change of the heart by those effectual persuasions and exhibitions contained in this great message of the divine love and will communicated to the world by Jesus Christ, and those great and powerful motives to a virtuous and obedient life in the discovery of the future state of rewards and punishments.[86]

By 1673, he had moved towards this alternative position. He thought it not improbable that the human race collectively enjoyed some kind of communal assistance, but he attacked the view that this assistance raises man to an intellectual level:

Although the supposition of an Intellectus Agens be very ancient and possibly true yet it may have other offices than to be spinning phantasms into species intelligibiles [transforming data from the sense into material for abstract thought] and such as be more natural and useful namely to be the instrument of the glorious god to infuse common notions of truth religion and piety into the minds of men . . .[87]

This *Intellectus Agens* was envisaged as enlightening the sinner, rather than constituting his restoration to his former state.

It is hard to read Hale's works without being struck by the seamlessness of his intellectual world. His views on the active intellect were no more than another expression of his shifting conception of grace. As Chapter 10 explained, he had turned from understanding faith as an act of God *in* man to seeing it as an act *of* man, assisted by God's power. The means of divine assistance was by imparting certain moral truths, especially the 'great and

---

[83] See above, p. 169.   [84] Lambeth 3490, 75.   [85] *Ibid.*, 78v.–79.
[86] *Ibid.*, 93.
[87] Lambeth 3500, 93.

powerful motives' supplied by the promise of heaven and threat of hell. These were the ultimate sanctions behind every human law, and therefore the foundation of any tolerable social life. By the end of his life, Hale had come to believe that religion was identical with the duties that society imposed. It is no surprise that this ethical religion, a religion of enlightenment, not of emotional experience, conditioned his late writings on the soul.

Conclusion

Hale opted to finish his most ambitious work with a brief summary of implications: 'a collection of certain evident and profitable consequences from this consideration, that the first individuals of human nature had their original from a great, powerful, wise, intelligent being'.[1] He had shown, at least by consequence, that Man 'is not himself his own, he owes his being to God, and therefore without the help of divine indulgence his acquests are like the acquests of a servant, acquirit domino'.[2] Creation out of nothing gave the Creator 'absolute dominion' over the world that he had freely made:

Almighty God tells us, Jeremiah xviii, that as the clay is in the potter's hand, so are mankind in his hand, yea and in a far greater subordination and subjection to his power; the power of the potter over his clay is a finite limited power, we see in the same place it resisted and disappointed its intention by its untractableness. But the power of God over his creature is an infinite power . . .[3]

'Here therefore', he assured his readers, 'we have that great question among some of the ancients satisfactorily answered, What is the root of all obligation in mankind, what is it that binds men to keep their faith, their promises?'[4]

The text he chose to illustrate his point had a terrifying resonance for any Calvinist. The image of clay and the potter was echoed by Paul in perhaps the best known of predestinarian texts: 'hath not the potter power over the clay, of the same lump to make one vessel unto honour and another unto dishonour?'[5] Hale never lost the Calvinist sense of absolute

---

[1] Hale, *Primitive origination*, 347.
[2] *Ibid.*, 354. Compare Locke, *Two treatises*, 271: 'Men being all the workmanship of one omnipotent, and equally wise maker; all the servants of one sovereign master, sent into the world at his pleasure and about his business, they are his property whose workmanship they are, made to last during his, not one another's pleasure'.
[3] Hale, *Primitive origination*, 355.   [4] *Ibid.*
[5] Romans ix 21. This complex of ideas had once been paraphrased by Hale himself: 'the potter forms one piece of clay to a vessel of honour and another to a vessel of dishonour, and when he hath that done, he dasheth it may be both to pieces, and this without any injustice or cause of complaint, yet the potter hath no absolute sovereignty over the clay, for it hath neither its being nor its continuance from him' (Lambeth 3488, 151v.).

dependence on an almighty power, but he came to experience his duty to God in the demands of natural moral law. God had created man as the 'high priest of nature', the awed 'spectator' of his handiwork, but also as a labourer in his sight, 'put into the Garden of Eden to dress and keep it',[6] 'idleness not being indulged even in paradise'.[7] God's purpose for man, an existence of sanctified labour, was unchanged by Adam's sin, but the wickedness of the mass of human beings made social life impossible in the absence of positive laws. The Fall had put 'the lower faculties in rebellion against the superior; so that the wiser and more morate[8] part of mankind were forced to set up laws and punishments to keep the generality of mankind in some sort of order'.[9] These laws were made by contract, agreed upon by humans but enforced by the omnipotence of God.

A good society, for Hale, was one composed of rational Protestants, keeping their contracts, labouring in their callings, enforcing godliness on the ungodly, and 'converting those acts that are materially and naturally civil into acts truly and formally religious'.[10] In such a society even the church itself was a department of the legal order. His grandchildren were to obey their parish minister, placed over them by 'providence', but also 'by the laws';[11] they were also to take communion at least three times a year, in part because 'the laws of the land require this'.[12]

It was always Hale's intention, as should by now be clear, to broaden and intensify his own religious life, to the point where a falling stone or a parish boundary were seen to manifest the will of God. The Christian faith 're-published' an innate morality, but the light of nature was itself a *super*natural light. Grace was communicated through the illumination of moral principles, and through the revelation that those principles were actually commands. The knowledge of God was a knowledge of God as a sovereign, and it was the mark of a sovereign to govern his subjects through laws. Omnipotence expressed itself in law-like regularity of action, in the 'settled and regular' motions established in the visible creation, and in the choice of 'rational ways' for securing the salvation of mankind.

In this, of course, Hale typified his culture. The English revolution had dramatised the dangers in Calvinist thinking on grace. The real or imagined excesses of the 'enthusiasts' had made it very urgent to reappraise the holy spirit's role. It was not surprising, then, that religious expectations were revolutionised, that the spirit was detected in the communication of

---

6 Hale, *Primitive origination*, 370.   7 *Ibid.*, 317.
8 The word exists: 'mannered; well-mannered, respectably conducted, moral' (OED). It seems just as likely, however, to be 'moderate' misprinted.
9 Hale, *Primitive origination*, 355–6.   10 Hale, *Works*, II, 246.   11 *Ibid.*, I, 210.
12 *Ibid.*, I, 207.

general moral rules, and not in the emotions of the godly. The divine was mediated to latitudinarian believers through the order of the universe and the dictates of natural law. Where Hale rebelled against the new consensus was in hankering after immediate experience of God. The tensions in his thought – between individual liberties and parliamentary contract, between sympathy with Quakers and contempt for their claims to inner inspiration, between suspicion of mechanistic science and admiration for the world's design – reflected the strain this hankering induced. The English made a choice, leaving their Calvinist heritage to a dwindling puritan minority for the sake of a comfortable pattern of thought in which 'enthusiasm' seemed not so much mistaken as absurd. The pathos of Hale's situation was that he did not know he had to choose.

Appendix: Hale and witchcraft

The text of this book leaves unmentioned the best-known episode in Hale's career. This was the trial for witchcraft of Amy Duny and Rose Cullender at the Bury St Edmunds Assizes in March 1662.[1] Both women had an evil reputation in their community. The matter had come to a head when they were accused of bewitching certain children. Five girls from four separate families, the eldest eighteen and the youngest only nine, had started to suffer from fits, in the course of which they vomited up pins. They blamed Rose Cullender and Amy Duny, and managed to convince surrounding adults, including at least one who was initially incredulous, that they had definitely been bewitched.[2]

The trial was conducted in an admirably scientific spirit. The court was influenced by the expert opinion of 'Dr Brown of Norwich, a person of great knowledge', who noted that the vomiting of pins was a symptom of bewitchment reported in a recent Danish case. He diagnosed 'the mother' [that is some kind of feminine hysteria], which had been 'heightened to a great excess by the subtlety of the devil, co-operating with the malice of these which we term witches'.[3] Three of the five accusers were well enough to be present, though not to testify, and were subjected to experiments. Though 'to all men's apprehension, wholly deprived of all sense and understanding', they screamed and went into a spasm when touched, however lightly, by the unfortunate Rose Cullender, 'which accident would not happen by the touch of any other'.[4] A test was organised, at the suggestion of 'an ingenious person', in which one of the children was confronted by Amy Duny; the apparently comatose child was then put in a blindfold, before she was touched by *another* stander by. The child reacted

---

[1] The principal source for the trial is the eyewitness account *A trial of witches at the Assizes held at Bury St Edmunds* (1682), conveniently reprinted in Cobbett, *State trials*, VI, 687–702. I am grateful to Gilbert Geis and Ivan Bunn for letting me see their work about the social context of the trial.

[2] Cobbett, *State trials*, VI, 693.

[3] *Ibid.*, 697. 'Dr Brown' was of course Thomas Browne (1605–82), the curiously learned master of English prose.

[4] Cobbett, *State trials*, VI, 697.

as before, convincing those who witnessed the event that all her symptoms were 'a mere imposture'.[5] It was pointed out, however, that the test was not conclusive; the girls might well enjoy their faculties in spite of their apparent paralysis, and might be driven to a desperate spasm by what they assumed was the touch of their tormentor. The decisive consideration was that

no man can suppose that they should all conspire together (being out of several families, and, as they affirm, no way related one to the other, and scarce of familiar acquaintance) to do an act of this nature whereby no benefit or advancement could redound to any of the parties, but a guilty conscience for perjuring themselves to take the lives of two poor simple women ...[6]

Nobody really answered the sceptical objection of John Kelyng (soon to become notorious as the authoritarian Chief Justice) that

admitting that the children were in truth bewitched ... it can never be applied to the prisoners, upon the imagination only of the parties bewitched. For if that might be allowed, no person whatsoever can be in safety, for perhaps they might fancy another person, who might altogether be innocent in such matters.[7]

The assembly appears to have been convinced, however, by the accumulation of circumstantial evidence that Cullender and Duny were the culprits; both of them were found guilty on all counts, and 'the judge and all the court were fully satisfied'.[8]

Hale took it for granted that witches exist, because, as he said to the jury, 'the scriptures had affirmed so much', and 'the wisdom of all nations had provided laws against such persons'.[9] He appears to have had no doubt that the women were guilty. Although he was quite ready, on occasion, to offer juries very detailed guidance,[10] he failed to sum up the evidence presented to the court; given the prejudices to be expected of the jurymen, this was an invitation to convict. The night before the women were hanged by the neck until dead, he wrote a devotional essay on the subject. It endorses the practice of finding and punishing witches. He was delighted that 'the instrument, without which [the devil] cannot ordinarily work, is within reach of human justice and government'.[11]

There is no need to be surprised at his credulity, for a firm belief in witchcraft was not at all unusual among the liberal Protestants of Restoration times. A number of comparable figures (Joseph Glanvill, Richard Baxter, Henry More) collected well authenticated stories about the spirit world. It was widely believed that the existence of witches and ghosts was an empirical disproof of Hobbesian materialist ideas. The truly surprising feature of Hale's behaviour was that none of his apologetic writings made

[5] *Ibid.*, 698.   [6] *Ibid.*, 698.   [7] *Ibid.*, 697.   [8] *Ibid.*, 702.   [9] *Ibid.*, 700.
[10] *Ibid.*, 948–51. I owe this point to Bunn and Geis.   [11] Lambeth 3506, fo. 114.

any mention of the whole affair.[12] Given his fascination with the inadequacies of mechanistic physics, he might have been expected to make extensive use of a personal experience of witchcraft. His puzzling silence may suggest a certain subsequent uneasiness. His criminal law textbook remarked that rape and witchcraft accusations were both extremely difficult to prove, and that the classic common law left witchcraft, as a 'secret thing', to God.[13] He gave a brief account of the Jacobean statute against witches, but did not try to justify the measure, still less to explore its workings with reference to the famous Bury case. His reticence offers some support to the eighteenth-century story that 'he was afterwards much altered in his notions as to this matter and had great concern upon him for what had befallen those persons'.[14]

---

[12] Not even, for example, when corresponding with Richard Baxter, who cites Bodin, Remigius and the *Malleus maleficarum* in support of the existence of 'spirit' (Lambeth Palace MS 3499, fos. 63–115.

[13] Hale, *Historia*, II, 380; I, 429.

[14] *Historical manuscripts commission*, Fourteenth report, Part 9, p. 480. The source is Arthur Onslow (1691–1768), whose brief but accurate sketch of Hale's career includes some information which was not then available in print.

BIBLIOGRAPHY

This bibliography contains a list of Hale's writings, a list of all the law reports consulted, and a list of works mentioned in the text or cited in notes.

HALE'S WRITINGS

UNPRINTED

A number of Hale's works achieved a circulation in an unprinted form. The Bodleian Library alone has five manuscript copies of the *History of the common law of England*. The following lists all manuscripts that are written in Hale's own distinctive hand, except for his professional opinions. Where no autograph version survives, it lists the most authoritative copy.

Australian National Library

7211 (Letter to second wife: copy). Printed 1993a.

Beinecke Rare Book and Manuscript Library, New Haven

Osborn files, Hale
 ALS to unnamed recipient (n.d.).
 ALS to John Conant and unsigned draft (April 1660). Printed 1835.
 ALS to G. Estcourt (n.d.).
 ALS to Lord Herbert (n.d.).
 'Catalogus librorum meorum' with 'Books at Serjeants' Inn'.
 'Considerations touching the present and late occurrences'. Printed 1835.
 'Considerations on my late sickness'. Printed 1835.
 Notes on scientific experiments.
 'Observations touching the present providences'. Printed 1835.
 Writings from 'circuitus autumnalis 1668'. Printed 1988.

Bodleian library, Oxford

Rawlinson A 400 ('Considerations concerning trade': copy).
Selden supra 112 ('Observations touching . . . King's Bench').

British Library, London

Additional 33, 589, fo. 79 (Letter to John Smyth of Nibley).

Additional 41, 661
  fos. 156–92 ('Concerning the court of the Marches': copy).
  fos. 192v.–216. ('A short treatise touching Sheriffs' Accounts': copy). Printed
    1683 b.
  fos. 227–235v. (On 'enrolment of deeds': copy). Printed 1694.
Hargrave 98, fos. 2–30v. (A narrative . . . touching the customs'). Printed 1888.
Hargrave 137 (A disquisition . . . touching the Admiralty': copy).
Hargrave 485 ('Of the nature of laws': copy).
Stowe 163, fos. 146–55 ('Considerations against a . . . naturalisation').

Clark library, Los Angeles

Selden–Hale Add. 1 ('History of the common law'). Part printed 1699 and printed
    1713.
Selden–Hale Add. 2 (Additions to Rolle's *Abridgement*).
Selden–Hale Add. 3 (Notes from parliament rolls).
Selden–Hale Add. 5 ('Concerning . . . the customs': copy). Printed 1787a.

Gloucester Record Office

D1086 F72
  On liberty of the will: fragment.
  Corruption in the intellectual faculties: fragment.
D1086 F71
  ALS to Alexander Digges (5 December 1671).

John Rylands Library, Manchester

59 (History of the pleas of the Crown). Printed 1736.

Lambeth Palace Library, London

The papers now at Lambeth form the overwhelming bulk of material for the study
of Matthew Hale. Any serious scholar will wish to consult the admirable catalogue
by Dr Geoffrey Bill. There would be no advantage here in duplicating Bill's
meticulous labours. The following list confines itself to listing the manuscript
volumes and indicating the whereabouts of writings that were subsequently
printed.

47/11 (Rejection of office under Richard Cromwell).
3475 (Legal papers and draft bills).
3476 (Miscellaneous).
3477 (Miscellaneous: some relating to sheriffs' accounts).
3478 (Judicial notebook).
3479 (Miscellaneous). Part printed 1787b, 1797c, and 1921.
3480 (Miscellaneous).
3481 (On 'chief end of man').
3482 ('Quod Deus est').
3483 (On Philip iii 8).
3484 (Sequel to 3481?).
3485 (On the 'evidence of the Gospel'). Part printed 1684.
3486 (Chronological calculations).
3487 (Transcripts from Ussher).
3488 (Miscellaneous).

3489 ('Of man: pars prima').
3490 (Sequel to 3489).
3491 ('De Deo': Books I–II).
3492 ('De Deo': Books III–V).
3493 ('De Deo': Books VI–VIII).
3494 ('De Deo': Books IX–X).
3495 ('De Deo': 'pars nona': draft for 3494?).
3496 ('Of policy ... in matters of religion').
3497 (Miscellaneous).
3498 (Miscellaneous). Part printed 1676.
3499 (Miscellaneous: mostly 'de anima'). Part printed 1677a.
3500 ('Tentamina de ortu, natura et immortalitate animae').
3501 ('Magnetismus magneticus').
3502 ('Magnetical observations').
3503 ('Magnetismus magnus'). Printed 1695.
3504 ('De generatione vegetabilium et animalium').
3505 ('Contemplationes meae'). Printed 1688.
3506 (Miscellaneous). Part printed 1676, 1693.
3507 (Miscellaneous 'ab anno 1655'). Part printed 1676.
3508 (Miscellaneous). Part printed 1676.
3509 (Miscellaneous).
3510 ('Obstructions'). Printed 1677.
3511 (Draft work on Torricellian experiment).
3512 (Miscellaneous). Part printed 1787d.
3513 (Miscellaneous).
3516 (Miscellaneous). Part printed 1680a.

Lincoln's Inn Library, London

Hale 121 (191) ('The Black Book of the New Law').
Hargrave 1 ('Prerogativa regis'). Printed 1975.
Hargrave 5 ('Incepta de juribus coronae').
Hargrave 6 ('Notes touching parliamentary proceedings': copy).
Hargrave 11 ('Discourse ... concerning the power of judicature').
Hargrave 12 (Jurisdiction of the Lords House). Printed 1796.
Miscellaneous 48 ('Notes touching the rights of the Crown'). Part printed c. 1885, 1975.

PRINTED

This list is chronological, by the date of first known printed publication. It is cross-referenced with autograph manuscripts only.

1668. Preface to Henry Rolle, *Un abridgement des plusieurs cases et resolutions del common ley alphabeticalment digest desouth severall titles.*
1673. *An Essay touching the gravitation, or non-gravitation of fluids and the reasons thereof.*
1674. *Difficiles nugae, or observations touching the Torricellian experiment and the various solutions of the same but especially touching the weight and elasticity of the air.*
1675. The same with 'Occasional additions'.

1676. *Contemplations moral and divine* (Drawn from Lambeth 3498, 3506, 3507, 3508).

1677a. *The life and death of Pomponius Atticus written by his contemporary and acquaintance Cornelius Nepos translated out of his fragments, together with observations political and moral thereon.* (Lambeth 3499, 257–65v).

1677b. *Observations touching the principles of natural motions together with a reply to certain remarks touching the gravitation of fluids.* (Lambeth 3510).

1677c. *The primitive origination of mankind, considered and examined according to the light of nature.*

1680a. *A letter from Sir Matthew Hale, Knight, some time Lord Chief Justice of England, to one of his sons after recovery from the small-pox.*

1680b. *A letter to his children, advising them how to behave themselves in their speech.*

1680c. *Two arguments in the Exchequer by Sir Matthew Hale when Lord Chief Baron* (Lambeth 3479, 138–162).

1680d. 'Judge Hale his opinion on some select cases' in *The excellency and preheminence of the common law of England over all other human law in the world,* ed. W. B.

1682. *Pleas of the Crown or a methodical summary of the principal matters relating to that subject.*

1683a. *A discourse touching provision for the poor.*

1683b. *A short treatise touching sheriffs accompts.*

1688. *A discourse of the knowledge of God and of ourselves* (Lambeth 3505)

1684. *The judgement of the late Sir Matthew Hale ... of the nature of true religion* (Lambeth 3485, 104–126v.)

1693. 'Concerning the great mercy of God in preserving us from the power and malice of evil angels', in *A collection of modern relations of matter of fact concerning witches and witchcraft,* 1693 (Lambeth 3506, 111–14).

1694. *A treatise showing how useful the enrolling and registering of all conveyances of land may be.*

1695. *Magnetismus magnus, or metaphysical and divine contemplations on the magnet, or load-stone* (Lambeth 3503).

1696. *Contemplations moral and divine: the third part.*

1699. *Tractatus de successionibus apud Anglos, or a treatise on hereditary descents* (Chapter 11 of 1713a).

1713a. *The history of the common law of England* (Clark, Selden–Hale Add. 1).

1713b. *The analysis of the law* (Clark, Selden–Hale Add. 1).

1736. *Historia placitorum coronae,* ed. S. Emlyn, 2 vols. (John Rylands 59).

1787a. 'A treatise in three parts: pars prima de jure maris et brachiorum eiusdem; pars secunda de portubus maris; pars tertia concerning the customs of goods imported and exported' in Francis Hargrave (ed.), *A collection of tracts relating to the law of England,* Dublin, pp. 1–248.

1787b. 'Considerations touching the amendment or alteration of laws', in Hargrave, *Collection,* 253–89 (Lambeth 3479, 207–30).

1787c. 'A discourse touching the courts of King's Bench and Common Pleas', in Hargrave, *Collection,* 357–76. (Lambeth 3479, 2–8).

1796. *The jurisdiction of the Lords' House, or parliament considered according to ancient records,* ed. Francis Hargrave (Lincoln's Inn, Hargrave 12).

1816. *A letter of advice to his grandchildren, Mary, Gabriel, Anne, Mary and Frances Hale.*

1835. 'Considerations touching present and late occurrences', in J. B. Williams, *Memoirs of the life, character and writings of Sir Matthew Hale*, pp. 53–78 (Lambeth 3507, 175–88v.).

c. 1885. *The royal supremacy by Matthew Hale*, The 'Record' Office, 1 Red Lion Court E.C., for private circulation (drawn from Lincoln's Inn, Miscellaneous 48).

1888. 'A narrative legal and historical touching the customs', in Stuart A. Moore, *A history of the foreshore*, pp. 318–69 (British Library, Hargrave 98, 2–30v.).

1921. 'Reflections by the Lord Chief Justice Hale on Mr Hobbes his Dialogue of the law', ed. W. Holdsworth, *Law Quarterly Review*, 37: 286–303 (Lambeth 3479, 68–78).

1975. *Hale's Prerogatives of the King*, ed. D. E. C. Yale, Selden Society (Lincoln's Inn, Hargrave 1 and part of Miscellaneous 48).

1988. 'Matthew Hale on judges and judging', ed. Maija Jansson, *Journal of Legal History*, 9: 204–12 (Beinecke, Osborne files, Hale: 'Notes on circuitus autumnalis').

1993a. 'Hale as husband', ed. W. R. Prest, *Journal of Legal History*, 14: 142–4 (Australian National Library 7211).

1993b. *Hale and Fleetwood on Admiralty jurisdiction*, ed. M. J. Prichard and D. E. C. Yale, Selden Society.

LAW REPORTS

I have scanned the relevant years (1636–76) of the following reports and compilations for matter relating to Hale:

The English Reports (1900–32)

J. H. Baker (ed.), *The English legal manuscript project*, Microfiche, Zug 1975.

British Library, London
  Additional 10, 619
  Additional 16, 172
  Additional 32, 519
  Additional 35, 971
  Additional 35, 973
  Additional 35, 975–6
  Hargrave 23
  Hargrave 42
  Hargrave 47
  Hargrave 49
  Hargrave 53
  Hargrave 59
  Hargrave 63
  Hargrave 64–5
  Hargrave 150
  Lansdowne 596
  Lansdowne 1066
  Lansdowne 1109

Folger Shakespeare Library
  V.b.6

SOURCES MENTIONED IN THE TEXT OR CITED IN NOTES

MANUSCRIPTS

British Library:
  Additional 25, 250
  Additional 35, 972
  Additional 35, 976
  Additional 35, 863
Bodleian Library, Oxford:
  B.14.15.Linc. (bound with printed material).
  Dom. b. 8
  Rawlinson A 400
  Rawlinson C 719
  Selden supra 109
  Selden supra 123–4
  Smith 21
Cambridge University Library
  Add. 3820
Clark Library, Los Angeles:
  Selden–Hale 14
  Selden–Hale Additional 1
  Selden–Hale Additional 4
Gloucester Record Office: D 1086/F72
Gray's Inn Library: 33–34
Lambeth Palace Library: 3475–3516 (The Fairhurst Papers)
  47/11
Lincoln's Inn Library:
  Hargrave 5
  Hargrave 6
  Hargrave 11
  Miscellaneous 48
  Miscellaneous 496
  Miscellaneous 501
  Miscellaneous 555
Public Record Office: Assizes 35/99/4
  King's Bench 33/1/1
  State Papers 19/75
  State Papers 19/76
  State Papers 25/75
  State Papers 104/177
Yale: Beinecke Rare Book and Manuscript Library:
  Osborn Files, Hale
Yale: Law School: G.R. 29.25

PRINTED WORKS

Ames, William, *Conscience with the power and cases thereof*, 1639.
  The marrow of theology, translated from the third Latin edition and edited by
  John Eusden, Boston 1968.

Annesley, Arthur, *England's confusion*, 1659.

Aristotle, *De anima*, tr. J. A. Smith, Oxford 1931.

Ashe, Thomas, *Fasciculus florum, or a handful of flowers gathered out of the several books of the right honourable Sir Edward Coke*, 1618.

Un general table a tous les several livres de le darreine tresreverend judge, Sir Edward Coke, 1618.

Aubrey, John, *Aubrey's brief lives*, ed. Andrew Clark, 2 vols., Oxford 1898.

Augustine, *see* Migne, J.-P.

Bacon, Francis, *The works of Francis Bacon*, ed. R. L. Ellis, J. Spedding, and D. D. Heath, 14 vols., 1857–74.

Baillie, Robert, *Letters and journals of Robert Baillie*, ed. D. Laing, Edinburgh 1861.

Bartolus, *In ius universum civile commentaria*, ed. Froben, 3 vols., Basel 1562.

Baxter, Richard, *Reliquiae Baxterianae*, ed. M. Sylvester, 1696.

Richard Baxter's penitent confession, 1691.

Richard Baxter's catholick theology: plain, pure, peaceable: for pacification of the dogmatical word warriors, 1675.

Additional notes on the life and death of Sir Matthew Hale, 1682.

The Grotian religion discovered, 1659.

The Berkeley MSS, see Smyth, John.

Besse, Joseph, *A collection of the sufferings of the people called Quakers*, 2 vols., 1753.

Bodin, Jean, *Bodin on sovereignty: four chapters from the Six books of the Commonwealth*, ed. and tr. Julian H. Franklin, Cambridge 1992.

New experiments physico-mechanical touching the Air, 2nd edn, Oxford 1662.

The works of the Hon. Robert Boyle, 5 vols., ed. T. Birch, 1744.

Bracton, *On the laws and customs of England*, ed. G. E. Woodbine, tr. S. E. Thorne, 4 vols., 1968.

Brooke, E. and R. (eds.), *Collectanea juridica*, 1791.

Brooke, Robert, *La graunde abridgement, collect et escrie per le judge tresreverend Syr Robert Brooke*, 1573.

Bunyan, John, *Grace abounding to the chief of sinners*, ed. R. Sharrock, Oxford 1962.

Burnet, Gilbert, *History of his own time*, ed. Osmund Airy, 2 vols., Oxford 1897.

The life and death of Sir Matthew Hale, 1682.

Burton Thomas, *The diary of Thomas Burton, esq, Member in the Parliaments of Oliver and Richard Cromwell*, 4 vols., 1828.

Calendar of State Papers Domestic.

Calvin, Jean, *Calvin's commentaries: the Gospel according to St John i–x*, tr. T. H. L. Parker, ed. D. W. and T. F. Torrance, 1959.

Institutes of the Christian religion, tr. John Allen, 2 vols., Philadelphia 1935.

Camden, *Britannia*, ed. Gibson, 2nd edn, 1722.

Camero, Johannes, *Defensio Johannis Cameronis sancti evangelii ministri*, Saumur 1624.

Chillingworth, William, *The religion of Protestants a safe way to salvation*, 1638.

Choppin, René, *De Domanio Franciae*, Frankfurt 1701.

Cicero, *The works of Cicero: De republica, de legibus*, tr. C. W. Keyes, 1928.

Clarendon, Edward Hyde, Earl of, *The Life of Edward Earl of Clarendon containing . . . the continuation of the life*, Oxford 1759.

Calendar of the Clarendon State Papers preserved in the Bodleian Library, 5 vols., Oxford 1932.

Clarendon, Henry Hyde, Earl of, *Correspondence of Henry Hyde, Earl of Clarendon, and of his brother, Laurence Hyde, Earl of Rochester*, ed. S. W. Singer, 1828.

Cobbett, William, *Complete collection of state trials*, 1810.

Cocke, Charles James, *England's complete law-judge and lawyer*, 1656.

Coke, Edward, *The first part of the Institutes of the laws of England*, ed. C. Butler and F. Hargrave, 1793.

    The institutes of the law of England, second to fourth parts, ed. E. and R. Brooke, 1797.

    The reports of Sir Edward Coke, Knt., ed. J. H. Thomas and J. F. Fraser, 1826.

Commons Journal.

Cotton, Sir Robert, *Cottoni posthuma*, 1672.

Crompton, Richard, *L'authoritie et jurisdiction des courts de la Majeste de la Roigne*, 1637.

Cromwell, Oliver, *The writings and speeches of Oliver Cromwell*, ed. W. C. Abbott, Harvard 1945.

Culverwell, Nathaniel, *An elegant and learned discourse of the light of nature*, ed. Robert A. Greene and Hugh MacCallum, Toronto 1971.

Cumberland, Richard, *De legibus Naturae disquisitio philosophica*, 1672.

Dalton, Michael, *The country justice*, 1618.

Davies, Sir John, *A perfect abridgement of the eleven books of Coke's reports*, 1651.

Davies, Sir John, *Irish reports*, Dublin 1762.

A declaration of the parliament of England, expressing the grounds of their late proceedings and of settling the present government in the way of a free state, 1649.

Descartes, René, *Correspondance avec Arnauld et Morus*, Latin and French edn, Paris 1953.

    Principles of philosophy, tr. V. R. and R. P. Miller, 1983.

Digby, Kenelm, *Two treatises, in the one of which, the nature of bodies; in the other, the nature of man's soul, is looked into*, Paris 1644.

[Dort, Synod of], *The judgement of the synod holden at Dort concerning the Five Articles*, 1619.

Dryden, *Essays of John Dryden*, ed. W. P. Ker, Oxford 1926.

Evelyn, John, *The Diary of John Evelyn*, ed. W. Bray, 1907, vol. II.

Fabri, Honoratus, *Dialogi Phisici*, Lyons 1665.

    Dialogi Phisici, Lyons 1669.

Featley, Daniel, *Clavis mystica: a key opening divers difficult and mysterious texts of Scripture*, 1636.

Filmer, Robert, *Patriarcha and other writings*, ed. Johann P. Sommerville, Cambridge 1991.

Finch, Henry, *A description of the common laws of England*, 1759.

Firth, C. H. and Rait, R. S., *Acts and ordinances of the interregnum*, 3 vols., 1911.

Fitzherbert, Anthony, *La grande abridgement*, 1565.

Fortescue, John, *De laudibus legum Angliae*, ed. and tr. S. B. Chrimes, Cambridge 1942.

Foss, Edward, *The judges of England*, 1864.

Foster, E. R. (ed.), *Proceedings in parliament 1610*, Yale 1966.

Foster, Joseph, *Alumni Oxonienses: 1500–1714*, 4 vols., Oxford 1891–2.

Fulbecke, William, *A direction or preparative to the study of law*, 1600.

    A parallele or conference of the civill law, the common law, and the common law of England, 1601–2.

Fuller, Nicholas, *The argument in the case of Thomas Lad*, 1607.

Gadbury, John, *The just and pious scorpionist or the nativity of that thrice excellent man Sir Matthew Hales*, 1677.

Gassendi, Pierre, *Opera omnia*, Lyons 1658.

Gentili, Alberico, *De jure belli*, Libri tres, Latin and English edn, 2 vols., Oxford 1933.

Gilbert, William, *On the loadstone and magnetic bodies*, tr. P. Fleury Mottelay, 1893.

Glanvill, Joseph, *Lux orientalis, or an enquiry into the opinion of the eastern sages, concerning the prae-existence of souls*, 1662.

Glanville, ed. and tr. G. D. G. Hall, 1965.

Glisson, Francis, *Tractatus de natura substantiae energetica*, 1672.

Grey, Anchitell (ed.), *Debates of the House of Commons from the year 1667 to the year 1694*, 10 vols., 1769.

Grotius, Hugo, *Of the freedom of the sea 1609*, Latin and English edn, Oxford 1916.

    De jure belli ac pacis libri tres, Latin and English edn, tr. Francis W. Kelsey, Oxford 1925.

Hale, Matthew, *An essay touching the gravitation , or non-gravitation of fluids*, 1673.

    Difficiles nugae, or observations concerning the Torricellian experiment, 1674.

    The life and death of Pomponius Atticus written by his contemporary and acquaintance Cornelius Nepos, 1677.

    Observations touching the principles of natural motion, 1677.

    The primitive origination of mankind, considered and examined according to the light of nature, 1677.

    A discourse touching provision for the poor, 1683.

    The judgement of the late Sir Matthew Hale ... of the nature of true religion, 1684.

    A treatise showing how useful the enrolling and registering of all conveyances of land may be, 1694.

    Magnetismus magnus, or metaphysical and divine contemplations on the magnet, or load-stone, 1695.

    'Matthew Hale on judges and judging', ed. M. Jansson, *Journal of Legal History*, 9 (1988).

    A discourse of the knowledge of God and of ourselves, ed. R. Baxter, 1688.

    Historia placitorum coronae, ed. S. Emlyn, 1736.

    A treatise on the admiralty jurisdiction, ed. F. Hargrave, 1787.

    Jurisdiction of the Lords House, or parliament, considered according to ancient records, ed. Francis Hargrave, 1796.

    Works moral and religious, ed. Thomas Thirlwall, 1805.

    The history of the common law of England, ed. C. M. Gray, Chicago 1971.

    Hale's prerogatives of the king, ed. D. E. C. Yale, Selden Society 1975.

Hammond, Henry, *To the Rt. Hon. the Lord Fairfax and his council of war, the humble address of Henry Hammond*, 1649.

The Harleian miscellany, ed. J. Malham, 12 vols., 1808–11.

Hargrave, Francis (ed.), *A collection of tracts relating to the law of England*, 1787.
Harvey, William, *Anatomical exercitations, concerning the generation of living creatures*, 1653.
    Movement of the heart and blood in animals: an anatomical essay, Latin and English edn, tr. K. Franklin, Oxford 1957.
Hatton, *Correspondence of the family of Hatton*, ed. E. M. Thompson, 2 vols., Camden Society 1878.
Hearne, Thomas, *A collection of curious discourses*, Oxford 1720.
Helmont, John Baptist van, *Oriatrike, or physic refined*, tr. J. Chandler, 1662.
Herle, Charles, *A fuller answer to a treatise written by Dr Ferne*, 1642.
Highmore, Nathaniel, *The history of generation*, 1651.
Hobbes, Thomas, *Dialogus physicus, see* Schaffer, Simon and Shapin, Steven.
    The English works of Thomas Hobbes, ed. W. Molesworth, 11 vols., 1839–45.
    Leviathan, ed. C. B. Macpherson, 1968.
A dialogue between a philosopher and a student of the common laws of England, ed. Joseph Cropsey, Chicago 1971.
    De cive: the Latin version, ed. Howard Warrender, Oxford 1985.
Holdsworth, William, *A history of English law*, 15 vols., 1922–65.
Holles, Denzil, *The grand question concerning the judicature in the House of peers stated and argued*, 1669.
Hooker, Richard, *The laws of ecclesiastical polity*, ed. J. Keble, Oxford 1835.
Hunton, Philip, *A treatise of monarchie*, 1643.
Husbands, Edward (ed.), *An exact collection of all remonstrances, declarations, votes, orders, ordinances, proclamations, petitions, messages, answers and other remarkable passages between the King's most excellent majesty and his high court of parliament*, 1643.
Ireland, Sir John, *An exact abridgement in English of the eleven books of reports of Sir Edward Coke*, 1651.
Jenkins, David, *Lex terrae*, 1647.
Johnson, Ben, *Works*, ed C. H. Herford and P. Simpson, 11 vols., Oxford 1925–52.
Johnson, R. C., Keeler, M. F., Cole, M. J. and Bidwell, W. B. (eds.), *Commons debates 1628*, 4 vols., Yale 1977–78.
Jones, John, *The cry of blood*, 1651.
The jovial crew or the devil turned ranter, 1651.
Justinian, *The digest of Justinian*, ed. T. Mommsen, tr. A. Watson, Philadelphia 1985.
Justinian, *Institutes, see* Lee, R. W.
Kircherus, Athanasius, *Magnes, sive de arte magnetica*, 3rd edn, Rome 1654.
Knafla, Louis A., *Law and politics in Jacobean England*, Cambridge 1977.
Lambarde, William, *Archeion, or the High Courts of Justice in England*, 1635.
    Eirenarcha, or of the office of justices of the peace, 1619.
Lee, R. W., *The elements of Roman Law, with a translation of the Institutes of Justinian*, 4th edn, 1956.
Lilburne, John, *London's liberty in chains discovered*, 1646.
    Royal tyranny discovered, 1647.
Lincoln's Inn, *Records of the Honourable Society of Lincoln's Inn: the Black Books*, 1898.
Linus, Franciscus, *De inseparabilitate corporum*, 1661.
Locke, John, *An essay concerning human understanding*, ed. P. H. Nidditch, Oxford 1979.

Two treatises of government, ed. P. Laslett, Cambridge 1988.

London's liberties, or a learned argument of law and reason, 1651.

Lower, Richard, *Tractatus de corde, item de motu et colore sanguinis et chyli in eum transitu* 1669.

Ludlow, Edmund, *The memoirs of Edmund Ludlow*, ed. C. H. Firth, 2 vols., Oxford 1894.

   A voyce from the watchtower: part five: 1660–62, ed. A. B. Worden, Camden Society, 4th series, XXI (1978).

Machiavelli, Niccolo, *The discourses of Niccolo Machiavelli*, ed. B. Crick, 1970.

Marshall, Stephen, *A copie of a letter written by Mr Stephen Marshall to a friend of his in the city*, 1643.

Mason, Francis, *Of the authority of the Church in making canons and constitutions concerning things indifferent*, 2nd edn, revised, Oxford 1634.

Migne, J.-P., *Patrologiae cursus completus*, vol. XLIV, Paris 1845.

Milton, John, *The complete works*, Columbia 1932–38.

Molloy, Charles, *De jure maritimo et navali, or a treatise of affairs maritime and of commerce*, 1676.

More, Henry, *The immortality of the soul, so far forth as it is demonstrable by the light of nature*, 1659.

   Enchiridion metaphysicum, sive de rebus incorporeis succincta et luculenta dissertatio, 1671.

   Remarks on two late ingenious discourses, 1676.

Natura Brevium newly corrected in Englysshe, with divers addicons, 1543.

Nicholas, Edward, *The Nicholas Papers*, vol. II, ed. G. F. Warner, Camden Society 1892.

North, Roger, *Examen, or an enquiry into the credit and veracity of a pretended complete history*, 1740.

   The life of the Lord Keeper Guilford, 1742.

   A discourse on the study of laws, 1824.

   The autobiography of the Hon. Roger North, ed. Augustus Jessopp, 1887.

Notestein, W., Relf, F. H. and Simpson, H., *Commons debates 1621*, 7 vols., Yale 1935.

Noy, William, *A treatise of the principal grounds and maxims of the laws of this kingdom*, 1641.

Oldenburg, *The correspondence of Henry Oldenburg*, ed. and tr. A. R. and M. B. Hall, Madison 1965.

Parker, Samuel, *A discourse of ecclesiastical polity*, 1670.

[Parsons, Robert], *An answer to the fifth part of the reports set forth by Sir Edward Coke, Knight*, 1606.

Patrick, Simon, *Friendly debate between a conformist and a non-conformist*, 1669.

   A continuation of the friendly debate, 1669.

Patrides, C. A., *The Cambridge Platonists*, Cambridge 1969.

Perkins, William, *A reformed Catholic or a declaration showing how near we may come to the present church of Rome and wherein we must forever depart from them*, Cambridge 1597.

   The works of that famous and godly minister of Christ in the University of Cambridge William Perkins, 1609.

A poem of the history of Queen Hesther, an elegy on the death of the Lord Chief Justice Hales and other occasional poems, For William Leech, n.d.

Quarles, Francis, *The loyal convert*, 1643.

Registrum omnium brevium tam originalium quam iudicialium, 1531.

Ray, John, *Observations topographical, moral and physiological made in a journey through part of the Low Countries, Germany, Italy and France*, 1673.

Ridley, Mark, *A short treatise of magnetical bodies and motions*, 1613.

Roberts, Michael (tr. and ed.), *Swedish diplomats at Cromwell's court 1655–56: the missions of Peter Julius Coyet and Christer Bonde*, Camden Society, 4th series, XXXVI (1988).

Roots, Ivan, 'Cromwell's ordinances: the early legislation of the Protectorate', in G. E. Aylmer (ed.), *The Interregnum: the quest for a settlement 1640–60*, 1972.

Roskell, J. S., 'The office and dignity of a Protector of England with special reference to its origins', *English Historical Review*, 68 (1953), 193–233.

St German, Christopher, *Dialogue between a Doctor of Divinity and a student of the common law of England*, ed. T. F. T. Plucknett and J. L. Barton, Selden Society, 1974.

Sanderson, *The works of Robert Sanderson*, ed. W. Jacobson, 6 vols., Oxford 1854.

Sedgwick, Obadiah, *An ark against the deluge*, 1644.

The nature and danger of heresies, 1647.

The bowels of tender mercy sealed in the everlasting covenant, 1661.

Selden, John, *Mare clausum*, tr. Marchamont Nedham, 1651.

Titles of honour, 3rd edn, 1672.

Tracts written by John Selden, tr. Redman Westcot, 1683.

Opera omnia, ed. D. Wilkins, 1726.

Table talk, ed. F. Pollock, Selden Society 1927.

Ad fletam dissertatio, ed. and tr. D. Ogg, Cambridge 1936.

Selwood, Samuel, *A narrative of the proceedings of the committee for the preservation of the customs in the case of Mr George Cony, Merchant*, 1655.

Schott, Gaspar, *Technica curiosa sive mirabilia artis*, Wurzburg 1664.

Sharrock, *The History of the Propagation and Improvement of Vegetables by the concurrence of art and nature*, Oxford 1660.

Sherlock, William, *A vindication of the rights of ecclesiastical authority*, 1685.

Smith, Thomas, *De republica Anglorum*, ed. L. Alston, Cambridge 1906.

Smyth, John of Nibley, *The Berkeley MSS: a description of the Hundred of Berkeley*, ed. Sir John Maclean, 1885.

[Somers' tracts], *A collection of scarce and valuable tracts*, ed. Walter Scott, 1811.

Spelman, Henry, *Archaeologus*, 1626.

Spelman, John, *The reports of Sir John Spelman*, ed. J. H. Baker, 2 vols., Selden Society, 1978.

The statutes of the realm, 11 vols., 1963.

Staunford, William, *An exposition of the king's prerogative collected out of the great abridgement of Justice Fitzherbert*, 1567.

Stillingfleet, Edward, *A discourse concerning the doctrine of Christ's satisfaction*, 1696.

Stubbe, Henry, *Essay in defence of the Good Old Cause*, 1659.

Suarez, Franciscus, *De legibus ac deo legislatore*, Coimbra 1612.

Thorne, S. E. (ed.), *A discourse upon the exposition and understanding of statutes*, San Marino 1942.

Thurloe, John, *Thurloe state papers*, ed. Thomas Birch, 7 vols., 1742.

Tillotson, John, *The rule of faith*, 1666.

Twysden, Roger, *Certaine considerations on the government of England*, ed. J. M. Kemble, Camden Society 1899.

Vazquez y Menchaca, Ferdinand, *Illustrium controversiarium aliarumque usu frequentium*, Book 6, Frankfurt 1668.

Verney, *Memoirs of the family of Verney during the seventeenth century*, ed. F. P. and M. M. Verney, 1907.

Vitoria, Franciscus de, *The Spanish origins of international law: Franciscus de Vitoria and his Law of Nations*, J. B. Scott, Oxford 1934.

Wallis, John, *A discourse of gravity and gravitation grounded in experimental observations presented to the Royal Society November 12 1674*, 1675.

Ward, Samuel, *The wonders of the load-stone, or the load-stone newly reduced into a divine and moral use*, tr. Harbottle Grimston, 1640.

[Westminster Assembly], *The Westminster confession of faith*, ed. S. W. Carruthers, Presbyterian Historical Society of England, Extra publications, no. 2, Manchester, n.d.

Wharton, Thomas, *Adenographia, sive glandularum totius corporum descriptio*, 1656.

Whitelocke, Sir James, *The liber famelicus of Sir James Whitelocke*, Camden Society, 1858.

Williams, J. B., *Memoirs of the life, character, and writings of Sir Matthew Hale*, 1835.

Wood, Anthony a, *Athenae Oxonienses*, 3rd edn, 1813.

SECONDARY SOURCES

Allison, C. F., *The rise of moralism: the proclamation of the Gospel from Hooker to Baxter*, 1966.

Abernethy, G. R., 'Clarendon and the Declaration of Indulgence', *Journal of Ecclesiastical History*, 11 (1960).

Ashcraft, Richard, 'Latitudinarianism and toleration: historical myth versus political history' in Ashcraft, Perez Zagorin and Richard Kroll (eds.), *Philosophy, science and religion in England 1640–1700*, Cambridge 1992.

Ashcraft Richard, *Revolutionary politics and Locke's Two Treatises of government*, Princeton 1986.

Baker, J. H., 'The Inns of court and legal doctrine', in T. M. Charles-Edwards, M. E. Owen and D. B. Walters (eds.), *Lawyers and laymen: studies in the history of law presented to Professor Dafydd Jenkins*, pp. 274–83.

Baker, J. H., *The legal profession and the common law*, 1986.

Bellamy, John, *The Tudor law of treason*, Toronto 1979.

Berkowitz, David S., *John Selden's formative years: politics and society in early seventeenth-century England*, Washington 1988.

Black, Stephen F., 'Coram protectore: the judges of Westminster Hall under the protectorate of Oliver Cromwell', *American Journal of Legal History*, 20 (1976). 'The courts and judges of Westminster Hall during the Great Rebellion', *Journal of Legal History*, 7 (1986).

Bryson, W. H., *The equity side of the exchequer*, Cambridge 1975.

Burgess, Glenn, *The politics of the English constitution: an introduction to English political thought 1603–42*, 1992.

Calamy revised: being a revision of Edmund Calamy's account of the minister and others ejected and silenced 1660–62, ed. A. G. Mathews, Oxford 1934.

Cairns, John W., 'Blackstone, an English institutist: legal literature and the rise of the nation state', *Oxford Journal of Legal Studies*, 4 (1984).

Chrimes, S. B., *English constitutional ideas in the fifteenth century*, Cambridge 1936.

Christianson, Paul, 'Young John Selden and the Ancient Constitution *c.* 1610–18', *Proceedings of the American Philosophical Society*. 128 (1984).

'Royal and parliamentary voices on the ancient constitution *c.* 1604–21', in Linda Levy Peck (ed.), *The mental world of the Jacobean court*, Cambridge 1991.

Clifford, Alan C., *Atonement and justification: English evangelical theology: an evaluation*, Oxford 1990.

Cockburn, J. S., *A history of English assizes, 1558–1714*, Cambridge 1972.

Collinson, Patrick, *The religion of Protestants: the Church in English society 1559–1625*, Oxford 1982.

Coolidge, John S., *The Pauline Renaissance in England: Puritanism and the Bible*, Oxford 1970.

Coquillette, Daniel R., *The civilian writers of Doctors' Commons, London: Three centuries of juristic innovation in comparative, commercial and international law*, Berlin 1988.

Costello, W. T., *The scholastic curriculum in early seventeenth-century Cambridge*, Harvard 1958.

Cotterell, Mary, 'Interregnum law reform: the Hale Commission of 1652', *English Historical Review*, 83 (1968).

Dean, D. M., and Jones, N. L., *The parliaments of Elizabethan England*, Oxford 1990.

Debus, Allen G., *The chemical philosophy: paracelsian science and medicine in the sixteenth and seventeenth centuries*, 2 vols., New York 1977.

Disley, Emma, 'Degrees of glory: Protestant doctrine and the concept of rewards hereafter', *Journal of Theological Studies*, NS, 42 (1991).

Doe, Norman, *Fundamental authority in late medieval law*, Cambridge 1990.

Dworkin, Ronald, *Law's empire*, Harvard 1986.

Edie, Carolyn A., 'Tactics and strategies: Parliament's attack on the royal dispensing power, 1597–1689', *American Journal of Legal History*, 29 (1985).

Elton, Sir Geoffrey R., *The Tudor Constitution: documents and commentary*, 2nd edn, Cambridge 1982.

The parliament of England 1559–81, Cambridge 1986.

Ferguson, Arthur B., *Clio unbound: perception of the social and cultural past in renaissance England*, Duke 1979.

Finberg, H. P. R., *Gloucestershire studies*, Leicester 1957.

Fix, Andrew C., *Prophecy and reason: the Dutch collegiants in the early Enlightenment*, Princeton 1991.

Foster, Elizabeth Read, *Proceedings in parliament 1610*, 2 vols., New Haven 1966.

Gabbey, Alan, 'Henry More and the limits of mechanism', in Hutton, Sarah (ed.), *Henry More: tercentenary studies*, Dordrecht 1991.

Gough, J. W., *Fundamental law in English history*, Oxford 1955.

Gray, Charles M., 'Bonham's case reviewed', *Proceedings of the American Philosophical Society*, 1972.

'Boundaries of the equitable function', *American Journal of Legal History*, 20 (1976).

'Reason, authority and the imagination: the jurisprudence of Sir Edward Coke', in Perez Zagorin (ed.), *Culture and politics from puritanism to the Enlightenment*, Berkeley 1980.

'Parliament, liberty and the law', in J. H. Hexter (ed.), *Parliament and liberty: from the reign of Elizabeth to the English civil war*, Stanford 1992.

Green, Thomas Andrew, *Verdict according to conscience: perspectives on the English trial jury 1200–1800*, Chicago 1985.

Guy, John, *St German on equity and statute*, Selden Society, Supplementary series, no. 6, 1985.

Hall, A. Rupert, *Henry More: magic, religion and experiment*, Oxford 1990.

Harris, Tim, *London crowds in the reign of Charles II: propaganda and politics from the Restoration until the exclusion crisis*, Cambridge 1987.

Harris, Tim, Seaward, Paul and Goldie, Mark (eds.), *The politics of religion in Restoration England*, 1990.

Hart, James S., *Justice upon petition: The house of Lords and the reformation of justice 1621–1675*, 1991.

Hast, Adele, 'State treason trials during the puritan revolution', *Historical Journal*, 15 (1972).

Havighurst, A. L., 'The judiciary in the reign of Charles II', *Law Quarterly Review*, 66 (1950).

Henderson, Edith G., *Foundations of English administrative law: certioriari and mandamus in the seventeenth century*, Cambridge, Mass. 1963.

Henning, B. D. (ed.), *The history of parliament: the House of Commons 1660–1690*, vol. II, 1983.

Henry, John C., 'Medicine and pneumatology: Henry More, Richard Baxter and Francis Glisson's treatise on the energetic nature of substance', *Medical History* 31 (1987).

Heward, Edmund, *Matthew Hale*, 1972.

Hill, Christopher, *Puritanism and revolution: studies in the interpretation of the English revolution in the seventeenth century*, 1958.

Hutton, Ronald, *The Restoration: a political history of England and Wales 1658–1667*, Oxford 1985.

Charles the Second: King of England, Scotland and Ireland, Oxford 1991.

Hutton, Sarah (ed.), *Henry More: tercentenary studies*, Dordrecht 1991.

Inderwick, F. A., *The interregnum (AD 1648–1660): studies of the commonwealth: legislative, social and legal*, 1891.

Isler, Hansruedi, *Thomas Willis MD, 1621–75*, 1968.

Ives, E. W., *The common lawyers of pre-reformation England: Thomas Kebell: a case study*, Cambridge 1983.

Jones, William, 'Conflict or collaboration? Chancery attitudes in the reign of Elizabeth', *American Journal of Legal History*, 5 (1961).

The Elizabethan Court of Chancery, Oxford 1967.

Jones, W. J., 'The great Gamaliel of the law: Mr Attorney Noye', *Huntingdon Library Quarterly*, 40 (1977).

Judson, M. A., *From tradition to political reality: a study of the arguments set forth in support of the Commonwealth government in England 1649–53*, Hamden, Conn. 1980.

Kendall, R. T., *Calvin and English Calvinism to 1649*, Oxford 1979.

Kenyon, J. P., 'The acquittal of Sir George Wakeman: 18 July 1679', *Historical Journal*, 14 (1971).

Kenyon, J. P. (ed.), *The Stuart constitution 1603–1688: documents and commentary*, 2nd edn, Cambridge 1986.

Key, Newton E., 'Comprehension and the breakdown of consensus in Restoration Herefordshire', in Tim Harris, Paul Seaward and Mark Goldie (eds.), *The politics of religion in Restoration England*, 1990.

Krapp, Robert Martin, *Liberal Anglicanism 1636–47: an historical essay*, Ridgefield, Conn. 1944.

Krautheim, Ulrike, *Die Souveränitätskonzeption in den englischen Verfassungskonflikten des 17. Jahrhunderts*, Frankfurt 1977.

Lake, Peter, 'Calvinism and the English church, 1570–1635', *Past and Present*, 114 (1987).

Lamont, William M., *Godly rule: politics and religion 1603–60*, 1969.

Richard Baxter and the millennium: Protestant imperialism and the English, 1979.

Lassiter, John C., 'Defamation of peers; the rise and fall of the action for scandalum magnatum', *American Journal of Legal History*, 22 (1978).

Lewis, J. U., 'Sir Edward Coke (1552–1633): his theory of artificial reason as a context for modern basic political theory', *Law Quarterly Review*, 84 (1968).

Liebermann, David, *The province of legislation determined: legal theory in eighteenth-century Britain*, Cambridge 1989.

Lindley, E. S., *Wotton-under-Edge: men and affairs of a Cotswold wool town*, Dursley, Gloucestershire 1977.

McAdoo, H. R., *The structure of Caroline moral theology*, 1949.

McGee, J. Sears, *The Godly man in Stuart England: Anglicans, puritans and the two tables, 1620–1670*, New Haven 1976.

McGuire, J. E., 'Boyle's conception of nature', *Journal of the History of Ideas*, 33 (1972).

McIlwain, C. H., *The high court of parliament*, 1910.

Constitutionalism in a changing world: collected papers, Cambridge 1939.

Constitutionalism ancient and modern, Revised edn, Cornell, 1947.

Maitland, F. W., *Roman canon law in the Church of England: six essays*, 1898.

The letters of Frederic William Maitland, ed. C. H. S. Fifoot, Selden Society, Supplementary series, 1965.

Marshall, John, 'The ecclesiology of the Latitude-men 1660–89: Stillingfleet, Tillotson, and "Hobbism"', *Journal of Ecclesiastical History*, 36 (1985).

Martin, Julian, *Francis Bacon, the state, and the reform of natural philosophy*, Cambridge 1992.

Matthews, Nancy, *William Sheppard: Cromwell's law reformer*, Cambridge 1984.

Mendle, Michael J., 'The Ship Money case, *The case of Ship Mony*, and the origins of Heney Parker's parliamentary absolutism', *Historical Journal*, 32 (1989).

'The great council of parliament and the first ordinances: the constitutional theory of the first civil war', *Journal of British Studies*, 31 (1992).

Milsom, S. F. C., *Historical foundations of the English common law*, 2nd edn, 1981.

Morrill, J. S. (ed.), *Reactions to the English civil war 1642–49*, 1982.

Nenner, Howard, *By colour of law: legal culture and constitutional politics in England*, Chicago 1977.

Oakeshott, Michael, *Rationalism in politics and other essays*, 1962.

Orr, Robert R., *Reason and authority: the thought of William Chillingworth*, Oxford 1967.

Osler, Margaret J., 'Baptising Epicurean atomism: Pierre Gassendi on the immortality of the soul', in *Religion, science and world-view: essays in honour of Richard S. Westfall*, Cambridge 1985.

Pagel, Walter, *Joan Baptista van Helmont*, Cambridge 1982.

Pocock, J. G. A., *The Machiavellian moment: Florentine political thought and the Atlantic republican tradition*, Princeton 1975.

The ancient constitution and the feudal law: a reissue with a retrospect, Cambridge 1985.

Popkin, Richard, H., *The history of scepticism from Erasmus to Spinoza*, Berkeley 1979.

Postema, Gerald J., *Bentham and the common law tradition*, Oxford 1986.

Prall, Stuart E., *The agitation for law reform in the puritan revolution, 1640–60*, The Hague 1966.

Prest, W. R., *The Inns of court*, 1972.

'The dialectical origins of Finch's Law', *Cambridge Law Journal*, 1977.

The rise of the barristers, Oxford 1986.

Reilly, C., *Francis Line, S.J.: an exiled English scientist, 1525–1675*, Rome 1969.

Richardson, W. C., *A history of the Inns of court: with special reference to the time of the Renaissance*, Baton Rouge 1975.

Rivers, Isabel, *Reason, grace and sentiment: a study of the language of religion and grace in England*, Cambridge 1991.

Roberts, Clayton, *The growth of responsible government in Stuart England*, Cambridge 1966.

Russell, Conrad, *The origins of the English civil war*, 1973.

The fall of the British monarchies, Oxford 1991.

Schaffer, Simon, and Shapin, Steven, *Leviathan and the air-pump: Hobbes, Boyle and the experimental life*, Princeton 1985.

Seaward, Paul, *The cavalier parliament and the reconstruction of the old regime, 1661–1687*, Cambridge 1989.

Shapiro, Barbara J., *Probability and certainty in seventeenth-century England*, Princeton 1983.

'Beyond reasonable doubt' and 'probable cause', Berkeley 1991.

Sharp, Kevin, *Sir Robert Cotton 1586–1631: history and politics in early modern England*, Oxford 1979.

Simpson, A. W. B., 'The common law and legal theory', in Simpson (ed.), *Oxford Essays in Jurisprudence*, 2nd series, Oxford 1973.

A history of the common law of contract: the rise of the action of assumpsit, Oxford 1975.

'The rise and fall of the legal treatise: legal principles and the forms of legal literature', *University of Chicago Law Review*, 48 (1982).

Skinner, Quentin, 'History and ideology in the English revolution', *Historical Journal*, 8 (1965).

The foundations of modern political thought, 2 vols., Cambridge 1978.

Sommerville, J. P., *Politics and ideology in England, 1603–40*, 1986.

'History and theory: the Norman Conquest in Stuart political thought', *Political Studies*, 34 (1986), 249–61.

Spalding, Ruth, *Contemporaries of Bulstrode Whitelocke 1605–75*, British Academy, Oxford 1990.

Sprunger, Keith L., *The learned Dr William Ames: Dutch backgrounds of English and American puritanism*, Urbana 1972.

Spurr, John, 'Latitudinarianism and the Restoration Church', *Historical Journal*, 31 (1988).

'Schism and the Restoration church', *Journal of Ecclesiastical History*, 41 (1990).

The Restoration Church of England 1646–1689, Yale 1991.

Stein, Peter, *Regulae juris: from juristic rules to legal maxims*, Edinburgh 1966.

Thorne, S. E., 'Dr Bonham's Case', *Law Quarterly Review*, 54 (1938).

Thorne, S. E. (ed.), *A discourse upon the exposition and understanding of statutes*, San Marino 1942.

Tite, C. C. G., *Impeachment and parliamentary judicature in early Stuart England*, 1974.

Tolmie, Murray, *The triumph of the saints: the separate churches of London 1616–49*, Cambridge 1977.

Trevallyn Jones, G. F., 'The composition and leadership of the presbyterian party in the Convention', *English Historical Review*, 79 (1964).

Trevor-Roper, Hugh, *Catholics, Anglicans, and Puritans*, 1987.

Tuck, Richard, *Natural rights theories: their origin and development*, Cambridge 1979.

Hobbes, Oxford 1989.

Tully, James, *A discourse on property: John Locke and his adversaries*, Cambridge 1980.

'A reply to Waldron and Baldwin', *The Locke Newsletter*, 13 (1982).

Tyacke, Nicholas, *Anti-Calvinists: the rise of English Arminianism 1590–1640*, Oxford 1987.

Veall, Donald, *The popular movement for law reform 1640–1660*, Oxford 1970.

Von Rohr, John, *The covenant of grace in puritan thought*, American Academy of Religion, Studies in religion, no. 45 (1986).

Wallace, Dewey, D., *Puritans and pre-destination: grace in English Protestant theology 1525–1695*, Chapel Hill 1982.

Weber, Max, *The protestant ethic and the spirit of capitalism*, tr. T. Parsons, 2nd edn, 1976.

Webster, Charles, *The great instauration: science, medicine and reform 1626–1660*, 1975.

White, Peter, *Predestination, policy and polemic*, Cambridge 1992.

White, S. D., *Sir Edward Coke and the grievances of the commonwealth*, Manchester 1979.

Willcox, W. B., *Gloucestershire: a study in local government 1590–1640*, Yale 1940.

Woolf, C. N. S., *Bartolus of Sassoferrato*, Cambridge 1913.

Woolrych, Austin, *Commonwealth to protectorate*, Oxford 1982.

Worden, A. B., *The rump parliament*, Cambridge 1974.

Yale, D. E. C., 'Hale and Hobbes on law, legislation and the sovereign', *Cambridge Law Journal*, 31 (1972).

'A view of the Admiralty jurisdiction: Sir Matthew Hale and the civilians', in Dafydd Jenkins (ed.), *Legal history studies 1972*, Cardiff 1975.

Index

Cambridge Studies in Early Modern British History

Titles in the series